Shakespeare has long been considered the preeminent poet and dramatist of the English-speaking world. Shakespearean criticism has been largely Anglo-centered, stressing his mastery of the English language; even commentary on performance has normally assumed the original English text as the basis of judgment. Though Shakespeare is the most frequently performed playwright in the world, little attention has been paid to theatrical production outside the English language.

This is the first collection to offer a considered account of contemporary Shakespeare performance in non-English-speaking theatres. The essays investigate text and translation theory, the significance of the visual, divergent strategies of acting, directing and of audience culture, intercultural performance, political appropriation and dissent. Focusing on productions in Europe, with some lesser attention to Asia, the volume suggests that "foreign Shakespeare" has much to teach us about Shakespeare's cultural place in the world at large. Dennis Kennedy introduces the topic within the context of postwar performance, and an Afterword suggests how foreign productions challenge Anglocentric standards of Shakespeare interpretation.

FOREIGN SHAKESPEARE

FOREIGN SHAKESPEARE

Contemporary performance

EDITED BY

DENNIS KENNEDY

Published by the Press Syndicate of the University of Cambridge
The Pitt Building, Trumpington Street, Cambridge CB2 1RP
40 West 20th Street, New York, NY 10011–4211, USA
10 Stamford Road, Oakleigh, Melbourne 3166, Australia

First published 1993
Reprinted 1995

Transferred to digital printing 2000

Printed in Great Britain by Biddles Short Run Books

A catalogue record for this book is available from the British Library

Library of Congress cataloguing in publication data

Foreign Shakespeare: contemporary performance / edited by Dennis Kennedy.
p.   cm.
Includes bibliographical references and index.
ISBN 0 521 42025 3
1. Shakespeare, William, 1564–1616 – Stage history – Foreign
countries. 2. Shakespeare, William, 1564–1616 – Stage history – 1950–
3. English drama – Appreciation – Foreign countries. 4. Theater –
history – 20th century. I. Kennedy, Dennis.
PR2971.F.66F66   1993
792.9'5 – dc20   92–47235   CIP

ISBN 0 521 42025 3

For Ann
again and always

Contents

Illustrations

Contributors

JOHN RUSSELL BROWN is Professor of Theatre at the University of Michigan, general editor of Theatre Production Studies (Routledge), and editor of the forthcoming *Oxford Illustrated History of the Theatre*. He is author of numerous books on Shakespeare and twentieth-century theatre: *Shakespeare's Plays in Performance*, *Free Shakespeare*, *Theatre Language*, etc. He was an Associate Director of the National Theatre in London and is currently a freelance director.

JARKA M. BURIAN is Professor Emeritus of Theatre at the State University of New York, Albany. His publications include *The Scenography of Joseph Svoboda*, *Svoboda : Wagner*, and numerous studies of Czech theatre and international scenography. Most recently he translated and edited Svoboda's *The Secret of Theatrical Space*.

MARVIN CARLSON is Sidney E. Cohn Professor of Theatre and Comparative Literature at the Graduate Center of the City University of New York, and is founding editor of *Western European Stages*. His recent books include *The Italian Shakespearians*, *Places of Performance*, and *Theatre Semiotics: Signs of Life*.

RON ENGLE is Chester Fritz Distinguished Professor of Theatre Arts at the University of North Dakota, and founding editor of *Theatre History Studies*. His books include *Shakespeare Festivals and Companies: An International Guide* (edited with Daniel Watermeier and Felicia Londré) and *The American Stage: Social and Economic Issues from the Colonial Period to the Present* (edited with Tice Miller). He was visiting professor in the Institut für Theaterwissenschaft at Munich University in 1989.

SPENCER GOLUB is Associate Professor of Theatre and Comparative Literature at Brown University. He is the author of *Evreinov: The*

Theatre of Paradox and Transformation, and of the Russian theatre and drama entries for *The Cambridge Guide to World Theatre*, as well as numerous essays and reviews. His book, *The Recurrence of Fate: Theatre and Memory in Twentieth-Century Russia*, is forthcoming.

DOMINIQUE GOY-BLANQUET is Professor of English Literature at the University of Amiens, a member of the CRNS Laboratoire des Arts de Spectacle, and a regular contributor to the drama section of *The Times Literary Supplement*. Her books include *Le roi mis à nu: histoire d'Henry VI de Hall à Shakespeare*, and she is part author of *Shakespeare de A à Z . . . ou presque*. She has also translated various works on the theatre, among them John Dover Wilson's *What Happens in Hamlet* for Patrice Chéreau's production of 1988.

J. LAWRENCE GUNTNER teaches English and American literature at the Technical University of Braunschweig. He has published articles on Shakespeare and on Shakespeare on film. He is co-editing *Redefining Shakespeare: Literary Criticism and Theatre Practice in the German Democratic Republic*, as well as a book on teaching Shakespeare as a foreign-language text.

WILHELM HORTMANN is Professor of English at the University of Duisburg in Germany. His publications include *Englische Literatur im 20. Jahrhundert*, *Wenn die Kunst stirbt*, as well as articles on contemporary German theatre and productions of Shakespeare. He is now completing *Shakespeare on the German Stage, 1914–1990*.

DENNIS KENNEDY is Professor of Theatre Arts at the University of Pittsburgh. His books include *Granville Barker and the Dream of Theatre*, *Plays by Harley Granville Barker* (editor), and *Looking at Shakespeare: A Visual History of Twentieth-Century Performance*. He is the general editor of Pittsburgh Studies in Theatre and Culture (Peter Lang Publishing). His own plays have been performed in New York, London, and at regional theatres across the United States, and he works frequently as a dramaturg.

PIA KLEBER, trained as costume designer in France and Germany, is Associate Professor and Director of the University College Drama Programme at the University of Toronto. Her publications include *Exceptions and Rules: Brecht, Planchon, and The Good Person of Szechwan*, and *Re-Interpreting Brecht: His Influence on Contemporary Drama and Film* (co-editor). She is also co-editor and contributor to the series "Sources of Dramatic Theory."

LEANORE LIEBLEIN is Associate Professor of English at McGill University in Montreal. She has published articles on medieval and Renaissance drama in performance, and has directed medieval and Renaissance plays. She also co-translated *Les Eshabis (Taken by Surprise)* by Jacques Grévin (1561).

IRENA R. MAKARYK is Associate Professor and Director of Graduate Studies of English at the University of Ottawa. Her books include *Comic Justice in Shakespeare, About the Harrowing of Hell: A Seventeenth-Century Ukrainian Play in its European Context*, and *Contemporary Criticism: Approaches, Scholars, Terms*.

ANDREA J. NOURYEH is Assistant Professor of Theatre at St Lawrence University. Her recent articles include "Understanding Xanadu," about Orson Welles' approach to Shakespeare, and "JoAnne Akalaitis: Postmodern Director or Socio-Sexual Critic." She is also an archivist and dramaturg.

AVRAHAM OZ lectures on theatre at the Universities of Haifa and Tel Aviv. His books include *The Yoke of Love: Prophetic Riddles in The Merchant of Venice*, and a forthcoming work on political theatre. He served as associate artistic director and dramaturg at the Cameri Theatre and at the Municipal Theatre of Haifa, and has translated operas and numerous plays (including Shakespeare) for Israeli theatres. He is the general editor of the Hebrew edition of the works of Shakespeare.

PATRICE PAVIS is Professor in the Department of Theatre at the University of Paris VIII, and the author of many works. Among his books available in English are *Languages of the Stage, Theatre at the Crossroads of Culture, A Reader in Intercultural Performance* (editor), and *Dictionary of the Theatre* (forthcoming).

Preface

This collection hopes to open a discourse for a subject much ignored by Anglo-centered Shakespearean commentators. As a first attempt, it cannot pretend to inclusive coverage, whether geographical or canonical, and I certainly do not wish to suggest that it somehow contains its topic. I have selected essays that are provocative in that they make different kinds of entrances. They discuss Shakespeare performance outside of the English-speaking theatre of the last three decades or so, attempting to map out small plots of that vast ground, charting how foreign performances differ from familiar models. They do not proceed by a common methodology or share a political or philosophical viewpoint. Most of the essays are historical to some degree, in that they record details of and ascribe meanings to actual performances, though they do not follow a single historiographical method. What they do share is a concern for how Shakespeare appears and works on stage and in the mind in countries that lie beyond the usual exploration of critics and performance historians.

Obviously a great number of important productions, along with their directors, designers, and actors, cannot be treated here. Their absence results from the limitations of an introductory project, and does not constitute a judgment about value. If the complete Shakespeare work of major directors like Ingmar Bergman, Ariane Mnouchkine, Peter Stein, and Giorgio Strehler were given its due, there would be no room left for other important figures and issues, who are often unknown outside their own countries. In the same vein, with the exceptions of Andrea Nouryeh's essay on Japan and my Afterword, the attention here is on European and Soviet performance. In objecting to Anglo-centric approaches to Shakespeare, the volume thus runs the risk of merely substituting European ones. To a certain extent this is inevitable, since most Shakespeare production outside of English still occurs in Europe, and European theatres have led the way in redefining performance models. But it's also worth noting that there is no such thing as a "European value system" for Shakespeare; as the essays reveal, the values and the methods of production vary enormously, and often contradict one another.

Mapping out the larger areas for global Shakespeare performance is clearly going to take more time, more thought, and more scholarship. Since the full significance of foreign Shakespeare in the contemporary theatre is beyond the capabilities of a single volume, what is here should be read as an early sketch of a (mostly) undiscovered country.

I owe debts to many people – scholars, translators, theatre practitioners, archivists, and administrators – who aided this project at various stages and who helped define its contours. For insightful discussion and conversation I particularly thank Gerhard Blashe, John Russell Brown, Jean-Claude Carrière, Bob Crowley, Hank Dobin, Fan Yi Song, Spencer Golub, Dominique Goy-Blanquet, Wolfgang Greisenegger, Maik Hamburger, Wilhelm Hortmann, Pamela Howard, Pia Kleber, Michal Kobialka, Ania Loomba, Milan Lukeš, Mao-Sheng Hu, Cary Mazer, Zdeněk Stříbrný, Atul Tiwari, and Simon Williams. A seminar at a meeting of the Shakespeare Association of America brought some of the essayists together for early and fruitful discussion. Louis Fantasia kindly invited me to try out my own ideas in two lectures at the festival "Shakespeare in the Non-English Speaking World" in Los Angeles in 1991. Martha Coigney of the New York office of the International Theatre Institute was extremely useful in arranging my research visits abroad, and Sarah Stanton of Cambridge University Press made many valuable contributions. My colleagues Benjamin Hicks, Marianne Novy, and Thomas Rimer graciously helped improve different parts of the manuscript; Anthony Parise read and commented on the Introduction and Afterword with his customary discernment. Rachel Resinski, my research assistant for this project, was particularly helpful and efficient, and Melissa Gibson prepared an assiduous index.

Two of these essays have appeared in print before: Leanore Lieblein's "Translation and Mise en Scène" in *The Journal of Dramatic Theory and Criticism* in 1990, and Avraham Oz's "Transformations of Authenticity" in *Shakespeare Jahrbuch/West* in 1983. Both have been substantially revised. The others have been written for this volume.

University of Pittsburgh   D.K.

Introduction: Shakespeare without his language

Dennis Kennedy

There is a typical Hungarian story, about the very well-known Hungarian theatre director, Arthur Bardos, who left Hungary in 1949 to direct *Hamlet* in England; and he was asked by the BBC what it was like to do so. Mr Bardos answered: "Of course, it is a great honour and a challenge, but to tell you the truth, it's strange to hear the text in English because I am used to the original version, translated by Janos Arany."[1]

Foreign Shakespeare? The moderately impertinent title of this volume implies a perspective on Shakespeare's stature, and on his place in world culture, which is normally obscured in the academic and theatrical enterprises that have adopted his name. It's both natural and logical that Shakespearean studies and theatrical production have been Anglo-centered: Shakespeare was an English writer, after all, and since the eighteenth century the understanding and formal assessment of his work have been in the hands of critics and editors with profound allegiances to English literature. These days the situation is more secure than ever, for the great majority of Shakespearean commentators are professional interpreters connected to university departments of English in English-speaking countries. In many cases the officials connected to placing his work on stage have had parallel backgrounds: the leading directors and administrators of the Royal Shakespeare Company for its first two decades, for instance, read English at Cambridge under the influence of F. R. Leavis. Both the teaching and the acting of Shakespeare in English customarily start with a deep study of the linguistic clues in the text, and most English-speakers initially encounter Shakespeare as a literary creator, the champion example of a distinctive and abiding literary tradition.

Though the condition of Shakespearean studies is natural it has been unfortunate in at least one regard, for it has tended to cloak

Shakespeare's vast importance in the theatre in languages other than English. A simple test will demonstrate my point: look at the stage histories that are usually included in the introductions to the numerous single-play editions of Shakespeare. Almost none will mention performances outside of the Anglo-American theatre. Three British publishers now offer series of performance histories, also in single-play formats; their record is no better.[2] Yet Shakespeare, by far the most popular playwright in England and North America, is actually the most performed playwright in the world at large. He regularly crosses national and linguistic boundaries with apparent ease. Does he cross into Poland or China as the same dramatist who is played at Stratford?

It would fit the notion of Shakespeare as the transcendent humanist to answer yes, but the truth is more complex. As these essays reveal, the performance history of Shakespeare's plays abroad suggests the opposite, and also suggests a reason why commentators normally pass over the subject. The cultural attitudes that inhere in the work, and that the Anglo-centered approach has assumed to be the common heritage of Shakespeare's art, require not only linguistic translation but also cultural adaptation when they are transferred to a foreign environment. While Anglophone critics have not ignored the alternative traditions, they have tended to look upon Shakespeare's popularity in other countries as an example of his comprehensive appeal. Rather than seeing the use of Shakespeare's texts in foreign languages as a phenomenon separate from their use in English, they have normally chosen to see it as further vindication of the importance of their subject, and, by implication, of the superiority of English as the medium for Shakespearean cognition. They have constructed a universal Shakespeare based on the value of his original language.

Yet almost from the start of his importance as the idealized English dramatist there have been other Shakespeares, Shakespeares not dependent upon English and often at odds with it. The English Comedians may have played Shakespeare in the German lands in the sixteenth century, and English sailors may have played *Othello* on the African coast in the seventeenth century – the evidence is uncertain. If such performances did occur, they would have been based primarily upon gesture and extremely improvised speech. Tantalizing as these possibilities are as early global exportations of Shakespeare, it's obvious that their actors could not have been presenting the dramatist as a literary artist or his plays as subtle verbal creations. The almost absurd conditions under which the English Comedians first worked – as troupes of actors without German, attempting to present Elizabethan plays for audiences with little or no theatrical tradition, rendering the plays essentially as dumb-shows – emphatically point to the problematics of foreign Shakespeare.[3] The connections and cultural connotations that derive from playing Shakespeare in his own land in his own tongue are simply not applicable in another country and in another language. Whereas Shakespeare has been a given in English for some centuries, readers and audiences in linguistically foreign environments have had to *find* a desire for him.

The first major example of finding that desire outside of English occurred in German 200 years ago. The roughness and relatively sprawling nature of the plays, as well as their political stories, made them felicitous cultural material for an embryonic nationalist movement. Schiller's well-known project, to create a German literature and a German theatre that would transcend the petty principalities of the Holy Roman Empire and define the essence of a people, hoped to unite *das deutsche Volk* in a common, utopian resolve. Because Shakespeare was not French, and because his work violated neoclassic (i.e., aristocratic) principles, he became a rallying point for the new spirit of romantic democracy. It was, ironically, his very foreignness that made him useful as a model for the Germanic future: "*unser* Shakespeare" was an outright appropriation, dependent upon the absence of an existing tradition. Shakespeare could be made to signify what no familiar literature could signify, and simultaneously serve to validate Schiller's own dramaturgy.

In central and eastern Europe the same condition obtained in the mid-nineteenth century. In lands under the Austrian hegemony, Shakespeare's plays became part of the movement for a national literature and a bourgeois theatre separate from the court stages of the Habsburgs. Similarly, the first translations of Shakespeare in Poland were part of a nascent opposition to foreign cultural domination. This oppositional use of Shakespeare has received an intriguing variation more recently, when the plays were used in postwar eastern Europe and the Soviet Union as dissident texts. If new plays and films critical of a repressive regime are regularly censored, producers are sometimes tempted to make the classics into coded messages about the present: Shakespeare thus became a secret agent under deep cover.

Such a catalogue, however brief, serves as a reminder that Shakespeare's work has never stood above or outside history in Europe. Shakespeare is of course part of history in Great Britain and Ireland and North America and Australia too, and has often been made part of larger political and philosophic currents. But in continental Europe the absence of immersed linguistic and cultural connections to Shakespeare has meant that this appropriation has been more overt, and has met less official resistance from advocates of high culture than in the home countries. *Hamlet*, for example, has long been read in England and America inside the romantic tradition, as the outcry of an individual tortured soul, focusing on the poetic insights of the central character. This reading has been reinforced by the tendency to use the text as a star vehicle for an ardent and youthful actor. It's interesting to note how many Anglo-American productions in the past have been insensible of the fact that the play contains three rebellions – Claudius' against old Hamlet, Laertes' against Claudius, and young Hamlet's against Claudius – and that the ending shows a belligerent outsider taking over the Danish throne. In fact, a long theatrical tradition in England cuts Fortinbras entirely, preferring to conclude with the personalized, anguished overtones of Hamlet's death rather than its political implications.

But if to the liberal west *Hamlet* is an expression of the individual spirit, to a censor in a more repressive land it is a threat. In eastern Europe the play frequently received frank political readings at odds with the standard romantic interpretation. At various times in the nineteenth century the czarist regime banned performances in Warsaw out of fear of encouraging rebellion. Most notoriously, Stalin banned it during the war in the USSR, its political allusions too sensitive for a supreme dictator and its hero too tentative for the nation's militant cause. This tradition has continued to the present. In 1989, just before the collapse of the Stalinist government of the German Democratic Republic, I saw Siegfried Höchst's production at the Volksbühne in East Berlin, which treated Denmark as a literal prison from which almost everybody was trying to escape, just as almost everybody was trying to escape at that moment from East Germany. The stage was enclosed with three rows of wire fencing, and when Laertes was given permission to return to France in the second scene, he was handed a green document that looked suspiciously like the passports issued by West Germany. The audience howled in delight.[4] In these examples thinking about Shakespeare has been influenced by circumstances entirely foreign to those that apply in the Anglo-American tradition, where greater political stability has robbed Shakespeare of some of the danger and force that other countries have (re)discovered in his texts. It is worth remembering that there is no phrase in English equivalent to *coup d'état*.

English-speakers are apt to assume that foreign-language productions necessarily lose an essential element of Shakespeare in the process of linguistic and cultural transfer, and of course this is true. But it is also true, as I am suggesting, that some foreign performances may have a more direct access to the power of the plays. In this respect the modernity of translation is crucial. Shakespeare's poetry may be one of the glories of human life, but the archaism and remoteness of his language create enormous difficulties for audiences in the late twentieth century. The fact is, harsh as it may sound to some teachers of English, we do not speak the same language as Shakespeare: at best we speak a remote dialect of it. A foreign language, while missing the full value of the verse, can be said to have an advantage of great significance in the theatre. Even the oldest of the translations of Shakespeare in regular use today, the Schlegel–Tieck versions, are infinitely closer to the language spoken on the street in Berlin or Zurich or Vienna than Shakespeare's language is to that of London or Los Angeles or Melbourne. It is common practice in the contemporary theatre to commission new translations for new productions, so that the language is not only colloquial but also becomes tied to the interpretation and the mise en scène of the particular performance. As a result many foreign performances of Shakespeare sound similar to performances of new plays – just as performances in English of Molière or Schiller can do.

The idea of translating the plays into contemporary English is anathema to most Anglophone Shakespeareans, and probably to most Anglophone audiences. The reasons for this protectionism, however, may not be as obvious as they seem, especially when we remember that it was almost universal practice to adapt the language in the English theatre from the Restoration to the mid-nineteenth century. The reasons have as much to do with the traditions of modernist high culture and the entrenched position of the Shakespeare industry as with the inherent superiority of the originals. It's not necessary to argue the issue here; I only need to note that what is anathema in English is a fact of life elsewhere.

The differences that derive from performing in languages other than English have led to major differences in performance strategies. They are especially noticeable in the visual aspects of production; unable to place the same emphasis on Shakespeare's verbal resourcefulness, foreign performances have explored scenographic and physical modes more openly than their Anglophone counterparts, often redefining the meaning of the plays in the process. Though of course there have been, and continue to be, innovative and highly influential productions in English, the authoritative and thorough-going rethinkings of the plays we associate with Leopold Jessner or Giorgio Strehler or Ariane Mnouchkine have not occurred to the same degree in the home countries. Even Peter Brook, re-inventing the plays in English since 1945, has done his most radical work on Shakespeare in French. Those differences in performance traditions, which form the assorted themes of this volume, tell a complicated story about the interrelationships between an English dramatist, his performance in English, and his performance outside English. To begin to understand the importance of foreign productions, and to put them in the context of Anglophone Shakespeare, it will be useful here to look at the general history of Shakespeare performance since the Second World War.

International Shakespearean representation in our time has gone through many changes, and has not proceeded in anything so convenient as a straight line. But the dominant uses and styles of Shakespeare on the stage from about 1950 to about 1980 were established by a combination of two overriding forces: the open stage movement, and the movement to contemporize the meanings of the plays. Though it had predecessors in Germany in the nineteenth century, the open stage movement was essentially English in theory and Anglo-Canadian in practice. Its chief object was to demystify the dramatic event by stressing its non-illusionist nature. Tyrone Guthrie, modifying the urges of William Poel and Harley Granville Barker, demonstrated that a revised architectural structure would significantly alter how Shakespeare was received in the theatre, bringing the plays closer to their audiences in both the literal and the figurative sense. The Festival Theatre in Stratford, Ontario, designed by Tanya Moiseiwitsch and Guthrie, opened in

1953, the stage first covered by a tent; the theatre combined Elizabethan attributes with audience arrangements similar to those at the
ancient theatre at Epidauros, overtly welcoming spectators as
mutual creators of the dramatic fiction. New playhouses soon followed in Minneapolis, New York, Los Angeles, Chichester, Shef-
field, and around the world. Some of the discoveries of the open
stage movement were widely adapted elsewhere, even modifying the
interior architecture of proscenium theatres (like the Royal Shakespeare Theatre in Stratford, which resolutely divides actors from
spectators), and greatly increased the ease and the speed of performance. His producers at last seemed to free Shakespeare from nineteenth-century notions of Realism.

Though the movement claimed an authenticity deriving from
Elizabethan stage practice, it affected Anglophone production so
deeply in the 1950s and 1960s partly because it fit inside the
dominant, modernist interpretation of Shakespeare that stressed the
centrality of his subtle and imagistic poetry to his meaning. The
linguistic text became even more consequential to Shakespearean
enactment by situating the actor on a (relatively) bare stage in a
(relatively) Elizabethan mode, placing the main force of interpretation on the (relatively) unencumbered word. The movement,
though not much analyzed, was so taken for granted that when J. L.
Styan published *The Shakespeare Revolution* in 1977 his premise went
unquestioned. Shakespeare wrote for the non-illusionist stage, Styan
emphasized, and the production modalities of the twentieth century
have been moving to refulfill Shakespeare's Elizabethan assumptions through a combination of architectural and performance
tactics.

The second major postwar force in Shakespeare performance, the
movement to contemporize the plays, was foreign in origin, though
it was seized almost immediately by the Royal Shakespeare
Company. This movement had two separate European parts, both
thoroughly conditioned by the war: one derived from Marxist
theory and Bertolt Brecht, the other from Existentialist philosophy
and Jan Kott. Brecht's effect was achieved partly through his
writing but more directly through the work of the Berliner Ensemble,
probably the most influential theatre company in the world in the
third quarter of the century. This troupe, subsidized by the government of East Germany, stressed the combined responsibility of
actors, directors, designers, playwrights, and audiences to the

social and political issues that lay beyond the entertainment value or the high-art virtues of attending plays. Kott, on the other hand, wished to stress the relevance and immediacy of Shakespeare's texts to the excruciations of the postwar world, and asked for theatrical representations that would reveal what he saw as the underlying cruelty of Shakespeare's fables, a cruelty not limited by political issues.

Peter Hall, greatly impressed by the visit of the Berliner Ensemble to London in August of 1956 (the very month of Brecht's death), set out to capture its organizational structure and its social commitment for the Royal Shakespeare Company, founded in 1960–1. At the same time Hall and his colleagues like Peter Brook wanted to make British Shakespeare production relevant to the modern condition, firmly moving it away from the rather operatic, high-culture-is-good-for-you posture that had generally characterized it since the Victorian era.[5] The new mode of the RSC converged with European trends in the 1960s: at Stratford, in a variety of European cities from Moscow to Milan, and eventually even in North America, some of the chief directors and designers of the age began to accent the historical messages of Shakespeare's plays for the present, often in a committed or engaged context, and in simple scenographic environments deriving from Elizabethan practice.

These tendencies of postwar Shakespearean performance received substantial theoretical support. Though the procedures of the RSC and of other major companies were frequently attacked by traditional scholars, a number of critics and theatre historians in the 1960s and 1970s provided research and commentary that endorsed radical experimentation. The two most important of these for theatre, interestingly enough, were foreign. Both wrote under Socialist regimes in central and eastern Europe. Kott spoke for himself; the Brechtian strategies were best fortified by the scholarship of Robert Weimann.

Kott's *Shakespeare Our Contemporary* (published in Polish and French in 1962 and in English in 1964), probably the most widely read book of Shakespearean criticism since A. C. Bradley's *Shakespearean Tragedy*, overtly annexed the Elizabethan dramatist to the absurdist environment of postwar Europe. Kott wrote in implicit opposition to the Stalinist government of Poland, a nation whose identity had been forcibly redefined, and whose freedom had been savagely abridged, first by German and then by Soviet annexation.

Kott read Shakespeare, as it were, by the searchlights of a police state. In the histories he saw the "Grand Mechanism" of implacable human corruption, in the comedies a dark and bestial vision of sexuality, in the tragedies a kindred comic grimace reminiscent of Samuel Beckett. As Peter Brook said, "Kott is undoubtedly the only writer on Elizabethan matters who assumes without question that every one of his readers will at some point or other have been woken by the police in the middle of the night."[6] It was through Brook, in fact, that Kott affected the theatre most directly, especially through Brook's (in)famous RSC productions of *King Lear* in 1962 and *A Midsummer Night's Dream* in 1970.

It's hard to pinpoint how Kott altered performance traditions, since Shakespeare had normally been subject to contemporary revision and revaluation anyway. In the modernist period, however, critics were strongly inclined to see Shakespeare as somehow existing outside of time, a refuge of immutability secure from the insistent intrusions of the twentieth century.[7] Kott gave to the theatre of the 1960s and 1970s a theoretically backed fortitude to admit that Shakespeare, despite the cultural accretions that inevitably cling to the work, exists on stage in the present tense; and that representation of Shakespeare can exhibit powerful and intellectually provocative visions of the present. What was particularly new was Kott's injunction that Shakespeare should be read as a dramatist of pain. By drawing analogies to the apocalyptic nightmares of the European absurdists, he deprived Shakespeare of the comfortable status of a tamed classic. Of course, many commentators and some audiences found his ideas excessive or inappropriate; on the other side, by 1980 these ideas had themselves become a new kind of theatrical orthodoxy. But there can be no doubt that *Shakespeare Our Contemporary* broke down a number of artificial, Anglo-centric values that had dogged Shakespearean criticism and production into the postwar era.

Kott's working assumption was that human nature is unchanging and essentially comic in its absurdity. While he stressed the particularity of the postwar condition, he seemed to ratify a determinate universe in which human fate remained inscrutable, the black void our only end. The circus and the theatre, where human beings grapple with extreme issues that change nothing in the other world, became for him the pertinent metaphors for life, and Beckett's plays the characteristic comic expression of the era. Thus, thinking about

Gloucester's clownish leap from Dover Cliff in *Lear* Kott is immediately reminded of Didi and Gogo's clownish attempt to hang themselves in *Waiting for Godot*:

Gloucester did fall, and he got up again. He made his suicide attempt, but he failed to shake the world. Nothing changed ... If there are no gods, suicide makes no sense. Death exists in any case. Suicide cannot alter human fate, but only accelerate it. It ceases to be a protest. It is a surrender. It becomes the acceptance of world's greatest cruelty – death.[8]

Obviously indebted to Sartre and Camus, the passage also reflects a view of the world, congenial to the liberal western democracies, that privileges the anguish of the individual over the destiny of the social group. For Shakespeare the world was a cruel place, for us it is still a cruel place. We cannot affect our fates, only hasten them: personal survival and stoic perseverance are solemn protests against the cosmic odds, hugely stacked against us.

This kind of Kottian fatalism regularly appeared in numerous productions of the comedies in the period that liked to suggest that human beings were caught in a trap of their own making. Konrad Swinarski's *Midsummer Night's Dream* (Krakow, 1970) is an interesting example: a round of sinister sexuality was treated with nightmare intensity, with two secret policemen silently observing throughout; political power and sexual power were intertwined. In the histories and tragedies, productions under Kott's influence often suggested that evil was an unending, cyclical force. Borrowing a favorite dramaturgical structure from Beckett, directors sometimes added *da capo* endings to plays like *Lear* and *Macbeth*, codas that saw the same cycle of destruction replaying itself. Perhaps the most widely seen example of the *da capo* approach was in a version by another Polish director, Roman Polanski's 1972 film (in English) of *Macbeth*; after Shakespeare's final scene, the camera showed Donalbain as a disenfranchised younger brother climbing through a storm to seek out the witches, and hearing the same music Macbeth had heard at the beginning of the play.

While Kott's influence was vast and international in scope, his book spoke with the greatest immediacy in eastern Europe, as my examples tend to suggest. Just as his notion of the "contemporary" requires historicizing, his synchronic approach to Shakespeare was itself part of cold war history. Brook noticed this phenomenon with the 1962 *King Lear*, a production that many English-speaking commentators thought too "European" (i.e., foreign) anyway, which traveled both east and west over the next two years. On tour in the US, the director felt that it failed to connect with audiences rather remote from its themes of absence and loss; in eastern Europe, however, it found its true home. "The best performances," Brook wrote, "lay between Budapest and Moscow."[9]

Robert Weimann's effect on international Shakespeare has been less obvious, though the issues he set out have been equally powerful tools in the theatre. If Kott saw the world as cruel and unmitigated middle-earth, Weimann saw it as a space to be changed. Marxist in thought and historical in method, Weimann was especially interested in how the theatre could recover in Shakespeare a popular tradition, empowering general spectators with the status the playwright and his stage had given them in the sixteenth century. Weimann's major work, published in East Berlin in 1967 as *Shakespeare und die Tradition des Volkstheaters*, was translated and updated in 1978 as *Shakespeare and the Popular Tradition in the Theater*. It asked for a "unity of history and criticism by which the past significance and the present meaning of Shakespeare's theater" could be explained with reference to its "structural quality" and its "social function." Two overriding historical facts must condition everything we think about Shakespeare:

On the one hand, Shakespeare's theater is irremediably a thing of the past; on the other, his plays have survived the conditions from which they originated and are continually revitalized on the modern stage ... The tension between what is past and what lives for us today is obvious; and yet, from the point of view of the function of literary scholarship, it seems impossible to relegate the pastness of Shakespeare's theater to the "pure" historian and its contemporaneousness to the "pure" critic or modern producer.[10]

Accepting Marx's premise that art is "one of the special modes of production," Weimann insisted that we cannot sever Shakespeare's plays from the social and historical conditions of their original time (as literary critics as diverse as Bradley and Kott have tended to do). At the same time, when we fail to "separate pastness from what is alive, history from interpretation," we only compound the confusion by failing to distinguish between "the history of a work's origins in the past and the story of its effects in the present." As he put it in a separate essay, "today *any* Shakespeare staging has to come to terms with the tension between Renaissance values and modern evaluations."[11]

In dedicating the book to Manfred Wekwerth and Benno Besson – "my friends in the theater who have come closest to a modern Shakespeare in the popular tradition" – Weimann showed his colors most clearly. Wekwerth and Besson, who at various times worked at and were the managers of the three major theatres in East Berlin, the Deutsches Theater, the Volksbühne, and the Berliner Ensemble, were the leading Brechtian directors of Shakespeare in the 1960s and 1970s. Indeed, Wekwerth directed (with the collaboration of Joachim Tenschert, in 1964) Brecht's own adaptation of *Coriolanus*, one of the defining productions of the Berliner Ensemble. Thus for Weimann and for his friends, *die Tradition des Volkstheaters* meant more than the words *the Popular Tradition in Theater* convey in English: Weimann's title referred not only to Shakespeare's popular audience but also to the Marxist–Brechtian blueprint for theatrical production which privileged reception over intention, the minds of the spectators over the personalities and aspirations of the artists.

In the west, "Brechtian" has become a description of style. The term is often detached from the social and political commitment that underlay the comprehensive system of theatrical writing and performance that Brecht and his associates worked out in Berlin after the war. This is especially true with Shakespeare, and even became true at the RSC in the late 1960s, despite Peter Hall's early leftist leanings. But in the GDR, and on other important stages in Europe, Brechtian Shakespeare remained revolutionary. As Weimann counseled, its method of production emphasized the pastness of the texts and thus found itself free to redefine their meanings for the present. Populist directors like Roger Planchon in Lyon, Leopold Lindtberg in Vienna, and Giorgio Strehler in Milan, as well as Wekwerth, Besson, and Friedo Solter in Berlin, struck a bargain with Shakespeare: he delivered a Renaissance classic text, they overlaid it with a postwar social text. By stressing class distinctions among the characters, the recessive political tensions in the fable, or the complicity between terror and power, for example, they offered visions of Shakespeare that seemed to straddle the past and the present.

Unlike the Kottian method, which tended to suggest the unchanging nature of a cosmos ruled by cruel but invisible forces, Brechtian productions wished to suggest that human beings could control and thus change their own fates. Attempting to alienate the spectator from the purely emotive aspects of the drama, these productions hoped to prompt a new awareness of the spectator's position within the political and economic construct. An audience would be most connected to Shakespeare when it was distanced from him, when it ceased merely spectating and started acting, or at least thinking.

Thus Shakespearean performance after the war, whether influenced by Kott or by Brecht or by a mixture of the two, tended to discover contemporary themes and to stress the spectator's inclusion in those themes. Not all productions, of course, demonstrated the same inclinations. In Ontario, for example, the Stratford Festival Theatre was the architectural model for audience incorporation but, perhaps because of Guthrie's own apolitical stance, seemed devoid of social commentary. On the other hand, the New York Shakespeare Festival in Central Park worked hard (though not always successfully) to find a progressive American expression equal to the excitement generated by the European theatre thinkers. In general terms, by the mid-1960s Shakespeare performance, both Anglophone and foreign, sought a message in the play; whatever the message might be, the production almost always achieved its utterance by limiting the manifold possibilities of the raw text.

This method of handling classic texts, common in the twentieth century, has been greatly facilitated by the enormous growth in authority of the stage director. There are many things to say about the advent of the director as the chief artistic force in the theatrical enterprise, but one thing that perhaps hasn't been said enough is that the director's rise is intimately tied to theatrical modernism. The modernist ideal – planted by Appia and Craig and much cultivated in the early century by directors like Reinhardt and Meyerhold – encouraged the director to fuse the elements of scenography, acting style, and intellectual theme into a single aesthetic experience. The mediation of the theatre was channeled through the mediation of the director, and justified on the grounds that for complex dramas an audience wants a single concept or point of view provided. Needless to say this paradigm still has numerous adherents in the theatre, and is often the working assumption even in training programs. For modernist Shakespearean performance the director was a godsend: he became a manager of the formidable possibilities of a text otherwise too distant in time, language, and thought. (The gendered pronoun is deliberate; until quite recently almost all directors were male.) Despite their substantial differences, both Brecht and Kott countenanced the modernist inclination for

Shakespeare in that they proposed that the director control and shape theatrical meaning.

But starting in the mid-1970s the modernist ideal of unified production began to break down. For Shakespeare, a number of European directors and companies that had earlier subscribed to the Brechtian and Kottian modes started to experiment with expressions of diverse savor, particularly in the visual realm. As Europe moved out of the period dominated by the effects of the war, Shakespearean representation began to reflect a new set of concerns, often affected by a new internationalism and by the global effects of multinational capitalism. The burgeoning wealth of the west and Japan, encouraging vast tourism as well as an international consumer economy, moved Shakespeare, along with culture in general, from the stern faces of Socialism and absurdism. The work of directors like Planchon, Strehler, and Brook no longer seemed restrained by the distressed clothing and distressed ideas familiar from *Mother Courage* and *Waiting for Godot*, the two plays that defined the postwar era.

Peter Zadek's travesty versions, seen in West Germany starting in the 1960s, were pertinent transitions to an iconoclastic but less ideological Shakespeare. Meanwhile, young directors like Peter Stein and Ariane Mnouchkine, originally affected by Brecht and by Marxist dialectics, began to sketch the outlines of a self-consciously postmodern Shakespeare. As Kott himself noted, the contemporary distrust of politics in the west has caused theatre artists to substitute a "new visual expression" for Shakespeare in place of the rough-edged emphasis on intellectual meaning of the postwar avant-garde, whose workers were, in any event, "restricted to the limited resources of the small stage."[12]

Postmodern experiments with Shakespeare were held in check in Great Britain and North America until quite recently by the power-ful routines of the RSC and Ontario, which continued to assert the centrality of the text and of traditional acting based upon textual analysis. There is little doubt that the Elizabethan English language played a large part in this state of affairs. Peter Hall, for example, said in 1988 that out of his career as a director of about twenty-five Shakespeare productions, only one was not located by a Renais-sance reference: "unless what's on the stage looks like the language, I simply don't believe it."[13] In Europe and Asia, however, partly because of the freedom from an accustomed linguistic approach to

Shakespeare, no such control existed, and the postmodern delight in eclectic transtemporality has been given free rein. As a result some of the most innovative and exciting productions of Shakespeare in the past twenty years have come not from the RSC but from Europe, east, west, and central; from Soviet Georgia; and from Japan. These productions often made it their business to register the cultural differences between the original texts and the target audiences, going directly against Hall's precept. In other words, Shakespeare was again being presented for his foreignness rather than for his familiarity, as he had been in German in the eighteenth century. Just at the time that the number of Shakespeare performances around the globe vastly increased, the deviations between Anglophone and foreign performances have been heightened.

And yet postwar performance of Shakespeare has often demonstrated a fruitful tension between the foreign and the native. The pervasive internationalism of film has been crucial here, particularly the influential work of Grigori Kozintsev and of Akira Kurosawa, both of whom adapted Shakespeare's tragedies by a process of cultural transfer. The apparent ease by which these master filmmakers brought new meanings to old drama has in turn affected a number of stage directors. Brook, for example, was much struck by how Kurosawa's *Throne of Blood* (1957) recast the *Macbeth* story in cinematic images of a cross-cultural nature. From Kurosawa's samurai tale, Brook learned to leap over the archaism of the text by concentrating on fable and theme, and his Shakespeare work in Paris since 1974 has tended to pull away from the textual responsibility he had felt in his earlier productions at Stratford.[14] He told his translator, Jean-Claude Carrière, that the major danger of linguistic conversion was translationese, what Carrière refers to as a language of "traduit de." The ideal performance script for Paris, Brook said, would be one that appeared to be "a new play, written in French, and written by Shakespeare."[15] The cross-cultural method reached a peak of sorts with Brook's production of *The Tempest* in 1990, in which an interracial troupe of actors combined an African modality with performance tactics borrowed from Brook's version of *The Mahabharata*, which was also written by Carrière.

The internationalism of film, which depends only on a distribution system that is part of the normal procedures of capitalist commerce, has been paralleled in recent years by a more complicated theatrical internationalism. The rapidity and ease of jet transport has allowed touring by theatre companies on a large scale, just as it has done for professional sports teams, and has simultaneously brought spectators from all over the globe to theatrical centers like Tokyo, New York, Stratford, Paris, and Berlin. The Channel-hopping spectator of the past has been replaced by the ocean-hopping spectator and the ocean-hopping company, equally at home in Los Angeles or London, Toronto or Milan, Sidney or Prague – or, in keeping with contemporary aesthetics, equally *not* at home. For Shakespeare this postmodern condition of nearly borderless theatre, exaggerated even further by the collapse of the Soviet empire, has created great curiosities of playgoing: Korean spectators at Stratford laughing at three-and-a-half-hour performances of comedies in an ancient language they do not understand; the critic of *The Guardian* using "Euro-Shakespeare" to castigate British theatres for their lack of multi-racial casting; a Japanese company bringing a violently beautiful and thoroughly foreign *Macbeth* to Scotland.[16]

There is no one conclusion to draw from all of this, except that foreign Shakespeare is more present than ever before, interrogating the idea that Shakespeare can be contained by a single tradition or by a single culture or by a single language. Perhaps the native familiarity that English-speakers assume for Shakespeare is part of a larger illusion, which might be called the myth of cultural owner-ship. In the end Shakespeare doesn't belong to any nation or anybody: Shakespeare is foreign to all of us. In the theatre we will continue to see a range of attitudes to the ownership of the plays, just as we see in contemporary Shakespearean scholarship. Some pro-ductions will want to point up the otherness of the texts, others will continue to want to possess or absorb them.

Either way, the texts themselves remain both distant and elusive. The span is enormous between the original conditions of the texts and their performances today, and will grow greater. In Weimann's terms, the situation of the plays is completely gone; what we have left are the traces. These traces, of course, fascinate us, disturb our dreams, and make us knock on the door through which they came. In general, foreign productions of Shakespeare, freed from the burden imposed by centuries of admiring his language, have been more ready to admit that the door to the past is locked.

In English the language will always be important to our appreci-ation, yet our ability to reach the plays directly in their original language lessens year by year. Our own English continues to change, and eventually only specialists will be able to read the texts, much less listen to them comfortably in the theatre. This may well happen within the next fifty years. In fact, some of us teaching Shakespeare in universities in North America believe that it is happening now, at an accelerated pace. Reflecting on performances outside of English, we can see more clearly how Shakespeare is alien, as well as what we continue to find indigenous or domestic about him. What is it that endures when he is deprived of his tongue? It's a question that will haunt the future.

NOTES

1 Anna Földes, in a panel discussion transcribed in John Elsom (ed.), *Is Shakespeare Still Our Contemporary?* (London: Routledge, 1989), 94.

2 The three series are "Text and Performance" (London: Macmillan), "Shakespeare in Performance" (Manchester University Press), and "Plays in Performance" (Bristol Classical Press. Future titles to be published by Cambridge University Press). Of the numerous Shakespeare volumes now available, only David Hirst's *The Tempest* (Text and Performance, London, 1984) uses a major foreign example (Giorgio Strehler's 1978 production in Milan). Two volumes on *King Lear* treat Grigori Kozintsev's Russian film version of 1970: Alexander Leggatt's (Shakespeare in Performance, Manchester, 1991) and Gamini Salgado's (Text and Performance, London, 1984).

3 Simon Williams notes that the early English Comedians were more admired for musical and acrobatic qualities than for dramatic ones: see *Shakespeare on the German Stage, 1586–1914* (Cambridge University Press, 1990), 32–3. Williams also provides a detailed account of the formal arrival of Shakespeare in German in the eighteenth and nineteenth centuries. Jerzy Limon's *Gentlemen of a Company: English Players in Central and Eastern Europe, 1590–1660* (Cambridge University Press, 1985) treats the early playing conditions in detail.

4 For a more complete description, see my essay "Ich Bin ein (Ost) Berliner: *Hamlet* at the Volksbühne," *Western European Stages* 2 (1990): 11–15.

5 Discussed by David Addenbrooke, *The Royal Shakespeare Company: The Peter Hall Years* (London: Kimber, 1974), and by Sally Beauman, *The Royal Shakespeare Company: A History of Ten Decades* (Oxford University Press, 1982).

6 Peter Brook, *The Shifting Point, 1946–1987* (New York: Harper and Row, 1987), 44. Brook read Kott's essay "King Lear or Endgame" (which is the centerpiece of *Shakespeare Our Contemporary*) in French prior to its publication. But the influence went both ways: Kott saw Brook's

production of *Titus Andronicus* (Stratford, 1955) on tour in Warsaw in 1957. "*Titus Andronicus* has revealed to me a Shakespeare I dreamed of but have never before seen on the stage," Kott wrote in his review (reprinted in the Anchor Books edition of *Shakespeare Our Contemporary* [New York: Anchor Books, 1966], 353). See my discussion in chapter 6 of *Looking at Shakespeare: A Visual History of Twentieth-Century Performance* (Cambridge University Press, 1993).

7 Hugh Grady's *The Modernist Shakespeare: Critical Texts in a Material World* (Oxford: Clarendon Press, 1991) treats the literary aspects of this topic in detail.

8 Kott, *Shakespeare Our Contemporary*, 151.

9 Peter Brook, *The Empty Space* (New York; Atheneum, 1968), 21–3. Martin Esslin's introduction to the Anchor Books edition of *Shakespeare Our Contemporary* discusses its resonance in eastern Europe, and Kott's own position as a Polish Communist academic who broke with Stalinism in 1956. Kott spends a few paragraphs historicizing his position in his latest book, *The Gender of Rosalind* (Evanston: Northwestern University Press, 1992), 5–8.

10 Robert Weimann, *Shakespeare and the Popular Tradition in the Theater: Studies in the Social Dimension of Dramatic Form and Function*, trans. and ed. Robert Schwartz (Baltimore: Johns Hopkins University Press, 1978), xiii.

11 Weimann, "Shakespeare on the Modern Stage: Past Significance and Present Meaning," *Shakespeare Survey* 20 (1967): 115. Gary Taylor takes a similar approach to Weimann's work in *Reinventing Shakespeare: A Cultural History, from the Restoration to the Present* (New York: Oxford University Press, 1989), 301–2.

12 Quoted in Charles Marowitz, "Kott, Our Contemporary," *American Theatre*, Oct. 1988: 100.

13 Interview in Ralph Berry, *On Directing Shakespeare*, 2nd ed. (London: Hamish Hamilton, 1989), 209.

14 See David Williams, "'A Place Marked by Life': Brook at the Bouffes du Nord," *New Theatre Quarterly* 1 (1985): 42. I discuss this issue, and related ones, in the final chapter of *Looking at Shakespeare*.

15 Reported by Jean-Claude Carrière, in a talk in Los Angeles in 1991.

16 The critic was Michael Billington, "From the Stage of the Globe," *The Guardian Weekly*, 5 May 1991: 22. The Japanese production was Yukio Ninagawa's *Macbeth* at the Edinburgh Festival in 1985.

PART I

The foreignness of Shakespeare

The first substantial piece of Shakespearean criticism, Ben Jonson's dedicatory poem in the Folio edition of 1623, already claimed a universal Shakespeare. Jonson's voice, classical and serene, memorialized a poet who transcended time and who outshone all ancient and contemporary playwrights, from Aeschylus and Sophocles to Plautus and Terence, from Kyd and Marlowe to Francis Beaumont. The collected works afforded Jonson an opportunity to assert an international eminence for his tiny island kingdom as well as for his friend and rival:

> Triumph, my Britain, thou hast one to show
> To whom all scenes of Europe homage owe.
> He was not of an age, but for all time ...

The stake that the English have since had in the dramatist's reputation, as given voice by English-speaking Shakespearean commentators, has been partly dependent upon a similar claim of Shakespeare's universal nativeness: he belongs to the world by virtue of belonging to us.

That collective group of believers in Shakespeare's greatness, that hegemonic "we," was itself a cultural construct, one that earnestly formulated a high purpose and a humanist rationale for the study of the subject. But the old construct began to break down after 1975 or so, and the recent history of Shakespearean criticism has been a history of fractures. New forms of thinking about the plays, based on issues relating to gender, to performance, to materialist interpretations of history, and to an assortment of post-structuralist problematics, have redefined the nature of the task. While there is no longer a unity of purpose, it's safe to say that a Shakespearean today is not likely to be what she was a generation ago.

Despite the redefinition, however, Shakespeare has not lost much of his dominating position; the Shakespeare industry, especially in the theatre, is more active and more extensive than ever before. Further, new approaches to Shakespeare have tended to retain a major assumption of the old approaches: they start with the linguistic text, and in English. It's not much of an exaggeration to say that for the vast majority of thinkers in the present and the past, Shakespeare is his text.

What happens when Shakespeare manifestly is *not* his text, as in any translation and all foreign-language performances? That is the question John Russell Brown asks, and asks specifically from the standpoint of an English-speaking critic and director. Brown's essay queries some fundamental assumptions about Anglo-centered Shakespearean thinking, as do the other essays in this section. Dominique Goy-Blanquet looks further at Shakespeare's foreignness by comparing three recent productions, seen in Paris, of that very "foreign" play, *Titus Andronicus*: one in English (Deborah Warner), one in Italian by a German director (Peter Stein), and one in French (Daniel Mesguich). Based on interviews with all three directors, and upon detailed comparisons of the productions, the essay offers a model for international Shakespearean criticism.

Avraham Oz reminds us that social and political controversies connected to Shakespeare's English Renaissance texts shift significantly when their performance venue shifts. Tracing the history of *The Merchant of Venice* in Israel, Oz notes that the play – which has in fact become a new text since Hitler – remains particularly ambiguous and unstable in the homeland of the Jews, and that no production of it can occur there merely as art. Leanore Lieblein examines whether a translation of a Shakespeare play is limited by the production for which it was written, and touches on issues of translation theory rarely considered in a Shakespearean context. In a different vein, Ron Engle looks at one of the most transgressive of contemporary Shakespeare directors, Peter Zadek, whose outlandish productions have been driven in part by a conviction that it is impossible to convey Shakespeare's text adequately outside of English.

CHAPTER I

Foreign Shakespeare and English-speaking audiences

John Russell Brown

Hit in the eye by a production of Shakespeare in a foreign city, and understanding scarcely a word that is spoken, a theatre critic can find much to write about. Well-known characters seem to move on that stage according to unfamiliar principles or unforeseen impulses. Crowd scenes dominate the story-line. Soliloquies are both passionate and refined. The stage set compels attention, and starts an argument about meaning and significance. The audience is excited, talkative, restless, serious, or quiet beyond expectation. And among such provocation, a new sense of what had hitherto lain hidden begins to emerge from within the familiar Shakespeare text; or a moment, which had previously seemed unremarkable, becomes riveted into memory. Ordinary reactions are by-passed or displaced, and perception is quickened. The critic comes away with an enthusiasm not easy to explain.

Bells do not ring like this every time a Shakespeare play is performed in a language other than English, but they are heard so frequently that "foreign Shakespeare" deserves careful study. Inquiry might start by noting the most obvious differences from home-produced Shakespeare, even though these may serve only to emphasize what is merely eccentric or perverse, and may be limited to elements of production which are most open to manipulation – set, costumes, heavy underscoring of certain words, casting against convention, stylistic transposition from one theatrical tradition to another, or the use of a translation which changes original references with unmistakable boldness. Deletion of whole scenes, speeches, or characters, together with interpolation of new characters, speeches, songs, stage-business, or extravagant improvisations will also enter the reckoning very readily. But a critic does not have to travel to see Shakespeare treated in these ways, because the extraordinary imaginative energy that went into the making of these texts

21

encourages exciting and extravagant liberties in whatever language
they are performed. Perhaps all that is unusual about the interpreta-
tive license of foreign Shakespeare is that English-speaking companies have rather more inhibitions, or less active imaginations.

Inquiry should go beyond this elementary accounting. We should
ask why Shakespeare's plays are performed with such popular
success in so many languages and in so many different political
intellectual, social and artistic traditions. The international viability
of Shakespeare goes beyond that of any other dramatist. What lies at
the center of his art, what secret quality do these texts possess which
is not destroyed by adaptation, transposition, misrepresentation,
spectacular simplification, or novel accretion?

Everyone knows that a good and faithful translation of Shakespeare's
text into another language is an impossibility. Vocabulary, syntax,
word-order, idiom, phrasing, pointing, texture, weight, rhythm,
tempo have no exact counterparts in other languages. Changes in
those who speak the text must also be reckoned with: class, dialect,
mentality, tradition, individual histories will all be unfamiliar in
foreign Shakespeare. While the translation of prose raises multiple
problems, that of verse compounds the difficulties; any change in
sound, nuance, resonance is the more shattering for its disturbance of
the finely tuned music of the original. At best only approximations
can be assembled or an alternative poetry substituted.

So why pay attention to the performance of lamed and imperfect
texts, to a Shakespeare production which has lost the very words
which are our sole contact with the play's author? Literary critics
have believed that the minutest details of the original words embody
the very substance of Shakespeare's art and vision: that text is a fine
intellectual web in which the real presence of his mind may be
discovered. G. Wilson Knight, in his *Wheel of Fire* (1930) and *The
Shakespearean Tempest* (1932), the first of many books, demanded a
close examination:

While we view the plays primarily as studies in character, abstracting the
literary person from the close mesh of that poetic fabric into which he is
woven, we shall ... end by creating a chaos of the whole. If, however, we
give attention always to poetic colour and suggestion first ... we shall find
each play in turn appear more and more amazing in the delicacy of its
texture, and then, and not till then, will the whole of Shakespeare's work
begin to reveal its rich significance, its harmony, its unity.[1]

Attention paid to complex words and subtle images, to ingenious and arresting wordplay, to the smallest details of grammar, and to resonance and suggestion has opened new vistas of understanding and appreciation. Why should we be interested in productions of Shakespeare which have jettisoned this essential element?

Often the impress of poetry is given central place in our understanding of Shakespeare's characters: "it is, of course, the range and depth of the poetry that make Shakespeare's Antony and Cleopatra into universal figures," says L. C. Knights in *Some Shakespearean Themes* (1959).[2] A whole school of literary critics has drawn from the subtleties of Shakespeare's language an equally subtle view of his plays. Una Ellis-Fermor gave due weight to the physical presence required by performance, but she also argued that enactment could not be appreciated without a close study of the words; in the smallest details of the text we should try to discern hints, suggestions, fragmentary evocations, half-hidden energies of thought and feeling. Shakespeare's deepest meaning must be teased out of the verbal surface. Shakespeare

is bound, by the nature of dramatic art, to reveal his perceptions in terms of the end-product of the process he has discerned, in terms of that efflorescence upon the surface which is made up of the words and deeds of his characters ... having, after all, for the instrument of his expression, only the words contained in some 3000 lines.[3]

More recently, Shakespeare's text has been examined for ambiguities and tensions expressed in his use of crucial words of political and moral significance as they were valid in the context of the England of his day. In *Radical Tragedy* (1984), Jonathan Dollimore discovered essential oppositions in the plays by a careful watch for particular terminology. He argued that in *Coriolanus* Shakespeare was pitting a reaffirmation of "old class antagonisms" spoken by Menenius over against the political realism voiced by Aufidius. The essentialist mystification of a former master – "He wants nothing of a god but eternity, and a heaven to throne in" (5.4.23–4) – is here contrasted nicely with his enemy's judgment that "So our virtues / Lie in th' interpretation of the time" (4.7.50). Every word plays its part, every stress; the opposition is expressed in tone of voice and force of utterance, as well as in carefully chosen words. The critic puts Shakespeare on ideological trial and each word, or hesitation, or over-emphasis counts. Translate the text of the play into another language and these careful reflections, balances, insinuations, emphases will all evaporate, and some other simpler, bolder, or more diffused, or more muddled ideas will be substituted.

With no less assurance than the critics, English-speaking theatre directors have often insisted on the central importance of the verbal text in English. Granville Barker's *Preface to Antony and Cleopatra* (1930) anticipated Knights:

the vibrations of emotion that the sound of the poetry sets up seem to enlarge its sense, and break the bounds of the theatre to carry us into the lost world of romantic history. Conceive such a story and such characters so familiarly, and then tie their expression to prose – Dido will be in danger of becoming a dowdy indeed, and Cleopatra a gypsy.[4]

In his *Preface to King Lear*, Barker asserted that the individuality of the play "is made manifest by the form as well as the substance of the dialogue, by the shaping and colour of its verse and prose," and this this vital element, present only in the English text, "is, of course, of primary importance for producer and actors" (II.25).

Such ideas were echoed more than fifty years later by John Barton of the Royal Shakespeare Company:

the clues in the text are much richer and more numerous than at first appears. And though the possibilities are infinite, we can only sift the fruitful from the perverse by getting our teeth into the text and the verse itself. If the textual points are ignored, then it's pretty certain that Shakespeare's intentions will be ignored also or at least twisted ... Shakespeare *is* his text. So if you want to do him justice, you have to look for and follow the clues he offers. If an actor does that then he'll find that Shakespeare himself starts to direct him.[5]

If "Shakespeare *is* his text," in all its English and metrical niceties, what interest can we find in a foreign Shakespeare?

For a start, we should observe that advantage is not to the English text in all respects. Translation can shake off excrescences and obscurities which are injuries inflicted by the passage of time. The structural balance of *King Lear* and an audience's reception of its text were newly revealed to me when I saw a production in Ankara. Nowhere else have I heard audiences laugh when Mad Tom mocks the pretensions of advantaged persons (3.4). There was a surprising change of tone, a frisson between personal superiority and apparent degradation, an easy volubility, and comedy; and Edgar gained confidence through these speeches. If I had seen the production on tour to London or New York, so much would have been clear; but in

Ankara the audience helped to show me that Edgar had also gained
a new relationship with the theatre audience; he was now at ease
with them, despite his nakedness.

Speaking these speeches in contemporary England is hard work
for an actor:

Who gives anything to Poor Tom? Whom the foul fiend hath led through
fire and through flame, through ford and whirlpool, o'er bog and quag-
mire; that hath laid knives under his pillow and halters in his pew, set
ratsbane by his porridge, made him proud of heart, to ride on a bay
trotting horse over four-inched bridges, to course his own shadow for a
traitor. Bless thy five wits, Tom's a-cold. O, do, de, do, de, do, de. Bless thee
from whirlwinds, star-blasting, and taking. Do Poor Tom some charity,
whom the foul fiend vexes . . .(3.4.50ff)

Unless special effort is made to give them meaning and vivacity,
many words in English will pass the audience by, unregarded
because not understood. Not only are they unfamiliar, as they were
not when translated into contemporary Turkish, but in England, or
in North America, little is known today of halters, ratsbane, star-
blasting, or plackets; few people are familiar with hog, fox, or wolf;
serving-men are by no means common and "fellowship" has only
weak social and moral implications; traitors, obedience to parents,
or a "foul fiend" have little impact on daily life; poverty is seldom
absolute or without protection; madness in neither holy nor entirely
hopeless. In translation and in Ankara, the scene was not only
liberated from the chains of out-of-date language, but for some of
the audience it also had immediate reference to freshly lived experience. It provided a significantly different theatrical experience
which may have been much closer to that provided by this text in
Shakespeare's own day.

The truth is that all performances of Shakespeare are in some
sense "foreign" to Shakespeare's intentions. Changes in the meaning
of words, and to the lived experience which they reflect, ensure that
we can never experience the plays as Shakespeare thought an
audience might. Directors, designers, and actors will strive to miti-
gate these disadvantages – some new words can be sneaked in, some
gestures can illustrate what words should sufficiently communicate –
but the problem goes deeper than that. These difficulties infect the
very center of Shakespeare's art, the "range and depth" of poetry,
and the "shaping and colour" of verse and prose. Many elements of
speech have changed beyond recall: pronunciation, dialect, class

distinctions, idioms (especially conversational ones), modes of address, attitudes to formality, imagery, and versification, references to god and the devil, to kings and the people. Among English-speaking productions there are many varieties of speech, and each has its own resonance, impression of naturalness, distinction between characters. All these elements of performance prevent us from clearly experiencing the Shakespeare which "*is* his text": they interpose an obstacle between us and it. To become aware of what has happened, we can turn to an obviously foreign Shakespeare, where the filter through which we perceive the play is radically, even brutally, changed: while missing much by losing direct contact with the original text, we may find other strains in the writing which might not otherwise be heard.

In foreign languages, Shakespeare's plays often seem more political and polemical than in English. Partly this is because a director will underline his chosen political interpretation in many ways that are not verbal and in an unfamiliar language we pay more attention to these visual signals. But a translation, by being more attuned to contemporary parlance, can move the whole play much closer to our own political consciousness. In *Coriolanus* words like *god, eternity, heaven, throne, virtues,* and phrases like the "interpretation of the time," do not immediately alert an audience to political issues; indeed, they obscure them. Of course, many subtleties of "depth" and "colour" will be lost in translation, but what is lost in flavor or intellectual nicety is compensated in part by the use of words which are plainly and undeniably political, the very words in which opposing sides in contemporary politics popularize their policies.

Playing Shakespeare in translation can also alert audiences to some resonances, naturalistic impressions and intellectual distinctions which may not register in English-speaking theatres today. Perhaps this is especially so in scenes of close personal encounter, when the sexuality of the characters is involved, or their more instinctive reactions. The intensity and strangeness of Hamlet's encounter with Ophelia after "To be or not to be ..." cannot be doubted, but all that may be implied in their words will not register in contemporary spoken English:

HAMLET: I never gave you aught.
OPHELIA: My honour'd lord, you know right well you did,
           And with them words of so sweet breath compos'd
           As made the things more rich ...   (3.1.96ff)

Should "aught" sound archaic, as it does in England or North America today? Might a foreign but inflected language show more clearly the force of the second person plural used by both Hamlet and Ophelia, compared with Hamlet's *thee, thou,* and *thy* only a few speeches later? How should "right well" sound in Hamlet's ears, and in the audience's? Is a pedagogic tone and emphasis appropriate here or was the phrase added by Shakespeare to suggest a careful moral insistence? Or is earnestness required? These two words can sound trite or childlike, or combative, to present-day audiences, for reasons which were not operative in Shakespeare's day. But then how precious, precocious, or precise is "of so sweet breath compos'd"? "Sweet" is not an easy word to use today; "composed" can sound oddly stiff, or cunningly taunting, when spoken to a Hamlet who is said to be no longer in "his wonted way" of speech or behavior (lines 40–1).

Only a moment later another huge difficulty arises, as Hamlet asks "Are you honest?" and speaks of Ophelia's "beauty." The sexual implications of "honest" have often been noted by critics and audiences, and also those that may be involved with Ophelia's use of "commerce" only one line later; but what is the exact force of "beauty"? Shakespeare and his contemporaries used the same word for the most idealistic or spiritual beauty and for the most sensually attractive or sexually provocative. The word "sex," as we use it today, and all the words we associate with it, were not available in English in their day, and so they used other means to refer to such matters, in ways which are very rare today. No words are more difficult to evaluate for performance today than *affection, fancy, love, delight, beauty.* Translators have difficulty with them too, but at least they can make a choice between a wide range of possibilities, or use an ambiguous word in a context which makes the dominant meaning clear enough. In an English-language performance an actor may accept the word as given by Shakespeare without being aware that it could have meanings other than those current today. "Can beauty my lord, have better commerce than with honesty?" – what does Ophelia mean, and what does Hamlet hear? Sometimes an actor performing in a translation is able to reanimate suggestions which must remain obscure or dormant in the original text.

Actors and audiences lose greatly when Shakespeare's plays are performed in languages other than English, but they may also profit. Certain ideas and experiences will be more potent or more probing,

and some scenes more animated. Theatre-going critics may well
return to the original text with a fuller appreciation of some of its
implications and with a keener sense – which they will share with all
actors – that to read or perform Shakespeare today is always to be
involved in a kind of translation; there is no one who can claim to
present the plays in their own language. Shakespeare may be "his
text," but our possession of that is won only with difficulty and is
never complete.

A single review of a production of *The Winter's Tale* in Berlin in
1991 illustrates how a release from the original language gives to
performers a freedom to strike out of accepted norms and to invite
permanent reappraisal of the text. The production at the Schaubühne was by Luc Bondy, the translation by Peter Handke. According to *The Times* of London for 3 January, Paulina became "a
marvellous comic creation of righteous harridanism," while the
clown Autolycus became more dangerous –

instantly recognisable as one of the new breed of East European wide-boys,
who have made Berlin their headquarters since the opening up of the Wall
in November 1989, selling smuggled knick-knacks, changing currency and
playing games of chance.

Camillo and his colleagues at court were high-ranking bureaucrats
"to whom nothing is less welcome than change or disruption." The
last scenes were joyless:

Leontes greets the young lovers by groping at his own daughter like a
depraved old man. When the statue of Hermione comes to life, the queen
returns to a world irremediably poisoned by the events of 16 years before
and to a husband who has lost the capacity to give and receive love.

A quick reaction might be to dismiss the production as a distortion,
but critics, instead of casting stones, might use these interpretations
as a means of reassessing the possibilities of the original text. They
might find their own readings incomplete: perhaps the innate
dignity of an old language has obscured comic aspects of Paulina
and unassuageable instincts in Leontes? The silences of courtiers
may have been undervalued. Who can say that he or she has
responded fully to what any Shakespearean text may have power
and authority to suggest?

A production involves more than giving life to a text: a company of
actors is drawn into the play's action and sustains it before an

audience, using all its various members and all their art and craft. In assessing these aspects of performance, foreign productions of Shakespeare are especially rewarding because the actors of no single country can represent all strands of theatre tradition and all modes of performance. In some ways foreign companies playing Shakespeare may come closer than English-speaking companies to conditions of performance in Shakespeare's day.

The Royal Shakespeare Company has a continuous commitment to staging the plays and has maintained a small group of directors, with one or two in overall control, to carry out this task. And so the RSC has developed, in recent years, a strong, considered and frontal kind of performance, a style which suits their two main theatres, at Stratford and at the London Barbican. To reach to the back of the stretched and cinema-shaped auditorium at Stratford, the actors are directed to speak out front, rather than in intimate interaction with each other. At the Barbican, they are often instructed to maintain considerable distances between each other in order to fill out the broad expanse of the acting area; it was a theatre planned for a large and active company, not for the shrunken numbers of the financially straitened 1980s and early 1990s. After being together in a small repertoire of plays for up to two consecutive years, the company members seem totally familiar with each other and with their text: the result is that they are tempted to trust the mechanism of the production, rather than to continue an exploration of the play. The productions do change over the long months of performance, but in the direction of assurance and boldness, not of innovation and excitement. Moreover, most of the company attend classes by the same voice and movement teachers, so that an impression of concerted response and effortless unity is often more striking than one of individual playing and personal risks; the action never seems liable to dislocation or discordance. While applauding the successes of this method of production, we may pause to consider whether the Shakespeare it presents is not alien to the text's inherent qualities.

Many opposite impressions are given in American regional theatres, where actors often come together from many different backgrounds to attempt a Shakespeare play in three or four weeks of rehearsal. In this time they can know neither each other nor the text with any thoroughness. Some of the actors may not have performed in Shakespeare, or in any stage play, for a year or more, having been busy in television or film. Such performers are most effective when they submit to clear directorial choices, after which they must survive by native wit and whatever training they have received from a variety of teachers in different studios. In these conditions, Shakespeare tends to be a visually impressive experience, but underpowered and unresolved in performance. The text is not always intelligible.

Foreign Shakespeare follows neither of these models and so presents alternative effects. In eastern Europe, actors have seldom been out of work, being engaged as members of permanent and generously subsidized companies. They know each other well, and their theatres and audiences; but they perform in a repertory of plays by a variety of authors, so that Shakespeare has not become a habitual task. In many countries actors have had a more musical training than in Britain or North America, being required to play on two instruments in order to complete their studies in an academy; so they know how to shape their performance as if they were instrumentalists, as well as persons in a play. Musical and dancing talents are not allowed to deteriorate when the company has musicals as well as dramas in its repertoire. Permanent companies under constant conditions of work can deliver routine productions, but a visitor to Prague, Budapest, Moscow, or Helsinki may well be amazed at the energy of a Shakespeare production: and this will not have been achieved by any lack of individuality. In the best of these companies each actor is very aware of fellow actors and has a musician's ability to phrase for maximum and careful effect, and knows how to improvise.

The administrative means by which a company makes provisions for staging Shakespeare may contribute to a revelatory performance. This is not to say that one way is better than another, or closer to what may deduced about Elizabethan and Jacobean practice, but rather that the relationships existing between actors, and between them and a director or teacher, will modify the kind of interplay which occurs on stage, and also between the stage and the audiences. These connections are like a cat's cradle in which change to any one line can throw some other line into prominence.

Very special conditions illuminate some features, as they obscure others. So *The Taming of the Shrew*, performed by a company practiced in that form of *commedia dell'arte* acting required for Goldoni's plays, will have a physicality and an elegance which lighten the play's combats and encourage unforced individuality in perform-

ance. So *Umabatha*, the Zulu adaptation of *Macbeth* which toured
Europe from Africa in the 1970s, is still remembered for showing
how the witches could enjoy their rituals, how the tremendous
implications of their words and deeds could combine with an almost
comic indulgence or thoughtlessness. These "weird sisters" were
confident and yet uncanny and awesome, familiar and yet possessed
by a power other than their own in everyday and individual existence. In English-speaking productions the witches are seldom credi-
ble, but here divergent elements required by the text were drawn
together with an unforced conviction. The production revalued the
play's action.

An actor performing a text written in a language which is not his
or her own is always liable to become aware of the translator's
intervention; and so any difficulty in rehearsal raises questions about
the meaning of words and suspicion that the trouble is due to faulty
translation. In such a situation the actor will insist on being understood, and will be very aware of the choices lying behind the use of
each particular word. In English-speaking theatre, however, it
sometimes seems that the actors have resorted to speaking the text
and hoping that the audience will understand what they have not:
Shakespeare's poetry may work, they suppose, in ways too deep for
comprehension. But this comforting retreat is not possible for actors
in foreign Shakespeare; they have to seek out the nature of each
moment in rehearsal, and sustain it in performance with each other.
By *not* trusting Shakespeare's text to do the work for them, these
actors are sometimes led to new discoveries and to performances that
have a remarkably complete committal to their parts.

In some ways a spectator at a Shakespeare performance in an
unfamiliar language has an analogous advantage. He or she will not
assume that to listen to the words is to understand the play well
enough. (This is a false assumption at any time, but one that is
instinctive to English-speakers, especially at moments when a text is
at its most intense or ambitious.) A member of an audience, at a loss
to understand any of the foreign words spoken, may become a more
penetrating *viewer*; to seek the heart of the mystery, he or she will
have to observe all "looks," and try to probe to the very "quick" of
each reaction. So the viewer will respond to physical tensions and
interactions, and will sense the danger or the achievement when
actors are reaching instinctively towards full performance of their
roles. Attention will shift repeatedly from speaker to speaker, and to

those who listen. A watch will be set on the whole stage, as the viewer responds to changes of grouping, pattern, movement, and physical activity. Because he or she is not straining in pursuit of verbal meaning, such a member of an audience can be acutely sensitive in other ways, free to discover lost repercussions within the drama and to absorb the most basic confrontations, crises, and resolutions.

When performances are less than good, so that they do not hold attention, the sense of distance, which comes from hearing persons speak in an unknown language, may allow a play to register quite differently. Then the spectator will observe the persons of the play in a relaxed, intermittent, and unpremeditated way, so that he or she may discern the structural form of the play with unusual clarity. In English-speaking productions the sheer fertility of Shakespeare's invention, in both speech and incident, can hide this deeper unity, or deflect attention from it.

A Japanese version of *Macbeth* which toured the world in the 1980s was considered by many critics to be remote and relentless, refined and yet sensual, symbolistic and yet, at times, realistic. Not every critic approved, but so many of the London journalists testified to revelatory experiences that a collection of their reviews illustrates most of the ways in which foreign Shakespeare can enlighten and move an audience. First, for Jack Tinker of the *Daily Mail* (18 September 1987), the language problem seems to have been bypassed:

Shakespeare's language is the last thing you miss in this all-Japanese version; the playing is the thing. And there are memories of this indelible production I know I will take with me to the grave.

Michael Billington in *The Guardian* (19 September) wrote that the performance of Komaki Kurihara as Lady Macbeth "leaps over the language barrier." Christopher Edwards in the *Spectator* (26 September), writing for a weekly journal and therefore less in haste, hailed the director, Yukio Ninagawa, as a "genius":

Strangely enough, the main missing ingredient – the poetry – is hardly noticed. Allowances are instinctively made, of course, and one is almost translating as the play unfolds. But ... what you come hoping to find is a realisation of something central and essential in the work's dramatic life. Ninagawa accomplishes exactly that, and does so with great intensity and exquisite visual beauty.

The effect of a different style of acting and production was to open up the texture of the drama, or to act like a magnifying glass through which to view significant moments. Christopher Edwards noted "an Eastern-seeming formality, stylisation and sense of ritual":

These elements create, for the actors, far greater freedom for the expression of poetic emotion than could any tradition of realistic Western theatre ... When, for instance, Macbeth (Masane Tsukayama) learns that the witches' prophecy has come true and that he is Thane of Cawdor, the force of the expression of his astonishment is remarkably dramatic. You might almost say the *available* force of his expression, because it is the emotional range open to him through formalised gesture that this actor taps so successfully. He is able to take a number of liberties without once seeming histrionic. Lady Macbeth ... is another case of emotional power coming out of stylised control.

Paul Taylor in *The Independent* (19 September) told how such acting allowed opposites to be drawn together in Komaki Murihara's "mesmerising performance as a youthful, doe-like Lady Macbeth." The effect of her control was an impression of the lack of control:

Her manner in the early scenes trembles uncontrollably between that of a coquettish sex-kitten and an unsmiling psychopath, suggesting a frigid nymphomaniac for whom the lust of power acts as a deep, compensatory mechanism. Lady Macbeth comes across as a woman bombarded by a blizzard of contradictory desires, for whom the witches' prophesy seems to offer the (tragically illusory) chance for some fixity of purpose.

Taylor also noted how attention could be focused on physical details in order to reveal inner, psychological tensions:

When Macbeth ... staggers on after the murder of Duncan, he stares down in disbelieving horror at the knives stuck unbudgingly to the congealed blood on his hands. Curiously, though, it looks as though it is Macbeth to whom the violence has been done – that his hands have been bloodily amputated and their stumps refitted, against his will, with viciously inhuman, claw-like blades. Ninagawa never lets you forget that, in murdering Duncan, the Macbeths maim themselves and that, henceforth, it is they who are the central victims.

For Martin Hoyle in *The Financial Times* (18 September), the effect was to draw attention to the working of the play's plot and to emphasize the role of destiny in the action:

As Macbeth, Masane Tsukayama grows paradoxically noble with guilt and therefore resignation. The stylised battle, where he disposes of a stage full of enemies watched by the immobile Macduff, as inexorable as fate itself, has a dash of the Fairbanks; but an inescapable destiny hovers in the "fog and filthy air" that so often wraps the stage action in mist. The unfailing pictorial quality of Yukio Ninagawa's direction on Kappa Senoh's set, poetically lit by Sumio Yoshii, is always at the service of the plot and characters. It adds another dimension to the mere story.

Critics who travel around the world have another kind of tale which illustrates a further impact of foreign Shakespeare, since audiences are also part of performance. *Hamlet* in Bratislava, in the years following the Prague Spring, presented a hero whose energy and helplessness alike caught the feelings of the audience. Estranged even from Ophelia, distrusting his most intimate relationship and so corrupting it, Hamlet in the nunnery scene questioned the world of Elsinore far more than his feelings toward Ophelia, or toward his mother. The audience's attention allowed the actors to hold long, intense, and questioning silences, as the two figures remained far apart on the stage; and from this impasse it was the political situation, more than personal and intimate feeling, which was revalued.

Such experiences are hard to validate when the traveler reaches home, but others which stem from the place of performance and the physical disposition of the audience are more readily communicated. In English-speaking theatres, Shakespeare is not often performed against the decaying walls of a great fortress, as at Dubrovnik, or in an ancient and spacious Riding School, as in Salzburg; and in consequence his plays seldom have a similar sweep of action and such a wide relevance. In villages far from any theatre, and still further from Shakespeare's homeland, *Hamlet* is performed regularly as a yearly celebration or game, an event for players and spectators alike; it changes without forethought as the seasons change, and as the participants grow older, more sceptical, or more aware of what they do. On a small island, for a special festival, *The Tempest* could be performed for a select audience. *Richard II* might be produced on the night before a military coup, *Twelfth Night* on a day of total carnival.

Even without the power of Shakespeare's own words and sounds, the plays are resilient and evocative. Experience of them in new and "foreign" circumstances may not discover the indestructible center of Shakespeare's art and purposes, but it can bring new sightings of the imaginative vision that created the plays, and new ways in which we can call them our own.

NOTES

1 G. Wilson Knight, *The Shakespearean Tempest* (London: H. Milford, 1932), 3–4.
2 L. C. Knights, *Some Shakespearean Themes* (London: Chatto and Windus, 1959), 149.
3 Una Ellis-Fermor, *Shakespeare's Drama*, ed. K. Muir (London: Methuen, 1980), 31.
4 Harley Granville Barker, *Prefaces to Shakespeare* (London: Batsford, 1970), II: 127.
5 John Barton, *Playing Shakespeare* (London: Methuen, 1984), 167–8.

Titus resartus:
Deborah Warner, Peter Stein and Daniel Mesguich have a cut at Titus Andronicus

Dominique Goy-Blanquet

Between March 1989 and May 1990, less than fifteen months, Paris saw three different productions of *Titus Andronicus* in three different languages: English, French, and Italian. Since Peter Brook's famous version (Stratford, 1955), shown at the Théâtre des Nations in 1957, only a few unmemorable attempts[1] had been made in France to stage this play, which T. S. Eliot thought one of the stupidest ever written. What hidden quality had emerged to make it so popular, all of a sudden? Too popular, was the uneasy suspicion. "However unknowable Shakespeare's intentions may be elsewhere," said the *Times* critic, "they are perfectly clear in this old shocker: the aim is to satisfy a public taste for sadistic spectacle."[2]

Deborah Warner, Peter Stein, and Daniel Mesguich, the three directors of these productions, all disclaimed any such reasons for putting on a play which they found invaluable despite its ugly reputation, and all proved it to a degree with their audiences. Deborah Warner's production, the first to be seen in Paris, resulted from the obligation of the RSC to perform the entire canon at regular intervals; it was created in Stratford in May 1987, moved on to London, and traveled round the world for eighteen months before its triumphant welcome at the Bouffes du Nord in March 1989. Daniel Mesguich's was seen next, in October 1989 at the Athénée–Louis Jouvet, where it played for five weeks. (A revival occurred at the Centre Dramatique de Lille in late 1992, for the Paris run had been praised both by the press and the public.) Peter Stein's production opened in Rome just a month later, toured in Italy, went to Spain, and came to Paris at the Odéon–Théâtre de l'Europe in May 1990. Though the reception had been rather cool in Italy, it was still warm enough there and in other parts of Europe to make the Italian producers decide on a revival in November 1990.

Shakespeare's name was on the three programs, but the productions had little else in common. That their intentions were worlds apart, I was given ample confirmation by the three directors themselves.[3] Deborah Warner's could in obvious ways claim to be closest to the author's. Her text, the original English one, spoken by British actors, was an integral version, something the RSC had never attempted before; John Barton's in 1981, for instance, was 'savagely cut,' so Deborah Warner felt she owed it to the play to 'try and make everything work,' a decision which entailed a four-and-a-half-hour long production but turned out to be a help eventually, as otherwise she would often have been tempted to suppress unsolved difficulties.[4]

'Integral' has quite a different meaning for Daniel Mesguich, who ideally would like to direct 'l'intégrale Shakespeare' – all his plays – but who does not feel committed to any slavish submission to their texts. He adapted *Titus Andronicus* himself into French, with the generous help of François–Victor Hugo's standard translation and generous helpings of other plays, spiced up by Kafka and various unknown Jewish or Tibetan sages. These inserts were compensated by large cuts in the speeches judged needlessly repetitive or prosy, so that the performance lasted just over two hours.

As for Peter Stein, the origin of his production was an invitation in 1989 by the University of Rome to direct a workshop on the Elizabethan theatre at their Centro Teatro Ateneo. The enthusiasm of the students tempted him to follow up the seminar with a production of *Titus Andronicus*, the most 'Elizabethan' of Shakespeare's plays, and drove him to a contract with the Teatro Stabile di Genova for a full professional tour, precisely what he had successfully avoided for twenty-five years. He fought every inch of the way with the management to maintain his standards of work, which are thoroughly at odds with touring in general and more particularly of the Italian kind, but he was caught in a commercial machine which led him steadily away from his original plan.

Of the three directors, it was certainly Stein who suffered most from the prevailing conditions. At the time, Deborah Warner found the RSC ideal in that respect, and the limits of Daniel Mesguich's dreams were those of his not very large budget, but Stein stood on foreign ground in every sense of the word, besides interpreting Shakespeare through a double screen of alienness.

Part of the original seminar with the Roman students had been dedicated to exercises on the original text of *Titus*. When the project developed, Stein, who speaks both English and Italian, supervised an adaptation by Agostino Lombardo, Giorgio Strehler's current translator, while retaining the principle of the seminar: the actors were invited to discuss Lombardo's text and offer suggestions, a number of which were kept in the final version.[5] No staging of a Shakespeare text can ever be satisfactory to Stein – "the loss of value in a production is 85%, not to mention the previous loss in translation, already 50% of the original"[6] – yet he, like Mesguich, finds *Titus* excessively verbose. He made it his point to cut exactly the same number of lines as Peter Brook had, about one-third of the whole, namely all the passages where he suspected the young Shakespeare of 'peacocking.' His first requirement was for clarity: the language sounded close to modern Italian, and intelligible even to untaught French ears; the original variations were transposed by contrasting everyday speech with the deliberate intricacies of politicians' syntax.

The three directors are positive that they had no pre-set theory about the play, no independent creativity, that all they did was to develop 'the actors' ideas.' Getting very familiar with the text is the only preparation they will own to; direction, they claim, is a collective process. To Deborah Warner, 'if you go to a Shakespeare play with drawn concepts, you stop the possibility of discovering what else the play is, you deny the actors' chance to explore and find out.' Stein asserts he has 'no imagination': he is 'too banal,' too irretrievably 'bound to the text' to impose on it brilliantly devised conceits like his more gifted colleagues. His assistant Fabio Sartor is equally critical of those unnamed directors who 'force the text to say something instead of writing their own play to state their problem.' Mesguich must 'think aloud in the rehearsal room, work on the actors' propositions, to find out what the play means.'

Actually, Stein began by doing intensive research before he felt able to confront Shakespeare at all. His *Shakespeare's Memory* for the Schaubühne in 1976 was itself a huge seminar preparatory to his first production, *As You Like It*, the following year.[7] "I feel an enormous lack of contact with the Shakespearean world, and therewith a lack of imagination. I have to collect as much information as I possibly can, to be able to answer the actors' questions. The more I know, the better I can see, hear, and understand." "To hell with Oxford and Cambridge," was Peter Brook's answer, when they met at the 1990 Braunschweig Festival for a "duet of titans."[8] Like Brook, who claims to have read "no more than three books about

Shakespeare," Deborah Warner is glad that she 'was not taught how to read Shakespeare but learnt everything in the theatre,' by going to see plays five times a week, and by working for years as Steven Berkoff's stage manager before she set up her own company, the Kick Theatre. As for Mesguich, a voracious reader, he is a law unto himself and will waste little time on specialized scholarship if it fails to stir his imagination.

Deborah Warner thinks of herself as a 'monitor of taste.' She talks very little in rehearsal and gives few directions. Again like Peter Brook, whom she greatly admires, she prefers to wait for natural growth, to leave her actors a great deal of freedom and – revealingly – have them assume that what they do is 'their own idea.' Disagreeing too often with an actor's choices is a clear indication that he or she was miscast. Mesguich talks in abundance during rehearsal and rebounds on his own words: he gives his actors a free start, comments on all the performances, including his own commentary, enlarges on them and selects from this variety to reach some degree of coherence. He feels that his *Titus* would have taken a completely different shape, and been as consistent and legitimate, or illegitimate, with another group of actors. The major choices are made in casting, which he and Warner agree is basically motivated by a desire to work with some particular actor, a vague idea that he or she would be 'interesting' in this part. This naturally implies that one does have a vague idea of what the part should be, yet both directors insist that it is minimal, or can only tell, as Deborah Warner puts it, 'what it feels like and what it tastes like.' All three directors feel their responsibility is to 'correct' and 'eliminate,' to select what is 'right,' 'bon,' or 'giusto' in the free creations they encourage. As to the nature of right and wrong in the final decision, there can be no argument; their judgment in this area is absolute. All three came to rehearsal with a stage design ready, a choice in Deborah Warner's case but difficult to avoid anyway, so admittedly there was a limit to the actors' part in the creative act.

Brian Cox had already been cast as Titus when Deborah Warner was called in by the RSC. The rest of the casting had to fit in with the complex network of the Company's season, in which all her actors held several parts. She chose them quite young, full of energy and eager to experiment, with Brian Cox, a 'brilliant anarchist,' more than eager to lead the way. The danger was to over-balance, but working with Shakespeare gave her confidence, for he had 'managed to keep the text on a knife-edge.' Her most delicate task was to create a company inside the Company, to 'build a protective bubble around them.' There also Shakespeare was an invaluable help, for 'no matter how tragic the scene, his warmth binds the actors.' First plays can be tricky, though, because it is easy to miss the way in, and *Titus* is definitely "an apprentice masterpiece,"[9] yet, for all its flaws, rewarding.

Again Daniel Mesguich has something else in mind than guilds and crafts when he uses the same word. *Titus Andronicus*, he argues, is a fully-fledged masterpiece; it contains all the other plays, which all have fragments of *Titus* in them, only better written, from which he freely borrowed on this principle. In Mesguich's view, there are no minor works of Shakespeare, and each play is a complete statement of his philosophy: a soaked copy of *Romeo and Juliet* would show by transparence fragments of *Macbeth* or *Hamlet*. Numerous critics before him have drawn such parallels. What makes Mesguich's claim original is that he actually puts those fragments on stage, where they become part of the performance as part of the play's history, in the way his *Hamlet* represented both Shakespeare's play and its wide imprint on the European consciousness. Against the insular viewpoint, he upholds his vision of a 'Shakespeare continent,' and he chose *Titus* out of a general liking for first plays, where the seeds of a writer's universe are concentrated. His actors also were quite young, recruits from the Jeune Théâtre National, most of whom he had already worked with.

The element of youth was also dominant in the early stages of Peter Stein's seminar with his Roman students, yet he did not, or could not, cast beginners for a professional show, and he 'had to call in' experienced actors for the leads. That they happened to be already famous, and somewhat inclined to behave like 'divas' in Stein's opinion, was not really his choice, but a consequence of the Italian system which makes it imperative to 'sell' the show around before it even exists. Raf Vallone, for instance, otherwise no great asset to the company, was still a name to be reckoned with when it came to booking a tour.

Casting was a more momentous decision for Deborah Warner, or even for Peter Stein, who both spent much thought on the inner coherence of each part, than it was for Mesguich who 'does not believe in characters.' In *Hamlet*, he had doubled or trebled them into nonentity, reallocating cues or even whole parts without much regard for the original speech-headings; here he organized them as a well-oiled team of near-anonymous vehicles. Where Brian Cox, and, to a lesser degree, Eros Pagni, gave memorable impersonations of the title part, it was quite meaningless to detach Mesguich's Titus from the rest of the cast, and difficult to remember its interpreter Christian Blanc as an independent performer. These three noble Romans belonged to different worlds.

The critics united in describing Deborah Warner's *Titus* as a trial run for *King Lear*, which she substantiated three years later by directing *Lear* for the National Theatre, again with Brian Cox in the title role. Their relationship had noticeably soured by then,[10] but their teamwork for *Titus* was excellent. That it may indeed have been a study for *Lear* is confirmed by Warner's account of the play as 'an exploration of grief' and her wish to test how much pain could be endured before it crushed the mind into insanity. Working more or less consciously against the learned opinion that in *Titus Androni-cus* "the horrors are classical and quite unfelt,"[11] she set out to demonstrate that the play had a strong emotional appeal. She 'wanted it to hurt,' to 'find ways of making it unbearable,' 'of making the audience scream out they could not take any more.' Judging by the history of faintings, heart-failures and other violent disorders which followed in her wake, she succeeded with a vengeance. The actors learned to recognize the symptoms after a while, and she felt that reports running ahead of them were developing a sort of mass hysteria, which might have spread to England had the production been revived there after their tour. She owned herself rather scared by the intensity of emotion she had released, wondering what hidden areas of guilt and remorse had been touched by Lavinia's plight. To her, there was never the least doubt that this and not Titus' extremity of grief was what some spectators could not take.

The company did their best to involve the public in the action, turning the lights on them, "placing tribunes in the house and addressing the Pit sensation-seekers as Romans seriously concerned about the decline in administrative standards," as Irving Wardle put it. Titus, entering in triumph from the back of the auditorium, looked "decidedly put out when the house fail[ed] to rise to its feet in his honour."[12] No scenery was used, no attempt made to disguise the theatre of operations into anything but what it actually was. The props were few and economical: the stepladders used to carry Titus on stage served also as yokes for his prisoners, traps for his sons, and finally gallows for Aaron. The costumes, which had been left somewhat to the decision of the actors, reflected a miscellany of tastes and intentions. The mud they were spattered with provided the only unifying design, as the actors found more and more uses for it. Originally it was meant for Lavinia's fall in the ditch; some of the audience thought it stood for blood until they saw "real" blood trickle from her mouth. The mud looked like ritual warpaint on the more brutal characters, and was thickly spread on Titus to represent "the grime of his trade, a particular kind of workhouse."[13] The point of the dark faded colours was to 'put decay in clothes,' while an attempt had been made to present the Goths as more sophisticated than the Romans. Otherwise, in Deborah Warner's lucid self-criticism, 'the costumes did not do very much,' rather a heavy price to pay just to have the actors feel at home in them.

There are other drawbacks to Deborah Warner's 'anti-interventional techniques,' which imply a very slow maturation. Being new to the RSC, the young but by no means inexperienced director had been allowed twelve weeks of rehearsals and a large number of previews. The long run of performances was another luxury she had never enjoyed before with her unsubsidized company, and, as she remembers, she 'needed all of that time.' Important changes were made during the previews, but the 'natural growth' she was cultivating only came to full fruition after months of touring. How to deal with the mutilations and when and how to use blood were a couple of the points discussed at length with the actors. The idea of breaking Lavinia's neck in a deadly embrace came to Brian Cox while the actress was sitting on his knee at an early reading: hers being a mute part in that scene, no chair had been provided for her. Not all the suggestions were as good. Some, eventually judged 'very bad,' were only abandoned after several performances. Others were kept on to the end, which appeared on reflection to have been serious mistakes – the Dwarfs' song, for instance ("Hi-ho, Hi-ho" from the film *Snow White*), which Warner later regretted because 'it took some people right out of the play. The idea was to push them into a world so absurd they would have to laugh, not to lift them out.' The process of selection was guided by instinct or personal taste, rather than by any overall concept. The casting itself was not entirely felicitous: opposed to a powerful Titus, the weaker Aaron of Peter Polycarpou caused "a deficiency of evil,"[14] which even Estelle

Kohler's superbly vicious Tamora could not quite compensate for, and Deborah Warner agreed afterwards that Aaron should have been 'a black, black, black man.'

A degree of stylization was thought necessary to maintain some hold on the audience's nerves instead of inuring them to the horror, as usually happens after half an hour of the goriest movies. Warner's original plan, to do the whole play without showing any blood whatsoever, had been discarded quite early, but the first blood trickled from Lavina's mouth only after Marcus' speech had imaginatively drawn it: 'We needed something horrific to push the audience one step further. The effect was greater because they had been denied it before.' Technically, the main difficulty was to keep up a state of emotional tension to the end of the play, almost an impossible feat when four corpses have to fall in less than 35 seconds, and each death must add to and not detract from the intensity of pain. It was easy enough to kill Lavinia and affect the audience, but very hard to get the third and fourth deaths to hurt. 'We only got the sequence right, and the audience's reaction as we wanted it, months after we opened, and even then we did not always get it.' This was achieved by delicate balance between a cartoon-strip style and raw emotions played up without distancing irony. The device was to 'get the laughter out,' as Michael Billington spotted: "Ms Warner's wiliest tactic is to pre-empt possible laughter at the play's grosser cruelties by launching them in a spirit of dangerous jocularity ... Even the final cannibalistic banquet stills our nervous laughter precisely because Ms Warner prefaces it with servants merrily whistling like the Seven Dwarfs as they set up the tables and usher in the dubious feast." When the production came to London, Billington went one step further, noting that she "shrewdly pre-empts nervous laughter by showing how often cruelty springs out of dangerous levity."[15] This moralistic turn of mind came very close to the actors' concerns. Brian Cox's declared aim was to 'get people to laugh, then kick them for it.' There again, judging by the critics' reaction, he was entirely successful: "The play renews for us a sense of shame and horror at the infliction of rape and casual mutilation."[16]

Brian Cox's Titus started as a noble but somewhat ludicrous figure. The image he had in mind was of 'a corroded statue, with its face half eaten away and pigeon-shit on its head.' Its comic potentialities and nihilistic gallows humor had a cue in the text: "Why dost thou laugh?" – "Why, I have not another tear to shed"

(3.1.266). Both he and Deborah Warner felt that the key to the release of tragic emotion lay in the comedy, an element which they were planning to develop in *King Lear* even before the critics invited them in one voice to follow up with the later play. The father–daughter relationship was crucial to their treatment of Titus. His allegiance to Rome has superseded any domestic or personal concerns, Brian Cox comments, "but if he can afford to lose a few sons in the service of Rome, he has only the one daughter, and the society he has placed his faith in allows her to be defiled, putting all his values into question."[17] The image of the mute girl writing in the sand, which Deborah Warner had 'scorched on the brain,' was initially what made her want to direct the play. She remembers Sonia Ritter's interpretation of Lavinia as 'almost Grotowski-like, but very dangerous, working off tension instead of using technique,' and though she was 'immensely grateful,' she found it 'almost frightening at times.'

The emotional involvement of the company, and the moral undertones of its effect on the public, took precedence over the political element in the play. Brian Cox saw Titus as a disastrous fundamentalist, but his work centered more on Titus' journey of self-discovery than on his society's brutality. As for Deborah Warner, she spent little time on the political issues, on the grounds that there are better plays in this regard. She was interested in creating the barbarous world men set up for themselves, but gave it very few specific references and hardly any Roman ones, leaving out what Rome meant in terms of Renaissance humanism. On the whole, British critics did not seem to feel the loss. Apart from Michael Coveney's reminder that "the catalogue of murder and torture characterises a gruesome interregnum between two imperial installations,"[18] most reviewers concentrated on the qualities of each performance, and found Warner's message "entirely consistent with Shakespeare's view: when one tribe oppresses another, mayhem follows," or praised the fact that "she discovers the humane values under the mountainous horrors." Some writers even discovered there "a redemptive quality which is persuasively underlined," though none questioned her most redemptive improvement on the text: the fact that Aaron's black baby ended the play safely in Marcus' arms. Brian Cox offered a tentative explanation for this rescue – 'because she is a woman, perhaps?' – but none of the critics were tactless enough to stress the feminine quality of mercy. They hardly dared mention that this particular director was a woman and wondered at her youth instead, possibly because women and children still belong to the same category of incomplete adults. Their hearts went out to the company for making the play watchable while still chastising evil, the first duty of the theatre now as it was in Elizabethan times.[19] It was left to Michael Coveney, reviewing Peter Stein's *Titus* in Paris, to deplore a general lack of interest for a "Directors' Theatre," and to berate the conservative critics who "seem to think there exists an ideal approach to the Bard that has no truck with modernism or intellectual intervention of any kind."[20]

This is also the gist of Stein's and Mesguich's opinion of British theatre. According to Mesguich, foreigners know Shakespeare much better than his own countrymen, who idolize him without properly reading his plays, and who pride themselves on their ignorance. As for dramaturgy, the least innovation which has been common practice on the continent for ages is hailed in England as genius, a delusion snobbishly entertained by France's uncritical love for all things British. Stein too finds the French applause empty and superficial.[21] The English are hardly any better, they know nothing about poetry, their reviewers have to have everything spelled twice, and all the meaning they can read in a production is in meaningless details of costumes – which caused Stein's Titus to be labeled "unequivocally a Fascist general."[22]

Stein's own reading was radically opposed to Deborah Warner's. If the play is more actable now than a few decades earlier, it is not because its horrors coincide with the contemporary taste, let alone prove too much for our sensitive nerves. They have become so banal, compared with what we commonly see on our TV sets, that they no longer hide the central picture: a major crisis of the state, in a family-based society totally unable to cope with the collapse of the old order. Stein's "giungla di tigri" was a world of rational evil, where Romans were no less barbarous than Goths, and rather less civilized in their ways. The city of empire-builders was seen to disintegrate into an urban jungle; a civil war was barely avoided at the beginning, only to take place in the final scene. The cast of *Titus Andronicus* were a pack of unattractive characters, including a Lavinia who was quite as arrogant as the rest of her tribe, undeserving of any sympathy before she got her comeuppance, and a creepy neuropath after. The patched-up peace at the end restored the Andronici to their former eminence: young Lucius stood by his father, the broken sequence of generations was resumed, and naturally there could be no salvation for Aaron's offspring in the gentlemen's agreement to close the accounts. Aaron was the scapegoat of a dubious return to legitimacy: a cut in the text gave him the last word, promising few happy days to the new state. The world goes on: such is the burden of all Shakespeare's plays.

To Peter Stein, there is no philosophical depth, no world vision of any magnitude, in *Titus*. In respect of its juvenile energy, it is a good play, and ideally suited for stage apprentices; but in respect of its immaturity, it is naught. It is typical of a brilliant beginner, 'one not yet corrupted by doubts about his own creation': Shakespeare displays his learning, repeats his effects, and succeeds in outkidding Kyd. At a point in his career when Stein needed a rest from German forceful trends of interpretation and search for meaning,[23] *Titus* offered an opportunity to reassess all aspects of stage business, to interpret its conflicts in terms of stage life, rivalries, power struggles, and general bustle. It was deliberately short on morals and poetry, which made it excellent training-ground for all concerned. Its scenic inventiveness was its most appealing quality, and Stein concentrated on stage business rather than on any soul-searching. The aim was to reach the highest speed and precision, combined with the maximum visibility. The 'rumorous activity' of Stein's ancient Rome being somewhat worse than Picadilly at the peak hour, most of his efforts were spent on organizing the traffic. The design was 'structural, not decorative,' and at the same time wholly consistent with Stein's political theme. The set was devised specifically for the first and last scenes, the others being variations of the opening one. Its clean architecture evoked Mussolini's monumental taste for Roman antiquity. Three practicable walls made of brick and travertine moved on chariots to widen or narrow the acting space, or fade in a green light for the forest scene. Two rows of openings on ground and upper levels aptly figured "the palace full of tongues, of eyes and ears" (2.1.127), offering full commodity for eavesdropping, but their main purpose was to give the actors quick access to center stage from any of the entrances available, while a cement floor served to muffle the noise of their movements. A small apron stage appended to the main one could be entered from the front of the house. It stood for the outside world as distinct from Rome, 'fuori,' where Tamora's corpse was thrown to the dogs once the civil war had cleared the stage.

The costumes and makeup were used literally as in ball games, 'to make up the teams' and underline the substance of the plot. The Romans' white marble was opposed to the brick-reds and pinks of the Goths, with the blackest of black men standing most visibly apart. Compared with the Goths' feline smoothness, the Romans seemed stiff, rough, and old-fashioned. The soldiers were thugs in football outfits and crash helmets, the civilians wore togas draped over prim suits, the court party looked like pop stars in silky oversmart clothes, until Lucius returned with his mud-coloured partisans to blur these differences: the final war was fought between two sets of gangsters wearing brown or beige coats but identical felt hats.

The contemporary relevance of this tale did not need to be underlined, and the Italian critics saw it without having to be told twice, noting for instance that Titus' indictments were pointedly addressed to the audience.[24] Apart from one clear allusion to the Mafia, when Titus' hand and the heads of his sons were returned to him wrapped up in clean plastic bags, Stein refrained from drawing too-easy parallels with specific events. In his view, the theatre must not emulate television but aim at some form of continuity and self-coherence. The critics who read fascism in Lucius' elevation to the title of "benigno duce di Roma" were too simple-minded: the references to modern Italy were not restricted to the 1930s nor to one particular set of politicians, but to more permanent traits like the connections of family and state affairs in a world where dynasties mean business. Stein insisted that Marcus Andronicus must take part in the final slaughter, along with the rest of his family. For this he had to fight the resistance of Raf Vallone, who was playing the part and did not like to forfeit the sympathy of his fans.

Vallone, who had handsomely lent his famous name to the project, confided his disappointment with Peter Stein to the press while in Paris.[25] The rest of the company did not advertise their disappointment with him, but united in flatly refusing to have him back when the production was revived. This was not by far Stein's only difficulty with his Italian 'divas.' He was constantly irritated by their lack of concentration, volatile memories, and generally slack routine, but there were other, deeper frustrations as well. He had thought the resources of the Italian language might be an answer to the unsolved question of classical rhetoric on the modern stage. The art of eloquence, the linguistic procedures it determined, have formed the basis of European theatre for 300 years. Now they are so stained with memories of the official turns they have served in our century, and Germany especially is so guilt-ridden in this respect, that any rhetorical mode of expression seems prohibited. Actors avoid it, and directors tend to neutralize it in the texts by cutting or breaking it into everyday speech. Stein had hoped that Italian actors would be freer from such inhibitions, that he could exploit the melodiousness of their language, the national taste for the ornaments of speech and elaborate arguments. He found instead that they could not play realistically, but cultivated musicality at the expense of meaning, and he often required them in rehearsal 'pensare di più e cantare di meno' – to think more and sing less. Their acting was 'troppo lento e pesante,' too slow and heavy. Rhythm, his first demand, should be a personal impulse, an inner energy drawn from their understanding of the play, of their characters' parts in it. Stein was looking for 'novelty, freshness, not just reflections of his own tricks'; he did not want to dictate to his actors. He gave them elbow-room where 'character' was concerned, but was adamant on all matters of physical activity. Each move was timed and measured, and the duels were endlessly rehearsed. The actors were not allowed, though, to relax in their interpretations of the parts. Stein paid lip-service to their talents but complained he had to be constantly there to keep them in mind of their roles, and there were indeed large variations from one performance to the next. Yet if he found them wanting in many ways, they enjoyed working with the famed director and tried hard to please him, acknowledging they had learnt much from his fastidious discipline.

To one trained, like Peter Stein, in the German fashion, the Italian production system was painfully erratic, and he could no more master its failings than Strehler or Luca Ronconi, who have repeatedly denounced the corruption of their public theatre, always in vain.[26] Touring is bad enough in any case, Stein avows; sets are reduced to bare essentials to save transport, and actors have nothing on their minds but lodgings or train tickets. Worse still, Italian designers 'can do operas, not plays.' They are not used to working with iron and cement, basic requirements in Germany where wood is prohibited on stage because of fire regulations. The theatres have no specialized workshops and must order everything outside, which makes building costs much higher. Having struck a bargain with the management of Teatro Stabile di Genova guaranteeing that the tour would imply no alteration of the initial set, Stein designed a production suited for touring which in his view was a paltry affair, but a most impressive one by all Italian standards. According to his assistant, and to the Italian press in general, the Teatro Stabile had made a very special effort in honor of Peter Stein: much larger financial and technical means were placed at his disposal than would have been judged necessary for any average Italian production – but these were found by him far from adequate. In answer to their grievances about costs, he objected that the Teatro must still have found it profitable if they decided on a revival, and that the overcharges were caused by mismanagement and lack of expertise more than by his own expensive tastes.[27]

The contrast between the rigidly clean look of the design and the flamboyance of the play reflected a war of styles which did not go unnoticed: Stein was promptly identified as "a barbarian descended from the North to tell us about another descent of barbarians."[28] His Teutonic vision of eternal Rome made little headway with the Italians.[29] Because it came too near home, in Stein's opinion – but which of its homes, one wonders? Though he was pleased with the reception in Germany, Stein's meeting with Brook caused more of a stir there than the performance of *Tito Andronico*.[30] On the whole, the reports of his compatriots were the harshest of the lot, the verdict being that the production was intelligent but strained, and that "Stein's journey to the Tiber was of little impact, except for himself."[31] Stein had tried to escape to Italy for lightness and uncomplicated readings; he wanted to 'learn from Shakespeare but not be made to feel small all the time,' yet even a coarse beginner's piece like *Titus*, which seemed safely straightforward, unnerved him, or so his nearest analysts diagnosed: "Peter Brook does not want to know anything, only to open his ears. Peter Stein wants to know everything, but this knowledge paralyzes him."[32]

There is no such anxiety in Daniel Mesguich. Where Stein vows himself so bound to the text that he must stick to Shakespeare's original lines, Mesguich treats them with studied independence. His free rendering of Shakespeare's original was undoubtedly the most inventive of the three productions. Not only did his text take great liberties with the body of the play, he even made short shrift of the stage directions so generally revered by the majority of his colleagues, for whom Shakespeare is an unerring theatrical guide. Both Stein and Warner built their design on three levels, as Shakespeare had prescribed, and showed the utmost reverence for his least instructions. But these are obsolete, says Mesguich, who dismisses the Bard as a poor director by modern standards: their only interest nowadays is to indicate the place where a piece of business is required, a plain invitation to directors to use their imagination. In our post-Einsteinian age, he claims, up and down, right and left have become meaningless and interchangeable. In French anyway, to move upstage is 'remonter vers le fond' – climb to the bottom. This is approximately what he did, by giving the public the sort of view one might get through a wide angle lens, lying on the floor of the Reading Room in the British Library. His designer, Louis Bercut, gave shape, a most entrancing one, to his cherished belief that all the world is a stage is a library.[33] A great admirer of Borges, Mesguich had repeatedly drawn on this concept before, but never with such relevance and inspiration. His defence of *Titus Andronicus* marshals Lévi-Strauss' categories, the raw and the cooked, to argue that there is nothing crude or primitive about a play where barbarous practices are carefully measured against traditional protective rites. By substituting the "raw" (i.e. human sacrifice) for the "cooked" (its symbolic figuration), Rome betrays a lack of trust in its time-honoured rituals and reverts to bloodshed, thus initiating its own decline into savagery. The revenge story and chain mutilations are but side-effects of the one and only tragedy of humanity, which is loss of faith in its civilized values. It matters little whether the Goths are more or less sophisticated than their cultured enemies. What is at stake is the process of change in the symbolic structure. The movement which pulls a culture to its own destruction creates a number of minor stories like so many ripples in its wake. None of the horrors are gratuitous; cutting hands and tongues means destroying the organs of speech and writing. When symbols can no longer be shared, no common language be found, blood is spilt. This regression was figured by the decayed library. Books were used as stepping-stones by men who had forgotten how to read. Lavinia held one out to Bassianus like a desperate remedy she did not know how to use. Each cut into human flesh was underlined by the fall of a burning book, and at the end of the play, brambles had invaded the shelves. After each killing, the corpses were thrown in two vivaria where they remained floating amid aquatic plants like bottled specimens. By the device of identical costumes, the top of one body seemed to be on a level with its lower half in the other glass case, adding a further touch of vertigo to this deadly confusion of species. Humanity had reached the peak of entropy.

Daniel Mesguich is absolutely convinced, and convincingly argues, that the 'adventure of the symbolic' dramatized in *Titus Andronicus* includes such political or emotional crises as Stein and Warner chose to represent. The play pinpoints the moment when a civilization begins to fall apart, when the Law itself has become a dead letter. The old sticklers want the first-born to be emperor, their opponents want a man of true worth, but the man elected for his worth raises the first-born to the throne, clearly an untenable situation. It would be absurd to dress the protagonists as barbarians in animal skins: they are decadent, not primitive. Because relative time never did run smooth, Shakespeare's distant past had to be made doubly relative to us, and Mesguich moved it back to the dawn of humanity. Dressing the actors in Hebrew robes and 1930s waistcoats told two different stories of origins, of our parents and of our first parents. *Titus* is 'the very matrix of Shakespeare's plays'; if it was indeed his first, then all the better. The first tragedy of humanity is the Old Testament. Rome is a metaphor for Jerusalem.

The dramatic reappearance of the source book, Ovid's *Metamorphoses*, at a turning-point in the action, is to Mesguich a sure symptom of Shakespeare's genius. Showing up the play for a palimpsest stresses the meaning of the written word, just as its emphatic theatricality calls attention to Shakespeare's exposure of 'passage à l'acte' – acting out – through acting itself. Mesguich quotes one of his favourite "proverbs" to account for the persistent misreadings of *Titus*: 'When the wise man points to the moon, the fool looks at the finger.' The enactment of violence points to the opposite way, out of a dead end: 'keep within the meaning of the act, play with it, do not adhere.' Titus' initial mistake is to believe one sacrifice will settle all accounts. Even the crushing out of Tamora's children in the last scene cannot be a 'final solution,' it will not prevent further massacre. 'The world is not kosher, Shakespeare warns us, play and represent flesh and blood, never use them raw, you might be eaten.' The implicit association of Shakespeare's source with the book of books pointed to the story of Abraham, when God's elected people put an end to human sacrifice by slaughtering a sheep. The defusing of 'passage à l'acte' into 'actuation' is the civilized answer to bloodshed. Mesguich compares this with Wagner's alleged Nazism: 'He had the same preconceptions, but writing operas, he remained within the limits of the symbolic, and whether he shared their views or not, he actually worked against Nazism. His operas could be analyzed, heard. Nazism is deaf and mute.' This is the crux of Mesguich's commitment to culture, especially drama: 'the theatre is the only place in the world where Abraham, Isaac, and the sheep all stand up at the end for the curtain call.' However pessimistic Shakespeare's plays may be, because they are plays they are optimistic.

Bearing this in mind, the main difficulty was to distinguish "real" from figurative bloodshed on the stage itself, and find a balance between sensational gore and sterilized symbols. Mesguich was not much given to bloody excesses, yet the recourse to signs like red ribbons – Peter Brook's answer to the problem – would obviously have been self-defeating in his case. Blood on a book is to Mesguich the most shocking of symbols. Some blood must be shown to mix with ink in unholy confusion, to stress the fading power of symbols. So Titus' hand was torn off like bread, his sons' heads were sent back wrapped up in red velvet, but Alarbus' ritual murder was executed with realistic blood-letting to make Mesguich's point: Titus hopes to add potency to the ritual with a drop of human blood, but to Tamora there is no symbolic value attached to the murder of her son.

The obsessive 'cutting' theme was carried into the dramaturgy: the remains of a much mangled text were sliced into short scenes by the guillotine drop of an iron curtain. This allowed swift changes in the mood or tonality, as the successive tableaux played modulations from black comedy to softer shades of nostalgia. The procession carrying the mutilated limbs danced out to the distant tune of a waltz. Supposedly months after the tragedy, Lavinia was seen to dine in solitary elegance with her father, a brief tender pause in the mounting irony. The curtain drop also served a practical necessity. The set drew in to a sharp perspective which left only some 40 square meters of the small Athénée stage available to the actors. To avoid monotony, the blackouts were used to change positions and offer a different viewpoint. Each scene was treated as a cinema shot – Take one: Exit Emperor with Lavinia / Take two: Exit Emperor with Tamora. The 'editing' of these shots suggested a series of variations on the first murder, in endless repetition. 'Joints' were also for Mesguich an opportunity to meditate on dividing lines, rupture and continuity: 'all Shakespeare's plays take place in the interregnum, at midnight, on the battlements.' *Titus Andronicus* shows them to be connected like body and limb, just as civilization breeds barbarity: the continuity is broken, then resumed after two hours, as if Saturninus' reign were just a bad joke, leading to Lucius Andronicus' final coronation. And who had suggested sacrificing Tamora's son in the first place? Lucius.

Mesguich's *Titus* was a beautifully controlled exposition of his views. There was nothing left for the critics to do but bow to his superior understanding of the play, meekly reproduce his statements, and admire his magic touch.[34] Since there was little prior experience of the play in France, it could be taken at its face value, or Mesguich's value, without qualms. It will no doubt figure now on the short list of eligible plays, thanks to Mesguich, who feels he has done much to save this imperilled work of art.

Titus, or is it Shakespeare, tells everyone the tale he needs to hear: old men lose their minds in woe, they have their exits and their entrances, they kill the boys and the books. The English tale was rough and emotional, the Italo-German one active and political, the French aesthetic and philosophical. Did they but reflect national traits? One hardly dares to draw conclusions from this European tour backstage, except that it might well take another 400 years to unite countries divided by a common love of Shakespeare.

NOTES

1 Three in the past ten years: Bruno Boëglin's with Bruce Myers, Avignon Festival, 1981; Pierre Peyron, Théâtre de la Villette, 1983; Michel Dubois, Théâtre de Chaillot, 1987.

2 Irving Wardle, "Titus Andronicus/Swan, Stratford," *The Times*, 13 May 1987.

3 All the quotations in single inverted commas are taken from various personal interviews held with the actors and directors in the course of 1990, or from notes at rehearsals.

4 The text of Deborah Warner's *Titus* was the Penguin Shakespeare.

5 *Tito Andronico* (Genoa: Edizioni Teatro di Genova, 1989). The English text used was the Oxford edition.

6 Gerhard Stadelmaier, "Das Ballett der Königsdiener – Peter Brook und Peter Stein auf der Suche nach Shakespeare," *Frankfurter Allgemeine*, 13 Nov. 1990.

7 See Michael Patterson, *Peter Stein, Germany's Leading Theatre Director* (Cambridge University Press, 1981), chap. 7.

8 Notiert von Der Gliewe, "Duett der Titanen," *Theater Heute*, Jan. 1991.

9 Brian Cox, in *Players of Shakespeare 3*, ed. Russell Jackson and Robert Smallwood (Cambridge University Press, 1993).

10 See Brian Cox's interview with Ceridwen Thomas, *Plays and Players*, Dec. 1990–Jan. 1991.

11 Muriel Bradbrook, *Themes and Conventions of Elizabethan Tragedy* (Cambridge University Press, 1973 [1935]), 98.

12 Irving Wardle, "Titus Andronicus/The Pit," *The Times*, 5 July 1988; "Titus Andronicus/Swan, Stratford," 13 May 1987.

13 Cox, *Players of Shakespeare 3*.

14 Michael Billington, "Horror and Humanity," *The Guardian*, 14 May 1987.

15 Billington, "Cruelty and Grief within Reason," *The Guardian*, 6 July 1988.

16 Michael Coveney, "Titus Andronicus/Stratford," *The Financial Times*, 13 May 1987.

17 Cox, in *Players of Shakespeare 3*.

18 Coveney, "Titus Andronicus / Stratford."

19 Jim Hiley, "Headless Wonders," *The Listener*, 14 July 1988; Billington, *The Guardian*, 14 May 1987; Gary O'Connor, "Titus Andronicus," *Plays and Players*, July 1987.

20 Coveney, "Vision of Plays without Frontiers," *The Observer*, 20 May 1990.

21 Interview with Odile Quirot, "De Shakespeare à Koltès dans la violence de Peter Stein," *Le Monde*, 8 Jan. 1990.

22 Billington, "Connoisseur of Cruelty," *The Guardian*, 10 Dec. 1989.

23 For a general discussion of this point, see chap. 7 of Patterson, *Peter Stein*.

24 Franco Quadri, "Tito Andronico in doppio petto," *La Repubblica*, 26–27 Nov. 1989.

25 Interview with Marion Thébaud, "Les curiosités de Raf Vallone," *Le Figaro*, 4 May 1990.

26 See Peter Iden, "Kopf Runter, Messer in den Hals-Shakespeare in Italien," *Theater Heute*, Jan. 1990.

27 The estimated cost of *Tito Andronico* was £90,000. Stein's budget for *As You Like It* at the Schaubühne was nearly £80,000, according to Patterson's figures, four times that of Deborah Warner's *Titus*. Mesguich's budget was 3 million French francs, approximately £30,000. These figures need to be qualified, though, since the budgets do not represent the sum total of what the shows actually cost, and may not cover the same list of items.

28 Quadri, "Tito Andronico in doppio petto."

29 Masolino d'Amico, "Andronico delle crudelta," *La Stampa*, 26 Nov. 1990.

30 Ludwig Zerull, "Die Geburt eines Neuen Festivals-'Theaterformen '90' – Peter Brook, Peter Stein & William Shakespeare in Braunschweig, in Wolfenbüttel," *Theater Heute*, Jan. 1991.

31 Iden, "Kopf Runter, Messer in den Hals-Shakespeare in Italien."

32 Stadelmaier, "Das Ballett der Königsdiener."
33 For a study of the scenography, see Marilyn August, "Staging Barbarism – Bercut, Poli and Forbin Create Shakespeare's Titus Andronicus," *Cue International*, Mar./Apr. 1990.
34 Michel Cournot, "La magie de Titus Andronicus," *Le Monde*, 21 Oct. 1989.

CHAPTER 3

Transformations of authenticity:
The Merchant of Venice in Israel

Avraham Oz

Rarely has a dramatic piece haunted a whole nation for centuries as *The Merchant of Venice* has the Jews. Shylock has penetrated the Jewish collective identity so deeply that no reader or spectator sensitized to Jewishness can approach Shylock without some sense of personal involvement. Discussing the play in a Jewish classroom often sounds like discussing the lot of an accused person awaiting his verdict in the next room. A few days after my own Hebrew version of the play was first produced on stage (1972), the Israeli Open University applied for the rights to include some passages in one of its newly written courses. That course, however, formed part of neither the drama nor the literature program: it was in Jewish history. More often than any other dramatic character, Shylock has visited the political columns of the Jewish press. A hard-line prime minister earned the name (by non-Jewish enemies) as a derogatory attribute; a Jewish guerilla fighter defended himself before a British court: "I am not a Shylock; I am a freedom fighter!"[1] An Israeli reporter in London compared the British press, urging pardon for John Damianiuk (sentenced to death by an Israeli court for atrocities against Jews in a Nazi concentration camp), to the Duke of Venice asking Shylock to show gentle mercy for Antonio (4.1.17–34).[2] The reporter's title was "Legitimation for Antisemitism 1988," and her main concern was the production of *The Merchant of Venice* by the Royal Shakespeare Company, which she had attended that same week:

From the very outset of the play, under Bill Alexander's direction, it becomes clear that contending Judaism and Christianity are not perceived on equal terms. On the stage background one sees a yellow star-of-David, painted in coarse lines with dripping colour, beside a neat church window with stained glass depicting Christian saints. The Christians are handsome and clean, while Shylock is clad like an oriental Jew in dirty coloured robes, his hair and beard curled, his speech and accent grotesque and detestable, and even the town's kids chase him, abuse him and spit on him. Antonio spits on him immediately after receiving the loan, and both lender and creditor are obviously enemies and Shylock has good reasons to wish for revenge.[3]

The journalist admitted that the 400-year-old Shakespearean text "does indeed present Shylock as a bloodthirsty, heartless persecutor," but she did not aquit the director of his responsibility for scenes prone to "legitimize antisemitism." She took particular note of the trial scene; Shylock (played by Anthony Sher, whom she did not forget to identify as "a South African-born Jew") ecstatically donned a *Talit* when about to cut his pound of flesh, and muttered the Hebrew prayer, "Pour thy rage over the gentiles who know thee not!" Knowing the Hebrew words, the journalist could not calm her own rage.

But whereas the reporter's rage sounded genuine, the same production was "scholarly," attacked an Israeli academic, professing "scientific objectivity." The writer, Eli Rozik, had attended what he called "an organized pilgrimage of the London Jewish community ... to take part in some inexorably recurring ritual ... to look again and again in the famous Shakespearean mirror and ask themselves again and again how are they reflected in the eyes of their host society."[4] This anthropological observation did not stop at the audience: it was soon applied to Sher as well, who was identified as "a Jew, born to a family of east European origin," who happens to be "by a happy coincidence ... also of South African origin," showing solidarity with the sufferings of his newly adopted "compatriots" (ironic inverted commas in text). Sher saw the production as an attack against apartheid, its silent accomplices (his own Jewish parents), and Jewish hypocrisy in general. "The former victims of racism turned racists themselves at their earliest opportunity," Sher was quoted as saying, while Rozik reached his own conclusion: "Surely the typical English reader was delighted to read these words." Having stereotyped the entire "host society" in phrases such as "the open consensus of the English society regarding racism," he noted that "the comparison with the Palestinians is not missing."

But Rozik's main argument had to do with the legitimacy of theatrical interpretation. The director's "line of interpretation" attempted to present Shylock as the victim of Christian racism, but this "is possible only if one abides by certain rules,"[5] which Rozik undertook to prescribe. Distinguishing between the presentation of "the play as it is" (an essentialist position taken for granted) and the director's deviations from it, he found the director guilty of "redistributing positivity and negativity between Christians and Jews, mainly between Antonio and Shylock," and diverting the original demonic, motiveless malignity of Shylock into a psychological reaction. The director chose, out of irrelevant historicist motivation, to present Shylock as "the oriental model" (namely, "a Jewish merchant of Turkish origin"). This anthropological model, Rozik argued, is alienated not only from the Christian society on stage but also from the audience: "undoubtedly, in my opinion, the natural tendency of the spectators is to identify with those who uphold the aesthetic and not with those who discard it." Thus the "oriental model" chosen by the director will not do, since racism cannot yield to psychological argumentation. Rozik would have preferred the mythical antisemitic stereotype to the insulting suggestion that "any historical Jew could act like Shylock." But there is still a surprising ending to his story, which seems to him bigger than life: contrary to all his theories, the London Jewish spectators did not protest. "Contrary to anything we know about communication, we were witnessing a miracle. The anti-racist message was taken in ... without resistance!" It never occurred to the writer that his "rules" themselves contradicted "anything we know about communication"; that perhaps even the "oriental model" could raise some sympathy at Stratford. He opted for another explanation, one which involves conspiracy and magic at once: there is, he suggested, a silent agreement between audience and artists, both of whom "would experience the anti-apartheid message to the point of neglecting [the rules of] theatre itself."[6]

Authorial intention, so radically abused by our academic writer, still frequently haunts directors and audiences in the theatre. It often seems a convenient historical refuge from the high-handed dictates of synchronic contemporary interpretations, into which a good number of classical productions fall nowadays. Furthermore, it is held by many to retain some inherent clue of authenticity which, set against the reality of the present, may capture the *kairos* investing "the revolution of the times."[7] Sought by both old and new historicists, intention is taken to shed some light on the particular discourse out of which a given work emanated.

It is against this background, then, that the question of "how was

Shylock intended to be" still matters to producers and audiences alike. This worn-out question seems to have embarrassed so many recent writers on *The Merchant of Venice*, that, if hardly able to escape its implications and consequences, they turn their backs upon its blunt wording whenever it awaits them at some dangerous corner. Others, who courageously address themselves to the question, are prone to blame Shakespeare for their own perplexities. Thus we are told by Francis Fergusson that "perhaps Shylock turned out to be more powerful than Shakespeare intended, for at that moment in his career he was not quite in control of the great characters that were taking possession of his imagination."[8] What this assertion suggests is that there exists a certain measurable model on which an ideal Shylock should rest, and of which the product of Shakespeare is an unintentionally inflated replica. The desirable proportions of a Shylock are dictated by the nature and properties of the play (in this case, mainly by the play's generic classification);[9] if the play as a whole, say, passes for a romantic comedy, then the character of the killjoy should spoil the fun only as far as the boundaries of romantic comedy will allow. Balance is all, as a good deal of the play's theatrical and critical history would seem to suggest: when Heine wishes to grant Shylock full tragic weight, he finds it necessary to attack fiercely every single member of Venetian society; and when M. C. Bradbrook describes him as a man reduced to a beast, she finds herself obliged to rehabilitate Bassanio from Heine's ferocious attack. This insistence on balance may of course be challenged by arguing for an intuitive attempt on Shakespeare's part to echo the imbalance characterizing the time in which the play was written, foreshadowing the notes of melancholy evident in the dénouements of *Much Ado about Nothing*, *As You Like It*, and *Twelfth Night*, or the sober realism that dominates the problem comedies.

The foregoing samples of conflicting interpretations are commonly based, however, on the belief that Shakespeare's view of Shylock and the play can be retraced and is to be taken into account if one wishes to make sense of, and do justice to, *The Merchant of Venice* on stage or in a critical study. But this position is in itself questionable. Even if one assumes that the constraints laid by the text upon the production are definable, it does not necessarily mean that these constraints can be identified with authorial intention. This point is driven home particularly, for instance, by that trend in the hermeneutic approach of which Gadamer is a notable proponent: "understanding means, primarily, to understand the content of what is said, and only secondarily to isolate and understand another's meaning as such." The "other" referred to is primarily the author, and it follows that

The real meaning of a text, as it speaks to the interpreter, does not depend on the contingencies of the author and whom he originally wrote for ... Not occasionally, but always, the meaning of a text goes beyond its author.[10]

There are not many instances in dramatic history which may better illustrate the unbridgeable gap between "intention" and interpretation than the case of the stage history of *The Merchant of Venice* in Israel. Shakespeare could hardly have anticipated the possibility of his play being performed for a Jewish audience, in Hebrew, in a Jewish state: for him, the probability of such a contingency would barely have exceeded that of an audience of fairies watching *A Midsummer Night's Dream* in fairyland (and, presumably, in fairytongue pentameters). It would seem that in such a context the whole question of the author's intention matters little, if at all. It did matter in Israel, however, as the public controversies surrounding each of the four major productions of the play since the establishment of the professional Hebrew stage in the twentieth century attest.

What lends particular interest to this case of stage history is the continuous dialogue taking place between a developing national consciousness – one which at no point could assume indifference towards Shylock – and a hypothetical original intention attributed to the text. The period concerned was, obviously, crucial for the development of such a national consciousness, and it may be a unique instance in the history of Shakespearean influence where a play readjusted its meaning to take an active part within the framework of a *kairos* totally different from the one in which it originated. For the significance of a Hebrew production of *The Merchant of Venice* clearly transcends the limited realm of the theatre in an age when a totally new national Jewish identity had emerged; in Israel the play is loaded simultaneously with the terror of extermination and the dilemma of might.

The first Hebrew production of *The Merchant of Venice* was mounted in 1936 at the Habimah Theatre (later to become the National Theatre of Israel). The director, Leopold Jessner (1878–

1945), one of the major figures in the rich theatrical life of Berlin during the 1920s, achieved fame as the director of the Staatstheater and the Schiller Theater. A pioneer of German Expressionism, he exerted much influence with his productions of Schiller, Wedekind, and Barlach, as well as Shakespeare's *Richard III* (1920, with Fritz Kortner in the title role), *Othello* (which he directed twice: 1921 and 1932), *Macbeth* (1922) and *Hamlet* (1926, in modern dress).[11] He arrived in Palestine a Jewish refugee, intending to wander on to Los Angeles, after having started his enforced exile in London.

Fifteen years prior to his engagement at the Habimah, Jessner must have attended the colorful and vivacious production of *The Merchant of Venice* by his contemporary and compatriot Max Reinhardt at the Grosses Schauspielhaus, where Werner Krauss's flat-footed, boisterous, almost farcical Shylock retained almost no trace of dignity in the character of the Jew.[12] For Jessner, who always differed from Reinhardt in stressing the conflict of ideas inherent in the plays rather than their spectacular effectiveness, following Reinhardt's example would have been inconceivable, particularly in the Palestine of 1936. As he explained (and he had a good deal of explaining to do), the play was supposed to remain a legend, though one in which the legendary harmony was upset by the special weight of Shylock's role. His was not to be a patient Shylock, accepting his tragic lot quietly; rather he would be a long-struggling Shylock, who eventually falls victim to the treacheries of his adversaries. Not just one Shylock who was beaten in his battle with Christian society: he was to be The Jew.[13]

Much about the spirit of Jessner's production can be gathered from the musical instructions sent with the score by his composer, Karl Rathaus: the overture juxtaposed a decadent Renaissance world (Italian in color), approaching its end, with a long-suffering Jewish one. In the opening scene, set in a lively cafe – the social center of Venetian "golden youth" – a tenor sang a tune associated with the "Hep-Hep," the well-known antisemitic cry of abuse. As was his wont, Jessner made clever use of his famous *Jessnertreppe*, a stairway designed to connect various stage levels – an external parallel to the play's immanent structure. A typical employment of this device to stress a point of meaning in a theatrical manner occurred at the trial scene: the Jew, ridiculed by the entire court, his yellow badge attached to the back of his Jewish gaberdine, stood upright on a higher level than the judge, who sat below, speaking his

lines in a thundering voice while everybody froze as if suddenly
hypnotized.[14]

Predictably, however, the play roused a public controversy. "In
spite of Jessner's promises in all his speeches that his production was
to stress only those points which will suit the Hebrew stage, most of
the gentiles appeared almost as decent human beings," one critic
typically complained. "Even Antonio betrayed that touch of somber
decency invested in him by the author." Attempting to guide his
readers to a better understanding of the spirit of Jessner's production, the same critic added:

Had our audience been more moderate and attentive, it would have sensed
in Shylock something closer to us, to our feelings, and perceived that maybe
even today (and perhaps *especially* today) the character of Shylock, as a
symbol, is the expression of the Jew's contempt of those who despise him, be
it for faults which are in him or such maliciously attributed to him. None of
the many details in the play would overshadow the main point, namely
that Shylock recognizes his right to detest his enemies, that he realizes his
moral advantage over them ... When Shylock is deserted by his daughter,
his last comfort in life, and when he leaves the courtroom, broken and
wronged to the core of his being, one gets the feeling that in this very
moment his rightfulness pierces the heavens. Yes, they have trodden him
under their feet; they have wounded his soul. Helpless, unable to utter a
word, to perform even one graceful gesture to fit fairly the tragic moment,
his fire of spirit extinct in a moment, he learns that there is no hope and
crashes into the abyss opening before him. But the fiery spirit of rage which
has left this broken Jew is to haunt the world for ages to come. That is what
Shylock symbolizes – the humiliation of Israel, for which there is no pardon
in the world for ever and ever![15]

While these were the words of one of Jessner's defenders, others
voiced different views. In a mock public trial, organized by the
theatre itself and in which Jessner took part as one of the three
prosecuted (the author, the theatre, and the director), Shakespeare,
though acknowledgment was made to his greatness as a writer, was
accused of writing "a play in which he invoked an anti-Jewish
theme without being informed enough to treat his subject, in a way
which produced a false, fictitious, impossible character, interpreted
with a strong antisemitic approach, if not on purpose then at least
erroneously."[16]

One of the witnesses for the prosecution, the writer Avraham
Kariv, a hard-line Jewish traditionalist, went so far as to deny the
Shakespearean character its Jewish identity. Shylock was the "hero

of revenge ... [whereas] we, the Jews, in whom an ancient spiritual culture is coupled with the long experience of humiliation and suffering, cannot possibly be prone to such a wild and sadistic act of revenge as that which Shylock so wilfully wants to commit."[17] Another witness for the prosecution, the well-known Communist poet Alexander Penn, reprimanded Jessner from a totally different stance:

Shylock and society – that is the question which was so utterly blurred by Jessner's interpretation ... If in an age like ours a director such as Jessner wanted to shed a fresh light upon the Shylock problem, he had to shift his focus to the one real, substantial point in the play: Shylock the "speculator." This is the Shylock which was really to be defended. A pound of flesh – absurd! And absurd is being apologetic in front of the absurd!... Instead of apologizing, we have the full right to accuse ... "You, who were angry at us for our success in accumulating money – *you* are to blame, because you never let us survive in any other way; you have turned us into usurers and profiteers."

In the recent history of Palestine, the year 1936 marks the outbreak of the Arab revolt. Penn, happy with the moderate reaction of the Jewish community at the early stage of the hostilities, did not shy from seasoning his reaction to Shakespeare's play with topical references. Addressing Jessner directly, he went on:

You have come to produce the play in Palestine! How did it not occur to you to disown hatefully anything which is fictitious in it? The way the Jewish community in this country behaved throughout these dangerous weeks, the very fact of its self-restraint is a decisive answer ... And if for the rest of the world a production of *The Merchant of Venice* should have served as a straightforward accusation ... for us, who came here in order to bring about a great spiritual–economical shift in our life, this show should have been a sharp reminder, an acute warning against all those petty Shylocks, those speculators and profiteers penetrating our country.[18]

The first production of *The Merchant of Venice* in Palestine, then, occurred at an heroic moment, where national pathos was a standard theme. Any attempt to deprive Shylock of at least some measure of his tragic pathos would have been self-defeating. On this occasion, reality proved stronger than the text in laying its constraints upon the limits of interpretation. The dictates of reality governed all facets of the production: the text bowdlerized, in the name of serenity, such vulgar references as Gratiano's "stake down" conceit in act 3, scene 2 and cut three-quarters of the same character's final speech at the end of the play, and the music and scenery served faithfully the director's solemn approach to its moral dilemma. So did the casting: the two rival leaders of the company, Aharon Meskin and Shim'on Finkel, alternated in the part, both denying the character of Shylock any trace of its inherent comic potential. Meskin was an heroic figure, making use of his commanding physical stature and resounding voice; Finkel emphasized Shylock's spiteful bitterness.

Twenty-three years later, the heroic pathos characterizing Jewish reality in Palestine was considerably modified. The struggle for liberation over, the Israeli community was undergoing a process of stabilization in its eleven-year-old state. And though the Israeli national character was still precarious and highly vulnerable, and the memory of the Jewish Holocaust still fresh, one could now more easily risk a presentation of *The Merchant of Venice* where Shylock was to be exempt from carrying the full weight of Jewish history on his shoulders. This time it was a non-Jewish director, Tyrone Guthrie, who came over to the Habimah (where he had directed a much-acclaimed production of *Oedipus Rex* in 1947) to revive the controversial play. And although the same two actors again alternated the part of Shylock, a significant change of focus was generally expected. Said Meskin:

When I first played Shylock, I stressed mainly the national, pathetic element. This time I shall endeavor to portray a more human Shylock: he has got a measure of fanaticism – but he has his weaknesses as well. Guthrie has told me that at the beginning of the play Shylock is a thriving merchant, a kind of Rothschild. This has given me much help. I have even obtained a picture of Rothschild.[19]

In Guthrie's modern-dress production, Shylock did indeed physically resemble "a kind of Rothschild." If Jessner's fame as a Shakespearean director rested mainly on his productions of the tragedies, Guthrie felt more at home in Shakespearean comedy, and his production attempted to coax the play as far as possible into that realm. In a busy Venice, he devised a lively and rapid succession of entrances and exits, with Salerio and Solanio portrayed as a pair of American businessmen holding their umbrellas in the rain while passing comments on city affairs, with Gratiano constantly on the move in a dancing step, humming merry jazz tunes – a persistent association of decadent Renaissance Italy with modern American life.

In his approach to Shylock, however, Guthrie remained pretty much faithful to the apologetic tradition. For him, the focal center of the action is the duel between Shylock and Portia in the trial scene, at the expense of Antonio, who is saved from being a bore only when his homosexual relation to Bassanio (Guthrie used the term "irregular" or "tender") is carefully established. But even so, "when all is said and done, in the theatre it is almost impossible to make Antonio dominate the play."[20]

In spite of the particular emphasis laid on the Shylock–Portia duel, Guthrie's actress for the Habimah production (Shoshana Ravid) failed to become an equal partner to the Jew. Anonymously referring to her in his introduction, Guthrie later described how her ineffectuality made him realize how important the part was:

Portia was entirely miscast – a sweet, motherly, young woman, the epitome of middle-class respectability. The more we stuck her with jewels and decked her up in pink satin, the more she resembled the Railway Queen of some remote junction; the harder she tried to be witty and sophisticated, the more she sounded like a hospital nurse reading a script prepared for somebody else.[21]

The scene, then, was left entirely to Shylock, and here Guthrie's excessive reverence for the Jew proved a major drawback. Guthrie's conception of Shylock in this production did not contradict his general view of the part, as his later commentary indicates:

It is my view that Shakespeare's portrait is not antisemitic, that the pound of flesh wager was entered upon as a jest and only turns to vengeance after Shylock has been robbed and his daughter abducted by young Venetians of Antonio's set. In fact, after the trial, and after Portia's great invocation of mercy it is the Christians who lack all mercy toward their enemy. The sadistic vengeance taken upon Shylock is as offensive to Christianity as it is legally outrageous.

And yet, as he realizes himself,

to say this to Jews in the present epoch is as useless as to beg the rain not to fall. There is a rooted tradition among Jews that the play is an antisemitic document, and it is indeed true that many Jewish boys at school have, through generations, been taunted and execrated as "Shylock" ... the remedy is ... to interpret it so that it becomes, *as its author intended*, a fantasia on the twin themes of mercy and justice ... in which none of the characters is either wholly good or wholly evil.[22]

Up to a point, Guthrie's colorful fantasia managed to work effectively. The problem of Shylock, however, proved recalcitrant:

in appearance reminiscent of "a liberal Rabbi, with a well-trimmed beard and a clever and pleasant expression,"[23] neither of the two Shylocks could avoid the pathos presumably remaining with them from the former production. Shylock's pathos stood in awkward contrast to the air of romantic comedy informing the production as a whole, to the detriment of the sought-for balance. Some of the problems of Guthrie's production anticipated the emergence of similar problems in Jonathan Miller's 1970 production at the National Theatre, London: can a liberal, fairly realistic modern-dress production accommodate the weird story of the pound of flesh and remain liberal and fairly realistic? Guthrie's production could not. It was removed from Habimah's repertory after a few months.

The next production of *The Merchant of Venice* on the Israeli stage occurred after the most significant experience undergone by national consciousness since the founding of the state in 1948: the 1967 war, which had a dramatic effect on the nation's mentality. The prevailing sense of persecution and self-defensiveness, so far an infinite resource for rationalizing any mistake made in the name of security or any moral conflict resulting from the rights, or "positive discrimination," of Jews in Israel, from now on had to allow for the manifest reality of occupation and might. The euphoric period which followed the war (at least until 1973) was characterized by growing feelings of national pride up to the point of vanity, not unlike those of the Elizabethans in the years immediately following the victory over the Armada. It was now reasonably safe to assume that the self-confident audience would be able to stomach a totally different, non-apologetic approach to the play.

This was the situation when, in 1972, an Israeli-born director addressed himself to the play for the first time in Israel. The "native view" permitted a portrayal of Shylock in the least favorable and most grotesque manner, as if coming directly from the heavily biased drawings of Jews in the Middle Ages. In Yossi Yzraeli's production of the play at the Cameri Theatre of Tel Aviv, everything was far removed from realism: Shylock, in a dark robe and a black bell-shaped hat, stood out among blonde Venetians, all clad in white, against abstract scenery consisting of a white back wall and a white rostrum. Tubal, in black, served only to underline the foreign look of the Jew, while Jessica (not unpredictably) wore a striped dress, with lines of black and white, following her conversion.

One of the major features which marked the production was its

persistent departure from the individuality of character. I have
dwelt elsewhere on one example of this practice, the experimental
doubling of Morocco and Arragon, both played by the actor playing
Bassanio, and thus lending a reinforced unity to the choice of the
three caskets.[24] If this device might still have been accommodated
within the boundaries of realistic characterization (e.g., Bassanio
eliminating alternatives in disguise), making all the Christians in
Venice look alike transcended the boundaries of individuality to the
point of rendering them, in some respects, as a collective entity.
Typical of this approach was the treatment of Antonio in the trial
scene: the stage was totally bare but for a black stool on which
Antonio sat with a huge black cross fastened to his back. Thus made
a type of Christ, Antonio himself did not become an object of
empathy; the pathos and compassion evoked by the scene were
directed to the figure of Christ beyond him rather than to Antonio in
person.

The action was further circumscribed by a surrounding framework: the show opened with a Passion-like procession, with mum-
mers in masks, and Shylock, his Jewish nose grotesquely prolonged, bending under the weight of the cross. Another symbolic
procession followed the trial scene. But the most dominant element
of this enveloping framework was the constant presence of a puppet
theatre peering over the white back wall, reflecting, reverberating,
and multiplying the action underneath by means of puppets in the
likeness of the actual characters on stage. The puppet-show was used
as a visual commentary on the action, sometimes comically imitating it, sometimes making visual interscenic connections, and
occasionally even providing alternative action. The most outstanding example of the latter practice occurred when, as the background
to Lorenzo's exhortation on music (act 5, scene 1), the puppet-play
enacted a symbolic ritual in which Shylock was baptized by the
Christians.

The production, though in many respects lively and entertaining,
was considered an artistic (and box-office) failure, its symbolism
much too obvious and far from convincing.[25] Predictably, much of
the critical controversy focused on the portrayal of Shylock. Even
though, in the final analysis, Yzraeli's interpretation was meant to
render Shylock as the victim of a sterile Christian society, his
intentions were thwarted, for much of the audience, by the Jew's
repellent appearance and mannerisms. Unlike Jessner and Guthrie,

who chose for the part typically heroic actors, Yzraeli gave the role to a notable comedian, Avner Hyskiahu, whose style of delivery generally consists of a nervous staccato. Under the director's instructions, Hyskiahu played Shylock as "a shrewd old Jew, his posture, his gait, his manner of speaking reflecting a life spent making shrewd, furtive money deals, a man accustomed to abuse. He delivers his key speech ('Hath not a Jew eyes?') snarling at the two *goyim* [gentiles], practically spitting in their faces. He is a worm turned, but still a worm."[26] The controversy over the production once again served to expose the age-old prejudices concerning the play:

It is but natural that we Jews are practically allergic to a typical antisemitic interpretation, which blurs Shylock's cry of pain and protest, stirring the heart of any human being, be it a Jew, a Christian, or other. In this the play was deprived of its tragic power and poetic flavour which are, in spite of the various amusing moments abounding in *The Merchant of Venice*, the very core of the play.[27]

This, however, was a fairly moderate reaction. Not surprisingly, the production in general, and the portrayal of Shylock in particular, were most fiercely attacked by the more radically nationalistic press.

Avner Hyskiahu repeated Shylock in yet a different production, in 1980, again at the Cameri Theatre, directed this time by a non-Jewish director from the Royal Shakespeare Company, Barry Kyle. In many ways Kyle's production was not distinguishable from any likely production of the play at his home theatre in Stratford. Set in no specific locality or period (Portia was dressed as a typical Renaissance lady while Launcelot Gobbo appeared on stage riding an ancient motorcycle), Christopher Morley's impressive scenery subtly captured the symbolism of the three caskets: a golden back wall (made of shutters typical of Tel Aviv verandas) and golden bridges, surrounding waters of silver hue, and a lead-colored central platform.

In his program note (entitled "Two Outcasts of Society: Shylock and Antonio") Kyle stressed the allegorical significance of the play, as his interpretation attempted to communicate it:

The money world, though bound by contracts and stamped by passion, must depend on friendship.

Kyle marked value as binding together the two stories of the plot: the value of friendship, of marriage pledge, and of money. Time has turned Shylock into a racist stereotype; yet in the play Shylock is

condemned not because of his Jewishness but because he lets money
rule him. This condemnation has nothing to do with antisemitism,
says Kyle, since it also applies to the Prince of Morocco and
Arragon, as well as to the young Christians of Venice, including
Bassanio. Shylock, whose world is stamped by gold and silver,
ignores the quality of mercy. Once wronged, Kyle said in his initial
talk to the actors, Shylock easily falls prey to revenge in succumbing
to the logic and mentality of terrorism. Triggering one of the most
charged terms in the life of the Middle East, Kyle allowed the tokens
of local topicality to penetrate his conception of the play.

Such an attitude towards "a fellow countryman," however,
proved an obstacle even for actors who took part in the production
itself. At a certain point during rehearsals, Kyle was persuaded by
some of the actors (though not before a thorough argument with
many of the others) that in order for the message of concord and love
to be accepted by the target audience, Antonio's first stipulation
regarding Shylock's conversion had better be dropped. Thus, while
in 1972 the ritual symbolizing Shylock's baptism was virtually
enacted on stage, no mention of his possible conversion was made to
the audience of 1980, polarized between cultural assimilation with
the west and a fervent, often fundamentalist search for traditional
roots. It was the radically nationalistic part of the audience who
failed to notice Kyle's conception of Shylock as "succumbing to the
logic and mentality of terrorism." Social, economic, and political
circumstances in Israel in the 1980s, a second decade of occupying
another people's homeland, have had their effect of the national
consciousness. Looking back on the long history of Jewish suffering
up to the Holocaust, many in Israel have made it a flag "not to be
made a soft and dull eyed fool, to shake the head, relent and sigh,
and yield to [gentile] intercessors" (3.3.14–16). For those, Shylock's
cry of defiance, "My deeds upon my head" (4.1.202) was justified in
context, since "Jewish" and "the logic and mentality of terrorism"
had become mutually exclusive concepts. This strange mixture of
resenting Shakespeare's alleged antisemitism and identifying with
Shylock's motives lent special significance to a topical image of a
terrorist act, which, in the political context of the Middle East, is
hardly confined to any one-sided allegorical interpretation.

Even though Kyle's production failed to make its political point,
it was a crucial step towards setting the play in the contemporary
Israeli context. Kyle's attitude towards Shylock surely would have

antagonized the old historicist school, for the term "terrorism" could enter neither the discourse nor the supposed "master narrative" of the Renaissance. But there is another, more basic difficulty. From the stance of normative social order, terrorism must signify crime. Terrorism may not necessarily be politically motivated; but Shylock convinces neither the Venetian court nor the majority of Shakespeare's critics in his motiveless malignity. What is he, then? A political dissenter? And if so, what would be the moral position of a political terrorist in the Renaissance? Within the discourse of crime, the term "political terrorism," meaning the use of violence to press individuals or society to meet political demands, may betray a peculiar sense of moral (if not legal) legitimation. As Uri Eisenzweig argues, the physical reality of terrorism "appears to be dramatically unquestionable," whereas its actual legal content is missing from most judicial systems.[28] While terrorism must emanate from a logical procedure which stands outside the normative order, it draws for its validity on a different, meta-normative order, which recognizes the dominant ideology as only one of several orders competing in the sociopolitical consciousness. Such an extra-official validity has no place in any legitimate code of values, and thus it may exist exclusively in the realm of text. The performative nature of the terrorist text thus becomes indispensable in this process. It is the word of Shylock's bond which becomes the symbolic, hence the essential, meaning of the terrorist act he performs. The consummation of the act of terrorism is not the actual deed (such as the cutting of the pound of flesh), nor is its author's real identity (as a Jew, a moneylender, or a Pantaloon) of necessary significance at the crucial moment. This may explain the discrepancy between Shylock's prominence in the play and his relatively brief presence on the scene, as well as his much-debated absence from the play after the trial scene.

And yet the legal content of terrorism, missing from most judicial systems, does reside in Shakespeare's Venetian book of laws. Any play composed during the reign of Elizabeth could not ignore the constant danger of contrivance by strangers, which may explain the peculiarly anti-alien nature of Shakespeare's Venetian legislation that otherwise pretends to be liberal and egalitarian. There is no sense in which such a private assault contrived by one individual against another should be distinguished ethnically or nationally, unless that distinction between alien and citizen implies an act of political subversion, or, in other words, political terrorism.

Shylock does not belong with those precursors of modern terrorism, such as Brutus, who use violence against tyranny. Yet if Shylock does not take hostages illegally, his act of appropriating the law itself is not entirely devoid of ideological grounds. Hardly an Iago-like "motive-hunter," Shylock provides some solid reasons for his stubborn insistence on his bond, none of which has to do with ideology; and yet some tokens of ideological motivation are still betrayed in his behavior. To cite but one example, whether or not we are to believe Jessica's evidence concerning her father's initial intentions to harm Antonio, her reference to Tubal and Chus as Shylock's "countrymen" (3.2.284) is telling. We do not know which is their common "country" of origin, but this expression, together with Shylock's repeated references to his "nation" and "tribe," casts an ideological shade on his attitude throughout the play.

Beside the particular case of his Jewishness, Shylock represents a more generally subversive element within the dominant Christian, capitalist order in Venice. Together with Othello he belongs in the company of "aliens," whose danger to the ideological integrity of the Venetian ruling class is so menacing that special legislation had to be issued to curb their rights and activities within the liberal state. Shylock is no self-styled machiavel like Marlowe's Barabas, who defies the law entirely. Thus his complaint cannot find any institutional outlet until his specific function within the trade–capitalist process which moves Venetian economy is directly addressed. Significantly enough, this opportunity occurs when emotion is mixed with business: the financial implications of courting Portia belong to the subversive parts of "pure" love in the same way that Shylock the alien is a necessary constituent of the Venetian economic system. Once Shylock is allowed to interfere with the financial operations of Venice's prince of merchants, the subversive process of rebellion is set in motion.

Throughout the play Shylock is consistently urged to adopt a "gentle" attitude ("We all expect a gentle answer, Jew"). This is but another way of demanding that he embrace a "gentile" ideology, a demand which is finally imposed on him legally with the verdict of the trial, which suddenly turns out to be his own. Shylock's perception of the law of Venice is indeed "alien," since the use he makes of the Venetian constitution rests on the word of the law but contradicts its spirit. It is, in fact, the very essence of Shylock's terrorism: he consciously subverts the soul of Venetian order, namely its book of laws, and turns it upon itself. The only counter-measure Venice could take against Shylock's act of legal terrorism is to subvert the spirit of language on which the law rests in order to re-establish the normal procedures of justice and social order by which Venice's mainstream ideology abides. And it is significant that this is brought about by an "alien" of a different order, a woman disguised as a man, a country feudal who comes from afar, in order and in time.

Unlike his modern counterparts, Shylock never dreams of insti-tuting a new order, where the ruling authorities will emanate from below, equally representing all the town's residents. His imaginary example of abolishing slavery (4.1.90–8) remains a parable, without anybody knowing his own opinion on the matter. We do not even know for sure whether he would have pursued his murderous act to the very end, had not Portia's "tarry" stopped him at the last moment. Nor is it crucial for us, or even for Shakespeare, to know, since, as we have noted before, the terrorist act performed by Shylock is consummated on the textual or symbolic level. As Grant Wardlaw is not alone in arguing, "terrorism is primarily theatre."[29] The gist of this notion is nothing but an extension of the textual identity of the terrorist act, as it is often expressed by a note or a telephone call which brings it to public attention, into the performa-tive ritual of the theatrical gesture. Shylock need not act further, since, as the play as a whole shows us, his function in the plot is nothing but that of a catalyst. It is, in other words, the reaction of normative society to an extraterritorial act that the play is about.

Without resorting to the critical fallacies of traditional histori-cism, *The Merchant of Venice* may still be made to show us the ways in which, by temporarily taking hostage the Venetian law, and while the entire audience of the theatre of terrorism hold their breath, Shylock manages to bring forth the very target of political terrorism, exposing the moral fragility of the dominant ideology. His act succeeds in undermining the notion of reality as integrated and rational, as appropriated by the dominant ideology. In his *Ge-schichtsphilosophische Thesen* Walter Benjamin tells us that only from the stance of the victors is history viewed as a unitary process. In this respect Shylock is a loser. But as a political terrorist he celebrates the losers' victory in naming the name of the game. In this he disappears as a Jew, or a Pantaloon, or even as an "alien" in the general sense. As the author and perpetrator of the "terrorist" text of his bond he coerces the legal system to produce a counter-terrorist text of a similar nature, whereby it exposes itself, at least for one cathartic moment, to its own ideological limitations.

It is hard to predict to what extent the future stage history of *The Merchant of Venice* in Israel will reflect sociopolitical developments in the way it has been doing in the past century, or what course it may take. I believe that the intricate view of Shylock as representing the ideological complexities of terrorism, initially propounded in Barry Kyle's production, may shed new light on the age-old apologetic approach to the play, adopted in its stage and critical history by Jews and non-Jews alike. The easy transformation of Shylock from one form of minority affiliation to another renders the ideological content of the play more general. In a very peculiar way it is expressed in Rafi Bokai's film *Avanti Popolo* (Israel, 1986), which depicts the escape of two Egyptian soldiers through the Israeli lines in Sinai in the attempt to reach the Egyptian border. When captured by a group of Israeli soldiers one of the two Egyptians starts to recite Shylock's "hath not a Jew eyes" speech. An Israeli soldier comments: "He has changed the parts!" Has he, indeed? Portia, clad as a young male judge, opens the process of justice in the Venetian court, asking: "Which is the merchant here? and which the Jew?" (4.1.170). It is the very question that any judicious reading of the play must attempt to leave open.

NOTES

1 Anshel Spielmann, member of the Stern Group fighting against British mandate of Palestine.
2 Citations from Shakespeare are from the New Arden editions, unless otherwise specified.
3 Dalia Sharon, "Legitimation for Antisemitism 1988," *Davar*, 27 May 1988: 28 (Hebrew). For a detailed account of Alexander's production, see James C. Bulman, *The Merchant of Venice*, Shakespeare in Performance (Manchester University Press, 1991), 117–42, and Russell Jackson and Robert Smallwood (eds.), *Players of Shakespeare 3* (Cambridge University Press, 1993).
4 Eli Rozik, "Apartheid in Venice," *Bamah* 111 (1988): 74 (Hebrew).
5 *Ibid.*, 75.
6 *Ibid.*, 84.
7 The present usage of the term *kairos* follows, e.g., that of Kermode; see Frank Kermode, *The Sense of an Ending* (New York: Oxford University Press, 1967), 47.

8 Fergusson, in the introduction to the Laurel (1958) edition of the play; reprinted in his *Shakespeare: The Pattern in His Carpet* (New York: Delta Books, 1971), 113.

9 See Northrop Frye, in whose view the play "seems almost an experiment in coming as close as possible to upsetting the comic balance": *Anatomy of Criticism* (Princeton University Press, 1957), 165.

10 Hans-Georg Gadamer, *Truth and Method* (London: Sheed & Ward, 1975), 262, 263–4.

11 See Herbert Ihering, *Reinhardt, Jessner, Piscator oder Klassikertod* (Berlin: Ernst Rohwolt, 1929); also Ernst Leopold Stahl, *Shakespeare und das deutsche Theater* (Stuttgart: W. Kohlhammer, 1947), 608–14 and *passim*. For a recent appraisal of Jessner's work, see David F. Kuhns, "Expressionism, Monumentalism, Politics: Emblematic Acting in Jessner's *Wilhelm Tell* and *Richard III*," *New Theatre Quarterly* 25 (1991): 35–48.

12 Stahl, *Shakespeare und das deutsche Theater*, 592. See also John Russell Brown's introduction to his New Arden edition of the play (London: Methuen, 1955), xxxvi.

13 Leopold Jessner, "On the Theatre in the Land of Israel and Its Vocation," *Bamah*, 10 (1936): 6 (Hebrew).

14 *Bamah* 11–12 (1937): 31 (Hebrew).

15 Ya'akov Fikhman, "On the Classical Theatre," *Bamah* 11–12 (1937): 8 (Hebrew).

16 *Bamah* 11–12: 24 (Hebrew).

17 *Ibid.*, 25. A similar line of argument was adopted, forty years later, by the Israeli Embassy in London, when given an opportunity by *The Sunday Times* to answer thorough research carried out by the paper's reporters into the practice of torture of detainees in the territories occupied by Israel. Rather than refuting the accusations point by point, the Embassy issued a statement to the effect that "the Nation of the Bible" was morally prevented from, and therefore unable to perform, acts of torture.

18 *Ibid.*, 26–8. Penn's is a typical reaction of a member of the pioneer groups who came to Palestine during the early 1920s, many of them strongly influenced by the ideals of the Russian Revolution, contrasting with the later "bourgeois" immigrants.

19 In an interview with Michael Ohad, *Dvar Hashavu'a* (Hebrew: February 1959). Guthrie himself opens his introduction to the play in *Shakespeare: Ten Great Plays* (New York, 1962) in the same spirit: "Who is the merchant of Venice? Shylock's part is the most striking and effective, and he is arguably a merchant." Reprinted in Guthrie, *In Various Directions: A View of Theatre* (London: Michael Joseph, 1965).

20 Guthrie, *In Various Directions*, 101.

21 *Ibid.*, 102.

22 *Ibid.*, 102–3 (italics mine).

23 Avitam, *Davar* (Hebrew), 6 Mar. 1959.

24 See Avraham Oz, "The Doubling of Parts in Shakespearean Comedy: Some Questions of Theory and Practice," in *Shakespearean Comedy*, ed. Maurice Charney (New York: New York Literary Forum, 1980), 175–82.

25 Originally, Yzraeli planned to set the play within a large cathedral, somewhere in Europe, where the townsfolk were mounting a Passion play with the local Jew forced to play the villain of the piece. This was abandoned during rehearsals, giving rise to a somewhat patched-up framework which eventually circumscribed the actual production.

26 M. Kohanski, *The Jerusalem Post*, 24 Mar. 1972.

27 Hayim Gamzu, *Ha'aretz* (Hebrew), 20 Mar. 1972.

28 See Uri Eisenzweig, "Terrorism in Life and in Real Literature," *Diacritics* (Fall 1988): 32.

29 Grant Wardlaw, *Political Terrorism* (Cambridge University Press, 1982), 38.

CHAPTER 4

Translation and mise en scène:
the example of contemporary French Shakespeare

Leanore Lieblein

The 1982 meeting of the Société Française Shakespeare contained a roundtable discussion on translating Shakespeare's plays. The issue was phrased by translator Jean-Michel Déprats: "Do you translate differently depending on whether a translation is to be read or to be staged?"[1] The answer seemed to be an unequivocal "yes." Translators and theatre people tended to agree that even if existing published translations of Shakespeare were (possibly) "faithful," or "literary," or "readable," they were problematic in performance.

On the other hand, translations for the stage, while performable, were felt to be as transient as the productions for which they were intended. According to Michel Grivelet, "Translation for the page and translation for the stage are two different things ... A translation for the theatre is immediately subordinated to the conception of the mise en scène." His view confirmed Jean-Claude Carrière's description of translating *Timon of Athens* for Peter Brook's Paris production in 1974: "For Peter Brook the very project of working on Shakespeare presupposed the updating of the text according to a strict equation: no new text, no new mise en scène."[2] In consequence Jean-Pierre Villequin pointed out, "Translations for the theatre age quickly and badly ... Every new mise en scène calls for a new translation." Theatrical translations were felt to reflect the language and sensibility of a given moment of reception and thus to narrow the range of possibility implicit in the original. Nevertheless, even in Germany, where the tyranny of the Schlegel–Tieck translations of Shakespeare has been greater than of those by François–Victor Hugo in France, there has emerged a definite movement toward re-translating the plays for new production.[3]

If a theatrical translation must be subordinated to the conception of the mise en scène why are such translations subsequently published, sold, and performed in new productions? Further reflection on dramatic translation has moved away from a facile contrast between translations for reading and for performance. This chapter explores the dynamic relationship between a dramatic translation and its production. On the one hand I argue that when a translation of a play is done for a specific production, it becomes part of the mise en scène. That is to say that the choices that are an inevitable feature of any translation interact with and are altered by the interpretive strategies that are implicit in the staging process. The translation is given voice and body in the production, the translated text becomes part of the historical record of a given production, and its publication and distribution are tied to the occasion of its performance. At the same time, successful productions, at least in France, create a demand for their own texts. These translations have a life of their own as published texts subsequent to the performance, and indeed may become subject to further stagings. Contrary to those who insist that each new mise en scène calls for a new translation, I examine recent work in the theory of dramatic translation to suggest that the process of translating for a given production does not necessarily inhibit a translation's subsequent production.

Recent translators of Shakespeare share a philosophy of translation that emphasizes, in addition to the sense of the words, the nature of dramatic language. They strive to preserve the Shakespearean text's potential for performance by making space in their translations for non-verbal codes of theatrical presentation. Translation theorists such as Susan Bassnett-McGuire and Patrice Pavis, and theorist/practitioners like Jean-Michel Déprats, focus not only on the "meaning" of the words to be translated but also on the relationship of those words to the body that speaks them and the cultural context in which they are spoken.

To illustrate my argument I draw upon some translations of Shakespeare that received performance in Paris in 1982–3. Though others could have been selected, I have chosen for my focus a comedy and a tragedy, because I saw them and because in the forms and contexts of their production they complement each other. *A Midsummer Night's Dream* was translated by director Stuart Seide for his production at the Théâtre National de Chaillot, while the translation of *Coriolanus* was commissioned by director Bernard Sobel for production at the community Théâtre de Gennevilliers. (Other French translations of Shakespeare for the stage from the same period on which I base my generalizations include: *Timon d'Athènes* by Jean-Claude Carrière, *Peines d'amour perdues* by Jean-Michel Déprats, *Hamlet* by Raymond Lepoutre, *La Nuit des rois* and *Richard II* by Ariane Mnouchkine, and *Periclès, Prince de Tyr* by Marika Prinçay and Jean-Michel Noiret.)

MISE EN SCÈNE AS TRANSLATION; TRANSLATION AS *MISE EN JEU*

A production itself is a "reading" – some might argue a "translation" – of a dramatic text. The words of any dramatic text are part of its rendering on the stage (though they may be subject to cuts and rearrangement), but they are transformed in performance by the intonation, the timing, the expression, and gesture with which they are spoken as well as by the scenic/material environment (including sound effects and music), and the spatial relationships between the speaker and the other performers and between the actors and the audience.[4] Performance clearly transforms a dramatic text, but it does so in chosen directions.

A mise en scène is of course of its own time and place; however, there are many possible productions in any given time and place. When a play is performed in its original language it will at any moment commit itself to one reading or interpretation over many others. A mise en scène of a play in translation will do the same. However, since there are more ways than one of rendering on the stage a given line or phrase in the source text, one may legitimately choose among not only a range of gestures and intonations to express a certain concept or set of words in the source language text, but also among a range of words or expressions in the receptor language.

That all dramatic translations are the result of a series of choices is emphasized by André-Michel Rousseau in his overview of the history of French translations of Shakespeare. What distinguishes one translation from another of the same play, he argues, are the reasons for the choices and the consistency with which they are deployed. Since no translation is neutral, a director opting to use an existing translation is buying into its special qualities and the kind of staging it makes possible.[5] Jean Jacquot points out, for example, that in choosing to stage *Hamlet* and *Antony and Cleopatra* in the translations of André Gide, Jean-Louis Barrault was striving for a reconciliation of Shakespearean language with classical French taste.

Barrault similarly chose the Yves Bonnefoy translation of *Julius Caesar* for its "poetic" qualities.[6]

These choices are consistent with the observations of polysystem theory, which points out that "Translating as a teleological activity *par excellence* is to a large extent conditioned by the goals it is designed to serve, and these goals are set in, and by, the prospective receptor system(s). Consequently, translators operate first and foremost in the interest of the culture *into* which they are translating, and not in the interest of the source text, let alone the source culture."[7] Or, to put it more simply, the goal of a translation, like that of a mise en scène, is to be understood and appreciated by its audience.

The case of dramatic translation is complicated by the nature of dramatic language. The dramatic text encodes not only its own meanings but also the conditions and possibilities of its performance. As Susan Bassnett-McGuire writes, "A theatre text exists in a dialectical relationship with the performance of that text." Patrice Pavis theorizes this as a "series of concretizations ... established in relation to an exchange between spoken *text* and speaking *body*, and with respect to the interaction of cultures juxtaposed in the hermeneutic act of intercultural exchange."[8] According to Pavis, the passage from the source dramatic text to the target dramatic text must take into account the "preverbal" as well as the verbal systems of both. The dramatic text, he argues, is the linguistic trace of a potential situation of enunciation which may include such elements as gesture and costume, indeed "all the sign systems that make up the theatrical situation of enunciation" and make possible an imagined potential performance or "*mise en jeu*" (34). A translation of a dramatic text thus requires the imagining of a corresponding preverbal situation of enunciation in the target culture, since a dramatic translation must not only communicate the meaning of the words of the source text but also, by deriving from a preverbal situation of enunciation in the target culture, make possible its mise en scène in the receptor culture. For this combination of verbal plus preverbal layers Pavis has coined the term *verbo-corps* (translated by Loren Kruger as *language-body*):

What we call the language-body, the union of thing-presentation and word-presentation, would in the context of theatrical enunciation be the union of spoken text and the gestures accompanying its enunciation, in other words, the specific link that text establishes with gesture. (36)

As a translator for the stage, Jean-Michel Déprats addresses the same issue in practical terms: "For me, the main requirement is to preserve the performability of the text."[9]

In the pages that follow I shall look at the verbal form of that "performability" in two French translations and productions of Shakespeare. In doing so I hope to suggest the relationship, in the case of Shakespeare, of recent translation theory to recent translation practice.

SEIDE'S *DREAM*

Stuart Seide is committed to creating through translation "an instrument for acting [*un instrument de jeu*]." His translation of *A Midsummer Night's Dream* proceeds from his sense of the importance of the words of the play.[10] Its rhythmic and metrical richness – the rhyming couplets and blank verse of the lovers, the prose of the mechanicals, the octosyllabics of the fairies, the incantations of Puck and Oberon – are an important part of the action for a director who sees himself as a "*metteur en jeu*." Indeed there are moments when, given the ludic and frenetic qualities of the lovers' language, "speech becomes the primary action" (p. 4). Seide points out that a translator is constantly making choices; for example, he must choose between the music of the words and their sense. His own choices were guided less by consistent principle than by the demands of the theatrical moment: "It was a dramaturgical choice which formed an integral part of my options as a director" (4). His object was to create a French text that would permit him to communicate not only Shakespeare's words, but his sense of Shakespearean performance, to his present audience.

Thus the translated text changed considerably between the study and the stage. The rehearsal process focused on the words: "I asked the actors to let themselves be carried away by the words, by their resonance."[11] But since the words were only the translator's, they were neither sacred nor final. The translator/director, together with the actors, constantly referred to the original in order to find out what the English text was asking them to do on the stage. They were seeking out, in Pavis's terms, the *verbo-corps*, the "*language-body* [that] is the orchestration, peculiar to a language and culture, of gesture, vocal rhythm and the text ... simultaneously *spoken action* and *speech-in-action*"(36). As a result, the French version evolved in the course of rehearsal. The publication of the text, which occurred in December 1982 during rehearsals for a revival in January 1983, interrupted but did not put an end to this process. As Seide found it necessary to remind the reader in his prefatory remarks: "The text published here is not completed. It is a stop-action photograph of work that is evolving" (4). In other words, the translation is not an object but part of a process of building the production. Although not quite the "co-operative translation" preferred by Susan Bassnett-McGuire in her summary of theatrical translation strategies, Seide's translation was constantly being tested, not only by the translator against its source, but also by the director and its actors against its destination.

Seide's translation is remarkably close to the Shakespearean text with, for a performance text, relatively few omissions.[12] It renders verse as verse and prose as prose, using for the verse a flexible line of varying length and meter that approximates the lineation of the Shakespearean verse. However, because of his commitment to the physical qualities of the language and the physicalization of the speech on the stage, as a translator Seide chooses to privilege, where possible, rhyme, alliteration, and word play.

Not that all of the English rhymes are preserved. The couplets of the lovers are largely abandoned, though they are often retained for exit lines. More important than fidelity to a specific rhyme is the preservation of such stylistic features as the tone and energy of the verse. Thus Puck's

> And the country proverb known,
> That every man should take his own,
> In your waking shall be shown.
>   Jack shall have Jill;
>   Nought shall go ill:
> The man shall have his mare again, and all shall be well.

> (3.2.458–63)

becomes

> Et le proverbe bien connu,
> que chacun doit avoir son dû,
> a votre réveil s'accomplira.
>
> Jeannot aura sa Jeannette
> le monde sera en fête.
> Chacun retrouvera sa jument,
> Et tout sera bien mieux qu'avant.

> (p. 75)

In some cases alliteration is present, even when it does not exist in Shakespeare. When Egeus says to Lysander

> [Thou hast] stol'n the impression of her fantasy
> With bracelets of thy hair, rings, gawds, conceits,
> Knacks, trifles, nosegays, sweetmeats   (1.1.32–4)

Seide translates:

> Tu t'es emparé de son imagination
> avec des bracelets de cheveux, des bagues, des babioles, des bijoux
>   chétifs,
> des breloques, des bouquets, des bonbons.   (p. 10)

Puns too make their appearance, sometimes even more forcefully than in Shakespeare or at the expense of the literal meaning. Bottom's "I could play Ercles rarely" (1.2.29) becomes "Je ferais un Mercule étonnant" (p. 21), and Demetrius' "wode within this wood" (2.1.192) becomes "aux abois dans ce bois" (p. 32). Similarly, Lysander's "For lying so, Hermia, I do not lie" (2.2.52), is rendered as "avec ce lit, Hermia, on se lie" (p. 38). The sound takes precedence over the sense. So too with Puck's "I go, I go, look how I go" (3.2.100), translated as "Je cours, je cours, je vole dare dare" (p. 57). In the absence of a literal French equivalent an alternative of similar playfulness has been invented. Thus Demetrius' comment on Snug the Joiner's lion – "The very best at a beast, my lord, that e'er I saw" (5.1.229–30) – turns into 'La pire âme, monseigneur, que j'aie jamais rencontrée chez une Thisbête" (p. 98).

Seide's commitment to the language of the play embraces not only its "meaning," but also its music. His translation attempts to render the material substance as well as the sense of the words in order to retain the dramatic energy of the text, its essential "play-ability."

DÉPRATS'S *CORIOLANUS*

In the case of *Coriolanus* directed by Bernard Sobel in a translation by Jean-Michel Déprats,[13] the socio-political dimension of the *verbo-corps* became apparent as well when midway through a performance I was surprised by the words of the Tribune Sicinius:

> Allez chercher le peuple, au nom duquel, moi,
> Je t'arrête comme traître révolutionnaire,
> Ennemi du bien public.   (p. 78)

Was "traître révolutionnaire" really "Shakespeare," I wondered? It seemed to bring into the world of the nascent Roman Republic the rhetoric of a more recent politics. So when I reached home that night I checked my *Complete Works*:

> Go call the people, in whose name myself
> Attach thee as a traitorous innovator,
> A foe to th' public weal.   (3.1.173–5)[14]

The prose translation of François–Victor Hugo renders "traitorous innovator" as "traître novateur."[15] Hugo's version is etymologically and phonically closer to Shakespeare than Déprats's, but is more abstract. In its choice of the word "révolutionnaire" Déprats's translation implicitly hypothesizes that the Shakespearean notion of "innovation" has the disruptive force of our modern western European sense of "revolution."

The Théâtre de Gennevilliers under the direction of Sobel has consistently striven to speak to the working-class community in which it is located. Sobel's production certainly did not turn the plebeians into the Maghrebian immigrant working class of the Gennevilliers community, and Déprats's translation did not for a minute insist that he do so. But the translation was enriched by the preverbal social and political situation of enunciation, shared by, though not exclusive to, that community, which provided the context of its performance.

Déprats's French version of *Coriolanus* keeps very close to the Shakespeare Folio text. It maintains the distinction between verse and prose, matching almost line for line and image for image and preserving, where possible, repetition, alliteration, etc. Certain choices, however, clarify the antagonism between Coriolanus and the citizens of Rome. The language of Shakespeare's citizens, to modern English ears, seems more abstract than it probably did in the Shakespearean context. Because Déprats takes from Shakespeare's English the sense that the plebeians pose a genuine threat in the play, he renders their language more concrete than a literal translation of the modern sense of the words would suggest. Along the same lines he intensifies the contempt of the patricians. Déprats's text, by sharpening contrasts, participates in Sobel's Marxist dialectical exploration of opposition and prepares for and helps to elucidate the antagonisms. It does not, however, impose an interpretation: "The translation must remain open, allow for play without dictating its terms; it must be animated by a specific rhythm without imposing it," Déprats said. "Translating for the stage does not mean twisting the text to suit what one has to show, or how or who will perform. It does not mean jumping the gun, predicting or proposing a mise en scène. It means making it possible."[16]

An extended example from the very beginning of the play can illustrate this:

2 CIT: One word, good citizens.
1 CIT: We are accounted poor citizens, the patricians good. What author-
         ity surfeits [on] would relieve us. If they would yield us but the
         superfluity while it were wholesome, we might guess they reliev'd us
         humanely; but they think we are too dear. The leanness that afflicts
         us, the object of our misery, is as an inventory to particularize their
         abundance; our sufferance is a gain to them. (1.1.14–22)

DEUXIEME CITOYEN:
Un mot, bons citoyens.
PREMIER CITOYEN:
On nous appelle pauvres citoyens. Le bien, c'est pour les patriciens. Ce
         pouvoir se gorge de ripailles dont l'excédent suffirait à nous secourir.
         S'ils voulaient bien nous céder leurs restes avant qu'ils soient pourris,
         on pourrait dire qu'ils nous secourent par humanité; mais nous leur
         sommes déjà trop chers: la maigreur qui nous afflige, le spectacle de
         notre misère est l'inventaire détaillé de leur abondance; notre souf-
         france est pour eux un gain. (p. 9)

To begin with, the translation understandably foregoes the repe-tition of the adjectival good ("good citizens ... patricians good") in order to preserve the pun implicit in the opposition between good and poor. It is the patricians who are good because they are possessed of goods or, in French, "des biens."

More revealing are the changes to the second sentence of the long speech. "What authority surfeits [on] would relieve us" is rendered as "Ce pouvoir se gorge de ripailles dont l'excédent suffirait à nous secourir" ("This power gorges itself on feasts of which the excess would suffice to save us"). Authority is no longer abstract but specifically pointed to by the demonstrative pronoun. The ante-cedent of "ce" is uncertain; possibly, since it is singular, it refers to Martius who has previously been alluded to as an enemy to the people, though it could refer to the patricians of the previous sentence. Furthermore, though "power" and "authority" are abstract nouns, both the Franch and English forms of "power" tend to connote physical force, while those of "authority" tend to connote judicial or moral force. The undefined "what" that authority sur-feits on in English has become "de ripailles," feasts which turn "ce pouvoir" into individuals eating and drinking, indeed "gorging" themselves. In the sentence that follows Déprats continues the metaphor of feasting he has introduced. The concessive "but" is omitted and the abstract noun "superfluity" is replaced by "leurs restes," not even "the" leftovers but "their" leavings. Also, the affirmatively phrased "while it were wholesome" becomes the nega-tively stated "avant qu'ils soient pourris." Similarly, "but they think we are too dear" is rendered as "mais nous leur sommes déjà trop chers," with the translation of "they think" by "nous leur sommes" and the addition of the intensifier "déjà." In the same vein the indefinite article in "an inventory to particularize" is replaced by the definite article in "l'inventaire détaillé."

The language given to the citizens preserves the Shakespearean sense of grievance while embodying this production's sense that the grievance is just. When Caius Martius insults them the First Citizen replies ironically in English, "We have ever your good word" (1.1.166), but asserts in French "Nous avons toujours *droit* à un mot aimable" (p. 15, emphasis added). In the production the citizens had more than the two or three articulate spokesmen who are identified in the Folio text, even in act 2, scene 3, where a stage direction specifies the entrance of "seven or eight" citizens who are asked by Coriolanus to give their voices in assent to his becoming Consul. Whereas the Ribner–Kittredge edition (1971) follows the Folio in numbering the speakers from one to three and the *Complete Pelican Shakespeare* (1969) increases this number to five, Déprats, like *The Riverside Shakespeare*, identifies seven separate speakers, inscrib-ing in his text the production's sense of them as a large and articulate group.

The gap between plebeians and patricians was made more con-spicuous by shifts in levels of diction to intensify contempt and abuse. This is especially apparent in the language of Coriolanus. Thus "Must these have their voices ...?" (3.1.34) becomes "Sont-ils *dignes* de s'exprimer ...?" (p. 73 – my emphasis). Similarly,

COR: Have you inform'd them [the citizens] sithence?
BRU: How? I inform them? (3.1.47)

becomes

CORIOLANUS: Vous avez donc joué les mouchards?
BRUTUS: Moi! Les mouchards! (p. 73)

Similarly, "Hence, rotten thing! or I shall shake thy bones / Out of thy garments" (3.1.178–9) becomes "Arrière carcasse pourrie! ou je te secoue les os / Hors de tes *guenilles*" (p. 79 – emphasis added).

For the scenes of dissension the translation employs terms associated with the politics of popular resistance. Thus "to chain up and restrain the poor" (1.1.84–5) becomes "pour enchaîner et *opprimer* les pauvres" (p. 12 – my emphasis), while "It is a purpos'd thing" (3.1.38) becomes "C'est un coup monté" (p. 73). "Traitor" occurs frequently in the English but "traître" more frequently in the French. "Commonwealth," which has no French equivalent, appears as "la République" (p. 119), but also as "le corps politique" (p. 68 – cf. "th' body of the weal": 2.3.181). "Emeute" is used a number of times to translate such terms as "riot," "broil," or "mutiny."

There is no doubt that such emphases work with rather than against the Shakespearean text. They put into the choice of target language words that a production in the source language might in any event communicate through intonation, facial expression, gesture, and other non-verbal means. And they place a priority on communication with the target culture. Thus it is not that the translator is advocating a particular interpretation of the play so much as making it possible. The translation keeps available a potentiality the director had found implicit in the original text. For this purpose interaction with the director is a constructive part of the task. Déprats sees this as "a collaboration whose goal is not to bend the text to the interpretive 'reading' of a director, but whose concern is above all to develop an instrument for acting."[17]

THE LIFETIME OF A TRANSLATION

In these two examples and others like them, the life of a translation is intimately tied to its mise en scène. It is born of a director's need for an actable version of the Shakespearean text that will communicate to its projected audience, and its existence is tied to the production that brings it to life. Its publisher is often the producing theatre company, its initial distribution takes place in the theatre lobby, and the text itself is a record of the translation's production.[18] The published versions of both *Coriolan* and *Le Songe d'une nuit d'été* list names of director, designers, and cast. That of Mnouchkine's *Richard II* contains the text of the acted version, including the inversion and redistribution of some speeches. It makes no mention of numerous substitutions to simplify names of people and places or lines omitted here and there throughout the text, although asterisks and an appendix containing the suppressed act 5, scene 2 enable the reader to reconstitute an "original" version of act 5. The text of Carrière's translation of *Timon* nowhere acknowledges something like 200 lines of cuts.[19] The text of the translation thus becomes for the spectator part of the experience of seeing and recalling the production, along with programs, posters, and other "souvenir" documents. (For example, available for purchase at the Cartoucherie de Vincennes during the run of *Richard II* was a table illustrating the kings of England and an "orchestra" plot of the numerous exotic instruments that provided the musical background to the production.)

Not surprisingly, such texts tend to go out of print once their productions have closed. Carrière's *Timon* is no longer available. Neither is Seide's *Dream* which, to my knowledge, has not received another production. On the other hand, the texts are still available in French libraries, if not in bookstores. And translations by Déprats, Mnouchkine, and others continue to be recommended, bought, and read. More important, translations by Déprats, at least, even though they have been done in close collaboration with directors and tied to their mises en scène, have begun to receive second productions. There have been subsequent productions of the 1983 *Hamlet* and the 1984 *Othello*, and *Coriolan* has been produced by the Théâtre National de Belgique. In recent texts of his translations, Déprats has taken care to ensure the publication of complete texts in spite of the theatrical necessity for cuts in production. He also is currently editing a new Pléiade edition which will consist exclusively of translations (presumably to be read) which were originally done for the stage.

As I have tried to suggest, the possibility of further productions arises from the philosophy of translation shared by the translators whose work we have been considering. These translators prefer to translate "without translating," to be literal rather than literary or idiomatic in order to preserve the gestural qualities of the Shakespearean text.[20] The choice is not a self-evident one. Given the theatre director's urgent need to communicate with an audience, the temptation to elaborate, clarify, and interpret as one goes along is great, and the decision not to do so is deliberate. As Richard Marienstras has said, "No interpretation or commentary was included in the translated phrase: the Shakespearean language is conceived as a mystery that it is better not to illuminate for the spectator."[21] It is the *mise en jeu* rather than the interpretations of a translator that must enable the audience to understand the text.

In practical terms, for Peter Brook and his translator of *Timon of Athens* and *Measure for Measure* this meant producing a French version of Shakespeare that would not, as usual, be longer than its English original. Similarly Jean-Michel Déprats says, "To follow the construction closely, to try to keep the word order and (as much as possible) the same number of words as in English is not to succumb to a mirage of impossible mimicry, it is to try to preserve the flow of the play [*l'influx de jeu*]."[22] Such translation is an attempt to overcome fundamental philosophical and structural differences between French and English. Both Déprats and Seide are committed to producing a version of Shakespeare that conveys the formal properties of the Shakespearean English as well as its content. They wish to preserve the body as well as the meaning of the language – "*l'influx de jeu*." They not only translate verse as verse and prose as prose but, where possible, line for line; sometimes – especially in the case of images or idioms that do not have French equivalents – word for word.

The result may sometimes be startling. Interviewer Georges Banu told Jean-Claude Carrière: "Personally, the impression that I have ... is that you do violence to the organization of the French language, that appears less structured, freer."[23] Ariane Mnouchkine frankly claims that it is not necessary that the translated text be beautiful or even that it be literary – only that it be there (fully) to be mined, since the text is one of the raw materials of her work. She is willing if necessary to suspend the idiom of the French language in order to retain some of the quality of the English: "In the translation there is a willingness to follow step by step the network of images without unpacking them."[24] And Déprats reports that some actors of his *Coriolan* initially found his text "hard to chew," though in the long run they felt it worked well.[25]

Mnouchkine's translations are consistent with her method of working and the scenography in which this results: "It's what we call throughout the rehearsal period the literal meaning [*pied de la lettre*] ... The actor takes into himself the text and invents its bodily symptoms, he embodies Shakespeare's poetry." Her attempt to translate literally is an attempt to create a text that remains itself even while being physicalized by the actors. The culturally remote theatrical traditions on which Mnouchkine draws (Japanese for *Richard II*, Indian and Indonesian among others for *La Nuit des rois*) allow her to isolate the text, which may be whispered, groaned, chanted, shouted, or hammered out by an actor whose gesture is expressive but frozen into immobility. As more than one critic has noted, for the Théâtre de Soleil "the text is king and the actors are here to serve it with their whole body."[26]

Déprats rejects the widespread view that the literal is the enemy of the precise and that a translator must make explicit an implied subtext in order to make clear the meaning of a line: "Sometimes... the word-for-word allows an immediate apprehension of the text that is more sensual than intellectual." Indeed, he has proposed that translating Shakespeare into French may be less a question of manipulating existing forms and turns of phrase than attempting to bring new forms to birth. Or looking at the matter another way, Antoine Vitez has suggested à propos of his own production of *Hamlet* (translated by Raymond Lepoutre) that the very purpose of a translation may be to reveal our distance from the original and to challenge a received conception of a play and the present experience of it. For Vitez, translation is one of the instruments of appropriating the text and of giving it new life.[27]

The attempt to translate literally is thus an attempt to create a text that remains tied to the *mot-à-mot* of its source even while it is being transformed by its *mise en espace*. The literal translation often seems strange – estranged, alien to the traditional structure of the French language. Its very literalness serves to make it concrete, but also elliptical. Its "otherness" and the gaps in its meaning reproduce the incomplete nature of the dramatic text, the *"texte troué,"* as Anne Ubersfeld calls it.[28] Thus if at one end of the spectrum the tyranny of a mise en scène may overdetermine a dramatic translation, at the other end the fact that a dramatic translation has been done for the stage may give it precisely the quality that invites its staging not only by the director who commissioned it, but again and again.

It is clear that in the last fifteen years the conception of the Shakespearean text in French has evolved enormously for most directors and hence for most audiences. The instability of the dramatic text, which is continually being demonstrated by its re-appropriation in successive performances, is made explicit when the

process of translation from one language to another becomes part of
the process of translating the play from the page to the stage.

NOTES

1 Research for this chapter was supported by a grant from the Social
 Sciences and Humanities Research Council of Canada through the
 Faculty of Graduate Studies and Research of McGill University.
 "Résumée des interventions sur la traduction théâtrale," in *Du texte à la
 scène: Langages du théâtre*, ed. M. T. Jones-Davies (Paris: Jean Touzot,
 1983), 277. The Grivelet and Villequin quotations that follow are from
 pp. 278, 281. All translations into English are my own unless otherwise
 indicated.
2 Georges Banu, "Naviguer au plus près: entretien avec Jean-Claude
 Carrière," *Théâtre/Public* 44 (Mar.–Apr. 1982): 41.
3 See also Christoph Müller, "Shakespeares Stücke sind komplexer als
 jede Aneignung – man braucht zu verschiedenen Zeiten verschiedene
 Übersetzungen," *Theater Heute* 7 (1975): 32–7. The Hugo translations
 are still admired if not performed. For example, Helen Bailey describes
 Hugo's *Hamlet* as "the most faithful in the French language to the
 imagery, if not the music, of Shakespeare" (*"Hamlet" in France from
 Voltaire to Lafargue* [Geneva: Droz, 1964], 83). And when asked about
 her preferred translation, Ariane Mnouchkine, whose work is discussed
 above, replied, "All of them are unplayable, but that of François-
 Victor Hugo is the most honest" (Anne Pons, "Ariane Mnouchkine et
 le Théâtre du Soleil," *Phosphore* [Mar. 1982], n.p. in the archival copy I
 consulted).
4 Anne Ubersfeld, *L'école du spectateur: Lire le théâtre 2* (Paris: Editions
 Sociales, 1981), 10–18. Tadeusz Kowzon, "The Sign in the Theatre:
 An Introduction to the Semiology of the Art of Spectacle," *Diogenes* 61
 (1968): 52–80.
5 André-Michel Rousseau, "Métamorphose ou anamorphose: les visages
 successifs de Shakespeare en français," *Canadian Review of Comparative
 Literature/Revue canadienne de littérature comparée* 7 (1980): 218.
6 Jean Jacquot, *Shakespeare en France: Mises en scène d'hier et d'aujourd'hui*
 (Paris: Le Temps, 1964), 96, 52, 57.
7 Gideon Toury, "A Rationale for Descriptive Translation Studies," in
 The Manipulation of Literature: Studies in Literary Translation, ed. Theo
 Hermans (New York: St. Martin's Press, 1985), 19. For an overview of
 polysystem theory see Itamar Even-Zohar, "Polysystem Theory," *Poetics
 Today* 1 (1979): 287–310, and Gideon Toury, *In Search of a Theory of
 Translation* (Tel Aviv: Porter Institute for Poetics and Semiotics, 1980).
8 Susan Bassnett-McGuire, "Ways Through the Labyrinth: Strategies
 and Methods for Translating Theatre Texts," *The Manipulation of
 Literature*, 87. Patrice Pavis, "Problems of Translation for the Stage:
2 of *Hamlet*, directed by Peter Zadek, in the Munich Circus

Interculturalism and Post-modern Theatre," trans. Loren Kruger, in *The Play out of Context: Transferring Plays from Culture to Culture*, ed. Hanna Scolnicov and Peter Holland (Cambridge University Press, 1989), 33. Subsequent references to this article will indicate page numbers in parentheses in the body of the text.

9 "Does Shakespeare Translate?" in *Is Shakespeare Still Our Contemporary?* ed. John Elsom (London: Routledge, 1989), 50.

10 William Shakespeare, *Le Songe d'une nuit d'été*, trans. Stuart Seide (Paris: Editions Théâtre National de Chaillot, 1982). "In developing a *mise en scène* of any Elizabethan play, my thoughts are in large measure determined by the articulations of meaning, the rhythms, and the support [*appuis de jeu*] that the words impose on the actors" (p. 3). Quotations from this edition will be documented with page numbers in parentheses in the body of the text.

11 Interview by Jean-Michel Déprats, "La Modestie du conteur: entretien avec François Marthouret et Stuart Seide," *Théâtre/Public* 46–7 (July–Oct. 1982): 15.

12 Seide nowhere indicates his source text. For lines I cite I have checked the readings of Q1, Q2 and F1 for significant variation. Without making an exhaustive study, I noted some half-dozen cuts of several lines each; however, since *MND* is shorter than many of the other plays, one would expect fewer cuts.

13 William Shakespeare, *La Tragédie de Coriolan*, trans. Jean-Michel Déprats (Gennevilliers: Editions Théâtre de Gennevilliers – Théâtre/Public, 1983). Quotations from this edition will be documented with page numbers in parentheses in the body of the text.

14 All quotations of Shakespeare's plays are from *The Riverside Shakespeare*, text ed. G. Blakemore Evans (Boston: Houghton Mifflin, 1974).

15 Shakespeare, *Œuvres complètes*, ed. Henri Fluchère (Paris: Gallimard, 1959), II: 1138.

16 Quoted in Pavis, "Problems of Translation," 32.

17 Jean-Michel Déprats, "Traduire Shakespeare pour le théâtre," *Théâtre/Public* 44 (Mar.–Apr. 1982): 48.

18 It is traditional in France to make the text of a production available at the time of its performance, and quite common for spectators to read the play before or even after seeing it. This is especially true of new plays and new translations. Thus most theatres have bookstalls in their lobbies, and specialized theatre bookstores feature displays of texts currently in production.

19 William Shakespeare, *Richard II*, trans. Ariane Mnouchkine (Paris: Solin, 1981). Mnouchkine nowhere indicates her source text. William Shakespeare, *Timon d'Athènes*, trans. Jean-Claude Carrière (Paris: Centre International de Créations Théâtrales, 1973). Richard Marienstras, "*Timon d'Athènes* de Shakespeare et sa mise en scène par Peter Brook," *Les voies de la création théâtrale* 5 (Paris: CNRS, 1977), 35, gives a

complete list. A parallel can be found in the series of "Swan plays" published by Methuen, performance texts of plays produced at the Swan Theatre in Stratford-upon-Avon.

20 Jane Koustas, "Traduire ou ne pas traduire le théâtre: l'approche sémiotique," *TTR: traduction, terminologie, rédaction*, 1.1 (1988): 127–38, summarizes the "translation versus assimilation" debate.

21 Marienstras, "*Timon d'Athènes* de Shakespeare," 34.

22 Banu, "Entretien avec Jean-Claude Carrière," 41. Déprats, "Traduire Shakespeare pour le théâtre," 47.

23 Banu, "Entretien avec Jean-Claude Carrière," 42.

24 Déprats, "Le besoin d'une forme: entretien avec Ariane Mnouchkine," *Théâtre/Public* 46–7 (Mar.–Apr. 1982): 11.

25 Interview, June 1988. I am grateful to M. Déprats for his generosity in providing materials and answering questions.

26 Sophie Moscoso, "Notes de répétitions," *Le Théâtre du Soleil: Shakespeare, 2ème partie*, ed. Martine Franck and Raymonde Temkine, *Double Page* 32 (1984): n.p. José Barthomeuf, "*Richard II* (Le texte est roi)," *Le Parisien Libéré*, 24 Dec. 1981. See also Anne Coppermann, "*Richard II*," *Les Echos*, 16 Dec. 1981.

27 Déprats, "Traduire Shakespeare pour le théâtre," 47, 46. "Rencontre sur *Hamlet* avec Antoine Vitez," *Théâtre/Public* 49 (Jan.–Feb. 1983): 20. On translation as appropriation see Annie Brisset, *Sociocritique de la traduction* (Montreal: Éditions le Préambule, 1990).

28 Ubersfeld, *L'École du spectateur*, 10.

CHAPTER 5

Audience, style, and language in the Shakespeare of Peter Zadek

Ron Engle

Shakespeare is a German tradition and no respectable theatre company in Germany would go more than a season without mounting a new Shakespeare production – many have two or more as a standard part of their repertory. Shakespeare's plays have become assimilated into the German repertory and frequently Shakespeare is the most produced playwright in the German language. In the 1988–89 theatre season, there were 103 new productions of thirty of Shakespeare's works, next to seventy productions of twenty-eight works by Bertolt Brecht, followed by Molière with forty-six productions of sixteen works.[1] The translations in the late eighteenth and early nineteenth centuries by A. W. Schlegel, Ludwig Tieck, and Graf Baudissin established a literary and performance tradition which was continued in this century by Hans Rothe, Erich Fried, up to the current controversial translations of Heiner Müller and a recent proliferation of translations and adaptations by individual artists. A variety of factors contribute to Shakespeare's popularity, but foremost are the romantic vitality with which the German language highlights Shakespeare's imagery and poetry, Shakespeare's thematic compatibility with German culture, and the virtuoso performance appeal of presentational and highly theatrical plays. These factors have supported a lively Shakespeare tradition in Germany.

Along with German appreciation of Shakespeare's poetry, there exists a directorial imagination in the tradition of staging Shakespeare – an imagination that has manifested itself in scenic design, production concept, and script interpretation – that recently has resulted in exotic, erotic, and slightly bastardized versions of Shakespeare. Often these productions have gone far beyond the fancy of the academic Shakespeare scholar, as if to remind us of the English Restoration bastardizations by Nahum Tate, Dryden, and

93

Davenant, among others. Recent translations have become statements of directorial intent in a manner parallel to the visual design of a production. German directors such as Claus Peymann, Peter Stein, Klaus Michael Grüber, Arie Zinger, and Hans Hollmann have produced unusual and provocative productions, but Peter Zadek perhaps best represents the German directorial vision that has aroused both praise and condemnation for its license with the text and interpretation.

In 1933 Peter Zadek at the age of seven emigrated with his Jewish parents from Germany to England, where he remained until the 1950s. From 1947 to 1958 Zadek worked in provincial English theatres and for a time was employed by BBC Television. In April 1957 he directed Jean Genet's *The Balcony* for a private production at the Arts Theatre Club in London. Zadek created an infamous controversy, in which Genet attacked him for obfuscating and debasing the integrity of the play and converting its ideal eroticism into putrid and vulgar sex acts. Genet appeared one day on stage with a revolver in hand and threatened to shoot Zadek if he did not stop the production. The dramatist wanted the production to be stylized and ritualized, whereas Zadek, directing in a realistic mode, transformed the play into a popular and insidious comic entertainment.[2]

Zadek returned to Germany in 1958 and during the mid-1960s gained a reputation as the most provocative young director in the German theatre. His early Shakespeare productions included *Measure for Measure* (1960), *The Merchant of Venice* and *Twelfth Night* (1961) in Ulm; *Cymbeline* (Hanover, 1962); *A Midsummer Night's Dream* (1963), *Henry V* (1964), and *Measure for Measure* (1967) in Bremen. In contrast to the prevailing realistic style of director Rudolf Noelte, Zadek now worked against German scholarly interpretation and historical accuracy, striving instead to popularize the plays through comedy, grotesquerie, eroticism, brutality, and highly visual imagery.

In the 1970s Zadek's Shakespeare productions received more attention and more press than those of any other director in the Federal Republic of Germany. Critics were unable to label his style, which seemed to change with each production. For some these productions were as trivial as trash, for others they were profound masterpieces; Peter Iden called his directing method "but one step from the sublime to the ridiculous."[3] As an iconoclastic director,

Zadek's productions were viewed as reflections of his own style rather than as legitimate interpretations of Shakespeare's text. His critics accused him of creating an individualistic brand of show, a circus spectacle, a comedy of the bizarre. The German tradition of merging political statements with theatre, and creating sensational staging effects to provoke controversy, is a legacy of such noted directors as Reinhardt, Piscator, and Brecht. Yet Zadek, who professes no desire to make political statements and has, indeed, expressed a disgust and boredom for political messages of any kind, especially for any allegiance to tradition, has offended both the left and the right. This element of provocation is essential to what he calls *Volkstheater*.

Zadek has invited audiences to vocalize their feelings and emotions while watching a production. In much the same way as spectators shout at a soccer game, audience members in the theatre should be provoked into participation. Zadek's *Volkstheater* called for a new audience, an invitation to the other 90 percent who do not attend the theatre. Without provocation the theatre becomes status quo, a self-serving temple where the audience members confirm their beliefs with what they see on stage. The audience becomes a ghetto for an ideology, and this can only be avoided, Zadek maintains, through provocation.[4]

In Zadek's 1972 *Merchant of Venice*, Hans Mahnke's Shylock reminded some of the Nazi 1940 *Jud Süss* film stereotype. The evil quality of Mahnke's Shylock created a stir in the German press and questions were raised as to Zadek's motives. After viewing this production and his later *Othello*, one critic asked if Zadek was masking his own bad experiences as a Jew.[5] On the contrary, Zadek responded that he had never suffered for being a Jew, but believed Shylock to be a character who could commit a murder. In Zadek's 1988 Vienna *Merchant*, Shylock, far from a ghetto figure, was a Wall Street broker. But in 1972 Shylock was a shouting, spitting Jew, and Mahnke was criticized for mumbling and creating deliberate anachronisms in speech delivery with Karsten Schälicke's contemporary translation. Responses to Rosel Zech's Portia were equally unflattering. She was described by one critic as a furious Marlene Dietrich on the war-path in a Wild West film, using forced language, swallowing words, and adding off-the-cuff verbal interjections such as "Tja."

Criticism was primarily focused on unmotivated stage business

and garbled language. Zadek was accused of slighting and distorting
the poetry and nuances of Shakespeare's language and colloquializ-
ing the speech patterns. While a few critics found this colloquial
quality refreshing, members of the Deutsche Shakespeare Gesell-
schaft-West, who were invited to a post-performance discussion with
Zadek, applauded the suggestion that to avoid passing off a
"counterfeit," Zadek should change the title to "The Life and Loves
of Launcelot Gobbo."[6]

German newspaper theatre critics are allotted ample space, write
lengthy reviews, and consequently have the opportunity to discourse
on their favorite themes and theories. Often productions are analyzed for their political views and Zadek's stark individualism has
made him more a target for political controversy than he has ever
imagined. Zadek's directorial statements provoke the status quo,
raise questions about traditional staging techniques and Shakespeare interpretation, and therefore are open to political interpretations. Theatre in Germany has long been the vehicle for making
statements of political or social significance. One only has to look at
the turbulent theatre of the 1920s during the Weimar Republic, or
the propaganda theatre of the Nazi era, for examples. German critics
espouse political and social significance in the theatre, perhaps much
more so than German audiences pay attention to them. But Zadek's
productions draw large audiences whether critics approve or chas-
tise his productions. "In Shakespeare," Zadek wrote in a 1967
program note for *Measure for Measure*, "belong both a lot of naïvety
and subtle distinctiveness. No theories, moral lessons, aesthetic principles, no fashionable statements [can] replace a lack of fantasy
through artificial contemporary quotes."[7]

In keeping with his *Volkstheater* philosophy, for his 1974 *King Lear*
in Bochum Zadek chose a vacant movie house as the physical plant
for the production rather than the two theatres available to him. He
reasoned that the movie house would provide an environment where
the average worker in the industrial region of Bochum would feel
more at home. The stage of the movie house was divided by two
tattered curtains and portable wall units. The actors were introduced as players and artists from the theatre, circus, and film world
who brought along their own costumes and properties for this
particular theatrical event. The production was almost an extension
of improvisations developed during the three-month rehearsal
period, a luxury which the subsidized German theatre system allows.

Throughout the action of the play original music composed by Werner Eggenhofer was performed on a trombone and a guitar, and occasionally records were played on a portable record player. The production created a bizarre vaudeville style of performance incorporating a conglomeration of diverse stage properties and mixed period costumes. Exaggerated stage business and slapstick farce created a comic enigma in Gloucester's use of a giant megaphone when speaking to Kent, the American Indian costume worn by Kent in Goneril's court, Goneril's "cardboard breasts," Kent and the Duke of Albany played by the same actor, or the King of France suddenly singing a *chanson* to guitar playing. For critic Volker Canaris such puzzling details and comic interludes were justified and fully explained in the context of the play by the comic, or in some cases, enigmatic act of revelation. For example, Gloucester appeared in a top hat and was "blinded" by the hat rammed down over his eyes. For some a mutilation of the text, for others an interpretation no less offensive than stage blood.[8]

Zadek rehearsed *King Lear* using an improvisational approach by providing a display of various properties and costumes for the actors in rehearsal. In time the most effective properties evolved and supported the actor's choices in a way which emphasized a "vaudeville" approach to the script, in a manner of American "brutal" vaudeville as opposed to French vaudeville. Zadek showed the cast films of Buster Keaton; Gloucester, played by Hans Mahnke, was encouraged to model himself on the character of W. C. Fields; while Goneril, played by Brigitte Janner, was encouraged to listen to recordings of Sophie Tucker.

Wigs, masks, and properties inspired by popular culture and *Karneval* fantasies were exploited for the sake of comic effect or shock value. The external objects replaced the internal motivation or expression of emotion almost as if an alternative semiotic relationship was being established with the audience. Ulrich Wildgruber's Lear, for example, developed character traits and personality shifts through the use of external items to transform himself into various stages of isolation, madness, and recognition. In the first scene, Lear wore a grotesque half mask and wig until the moment he banished Cordelia, dressed in a tutu, and then removed the mask. In the first mad scene, Lear wore "snail-feelers" on his head, monster false teeth in his mouth, and carried a toy Indian bow and arrow. All this was in stark contrast to the final scene of the play when Cordelia was carried naked over Lear's shoulder in a fashion verging on "incestuous" filial love. Yet the simplicity of this final scene provided a contrast and relief from the gruesome death scenes in which limbs were torn off, liters of blood flowed, and Regan drowned flailing in a water barrel. As one critic put it, "The *Grand Guignol* of the preceding deaths made the simplicity of this scene intensely meaningful."[9] Gunther Rühle of the *Frankfurter Allgemeine* wrote that "Peter Zadek has never been more poetic, nor worked with a more expressive fantasy ... Never have the most bizarre ideas in his productions added up and answered one another in quite this fashion."[10]

While some were outraged by his butchering of Shakespeare's text, others found the acting unrealistic and the characters without psychological truth. Zadek admits that Shakespeare is not psychological theatre in the sense of Ibsen or Chekhov, but he insists that his Shakespeare productions are based in a psychological process which begins with the establishment of the actor's relationship to the other actors, to the world, and to the director, followed by character relationships and their environment in rehearsal to prevent any appearance of artificiality on the stage.[11] This might seem to be contradictory, but psychological theatre for Zadek is not synonymous with coordinated period costuming and other traditional theatrical trappings. Psychological acting is the reality the actor creates. In Zadek's 1977 *Hamlet*, staged in a vacant factory workshop in Hamm, a suburb of Bochum, the audience was seated in arena fashion around a concrete performance space with a minimal set consisting of a podium for Polonius' room, a gigantic desk for the King, a virginal for Ophelia to relieve herself in, a cart for the players, etc. Costumes were a conglomeration of mixed periods and styles ranging from baroque to modern dress. Gertrude wore a crinoline skirt with red bull's eyes painted on her bare breasts (illustration 1). Hardly realistic in period, the sex and age of the actors underscored anomalies in the casting. Hamlet was older than his mother, a young woman played Polonius, Laertes was grossly overweight, and Rosencrantz and Guildenstern appeared to be gay men, but were later revealed to be transvestite females. Zadek explained why his Hamlet was played like a clown and madman directing a circus of performers. Simply put, tragedies can be stupid and comedies serious. For Zadek *Hamlet* was a serious comedy and Hamlet a character living in a chaotic world, a world of appearances,

1   Scene 2 of *Hamlet*, directed by Peter Zadek, in the Munich Circus (originally at
an abandoned factory outside Bochum in 1977). Claudius (Herman Lause),
Hamlet (Ulrich Wildgruber) in center with prayerbook and cane, Gertrude
(Eva Mattes) in hoop skirt and with red bullseyes painted on her breasts.
Photo: Gisela Scheidler.

a character who plays roles while watching others playing roles.[12]
Perhaps herein lies a key to Zadek's directorial process. Actors play
roles, often multiple roles that are like daydreams being acted out on
the fly – often outwardly unrelated to each other but from the
actor's vantage like viewing an improvised rehearsal. Shakespeare's
text and language provide the stimulus for suggestiveness and provocation. As Zadek stated in the *Hamlet* program notes, "Suggestion
is the probing of the channel between the fantasy of the artist and
the spectator. It is the way to plant images, thoughts, and dreams in
the head of the spectator that do not often overlap with what they
see on stage, that can be very different from what they physically see
or experience."[13] If this suggestion seems arbitrary, it is at the same
time an essential ingredient in comic technique. In Zadek's 1976

production of *Othello*, for example, both Iago and Desdemona appeared in bikini bathing trunks. While Iago stuffing the strawberry handkerchief as a bulge into his crotch may seem arbitrary, it suggested his cleverness and sexuality in a manner unlike traditional stagings.

Othello attracted a new audience to the theatre in Bochum, not only the curious and those who denounced Zadek as the butcher of Shakespeare, or those who viewed him as the saviour of mise en scène, but factory workers as well. Bochum had established a long tradition of producing the classics, beginning with Saladin Schmitt and followed by Hans Schalla's tightly conceived realistic Shakespeare productions while Intendant from 1949 to 1972. Liberation from these conventions of historical accuracy in staging Shakespeare was appealing, and the scenography for *Othello* achieved it. Designed by Zadek and Peter Pabst, it was minimal in concept and devoid of conventional set pieces. A bright red curtain, stretched across the width of the stage at 3 meters in height, was used by the characters to hide behind, to eavesdrop, or on occasion to reveal a new scene. A wicker chair, an upholstered chair, and a table were placed downstage in front of the curtain. Lights in the auditorium remained on, and again the costumes were anachronisms. Othello wore a dress military jacket with frilly ensigns on his shoulders, Desdemona appeared in a bikini, and Emilia sparkled in a glittering slinky evening gown with high heels (illustration 2).

Ulrich Wildgruber played Othello in blackface and makeup with no pretense that a white actor was presenting the role. Wearing a long, black, kinky wig, Othello's make-up was deliberately smeared onto Desdemona during the murder scene.[14] Wildgruber modeled his role on a stereotype – the image of a cartoon caricature of a black cannibal. He stalked about the stage, annoyed by lice in his hair, and mimicked the behavior of an ape. When Othello asked Iago for the "proof," Iago, the stud beach boy, proudly displayed the bulge of the handkerchief in his crotch. And during the "pr'ythee, unpin me" scene, Emilia, dressed as a vamp with designer sunglasses, completely undressed Desdemona and during the speech on "husbands' faults" pulled the "innocent" naked Desdemona on to her lap and vividly rubbed her breasts and "flipped" her nipples.[15] Perhaps no other Zadek production polarized the critics and public opinion as much, especially the brutal "sex murder" of Desdemona. Following a chase, Othello threw her on to a bed, straddled her

2   The arrival in Cyprus in *Othello*, directed by Peter Zadek, Deutsches
Schauspielhaus, Hamburg, 1976. Ulrich Wildgruber as Othello in minstrel
blackface, Eva Mattes as Desdemona in bikini. *Photo: Roswitha Hecke, courtesy of
Deutsches Theatermuseum, Munich.*

body, and strangled her as she kicked her legs. Demented, he hugged
the dead body and flung her over the curtain guide-line with her
bottom towards the audience. On display like a "slaughtered steer,"
he threw a kiss at her naked posterior. Othello's berserk state of mind
evoked laughter and shouts from the audience to which Othello
responded by shouting back. In the end, Othello cut his throat with
a knife as a fountain of blood spurted forth, which he proceeded to
smear over his body.[16]

Translations have always been a major concern for Zadek. Generally, he has experimented with many different versions and combined the best, including his own. In a recent interview with Bochum
dramaturg Gabriele Groenewold, who worked with Zadek on
several of his productions, I asked if she felt fortunate that the
Germans are able to mold Shakespeare's language in new translations to suit the sensibility of the time. "But, on the contrary, how
fortunate you are to have the original and avoid the clutter of a
foreign language," she said. Zadek's knowledge of English has led
him to conclude that no translation can ever hope to convey the original.[17] In the 1970s he favored the work of Erich Fried. The text of
Othello, for example, was 80 percent Fried and 10 percent Baudissin,
with a few lines from Eschenburg and two lines from Hans Rothe.
Zadak cut 600 lines and made several hundred word-choice alter-
ations during rehearsals. This improvised text worked for the production, but in hindsight Zadek found it appalling and totally
unreadable, because it had nothing to do with literature, he
admitted, and everything to do with the actors, the evolution in
rehearsals and production.[18] An irony perhaps, which exemplifies
Zadek's emphasis on performance technique rather than literary
analysis.

Zadek and his actors have been heavily criticized for sloppy language and relying on accents and dialects for characterization.
Wildgruber's Swabian accent as Launcelot Gobbo in *Merchant*, for
example, seemed to butcher the language and made it unintelligible
for many. But Zadek defends his use of colloquial language as being
natural. Why, he asks, when someone says "odaa" instead of "oder"
does the public cringe as if it were taboo? They wouldn't notice it in
life, so why on stage? They wouldn't dare take out a ruler and
measure the size of an apple in a Rubens. In essence, Zadek con-
cludes, one should only judge quality and not be concerned with the
artificial taboos of society. And most of all, whether it be in matters of

language or modern dress, what is important is to emphasize that aspect of the play that seems to be right for the time.[19]

Zadek's approach to the rehearsal period, to language, and to matters of style might be called a deconstruction of the text to achieve a reordering of the imagery and language. This reordering attempts to communicate non-esoteric visualization of stage action in a form and format accessible and meaningful to an audience, which Zadek believes can only be reached through "serious comedy," erotic images, provocation, and entertainment. Zadek views Shakespeare as belonging to the English tradition of popular theatre. And to appeal to the soccer crowd, the director must bring a modern relevance to the staging of the plays by discarding the notion that they are sacred and should be produced in an esoteric manner that caters to the fashionable or intellectual in society. Instead, Zadek creates a deliberate incongruity between the characters and the actors so that the image and style of the play are highlighted, not only in the reality of the characters but also by the vision of the actor playing the role. For this reason the rehearsal process and improvisation techniques are central to Zadek's productions. He deconstructs the imagery of the historical piece through modern relevance, which often reveals itself in the form of the grotesque and bizarre elements of pop art, circus, and slapstick comedy.

Zadek avoids "isms" and his iconoclastic directing eludes classification. It is more a product of his desire to entertain so as to attract the attention of the curious, the non-scholar, television and film devotees. Whether critics agree with his methods or not, the fact remains that his Shakespeare productions are usually sold out and pushed into extended runs. Andreas Höfele calls Zadek's appeal a form of audience seduction whose purpose is "intensification of experience, not explication," and where Zadek's relationship with the audience becomes a "relationship whose seductiveness expresses itself in the seducer's mixture of wooing and attacking" the "linearity of story," which is "discarded in favour of a network of correlated situations, a multilayered 'scenic text' constantly opening up references to other possible texts."[20] In the view of many German Shakespeare scholars Zadek has created little but apprehension, while raising questions about the validity of his texts. Zadek's non-literary approach has provoked not only scholars and audiences but also two centuries of theatrical conventions for Shakespeare in Germany.

Zadek's directorial approach and corruption of Shakespeare would, no doubt, be quite as foreign to an English-speaking audience as it is in German. Curiously, Zadek, despite his international reputation and his early experience with London theatre, has never directed Shakespeare in English. But were he invited to direct at the Royal Shakespeare Company, the results would be the same. His distinctive approach would prove to be as provocative and corrupt as in German, since Zadek transgresses not only German traditions but most Anglo-American traditions as well. Nevertheless, in German Zadek adds an additional level of connotation and "seduction" whereby the already "foreign" German Shakespeare is made foreign once again in its language and style. The language is removed twice from the original, once through the original translation and additionally through the adaptation and alteration. The style violates German conventions and audience appeal, based on a rejection of traditional taste, but essentially Zadek is merely giving a new twist to alienation technique by adding a layer of theatricality – appeal to sight and sound – which corrupts the literary Shakespeare but injects diversity and controversy into the global culture of Shakespeare.

NOTES

1 Deutschen Bühnenverein, *Was spielten die Theater? Werkstatistik 1988/89* (Remagen-Rolandseck: Verlag Rommerskirchen, 1989), 32.
2 Wend Kässens (ed.), *Theatermacher* (Frankfurt am Main: Athenäum, 1987), 180.
3 Peter Iden, *Theater als Widerspruch: Plädoyer für die zeitgenössische Bühne* (Munich: Kindler Verlag, 1984), 190.
4 Laszlo Kornitzer, comp., *Peter Zadek: Das wilde Ufer* (Cologne: Verlag Kiepenheuer & Witsch, 1990), 192–3.
5 Klaus Wagner, *Frankfurter Allgemeine Zeitung*, 14 May 1976.
6 Marvin Rosenberg, *The Shakespeare Newsletter* 23 (1973).
7 Kornitzer, *Peter Zadek*, 81.
8 Volker Canaris, *Theater Heute* 15.5 (1974).
9 Henning Rischbieter, *Theater Heute* 15 (Sonderheft 1974).
10 Gunther Rühle, *Frankfurter Allgemeine Zeitung*, 11 Jan. 1975.
11 Kässens, *Theatermacher*, 181.
12 Production program, *Hamlet*, Bochum Schauspielhaus, 1977. See also Volker Canaris, "Peter Zadek and *Hamlet*," *Drama Review* 24.1 (1980): 53–62.
13 Production program, *Hamlet*.
14 The idea for having the blackface makeup rub off came to Zadek as he

recalled a Pears soap ad from the nineteenth century, where a black baby appears in one box, then Pears soap, followed by a white baby. Doesn't every child ask its mother, "If you touch a black person, does it come off mommie?" This germinal idea developed through many stages for Zadek and Wildgruber, who applied blackface after the third rehearsal in as many different ways as possible. This could, of course, be seen as a method of audience alienation, a sort of skin dissolve unlinking race from the physical body. Wildgruber made the most of it. See "Anarchie der Gefühle," in Kornitzer, *Peter Zadek*, 149–50.

15 A production photo by Roswitha Hecke published in the July 1976 issue of *Theater Heute* shows an alternative staging with Emilia sitting on Desdemona's lap.
16 See Georg Hensel, "Karl Marx geht – Sigmund Freud kommt," *Frankfurter Allgemeine Zeitung*, 27 Sept. 1976.
17 Canaris, "Peter Zadek and *Hamlet*," 56.
18 "Probleme der Übersetzung," in Kornitzer, *Peter Zadek*, 250–1.
19 "Freiheit auf der Bühne," in *ibid.* 93–101.
20 Andreas Höfele, "The Erotic in the Theatre of Peter Zadek," *New Theatre Quarterly*, 7.27 (Aug. 1991): 234–6.

PART II

Political and national appropriations

The traditions of appropriation of Shakespeare in central and eastern Europe were reinforced after the war by the installation of Stalinist rule over the Second World. Whether a theatre used Shakespeare to confirm a Marxist view (as in East Germany), or used him to impugn a repressive government (as in Poland), heavy public subsidies permitted theatres to find interpretations of the plays that kept them vital and current. The political uses of Shakespeare in the Soviet Union and in its satellite countries in this period were clearly foreign to his normal representation in English. Equally foreign was a theatrical system that prohibited overt denunciation of its sponsoring regime but often tolerated crypto-criticism through performance of classic scripts.

Lawrence Guntner traces the history of Shakespeare in a country that no longer exists, the German Democratic Republic. With Brecht as its theatrical founder, the GDR's use of Shakespeare until 1990 shows the results of political appropriation more clearly than any other case, from Wekwerth's production of Brecht's *Coriolan* to Heiner Müller and the end of a tradition. Pia Kleber shows how Brechtian Socialist concerns have been modified outside the GDR in her treatment of one of the most important Shakespeare productions of our time, Giorgio Strehler's *The Tempest*, which combined a Marxist commitment with a commitment to *commedia dell'arte*.

Spencer Golub outlines the tradition of *Hamlet* in Russia, dealing with the effect of pre-revolutionary motifs on Soviet interpretations. The specific example is Lyubimov's famous production of 1972, precariously balanced on the political edge, with the main role played by the protest singer Vladimir Vysotsky. Irena Makaryk takes a different tack in her view of gender attitudes and *Antony and Cleopatra* in the USSR. By studying the printed reactions to an official production by Evgenii Simonov, she demonstrates that the challenges of Shakespeare were often met in the Soviet Union by subtle social adaptation. Finally, Jarka Burian's account of *Hamlet* in the postwar Czech theatre stresses how directors and designers have been committed to uncovering "Shakespeare's" themes rather than their own – yet in a social and theatrical environment vastly different to that of Britain.

CHAPTER 6

Brecht and beyond:
Shakespeare on the East German stage

Lawrence Guntner

East German scholar Robert Weimann has pointed out that modern Shakespeare performance is always characterized by a tension between "past significance and present meaning," that is, "between Renaissance values and modern evaluations."[1] Shakespeare in performance, Weimann argues, is always more than an interpretation of historical stage materials in terms of contemporary understanding, for through interaction between actor and spectator performance generates new and unpredictable meanings about both Shakespeare's past and the spectator's present. In 1967, the year in which Weimann's article appeared, East German theatres were making a concentrated effort to interpret Shakespeare's Elizabethan past in terms of an East German Socialist present, and Weimann's article, published interestingly enough outside the country, was a caveat against any attempt to appropriate Shakespeare for a particular political dogma. Shakespeare performance on the East German stage often involved interpreting Shakespeare's plays from a Marxist perspective, yet these same performances often subverted, wittingly or unwittingly, the very ideology about contemporary East German society they were supposed to validate. This is the context behind the actress Johanna Schall's remark that "the theatre had to act the part the media should play."[2] Schall, who is Bertolt Brecht's granddaughter, was referring to the enormous political changes that occurred in 1989 in the German Democratic Republic. On the stage things were said which would not or could not be said elsewhere; newspapers, books, and films can be censored, performance cannot – at least, not in advance. In the process, the East German stage became "the abstract and brief chronicles of the time," news commentator, political scientist, and historian, and any account of East German Shakespeare performance must keep this in mind. Shakespeare in performance as a representation of past history was often understood by the spectators to be a critical commentary on their own present, and Shakespeare came to enjoy a political relevance that he may not have had since the days of Elizabethan England.

Although technically speaking the history of Shakespeare performance in East Germany began with Gustav von Wangenheim's production of *Hamlet* at the Deutsches Theater in December 1945, the decisive impulses for a redefinition of the German Shakespeare tradition from a Socialist perspective stem from Bertolt Brecht and his ideas about an epic theatre and the alienation effect.[3] When Brecht returned to Berlin in October 1948 from his exile in the US, he quickly realized that not only the theatre buildings but also the theatre tradition and the minds of his audience lay in ruins. Brecht immediately prescribed a "withdrawal cure" from the drug of what he called "Göringtheater," a theatre of pomp and circumstance, rhetoric, spectacle, and technical perfection but empty of meaning and social relevance.[4] The first treatment was administered on 11 January 1949 when Mother Courage pulled her covered wagon across the brightly lit and sparsely decorated stage of the Chamber Theatre at the Deutsches Theater, and a new era in theatre history began. In 1951 Brecht turned his attention to Shakespeare's *Coriolanus*. He wanted to reinfuse Shakespeare with the original "grand passions," the fighting spirit and the power of language, by emphasizing acting rather than decoration, dramatic language rather than theatrics, meaning and *gestus* rather than rhetoric and "character."[5] The term *gestus*, the concept central to epic theatre and alienation effect, derives from "gesture." It implies both "bodily expression" and "attitude" but has nothing to do with "gesticulation." By *gestus* Brecht meant a rich ensemble of theatrical representation, including language, body stance, pitch, facial expression, speech rhythms, and sound patterns – any theatrical means through which actors could physically depict human beings as social creatures in a world governed by power struggles.[6]

Coriolanus had been a popular play under the Nazis, with performances which depicted the masses as confused, timid, fickle, and in need of a strong leader. Brecht discovered a new "reading" (*Lesart*) of the first scene, however, and adapted Shakespeare's material to fit what he thought to be the *Grundgestus*, or basic motif of the play: "heroes are dispensable." Brecht saw similarities between the political situation in Rome during the first years of the Roman Republic and the situation in postwar Germany. Accordingly his adaptation depicts the masses as taking an active role in bringing about and defending the Roman Republic and thereby provides role models with which the East German "masses" could identify and from which they could learn.[7] In fact the masses are more or less idealized as the decisive force for social development. Through the collective action of the masses, Roman society develops to a point where it no longer needs military heroes, and Coriolanus falls because he cannot comprehend that military specialists have now become redundant and even dangerous for the state. Thus his downfall is due to his own inflexibility and unwillingness to adjust to a new social situation, and any sympathy we might feel for him is negated. The real tragedy is society's, for it has lost a valuable individual and has had to pay a high price to boot. Through the means of epic theatre, the audience was to be confronted with Shakespeare's familiar dramatic material from a fresh and "alienated" point of view, which stressed fable and theme rather than character, social issues rather than private ones, and in so doing provoked a new insight into the immediate political relevance of the play.

Brecht's work on *Coriolan* was interrupted by the workers' uprising on 17 June 1953, and Brecht died in 1956 before he could see it staged. It was not until eight years later that Manfred Wekwerth and Joachim Tenschert had worked Brecht's incomplete translation and production notes into a stageable text.[8] Between Brecht's death in 1956 and the opening performance at the Berliner Ensemble on 25 September 1964, decisive economic and ideological developments had taken place in East Germany. State ownership of land and industrial production had taken effect, the first two Five-Year Plans had been carried out and a Seven-Year Plan was almost completed, the hero cult surrounding Stalin had been exposed and denounced by Khrushchev, and the Berlin Wall (called the "The Anti-Fascist Wall of Protection" by the East German government) had been erected, ostensibly to keep out capitalist aggressors from the west but in reality to halt the mass exodus of workers to West Berlin.[9] In other words, the economic prerequisites for a Socialist economy had been supposedly met, and the young republic seemed to be consolidating itself.

More important, however, was the fact that 1964 was also Shakespeare's four-hundredth anniversary and that this occasion was to be integrated into the Socialist Unity Party's cultural policy of "appropriation of the classical heritage" (*Erbeaneignung*). In the

1964 and 1965 seasons combined there were seventy-two productions of sixteen plays by Shakespeare, totaling more than 1,900 performances and seen by approximately 300,000 spectators.[10] In 1964, however, Brecht's "reading" of 1951 seemed too simple to the directing team of Manfred Werkwerth and Joachim Tenschert. In addition, Brecht himself had left various dramatic questions unresolved. First, how do you convince the audience that Coriolanus is an indispensable hero, yet dangerous to society? Second, how do you portray the masses of Rome as the decisive force for social progress when, in fact, they did lack political consciousness and were easily manipulated? Third, how do you stage the battle scenes? The German audience's first-hand experience of war would have made "realistic" battle scenes with tumult and chaos seem like comic relief, yet if Coriolanus' claim to being Consul rests solely on his expertise in war, then Coriolanus must have the opportunity to demonstrate his skills. In Wekwerth's words, Coriolanus must not be shown as a butcher gone berserk but as a specialist in manslaughter, necessary at a certain stage in society's development.

Wekwerth and Tenschert, with the help of Ruth Berghaus, solved these problems by emphasizing the personal motives and passions of the hero, his lifelong rivalry with Aufidius, and his Oedipal attachment to his mother Volumnia; by providing the plebeians with individual profiles and costumes; and by choreographing the battle scenes as a ritual ceremony. Whereas Brecht's message had been "the hero is dispensable," Wekwerth's and Tenschert's was "heroes are too expensive." In this production, the representatives of the lower orders were no longer Brecht's idealized replacement for the deposed Roman nobility but were shown as initially undecided, hesitant, and also responsible for making Coriolanus into the hero and despot he was to become.[11] The production was kept "grayish" in tone, with only two color accents: the copper-colored dress of raw silk worn by Volumnia (Helene Weigel) and the cloak of bright-red nappa leather worn by Coriolanus (Ekkehard Schall) when Consul. Special attention was given to the plebeian craftsman and their costumes. Whereas Brecht retained Shakespeare's "first citizen," "second citizen," etc., Wekwerth and Tenschert gave each plebeian a name, a profession, and an authentic costume: Sutor, the shoemaker, wore a leather shoemaker's apron, Hortulanus, the gardener, wore a straw hat, carried a seed bag, and had leather patches on his knees. As opposed to Brecht's earlier version, they were unarmed in scene 1 and could only protest against the price of bread (and olives) by refusing to volunteer for military service; "no wheat – no war." When Coriolanus pulled his sword and threatened them, they simply sat down. This stalemate represented the social contradiction at the base of Brecht's reading of the play. The plebeians are Coriolanus' class enemies, yet the very soldiers he needs to defend Rome from the Volscians. In the production directed by Wekwerth and Tenschert, the people's tribune Sicinius Velutus still thought that Coriolanus was worth the price to Rome at the end of scene 1, but in the final scene, he ignored Menenius' petition that Coriolanus' name be rehabilitated and moved on to the "business at hand." A new day and a new social order had dawned; the people would decide their fate by themselves.

The most spectacular scenes of the production were the battle scenes, choreographed by Ruth Berghaus, in which the military specialists Coriolanus and Aufidius (Hilmar Thate) transformed the barbarous chaos of war into an ordered ceremonial ritual reminiscent of the Peking Opera. Cymbals and gongs clanged, and the opposing armies lined up facing each other and chanted the name of their leader: "Caius Marcius!" "Aufidius!" Karl von Appen's set, one side a monumental white plaster gate for Rome, the other dark wooden palisades for Corioli, was mounted on a revolving stage, and as the battle began it slowly began to rotate back and forth to highlight the ebb and flow of the slaughter. It had the effect of transforming the scenes into a carousel of death. Likewise all activities in patrician Rome were depicted as ceremonial rituals to be orchestrated with the help of special skills, strategies, and tactics. When Coriolanus solicited the votes of the plebeians, for example, the stage began to revolve again, suggesting that such kinds of campaigning are but meaningless ritual. In contrast, the actions of the plebeians and their rise to power in Rome lacked this air of ceremony. When the plebeians were able to fend for themselves, the special skills of heroes and their rituals became unnecessary and even dangerous for society.

Critics, East and West German as well as English, were unanimous in their praise of the production and agreed that it set a new standard for interpreting Shakespeare.[12] Peter Brook wrote, "a triumph. Many aspects of the play were revealed as if for the first time, much of it can seldom have been so well staged.'[13] Stage decorations, costumes, the music, revolving stage, battle scenes, blocking, and acting style were carefully orchestrated into a *Gesamt-kunstwerk*. The close reading of Shakespeare's text from a sociological point of view, as well as the attention paid to the minor characters, set a standard against which later performances of Shakespeare in East Germany would be measured.

In April 1964, the annual meeting of the German Shakespeare Association in Weimar was extended from three to eight days, and even Walter Ulbricht, Prime Minister and head of the party, was in the audience when Alexander Abusch, Deputy Prime Minister and Secretary for Culture in the Central Committee, outlined his perspective on Shakespeare in a programmatic keynote address entitled "Shakespeare: Realist and Humanist, Genius of World Literature."[14] The address was televised live to the nation. Abusch presented Shakespeare as the great representative of a "humanist world view" and as a constituent force in the formation of a modern Socialist society. From this perspective, Shakespeare could be seen not only as a playwright but also as a social historian who had analyzed, interpreted, and forecast the course of history and of the masses in relationship to history. In his plays one could perceive that the historical development from the Renaissance to the culture of Socialism was inevitable and that progress under Socialism was exemplary of world progress at its best. In short, Shakespeare provided a role model for contemporary playwrights.[15] Abusch's speech had the effect of elevating Shakespeare to the status of a cultural monument, to be admired and praised but not to be critically examined. His plays were seen primarily as literature to be read and interpreted for explicit meanings and only secondarily as performance to be viewed and enjoyed; and if performed, then with a definite message: that Socialism had resolved the social conflicts which had destroyed Shakespeare's heroes.

At the Second Bitterfeld Conference for writers and artists held immediately after the Weimar meeting, Shakespeare was officially declared the normative standard for theatre, a classical monument to be emulated by playwrights and directors but not to be questioned. The message to the theatres was clear: no experiments in form, no ambiguities in content; stick to the illusionistic "literary" theatre of the past exemplified by postwar Socialist Realism. Walter Ulbricht and the Central Committee of the party were not interested in unresolvable social contradictions and disharmony in contemporary East German society, only in those conflicts in the past which had been seemingly resolved by Socialism.[16] One year later, at the notorious Eleventh Plenary Meeting of the Central Committee in December 1965, party spokesman Erich Honecker came down hard on writers such as Stefan Heym, Wolf Biermann, Robert Havemann, Heiner Müller, Günter Kunert, Volker Braun, and Peter Hacks, a veritable who's who of East German literature, who were accused of exhibiting "decadent" and "bourgeois" qualities.[17] It is in this context that Heiner Müller's cryptic remark to the annual meeting of the East German Shakespeare Association in Weimar in 1988, twenty-three years later, takes on a special meaning: "We haven't arrived at ourselves as long as Shakespeare is writing our plays."[18] Since contemporary plays critical of contemporary Socialist society were officially taboo, and could be kept off the stage, dramatists and theatre directors like Müller, B. K. Tragelehn, Adolf Dresen, and later Christoph Schroth and Alexander Lang, turned their attention to the Greek classics, to Goethe, Schiller, and Shakespeare as platforms from which to question the officially sanctioned version of history as well as official government policy which ignored the obvious conflicts in contemporary East German society.

The year 1964 marked the highpoint in a national consensus between official cultural policy, theatre practice, and literary scholarship on the aims and interpretation of Shakespeare. Its manifestation was the overwhelming official praise for the ideologically "valid" production of *Hamlet* in Karl-Marx-Stadt directed by Dieter Mäde, which uncritically idealized Hamlet as an early modern humanist and as a force for social progress and emancipation.[19] Hamlet in this performance was caught in an unresolvable conflict between the individual humanist potential of his ideals and the oppressive confines of his social situation. Mäde broke through the proscenium line to divide the sparsely decorated stage into the area of the court, feudal and corrupt, in the rear and the area of personal introspection and humanist ideals on the forestage. In the rear, in the absolutist past, Hamlet (Jürgen Hentsch) committed his bloody deeds: stabbing Polonius, killing Laertes in the final duel. On the apron jutting out into the auditorium, the Socialist present, he delivered his monologues, which supposedly contained his humanist ideals and the message of the play: that only contemporary Socialist (East German) society had resolved the contradictions between Hamlet's feudal reality and his (and Shakespeare's) humanist ideals.

Through this obvious distinction between past and present, distance and proximity to the audience, it was hoped that the spectators would identify Hamlet as their contemporary and empathize with him. The shortcoming of this performance, as Alexander Weigel pointed out, was that the conflict and its resolution lay outside the play itself. By relating Hamlet's actions to contemporary Socialist ideals rather than to the historical conditions of the play, the spectator was left with the impression of an unresolvable contradiction between a dramaturgical conception bent on portraying Hamlet as a man governed by reason and the gruesome unscrupulousness of his deeds.[20]

A fissure in this façade of cultural consensus was the theatre scandal associated with the 1964 production of *Hamlet* in Greifswald directed by Adolf Dresen. This performance put its finger squarely on the contradiction between Hamlet the humanist and Hamlet the executioner which had not been resolved by the production in Karl-Marx-Stadt. Dresen had noticed that whenever Shakespeare's Hamlet attempts to resolve the Renaissance ideals of Wittenberg with the feudal realities of Elsinore, the stage is left strewn with the corpses of innocent victims. Hamlet invents all kinds of excuses for not taking action, but whenever he does act he kills all the wrong persons. This contradiction became the *Grundgestus* of this production, a compressed version of which was "Buchenwald is near Weimar" (which, in fact, it is). The proximity of Weimar, the residence of Goethe, Schiller, and Liszt, the symbol of German idealism and enlightened humanism, to the death camp Buchenwald, symbol of Nazi atrocities, suggested that theoretical ideals, even in the name of reason and humanistic enlightenment, can be dangerous if they do not take historical circumstances into account. To emphasize the connection between Hamlet's hesitation and his unreflected revenge, there was no intermission between Hamlet's delayed revenge when he overhears Claudius confess his fratricide (3.2) and the unprecipitated murder of Polonius (3.4). Hamlet (Jürgen Holtz) was portrayed as a deranged and dangerous combination of feudal prince and bourgeois humanist intellectual whose bleating laughter suggested that he quite enjoyed playing the madman. Claudius (Kurt Radeke), on the other hand, was portrayed at the beginning as a competent administrator, politically expedient and historically necessary.[21]

The emphasis on the discrepancy between Hamlet's lofty ideals and the lethal reality of his deeds was a conscious attempt to provoke the audience. Although the Karl-Marx-Stadt production represented historical conflict on stage, it did not carry this conflict into the audience itself. The Greifswald production, on the other hand, consistently applied Brecht's ideas on epic theatre and the alienation effect to transplant Hamlet's historical dilemma into the audience's contemporary situation. This was a completely different idea of what theatre was supposed to be about in general and of what Shakespeare performance was supposed to be about in particular. It was not the interpretation of the present in terms of the past but the generation of new meanings through performance.

Dresen had questioned officially "valid" performances which idealized Hamlet in an attempt make him (and Shakespeare) into "our contemporary." According to official cultural policy at that time Shakespeare/Hamlet actually was to be seen as the "contemporary" of the audience. Thus it was not surprising that some party functionaries understood this production as a criticism of government policies, and for them remarks like "something is rotten in the state of Denmark" or "all Denmark is a prison" were tantamount to political treason. To top things off, the stagescript, a lively contemporary translation, rich in Brechtian *gestus*, rendered into German by Maik Hamburger and Dresen, was too radical for most cultural functionaries and academics alike. Despite enthusiastic audiences and lavish praise by fellow theatre people, the production was subjected to sharp attack and taken off the bill after only five performances. It was condemned as a denigration of the classical tradition, a false representation of humanity, and a misrepresentation of the view of history according to which Socialist culture was the legitimate heir of Renaissance humanism. Party functionaries were sent to disrupt performances, and official theatre journals published vindictive reviews.[22] Dresen was removed from his position as director and sent to work in a nearby oil refinery. Nevertheless, this scandalous *Hamlet* was to have two important consequences for East German theatre. First, Wolfgang Heinz, General Director of the Deutsches Theater, immediately hired Dresen. Together they directed a performance of Goethe's *Faust* in 1968 which was at least as provocative as the Greifswald *Hamlet* in that it brought out the humor in the play and highlighted the contradictions in Faust's personality and behavior, also a radical approach in East Germany at that time. Second, the Hamburger–Dresen translation of *Hamlet* set a new standard for German Shakespeare translations that lives on in Heiner Müller's often performed rendition, which is decisively indebted to it.

Another subversive, though subtler, thrust in the same direction came in 1967 with the publication of Robert Weimann's *Shakespeare and the Popular Tradition in the Theatre (Shakespeare und die Tradition des Volkstheaters)*.[23] At first glance it could be read as an exemplification of official cultural ideology which viewed Shakespeare as a synthesis of "high" and "popular"; at second glance, however, it demolished any notion of an "idealized" or "classical" Shakespeare representative of a particular ideology. Weimann's study proceeds from the assumption that Elizabethan theatre was not an institution of moral or political education but a melange of play (*Spass*) and politics in which moral issues were mixed with entertainment and official discourses were simultaneously reinforced and subverted. He also proves that contrary to the official East German view of Shakespeare, Elizabethan staging did not elicit emphatic identification with specific characters but that alienation and contradiction were inherent aspects of Shakespeare's plays and their staging. Weimann denies that "past significance and present meaning" can be equated and that to do so would be a simplistic and theatrically ineffective reduction of Shakespeare's mode of representation of his world and times. Shakespeare's theatre did not passively repeat a particular meaning explicit in a dramatic text but actively generated implicit meanings through performance. Thus Shakespeare's plays were not "literary" texts to be read and interpreted, but suggestions for performance. Such a theoretical framework categorically denied the primacy of the literary text and provided scholarly support for the Hamburger–Dresen *Hamlet* translation as well as its performance in Greifswald. It should, therefore, come as no surprise that the inspiration for Weimann's ideas about Elizabethan theatre did not come from Marxist theory but from performances of Brecht's *The Caucasian Chalk Circle* at the Berliner Ensemble (1954).

When Manfred Wekwerth directed *Richard III* at the Deutsches Theater in 1972, he turned to Weimann's study to resolve two dramaturgical problems which plague any director: why is such an abhorrent murderer so appealing on stage? How do you preserve the moral of the fable without destroying the fascinating appeal of the character and vice versa? The solution to this dilemma was provided by Weimann's theory of the "complementary perspective" of the

Elizabethan stage. Weimann argues that for the Elizabethan spectator Richard Gloucester was at once an image of Elizabethan historiography and the descendant of the grotesquely comic "Vice" figure from the morality plays. Richard's dual character elicited a dual response from the audience: it chuckled with the clown and shuddered at the killer. Wekwerth felt that this aesthetic and social contradiction could perhaps best be resolved by the tactics of epic theatre and the alienation effect, which undercut emphatic identification with the characters and thus portray and account for the ambivalence of Richard's nature.[24]

To approximate the Elizabethan stage, the stage of the Deutsches Theater was extended into the first rows of the auditorium. The stage decor (by Andreas Reinhardt) of gallows and torturers' equipment suggested a forest of human butchery and stood for the feudal social order in which today's hero became tomorrow's victim. Drums rolled and Richard Gloucester (Hilmar Thate) stomped down the ramp towards the audience, grinning and leering, full of personal charm and energy. He wore an oversized sword and carried a huge battleaxe. As Gloucester, Thate spoke the first lines of his opening monologue ("Now is the winter of our discontent ...") from the forestage to the audience. According to Weimann, Richard becomes Vice at line 14 ("But I, that am not shaped for sportive tricks ... "), and here Thate climbed down into the front row of the auditorium to speak directly with the audience. Whereas Laurence Olivier's Richard was dark and sinister with a wig of shiny straight black hair, piercing eyes, and a hooked nose of putty, Thate's was natural, familiar, and personal. Although Thate, too, had a humped back, lame arm, and limped, his disfigurement was almost unnoticeable. Whereas Olivier assumed the role of Richard, Thate moved back and forth between the role of Richard and Vice and in the character of Vice kept reminding the audience that he was still only Hilmar Thate, the actor. Here was Brechtian epic theatre, alienation effect, and *gestus* at work to demonstrate Richard's double nature to a contemporary audience.

According to Wekwerth, from acts 1 to 3 Shakespeare's Richard, as Vice, demonstrates to the audience that "divine right" is no match for cunning and willpower when it comes to gaining the crown; however, once in power, Richard becomes the victim of the very machinations he has exposed and spends the rest of the play justifying and defending his own "divine right" to the throne. At the pinnacle of his power, Richard lets his double identity drop and with it his audience, who, in turn, let him fall just as he lets Buckingham and Hastings fall. Consequently, in this performance, Richard once crowned was no longer the expansive and self-confident Vice but a suspicious and quarrelsome king, too small for his oversized robe and crown and too small for his throne, which was raised on a dais. In act 4 the dramatic action moved to the rear of the stage and became a series of discrete individual scenes dominated by the heraldic grouping of soldiers, drum rolls, chorales, and bells during the official ceremonies. In the background the ever-present forest of gallows remained visible. The performance built to a climax with a carefully choreographed emblematic battle scene inspired by medieval paintings (illustration 3). A screen was let down with the description of the Battle of Bosworth Field from *Holinshed's Chronicles*. Then the screen was raised, and Richard entered in golden armor and ornamental crown, battleaxe in hand, rocking from one outstretched leg to the other. Troops rushed in from both sides to surround and kill him with pikes, like a wild boar, all to the accompaniment of a monumental chorale.

Wekwerth was taken to task by West German critics for reducing Richard to a comic figure, as well as for ignoring the Elizabethan concept of fate and the Christian concept of guilt; and by East German critics for focusing on the individual rather than on the social background and the prospect for the future, as they claimed Brecht would have done.[25] In Brecht's adaptation of *Coriolanus*, the plebeians were on stage, and the audience learned from them through observation and identification. In Wekwerth's production of *Richard III*, the audience themselves became the plebeians whom Richard Gloucester, in the guise of Vice, instructed in the machinations of power. Through this device, the audience became emotionally involved with the character and became an integral part of the dramatic action. It was a new way of depicting the character of Richard and a step toward the development of Brecht's idea of a "philosophical folk theatre."[26]

By 1971 it was obvious that a Socialist revolution was not going to reshape the map of Europe within the foreseeable future, and thus it became official policy in the GDR to conserve and consolidate "already existing Socialism" (*realexistierender Sozialismus*) rather than to export Marxist–Leninist revolution. At the Eighth Party Congress old-guard Stalinist Walter Ulbricht was retired and replaced

3   Act 5 of *Richard III*, directed by Manfred Wekwerth, Deutsches Theater, Berlin, 1972. Hilmar Thate as King Richard in center with shadows of the gallows behind him. *Photo: Gisela Brandt, courtesy of Deutsches Theater, Berlin.*

by Erich Honecker and a younger generation of technocrats. With this changing of the guard came the hope of a "liberalization" in a cultural policy which had been increasingly restrictive since the erection of the Berlin Wall. This was encouraged by Honecker's statement to the Fourth Plenary Conference of the Central Committee (18 December 1971) that "there can, in my opinion, be no taboos in art and literature."[27] The years of suppression of contemporary drama containing any kind of critique of East German society had taken their toll, however, and the contemporary East German drama being performed was second-rate kitchen-sink fare.

For this reason dramatists and directors again turned to Shakespeare and other "classics": not only as a commentary on the East German condition but also to demonstrate to their audiences that another standard of drama, with other conflicts and characters, existed. Whereas Shakespeare performance in the 1960s had centered on the tragedies and histories, plays concerned with the conflict between humanistic ideals and a repressive social order, the role of the masses in shaping history, and the use and abuse of political power, Shakespeare performance in the 1970s focused on plays like *A Midsummer Night's Dream* and *Romeo and Juliet*, plays concerned with the conflicts between social duty and individual self-fulfillment, obedience to public authority and personal happiness, plays about young men and women who defy parental and state authority for the sake of love. *A Midsummer Night's Dream* is also about the role of theatre in society, a theme which played an important role in various productions.

There were a series of *Dream* productions which rejected the romantic illusionism of the Max Reinhardt tradition, still very much alive on the East German stage, in favor of highlighting the conflicts and contradictions in the play in the manner of Jan Kott and Peter Brook. In 1971 Christoph Schroth directed a production in Halle which highlighted the theme of the struggle for individual freedom in a rigid and restrictive society rather than celebrating a world of romantic harmony.[28] The script was a new translation by Maik Hamburger which foregrounded the theatrical *gestus* of Shakespeare's language rather than its "literary" qualities. Attention was paid to translating the emotional and social situation into physical expression which the players could perform. The woods were seen as "a mythologically alienated, distorted reflection of the Athenian court,"[29] and the roles of Thesus and Oberon were played by the same actor, Hippolyta and Titania by the same actress, an idea made popular by Peter Brook, but unknown to Schroth at the time. This production suggested that whereas the rigid authority of the court stifled individual self-fulfillment, the unbridled passion of the woods confused it. In the woods the male lust for domination was unrestricted and Oberon himself had to intervene to prevent the young men from killing each other.

On stage the Athenian court was depicted by broad white strips of cloth hung vertically in the back and on the sides to suggest rows of Greek columns, and when the scene shifted to the woods these strips of cloth were brought into a disarray through which the lovers staggered. The similarity between Theseus and Oberon became visible in act 4, scene 1 when Theseus, Duke of Athens, entered wearing a hunting outfit similar to the costume of Oberon, King of the Fairies, and even imitating Oberon's gestures. In this production the exact distinction between the two worlds remained unclear, and thus the woods always retained a dreamlike quality, which was emphasized by the colorfulness of the costumes. In keeping with the undefined border between the two worlds, Bottom was not totally transformed into an ass but remained an enchanted human being, and Titania's caresses contained a visible element of passion and desire. Bottom, as a member of the lower orders, was aggressive and unpredictable but also had a great capacity for love. Continuing in this vein, the "harmony" of the final scene in Athens was undercut by the behavior of the members of Thesus' court, including the young lovers, who ridiculed and laughed at the mechanicals' crude but well-meant amateur performance of "Pyramus and Thisbe," for Schroth the only true love story in the play. The young lovers had attained their niche in the restrictive social order of Athens, and in act 5 they could afford to laugh at notions of equality and freedom of choice in matters of love so important to them in act 1. This performance implied not only a criticism of how the state was treating its young people but was also a sad commentary on the official treatment of theatre by the East German government.

The decade of *Dream* performances culminated in two simultaneous productions in 1980 in Berlin: at the Deutsches Theater directed by Alexander Lang and at the Maxim Gorki Theater directed by Thomas Langhoff. Obviously influenced by Jan Kott in his dramaturgical concept, Lang rigorously cut or understated any passages which might suggest sweetness or harmony. The basic motif of Lang's production is summed up best by Lysander's remarks after being drugged:

> For, as a surfeit of the sweetest things
> The deepest loathing to the stomach brings;
> Or as the heresies that men do leave
> Are hated most of those they did deceive. (2.2.136–9)

For Lang, directing the play in Max Reinhardt's own theatre, Shakespeare's "dream" was on closer inspection a nightmare: Theseus' Athens an oppressive patriarchy, and Puck's love potion, "love in idleness," translated into German as "love in madness' (*Liebe im Wahnsinn*), a forcibly administered narcotic to insure the totalitarian power of the state.[30] In this performance Puck and Oberon, like muggers from a gangster film, chloroformed Demetrius and Lysander, who could only struggle sleepily against what was being done to them. When they awoke, they discovered in themselves not only new passion but also brutal aggression, and the utopian garden of delights became an arena of sexual violence in which Hermia and Helena were the victims. Gradually the narcotic took effect, however, and the four lovers ended up anesthetized, swaying back and forth, arms and legs entwined, barely able to mutter their lines. Lang rejected the traditional "poetic" Schlegel–Tieck translation in favor of the rough-hewn eighteenth-century translation by Johann Joachim Eschenburg, which lacks the lyrical qualities of Shakespeare's original and Schlegel's romanticism.[31] Gero Troike's set, a simple three-sided box of red paper, may have suggested the confinement of a restrictive East German society, yet it also emancipated the actors from illusionistic stage decorations and provided them with an almost Shakespearean "empty space" in which to perform. Here the influence of Brook's *Dream* on Lang became visible (Lang had seen it in Warsaw); however, the roles of Theseus/Oberon, Hippolyta/Titania were not doubled. This production explored the problems of authority on different levels of the dramatic action rather than dealing with character. Both levels – court and wood – were social orders of absolute male dominion and both stifled love and creative fantasy.

The performance opened with Theseus in ermine cape fondling his captive Hippolyta (Johanna Schall) who was obviously suffering. She also wore an ermine cape which had been quickly flung over her tight-fitting black amazon pants suit (illustration 4). Oberon (Jürgen Hentsch) in a black plastic coat (as was Puck) was, like Theseus (Otto Mellies), also a symbol of male dominion but aware of its price for his subjects. Titania (Katja Paryla), in an attempt at emancipation, wore the attire of a Hollywood vamp: tight-fitting off-the-shoulder dress, high-heeled shoes, blond wig, and coat with fur collar, but as with Hippolyta's ermine cape, it seemed to be a crude attempt to assume a role rather than an attempt to signify her real self. In the end, it was Bottom, not a plebeian craftsman but an amateur actor, in beat-up hat and baggy, broad-checked knickerbockers who, in his innocent and exuberant

4   The first scene of *A Midsummer Night's Dream*, directed by Alexander Lang,
Deutsches Theater, Berlin, 1980. Dieter Mann (Demetrius), Christian Stövesand
(Egeus), Otto Mellies (Theseus), Johanna Schall (Hippolyta). *Photo: Pepita Engel,
courtesy of Deutsches Theater, Berlin.*

affirmation of immediate experience and enthusiasm for role-
playing, was Lang's antidote for Theseus' oppressive "harmony."
For her night with Bottom, Titania shed her blond wig, coat, and
high heels, and when awakened, she cried and clung so tightly to her
animal lover that Oberon and Puck had to extract her forcibly from
his arms. With Bottom she had abandoned her assumed role to
discover her true self, and having experienced this was reluctant to
return to role-playing again in the harsh reality of Oberon's
kingdom (illustration 5).

Lang's critique was directed less at a romantic illusionistic theatre
tradition than at an official government policy of papering over

5 Lang's *Dream*: Katja Paryla as Titania and Dietrich Körner as Bottom in 3.1.
Photo: Pepita Engel, courtesy of Deutsches Theater, Berlin.

contradictions and unresolved conflicts in contemporary East German culture and society for the sake of an illusory social harmony. The officially proclaimed dream of self-fulfillment and personal happiness had become a nightmare for a younger generation in a restrictive society ruled by old men, and this was brought out in this performance. The rude mechanicals were not Brecht's plebeian craftsmen but tired actors struggling to be heard in an indifferent society. While they struggled with "Pyramus and Thisbe" in the rear, the young men lay disinterestedly on cushions on the forestage, between the players and the audience, and fondled their now silent fiancées. Now integrated into the Athenian establishment, the young lovers, like the rest of the court, were no longer interested in the issues of free choice in matters of love. From this perspective, with the courtiers between them and the players, the audience slowly realized how actors felt when they performed Shakespeare's innocent travesty of *Romeo and Juliet* for an officialdom not interested in theatre. Theseus interrupted their Bergomask dance and called for a song to disperse winter before the court tore down the paper walls of the set and went off to bed.

Thomas Langhoff's production of *A Midsummer Night's Dream*, like Lang's, celebrated the creative flexibility and regenerative capacities of theatre in general and Shakespeare in particular. However, Langhoff, also influenced by Peter Brook, had little quarrel with the Reinhardt tradition and tried to do justice to the amplitude of the play: to all three plots as well as the various levels of meaning and style. The roles of Theseus/Oberon and Hippolyta/Titania were doubled. The emphasis was on physical forms of theatrical expression, and little attention was given to the recitation of blank verse. Although Langhoff's Athens was less restrictive than Lang's, it too had little patience with a Hippolyta whose clothing (a mixture of amazon and late-hippie) did not match the Athenian norm. "Love in idleness" was not translated as "love in madness" but as "love in delusion" (*Liebe in Wahn*). In this production it was the wonderfully delusory power of love which drove young people to defy parental and state authority, disregard the social hierarchy of Athens, and probe their physical and emotional limits. This was celebrated with exuberance from the beginning of the performance. When they reached the woods by breaking through the paper walls of the stage decorations, the lovers entered a foggy, circus-like world inhabited by bizarre aberrations: a bald-headed Titania, a sex-crazed,

Pan-like Oberon, a wrestler, gnome-like Puck, a world in which nothing was stable, predictable, or dependable. The wood flooring suddenly became a trampoline on and off which the lovers and the fairies bounced and were bounced. The emphasis on the physicality of the performance freed the actors from the "literary" text and provided space for them to experiment with playful physical forms of theatrical expression. Back in Athens, when the dream was over, the flooring became stable again, and the young lovers were reincorporated into the world of adult social convention. In this performance, however, "Pyramus and Thisbe," acted with passion by the amateur players, was not ridiculed but was convincing to the members of the court. Theseus and Hippolyta changed back into the costumes of Oberon and Titania on stage, and, contradicting Lang's production, Puck, not Theseus, had the final word.

All three productions shared basic presuppositions about East German society and the role of theatre within it: that society was rigid and restricted young people or anyone else who did not fit the social norm, that the official representatives of this society were not particularly interested in theatre, that a cultural policy which expected actors to recite "literary" masterpieces paralyzed actors as well as Shakespeare's text, that there were real social conflicts and contradictions in East German society which should not be covered up for the sake of a superficial harmony, and that these unresolved conflicts prevented a communion between actors and audience at the end of the performance. All three *Dream* productions had exposed the contradictions in the societies ruled by Theseus and Oberon, but none provided an ending or interpretation which suggested that the social conflicts represented in the past by Shakespeare had been resolved in the present by Socialism. This was in marked contrast to the majority of Shakespeare productions in the 1960s. Although these three directors were more immediately influenced by the work of Peter Brook and Benno Besson than Bertolt Brecht, their approaches to Shakespeare performance were, nevertheless, the continuation of Brecht's ideas in that they did not simplistically ·resolve the social conflicts of Shakespeare's past in terms of the East German present but provoked their audiences to re-examine assumptions about their own time.

In the 1980s the tension between individual self-fulfillment and the constraints of society remained a central theme of East German Shakespeare performance – in, for example, *Troilus and Cressida* directed by Manfred Wekwerth (Berliner Ensemble 1985), *The Merchant of Venice* directed by Thomas Langhoff (Deutsches Theater 1985), or a double-bill of *Romeo and Juliet* and *A Winter's Tale* directed by Christoph Schroth (Schwerin 1986–7).[32] Despite possible differences in political outlook, they more or less agreed on what a Shakespeare performance was about: that plays told stories with a beginning, a middle and an end, that there was a relationship between text and performance, and that it was the job of the actors to perform this story for an audience in a manner which was comprehensible. At a deeper level, this consensus presupposed that the world itself was comprehensible, and that theatre's *raison d'être* was to help the audience better comprehend this world by representing it on stage.

Two other directors, Heiner Müller and Frank Castorf, took very different approaches to Shakespeare. For them the world was, and still is, incomprehensible according to traditional patterns of western thought, and they share with Robert Wilson an aversion to any specified "interpretation" of Shakespeare. They reassembled Shakespeare's text, characters as well as dramatic action, and transplanted Shakespeare's "past" into a postmodern landscape which would seem to deny any "present meaning." The adaptations and productions of Shakespeare by Müller and Castorf have been more symptomatic of avant-garde theatre of the 1980s and 1990s, where performance generates its own language and modes of representation independent of a historically mediated system of representation or verbal language, than they have been of previous East German Shakespeare performances. If the work of Brecht and Wekwerth may serve as a paradigm for East German Shakespeare performance of the earlier years, the work of Müller and Castorf suggests the ways that East German Shakespeare performance moved in the 1980s.

After the scandal associated with the 1961 production of his play about the redistribution of land, *Die Umsiedlerin oder das Leben auf dem Lande*, Heiner Müller's plays about contemporary East German society were kept off the East German stage. As a consequence he turned to reworking the classics, especially Greek drama and Shakespeare. Müller's characteristic mixture of the present and the past, of the profane and the sacred, of daily life and the classical heritage is suggested by the title of his Shakespeare translations and adaptations: *Shakespeare Factory*.[33] Whereas Brecht and his followers retold

Shakespeare's plays from a new point of view to gain fresh insights in Shakespeare's material, it is Müller's declared intention to destroy these plays, to reduce them to their skeleton. He has taken the plays apart, extracted disconnected images and reassembled them to confront the audience with the frailty of their assumptions about Shakespeare and the world they inhabit. While Brecht and Wekwerth placed Shakespeare within the context of history and used the conflict between protagonist and antagonist to demonstrate that social contradictions can be reconciled within history, Müller's adaptations suggest that neither the problems on stage nor in society could or can ever be reconciled in a world that is violent, cruel, and ultimately senseless. "No hope, no despair" is Müller's motto. In his Shakespeare adaptations, character, plot, and even the playwright become interchangeable and arbitrary.

The production of Müller's *Macbeth (Nach Shakespeare)* (Volksbühne, Berlin, 1982), directed by himself and Ginka Tscholokowa, reassembled Shakespeare's familiar fable as well as his characters.[34] Macbeth was played at different times by three different actors, the witches became three bald-headed women in evening gowns waltzing to "The Blue Danube," and Lady Macbeth was not a power-crazed witch who victimized Macbeth but an innocent young victim herself who ends her life trapped in a telephone booth. According to Müller, power – or evil – does not wear a specific mask, and any attempt to interpret either the witches or Lady Macbeth as inherently evil solely on the basis of appearance was negated. The stage design, an exact reproduction of three sides of the courtyard of a run-down East Berlin tenement, visually transplanted conflicts of Shakespeare's play into the contemporary situation of the audience without reconciling them.

Müller's own monumental seven-and-a-half-hour production of *Hamlet/Maschine: Shakespeare/Müller* at the Deutsches Theater (1990) consisted of his translation of *Hamlet* and a montage of his *Hamletmaschine*. At various points passages from *Hamletmaschine* were inserted into the dramatic action from loudspeakers in a vehicle which moved ominously back and forth on a track above the stage and the auditorium. These passages interrupted the story of an autistic Hamlet (Ulrich Mühe) who had isolated himself from political responsibility in the rotten state of Denmark. Television monitors leered out from the side boxes, and when the Ghost, naked but for a codpiece, stalked across the stage, the radio broadcast of Stalin's

6 Shakespeare/Müller, *Hamlet/Maschine*, directed by Heiner Müller, Deutsches Theater, Berlin, 1990. The second scene of *Hamlet*, with Ulrich Mühe as Hamlet in foreground. *Photo: Wolfhard Theile, courtesy of Deutsches Theater, Berlin.*

funeral could be heard in the background. Hamlet's gray Denmark was encased in a cube of ice depicted by a stage-high gauze screen which separated the stage from the audience. It served as a metaphor for Müller's own German Democratic Republic which "melted" and came to an end between the beginning of rehearsals and the opening performance on 24 March 1990. This "thaw" was also suggested by a large puddle in the middle of the stage and the sound of trickling water (illustration 6). Mühe's Hamlet himself

7   The Mousetrap (3.2) of *Hamlet/Maschine*, with disjunctive scenography.
Photo: Wolfhard Theile, courtesy of Deutsches Theater, Berlin.

became a metaphor for the East German intellectual, powerless to
influence political machinations, and the physical resemblance of
Horatio to Müller stamped him as the adaptor/translator's *alter ego*.
Despite all the heavy-duty metaphors, there was an air of light
entertainment about the performance, especially in acts 4 and 5 (see
illustration 7).

Hamlet and Claudius were nearly reconciled in the confession
scene, the graveyard scene was staged from the vantage point of the
gravedigger in the grave, and Laertes and Hamlet dueled in a slow

8   The slow motion duel in *Hamlet/Maschine*, with Dagmar Manzel (Gertrude),
Michael Kind (Laertes), and Jörg Gudzuhn (Claudius). *Photo: Wolfhard Theile,
courtesy of Deutsches Theater, Berlin.*

motion routine at a distance from each other (illustration 8). Before
Hamlet died, he stabbed everyone else on stage. Ophelia re-entered
from the auditorium, lifted Hamlet's body from where it hung over
the edge of the apron, and carried it back to the middle of the stage.
In a passage from *Hamletmaschine* she, like Electra, recanted the
world she had herself created before being consumed by a sheet of
fire. Fortinbras, a gold metallic figure, entered from the back of the
stage wearing a business suit and carrying a briefcase and covered

Hamlet's face with a gilded business folder. Müller himself once quipped that the key question for any East German performance of *Hamlet* was: "Who is Fortinbras?" Did he stand for Chancellor Helmut Kohl? The Deutsche Mark? The Deutsche Bank? The performance ended not with Shakespeare but a voice reading out Zbigniew Herbert's "Fortinbras' Lament" over the loudspeakers: "You were doomed to failure, Hamlet, you were not fit for life. You believed in crystalline concepts rather than in humanity." The performance could be understood as an epitaph for the GDR; Müller himself remarked that the GDR was so bad that it did not deserve even a decent burial.

A production of *Hamlet* directed by the East German Frank Castorf in Cologne in the fall of 1989 deconstructed not only Shakespeare's play but Müller's translation as well, a technique which Castorf himself has called "müllerizing" (*vermüllern*). Castorf's *Hamlet Material von Shakespeare* began with neither Shakespeare's nor Müller's text but with two actors, Hamlet and the ghost of his father, interacting on the stage. Plot, character, and text were broken apart and reassembled: the performance opened with Hamlet liberating the ghost of his father from a blue plastic garbage bag; Hamlet's father was also Claudius; Gertrude spoke Claudius' opening monologue; Ophelia, Rosencrantz, and Guildenstern were similar teenage actresses in 1950s dresses. In a version of the Cinderella story, they decided among themselves who was to play Ophelia on the basis of whose foot fit Ophelia's shoe. Fragments of Müller's translation were occasionally recited in fits and starts, only to degenerate into incomprehensible babbling and sign language interspersed with long periods of silence. The stage was the ring of a circus tent, covered with white paper and enclosed by an eyelevel wall of white paper which ran around it. Downstage right was an old refrigerator, downstage left a green dustbin, up left a soft leather couch, up right an old piano, and center an old wardrobe through which the actors could enter and exit. In the course of the evening, the paper on the floor was ripped up and the paper backdrop torn down. Theatre image and audience expectations were deconstructed before the spectator's eyes.

Whereas Brecht's approach to Shakespeare had its sources in Karl Marx, Renaissance humanism, and structuralism, Castorf's sources are Groucho Marx, surrealism, and postmodernism. In Castorf's *Hamlet*, European culture was reduced to the lowest common denominator: Claudius hammered out "Chopsticks" ("Der Floh-walzer") on the piano while Hamlet stammered through an incomprehensible monologue head down in the dustbin. This Shakespeare performance no longer interpreted the Elizabethan past in terms of the present but consisted of a disparate, almost surrealistic collection of quotes from popular and high culture arranged in discontinuous scenes: the slapstick of Charlie Chaplin, the unexpected absurdities of the Marx Brothers, fairy-tales, the dustbin from Beckett's *Endgame*, the caustic wit of W. C. Fields. What came across was the creative energy and fun of free association as well as the conscious rejection of any attempt to interpret or mediate. Castorf's *Hamlet* was not performed against a backdrop of history or a particular social order but presented us with a society in which history and systematic meaning have become irrelevant, replaced by private fantasy.

It is a subtle irony that the history of East German Shakespeare performance began and ended with *Hamlet*, that "most German" of Shakespeare's plays. In 1945 a conventional performance conveyed a heroic statement of hope for a Europe liberated from Fascism. In 1990 a gigantic *Hamlet* show opened with a monologue from Heiner Müller's *Hamletmaschine*: "I was Hamlet. I stood on the shore and spoke BLAH BLAH to the breakers, behind me the ruins of Europe. The bell tolls in the state funeral." For the first twenty-five years (1945–70) East German Shakespeare performance was characterized by a concern for public issues: interpretations of history and social order and the role of the individual in shaping them.[35] For the last twenty years (1970–90), East German Shakespeare performance was increasingly concerned with private issues: the possibilities for individual self-fulfillment in an increasingly rigid and restrictive society, and the personal disillusionment with a harmonizing social philosophy unable to admit or resolve obvious social contradictions. In both phases the application of Brecht's ideas about *gestus*, epic theatre, and the alienation effect actively involved spectators with fresh insights into Shakespeare's plays and their contemporary relevance. Now that the historical experiment known as the German Democratic Republic has come to an end, what will remain of this interesting but relatively unknown 45-year chapter in the history of Shakespeare performance? Certainly Brecht's close reading of texts from a sociological point of view, as well as his theatrical ideas, will live on in the work of individual directors, actors, and actresses. Certainly our appreciation of minor characters – the Gravedigger in *Hamlet*, the Gardener in *Richard II*, or the Chorus in *Henry V* – has been sharpened. The experienced ensembles which made these performances possible, however, have broken up. More importantly, the backdrop against which Shakespeare was performed has been removed and theatres no longer have to play the roles of the news media, of political scientists, or of historians. The stage is once again an undefined "empty space" and, to paraphrase a passage from *Hamletmaschine*, the actors can now reclaim their faces from the cloakroom where they have been hanging.

NOTES

1 Weimann, "Shakespeare on the Modern Stage: Past Significance and Present Meaning," *Shakespeare Survey* 20 (1967): 115.

2 "East Berlin Deutsches Theater Emerges as Force for Change," *The Chicago Tribune* 23 November 1989. Schall was quoted on 4 Nov. 1989, during the mass demonstration for social reform held on Alexanderplatz, which was organized primarily by theatre people.

3 For accounts of Shakespeare on the German stage in English, see Simon Williams, *Shakespeare on the German Stage, Vol.I:1586–1914* (Cambridge University Press, 1990) and the forthcoming *Vol.II:1915–90* by W. Hortmann with a special chapter on East German Shakespeare by Maik Hamburger.

4 "Einige Bemerkungen über mein Fach," *Schriften zum Theater* (Frankfurt am Main: Suhrkamp, 1963), 6:173–6; hereafter *SzT*. From 1933 to their closing in 1944, Berlin theatres were under the direct control of Hermann Göring, Governor of Prussia, who was married to Emmy Sonnemann, a second-rate actress.

5 See "Wie soll man heute Klassiker spielen" (1926), *SzT* 1: 89–91; "Notizen über die Dialektik auf dem Theater," *SzT* 7: 223–47; "Darstellung klassischer Werke ohne grosse Schauspieler," *SzT* 6:179–80; "Einschüchterung durch die Klassizität," *Stücke* (Frankfurt am Main: Suhrkamp, 1959), 11:5–8.

6 Hanns Eisler compared the importance of Brecht's discovery of *gestus* for art to Einstein's discovery of the theory of relativity for the natural sciences. See *Fragen Sie mehr über Brecht*, ed. Hans Bunge (Munich: Rogner and Bernhard, 1970), 26. For some of Brecht's scattered remarks on *gestus*, see "Über gestische Musik," *SzT* 3:281–5, "Über den gestus," *SzT* 4:31; "Gestik," *SzT* 6:213; "Kleines Organon," nos. 62, 63, 64, 65, 66, 70, 73, *SzT* 6; for a brief summary in English, see Patrice Pavis, "On Brecht's Notion of *gestus*," in *Linguistics and Literary Studies in Eastern Europe* (Amsterdam and Philadelphia: John Benjamins, 1984), 10:290–304.

7 "First Scene of *Coriolanus*," in John Willet, trans., *Brecht on Theatre* (New York: Hill and Wang, 1964), 252ff.

8 Wekwerth's and Tenschert's stagescript is reprinted in *Theater der Zeit* 21.14 (1966): 38–60 (hereafter *ThdZ*) and *Speculum VIII* (Frankfurt on Main: Suhrkamp, 1965).

9 See Manfred Wekwerth, "Das Theater Brechts und die Siebziger Jahre," *Schriften. Arbeiten mit Brecht* (Berlin: Henschel, 1975), 329ff; H. G. Huettich, *Theatre in the Planned Society. Contemporary Drama in the GDR in its Historical, Political and Cultural Context* (Chapel Hill: University of North Carolina Press, 1978), 56ff; *Theater in der Zeitenwende* (Berlin: Henschel, 1972), 2:11–38. The Wall was greeted at first by theatre people such as Heiner Müller, B. K. Tragelehn, Christoph Schroth, and even Wolf Biermann, as a temporary measure which would provide East Germany with an economic breathing spell and an opportunity to deal with specifically East German problems without having to account to the West.

10 Armin-Gerd Kuckhoff, "Shakespeare auf den Bühnen der DDR in den Jahren 1964 und 1965," *Shakespeare Jahrbuch* 103 (1967): 197–8; hereafter *ShJ*.

11 Cf. Wekwerth, *Notate: Über die Arbeit des Berliner Ensembles 1956 bis 1966* (Frankfurt am Main: Suhrkamp, 1966), 111–15.

12 See, for example, Ernst Schumacher, "Die Tragödie des Coriolans," *Berliner Zeitung*, 1 Oct. 1964; Christoph Funke, "Die Ersetzbarkeit des Coriolan," *Der Morgen*, 27 Oct. 1964; Rudolf Walter Leonhardt, "Können wir den Shakespeare ändern?" *Die Zeit*, 2 Oct. 1964; Michael Stone, "Brecht's *Coriolan*," *The Guardian*, 8 Oct. 1964; Kenneth Tynan, "Brecht on Shakespeare," *The Observer*, 4 Oct. 1964.

13 *The Empty Space* (London: McGibbon and Kee, 1968), 81.

14 Alexander Abusch, *Shakespeare: Realist und Humanist, Genius der Weltliteratur* (Berlin and Weimar: Aufbau, 1964), 19–21.

15 See Dieter Hoffmeier, "Lehrer über vier Jahrhunderte. Shakespeare und unsere Stückeschreiber," *ThdZ* 19.6 (1964): 6–8.

16 Walter Ulbricht, "Über die Entwicklung einer volkverbundenen sozialistischen Nationalkultur," in *Neues Deutschland*, 28 April 1964, reprinted in *Zweite Bitterfelder Konferenz 1964* (Berlin, 1964), 82ff.

17 See Huettich, *Theatre in the Planned Society*, 132ff.

18 "Shakespeare eine Differenz." *ShJ* 125 (1989): 21; English translation by Carl Weber, *Performing Arts Journal* 35/36 (1990): 32.

19 Hans-Dieter Mäde, "*Hamlet* und das Problem des Ideals," *ShJ* 102 (1966): 7–23; Christoph Funke und Ursula Püschel, "*Hamlet* in der Diskussion I" *ThdZ* 19.12 (1964): 9–11; Erika Stephan and Ulf Keyn, "*Hamlet* in der Diskussion II," *ThdZ* 19.13 (1964): 12–13; Armin-Gerd Kuckhoff, "Theaterschau," *ShJ* 103 (1967): 197ff; Weimann, "Shakespeare on the Modern Stage," 117–20.

20 *"Hamlet* in Karl-Marx-Stadt. Von der Schwierigkeit der Realisierung," *ThdZ* 19.8 (1964): 21.

21 See *"Hamlet* heute hier. Ein Gespräch über fünf Inszenierungen," *ThdZ* 19.17 (1964): 4–7 and *ThdZ* 19.18 (1964): 8–10; and Armin-Gerd Kuckhoff, "Theaterschau," *ShJ* 103 (1964): 206.

22 Alexander Weigel was one of the few critics who defended Dresen and Hamburger, see *"Hamlet* in der Diskussion III," *ThdZ* 19.15 (1964): 8–9.

23 *Shakespeare und die Tradition des Volkstheaters* (Berlin: Aufbau, 1967); English translation by Robert Schwartz: *Shakespeare and the Popular Tradition in the Theatre: Studies in the Social Dimension of Dramatic Form and Function* (Baltimore: Johns Hopkins University Press, 1978).

24 On Wekwerth's production of *Richard III,* see *"Leben und Tod von Richard des Dritten* am Deutschen Theater Berlin," *ShJ* 109 (1973): 125–35; "Vorschläge für ein Volkstheater," *ThdZ* 27.9 (1972), reprinted in Manfred Wekwerth, *Theater in Diskussion* (Berlin: Henschel, 1982), 83–5; "Lust und Last der Klassik oder wer besitzt wen?" *Neue Züricher Zeitung* (1973), reprinted in *Theater in Diskussion,* 95–100; see Weimann, *Shakespeare and the Popular Tradition,* 237ff for a discussion of the "complementary perspective."

25 For examples of West German criticism, see Helmut Karasek, "Harlekin Richard," *Die Zeit,* 31 Mar. 1972 and Rolf Michaelis, "Tyrannenmord als Volkstheater," *Frankfurter Allgemeine Zeitung* 24 Mar. 1972; for an example of East German criticism, see Ernst Schumacher, "Spektakulärer *Richard,*" reprinted in *Berliner Kritiken* (Berlin: Henschel, 1975), II: 560–75, as well as Wekwerth's response in "Das alte Thema: Gesellschaft und Individuum," *Theater in Diskussion,* 9–17.

26 See Wekwerth, "Vorschläge für ein Volkstheater," in *Theater in Diskussion,* 83–8, and "Fragen Brecht betreffend," in *Brecht 88,* ed. Wolfgang Heise (Berlin: Henschel, 1987), 301–24.

27 *Neues Deutschland,* 18 December 1971; quoted by Huettich, *Theatre in the Planned Society,* 151.

28 Maik Hamburger, "New Concepts of Staging *A Midsummer Night's Dream,*" *Shakespeare Survey* 40 (1988): 52ff; Armin-Gerd Kuckhoff, "Theaterschau," *ShJ* 109 (1973): 174–6; other productions were staged in Magdeburg 1972 (Dir.: Werner Freese), Dresden 1974 (Dir.: Klaus-Dieter Kirst), and Rudolstadt 1976 (Dir.: Klaus Fiedler).

29 Hamburger, "New Concepts," 52.

30 Martin Linzer (ed.), *Alexander Lang Abenteuer Theater* (Berlin: Henschel, 1983), 92.

31 On the Lang and Langhoff productions, see Hamburger, "New Concepts," 55–8; Martin Linzer, *"A Midsummer Night's Dream* in East Germany," *TDR* 25.2 (Summer 1981): 45–54; "Tag-Träume," *ThdZ* 35.7 (1980): 38–42; "Nacht-Träume," *ThdZ* 35.12 (1980): 13–15; *Alexander Lang,* 69–100; Armin-Gerd Kuckhoff, "Zur Shakespeare-

Rezeption in der DDR (1945–1980)," *ShJ* 118 (1982): 117ff; and "Theaterschau," *ShJ* 118 (1982): 142–51.

32 For descriptions and reviews of Wekwerth's productions of *Troilus and Cressida*, see Gary Taylor, *Reinventing Shakespeare* (London: Hogarth Press, 1989), 298ff, Armin-Gerd Kuckhoff, *ThdZ* 40.10 (1985): 21; for Langhoff's production of *A Merchant of Venice*, see Jochen Gleiss, *ThdZ* 40.6 (1985): 14–15, Armin-Gerd Kuckhoff, "Theaterschau," *ShJ* 123 (1987):159ff; for Schroth's *Romeo and Juliet* and *A Winter's Tale*, see Bernhard Scheller, *ThdZ* 42.4 (1987): 45ff, Armin-Gerd Kuckhoff, *ShJ* 124 (1988): 244ff.

33 *Shakespeare Factory*, 2 vols. (Berlin: Rotbuch, 1985/9), contains adaptations of *As You Like It*, *Macbeth (Macbeth. Nach Shakespeare)*, *A Midsummer Night's Dream (Waldstück)*, *Hamlet*, and *Titus Andronicus (Antatomie Titus Fall of Rome Ein Shakespearekommentar)*. *Hamletmaschine*, Müller's radical reworking of *Hamlet*, is in Theo Girshausen (ed.) *Hamletmaschine. Heiner Müller's Endspiel* (Cologne: Prometh, 1978); in English translation in *Hamletmachine and Other Texts for the Stage*, ed. and trans. Carl Weber (New York: Performing Arts Journal, 1984).

34 On the performance, Hans-Rainer John, "Zur *Macbeth*-Inszenierung der Volksbühne," *ThdZ* 37.12 (1982): 8–9; Hans-Thies Lehmann, "Das Ende der Macht – auf dem Theater," *Theater Heute* 23:12 (1982): 16–24.

35 On the first thirty-five years of East German Shakespeare tradition, see Kuckhoff, "Zur Shakespeare-Rezeption in der DDR," 107–19; Willi Schrader, "Shakespeare-Rezeption in der DDR im Lichte der Shakespeare-Tage in Weimar," *ShJ (West)* (1988): 68–87, and Günther Klotz, "Shakespeare Adaptionen in der DDR," *ShJ* 124 (1988): 223–4. The translation from *Hamletmaschine* is my own.

CHAPTER 7

Theatrical continuities in Giorgio Strehler's
The Tempest

Pia Kleber

When Giorgio Strehler staged *The Tempest* in 1978, it was greeted by the international press as "the most important Shakespeare production since Peter Brook's famous *A Midsummer Night's Dream* in 1970," and Strehler himself declared the play "the greatest work of theatre that was ever written":[1]

In only 2,000 lines, Shakespeare was able to treat the history of humanity, of culture, of politics, of theatre and illusion, of white as opposed to black magic, of the double. Caliban, for instance, is the double of Ariel. Ariel cannot live without Caliban. Caliban needs Prospero, Prospero Ariel, and Prospero cannot live without Caliban. Therefore we have once more a Faust and a Mephisto. This is synthesis at its very best. It is perhaps blasphemous to say so, but *The Tempest* may even be greater than Goethe's *Faust*.

Strehler expressed this overwhelming admiration for Shakespeare's play in an interview I conducted with him in Milan in German and French on 27 May 1991, only one day after he had finished the first run of *Faust II*, which he himself directed and in which he played Faust, a production which he considers to be the highlight of his career.[2]

Not only is *The Tempest* a synthesis of everything Strehler cherishes in the theatre, but his production of it can also be seen as a crystallization of all of Strehler's directorial art. It would be foolhardy to attempt, in a single article, to discuss all the elements of theatrical discourse present in this production, or to map the way in which he assimilated the influence of masters such as Constantin Stanislavsky, Jacques Copeau, Louis Jouvet, and Bertolt Brecht into this particular mise en scène. I intend instead to pursue the specifically Brechtian aspects of Strehler's *Tempest*, particularly as they are reflected in the reactions to it by the critic and Shakespearean commentator Jan Kott and by the director and playwright

Roger Planchon.[3] I shall, in addition, make a short excursion into the worlds of *commedia dell'arte*, the circus, and Strehler's production of *King Lear* (1972).

In the interview, Strehler spoke about his great love for Kott's book, *Shakespeare Our Contemporary*, and about how he sought to benefit from Kott's expertise in the preparatory phase of staging *The Tempest*:

I invited Kott for ten days to Milan and we talked daily for approximately four hours. I was looking for a dialectical discussion. Kott knew much more about Shakespeare and *The Tempest* than I did, and he explained to me many beautiful things. But we scarcely ever talked about the essential meaning of *The Tempest*.

Strehler found this preliminary collaboration fruitful; but Kott was subsequently highly critical of the production, calling Strehler "a prisoner of his imagination, of this theater, and of all the plays he has ever directed."[4] Kott's objections were directed specifically against Strehler's use of the clown tradition. He draws the parallel between Ariel, the "Pierrot from Watteau," and the Fool from Strehler's production of *King Lear*. Ariel and the Fool were both played by women; furthermore, Lear's Fool and Cordelia were played by the same actress, Ottavia Piccolo. Undoubtedly, Strehler quotes constantly from his own previous productions, particularly in regard to traditions of farce such as *commedia dell'arte* and the circus. But one person's exploitation is another's creative process. Strehler shares with Brecht the fundamental conviction that every theatrical element has to be re-evaluated and re-established for every new production. Strehler's adherence to this principle may be demonstrated by an analysis of his careful choice of clown motifs and his rethinking of *commedia* figures.

It might also be useful to weigh Kott's critique of Strehler's *The Tempest* in the context of Planchon's critique of Kott's view of Shakespeare's play. My procedure in this will be to sketch a three-way relationship involving Strehler, Kott, and Planchon – with Brecht as it were hovering above them all like Ariel.

Planchon's position proceeds from his belief that Shakespeare wrote the plays of his last years in order to communicate his discovery that "the supernatural is the core of reality and that the terrible is very close to us." He therefore began his address by attacking *all* left-wing theatre practitioners and thinkers for being unable to recognize or to admit that gods and goddesses, prophecies or, as he says, "mechanisms of predestination" play a fundamental role in Shakespeare. "They cut these passages, distort and rewrite them, without embarrassment." He throws Jan Kott and Bertolt Brecht into the pot with all these left-wing "freethinkers." "Jan Kott's analyses of *The Tempest*," for instance, "are well informed and competent as long as they concern the struggle for power. But what cheating or blindness there is when it has to do with the supra-natural! There Jan Kott and others set about altering the tale told by Shakespeare."[5]

Planchon continues his attack by quoting a single paragraph (no. 8) of Brecht's *A Short Organum* as proof of Brecht's lack of understanding of Shakespeare. He does so without looking, apparently, at Brecht's "The Theatre of Shakespeare," where Brecht lauds this theatre of ghosts and supernatural elements as the source of wonderful V-effects.[6] Planchon's article not only reveals his limited understanding of Brecht, but also his inability to recognize, as Brecht did, that Shakespeare had planted the seeds for a non-illusionistic theatre which not only questions reality but the very notion of theatre itself, a process which is now called metatheatrical, and which is at the base of Brecht's theatrical theory. As Agostino Lombardo puts it,

What this "tired and resigned" dramatist (Shakespeare) leaves us then, is nothing less than a great experiment – the most audacious maybe in the history of theatre. It was, moreover, centuries later before it was understood by such writers as Pirandello and Brecht.[7]

In the same interview, I discussed with Strehler Planchon's view that Brecht had failed to understand Shakespeare:

I never talked with Brecht about *The Tempest*, but I know that Brecht would have instantly understood that if one believes that theatre can sometimes change people or something, then *The Tempest* clearly demonstrates how one can alter people within the short span of a performance. However, the problem of the play is not illusion versus truth or magic, whatever one wants to call it – although, of course, all this is also contained in it – but it is a play where the magician at the end throws away his wand and book, walks down to the audience, completely naked, as a human being, and says: "Well, I've done my bit as actor and theatrical character, but now it's your turn. You're obliged to go on from here." The play's ending is highly didactic.

One might add that it is also open-ended, like Brecht's play *The Good Person of Szechwan*. Agostino Lombardo expands on Strehler's vision of the play's ending:

The real importance of the epilogue, however ... lies in the fact that it establishes the real protagonist of the research on theatre, namely the audience or the spectator. It is the spectator who must be asked everything ("Now, 'tis true / I must be here confin'd by you, / Or sent to Naples ... ") as Shakespeare has put him through the epistemological experience already described, by having him attend the performance of *The Tempest*.

This interaction between audience and stage, between life and theatre, is one of the reasons for Strehler's fascination with Brecht's theatre.

In his book *Un théâtre pour la vie*, Strehler admits that Brecht represents for him a sort of intersection of all the theoretical components he had cherished before. The lesson of Brecht "does not concern a theatre outside of history, outside of time, nor the eternal theatre for all time, or history as opposed to theatre, but *history* and *theatre*, the world and life at the same time, in a continuing dialectical relationship, difficult, sometimes painful, but always active, always concerned with a general evolution."[8] With Shakespeare's *The Tempest*, Strehler found the ideal text combining theatre and life, spectacle, illusion, and concrete social situations.

The theatrical illusions that Strehler created in this production did not cover up the fact that Prospero's magic is also a real activity: a function of his sovereignty, his planning, and his execution. It is work which has to manifest its own laws. Nor did Strehler hide his own art, but exposed the theatrical artifice in Brechtian fashion. In his discussion of *The Tempest*'s beginning, however, Kott accuses him of the opposite:

The director of *The Tempest* did not disclose his art, yet he did not conceal his power.[9]

The spectacular storm which opened Strehler's production of *The Tempest* has been described numerous times.[10] The sixteen operators hidden within the three corridors of the orchestra pit, who oscillated the blue silk, thus creating the enormous waves of the stormy sea, were not visible in the stage production as they are in the video of the production, and as they subsequently were in *Faust II*. Despite the spell this theatrical storm cast over the audience for about 5 minutes – interestingly, most critics speak of 15 minutes – the huge transparent cloth which dropped down from the "heavens," the splitting of the mast, the collapsing of the rigging, and the calming of the immense blue silk sea could not, and were not intended to, hide the fact that the storm was made by man.

Nevertheless, Kott had seen at a rehearsal of the production "the boys and girls carrying the blue sea on their raised arms." His disappointment at Strehler's subsequent decision to abandon the idea of making the human "machinery" visible, might have given rise to Kott's overall view. But there was no need to show everything. As Jack Viertel observed in his review of the play:

It is the most theatrical of "Tempests," one that celebrates, rather than disguises, its multiple uses of artifice and reveals its hand at every turn.[11]

The video provides us with another glimpse behind the scenes. The thunder and lightning of the storm were produced by eight drummers, a man running the wind machine, another the rain machine, and a couple of musicians pounding on strips of metal with hammers to make the crash of lightning. At one point we even see the technician pulling Ariel's rope.

The end of the production freed the audience from any residual illusions. Prospero lifted his wand over his head, broke it in two and threw it back into the orchestra pit/sea. Thunder crashed, lightning struck, and the entire setting fell apart, revealing all the mechanisms by which theatrical illusion is created. "Then with a wave of his hand," Stephen Holder comments, "the set reconstructs itself. Having taken away our world, Prospero, via Giorgio Strehler, graciously returns it to us in an act of supreme generosity."[12]

Luciano Damiani's set was a further guarantee that the theatre presented itself as theatre, as Brecht requires. Damiani did not attempt to create the illusion of an island by naturalistic means, but chose a wooden rectangular platform which was first the deck of the storm-tossed ship and then the island. Two wooden runways connected it to the wings, and the platform was bisected diagonally on both sides. Each side would be raised in order to present a different location on the island. The only other sign Damiani used to indicate a change of place was a shrub which "grows magically" in front of the wooden platform (2.1). The bareness of this shrub communicated clearly that to live on this island is toilsome for Prospero and pure horror for the courtiers; they are not in the Land of Cockaigne. There were three trap-doors in the wooden planks, two used to hold props and costumes, the third as Caliban's cave. This "island" was surrounded by three high white walls reminiscent of Brecht's legendary cycloramas. In the center of the space was a circular disk of sand referring to the closeness of the sea. A zodiac design around it outlined the magic circle. Only the most essential characteristics and elements necessary for the action and the narration of the fable were exhibited.

Damiani's design agreed with another of Brecht's requirements, that

it's more important nowadays for the set to tell the spectator he's in a theatre than to tell him he's in, say, Aulis. The theatre must acquire *qua* theatre the same fascinating reality as a sporting arena during a boxing match. The best thing is to show the machinery, the ropes and the flies.[13]

All machinery on Strehler's stage was readily apparent. The playing area was hydraulically raised and lowered, the trap-doors and storage cupboards opened and closed by actors on stage, in full sight of the audience. "Ropes" and "flies" were acknowledged by the rope which gave Ariel flight. This rope was obviously lowered from the flies, and clipped to a harness on the actress's back, a fact which was further strengthened when Ariel was released from the rope by Prospero and it audibly whined and clanged back up to the flies. This despite the fact that the audience was enchanted by the amazing arabesques and "flights" of Ariel throughout the perform-ance (see illustration 9).

Brecht further proposes that "the set needs to spring from the rehearsal of groupings, so in effect it must be a fellow-actor." The rope which gave Ariel flight but also held her captive is exactly Brecht's set/fellow-actor. Ariel yearns for liberty (1.2.245), and when Prospero delays the moment of liberation, "he [Ariel] tugs at the theatrical cable to which he is tied as to a chain. The prop suddenly becomes a metaphor."[14]

Throughout the play, every prop present was made use of, some-times even to produce a comic effect. After Prospero rebuked Ariel for having such a short memory and demanding her liberty before the project was finished, she tried to hide in embarrassment like a scolded child behind Prospero's stick, which had been stuck in the sand. The props were all realistic and beautifully executed, giving information about the social background of the courtiers trapped on the island or about the island itself. In the sand, for instance, there lay a large shell, and when Ariel collected all the props to put them into the prop cupboard after the second scene, she picked up the shell like the other objects but hesitated a second, then held it to her ear, listened to the "music" and put it back into the sand. The shell

9   Giorgio Strehler's *The Tempest*, Milan, 1978. Giulia Lazzarini as Ariel flies on a visible wire, Piccolo Teatro di Milano at Teatro Lirico. *Photo: Luigi Ciminaghi.*

was not only another indication of the proximity of the sea, but an allusion to the music which permeates the island.

Caliban's trap-door also had a meaningful function. Strehler commented on Caliban's exit at the end of the play, and the reason why the trap-door was left open:

This was a real problem. For weeks we contemplated how we could direct Caliban's exit. Should he leave the "lid" of his cave open or close it? In the end, we left it open, conveying the idea that Caliban does not want to have anything to do with this so-called civilized world, and crawls back into his cave, but the hole stays open, and he has the choice to come up if he wishes. This was a political decision.

Kott attacked this ending:

Of all the possible endings in *The Tempest*, Caliban's return to his rock-prison seems the most false and traditional. When Prospero and the newcomers from the Old World leave the island, Caliban should remain alone on the stage: deceived twice, he is richer in experience only.[15]

"Richer in experience" constitutes an important point for Strehler. While Kott suggests that Shakespeare's *The Tempest* reverts to its beginning when "the rightful ruler, the Lord non-anointed, was Caliban," this is only apparently so. For Strehler, *The Tempest* is:

a journey of knowledge, a road which leads to self-discovery for everyone. Prospero finds himself in a certain situation at the beginning of the play and during the play he undergoes a great development. Everybody is changed at the end and has learned to distinguish truth from illusion.

Caliban, played in this production by Michele Placido, has meanwhile learned the language of civilization, the language of science. Before Prospero's arrival, Caliban was able to communicate with nature, but Strehler notes that we don't know if he is still able to speak this language at the end of the play. He considers Caliban to be a remarkable political figure, because "already at the beginning of colonization, Shakespeare had understood where the danger lies in the colonization of black by white people. The blacks would be either corrupted or enslaved."

The language Caliban can learn from Prospero is made up of the "curses" he directs against his oppressor (1.2.365–6). One might say that resistance needs a language which has to be learned from the oppressor. But what a price to pay for this "journey of knowledge"! "The problem of civilization is enormous," reiterates Strehler. In his staging, the problem was raised but no answers were provided. At the end, with all the actors on stage, suddenly the music of Monteverdi's *Orfeo* began, and the actors exited right or left. Caliban remained alone and crawled into his hole, but this time the lid stayed open. Before Caliban entered his hole, he picked up a sword and Prospero's stick from the ground, lifted them majestically into the air, and threw them in disgust on the floor. It was now *his* choice or problem how to cope with his new situation.

Every art involved in a Brechtian production – whether of design, blocking, or acting – must tell the story from its own standpoint and bring out the contradictions both within and between the characters. Caliban's entrance on stage provided an excellent example and moreover demonstrated Strehler's ability to convey what Brecht called a *gestus*, by simple signs.[16] Indeed, the relationship between Prospero, Miranda, and Caliban was clearly spelled out even before Caliban appeared. Prospero took off his leather belt and held it like the whip of a slave-owner, while Miranda sought protection behind her father's back. Then very slowly, one black arm after the other emerged from the cave, holding onto the frame of the opening and heaving up the rest of Caliban's body. He looked more like a huge black spider than a human being. His body, painted coal-black, stood in sharp contrast to the white clothes of Prospero and his daughter. In act 2, scene 2, Caliban danced with a voodoo ritual prop reminiscent of an African witch-doctor's wand, neutralizing Prospero's magic. But Strehler did not make Caliban specifically an African tribesman. Stephen Holder observed that "rather than representing mankind's inherently brutish side, he seems to be an emblem of man's inhumanity to man in the form of slavery."[17] The slave Caliban, as Jack Viertel asserts,

is no half-man, as Shakespeare describes him, but only a black man in an all-white world. Yet this is not a simple racial metaphor: Caliban isn't a Negro, he's black as onyx, his skin dull as coal dust.[18]

Most of the time Caliban stayed close to the earth, often sitting, lying down, or crouching when he walked. His bodily postures and facial expressions disclosed in a social *gestus* the hatred for and fear of the man who had taken the island away from him and reduced him to slavery. These emotions were well illustrated when Caliban accused Prospero of teaching him "how to curse" (1.2.365). For a second, Caliban's crouching position was loaded with tension, as if

10   Michele Placido as Caliban and Tino Carraro as Prospero in Strehler's
Tempest. Photo: Luigi Ciminaghi.

he wished to attack Prospero. But Prospero quickly reversed the
situation by a body movement which physically threatened
Caliban, who instantly changed into a frightened position (see
illustration 10).

There were, however, several wonderful moments in the production when Caliban was shown as a "noble savage," the real king
of the island, full of tenderness, not hatred. Jan Kott describes one
such contradiction in the second scene: "when Miranda steps out
from behind Prospero, the face of Caliban suddenly changes. For an
instant he is desperately sad, shy, almost a timid boy."[19] A parallel
occurred when Prospero exclaimed "So slave; hence!" and Caliban
stood upright against the bright background, turned around, and
looked Prospero straight in the eye. His beautiful, majestic black
body defied Prospero's words.

According to Michel Bataillon, Planchon's dramaturge and longtime collaborator, Planchon did not like Strehler's treatment of Prospero. He expected Prospero to be more "black and white."[20] Could this mean that Planchon thought that the contradiction between the various roles Prospero takes on should have been more sharply delineated and thus more Brechtian? Jan Kott, on the other hand, missed the bitterness in Prospero's final soliloquy. Both men may have a point. According to Stephen Holder, Tino Carraro, who played Prospero,

imbues the character with a fine, measured dignity, balancing vengefulness and compassion, majesty and canniness, to suggest an artist who has sadly probed the depths of his artistic vision as he has entered the twilight of his years.[21]

There was no bitterness but also no joyous sense of reconciliation. Strehler's Prospero was a man who had learned that a Duke has duties. Strehler described him as

a bad political thinker, who was only preoccupied with his stars, magic, and his books, and with the fact that his brother took the power away from him. At the end, Prospero understood his mistakes. He will go back to Milan, to be a better leader who intends to dedicate the rest of his life to his people, without magic, and give "every third thought" to his "grave."

Strehler's interpretation of Prospero emphasized the education of those who wronged him rather than vengeance. This was a Prospero who passed through hate to understanding and reconciliation. "Shakespeare is a humanist rather than a pessimist. His pessimism is that of a humanist, because it leads to a deeper truth," Strehler said.[22] Strehler replaced Kott's "bitterness" with sadness, which was most obvious in the epilogue. Tino Carraro began his last speech in his own persona; he removed his magic cape, put on a simple shirt, and walked into the audience as the actor and not as Prospero.

The rather gentle characterization of Prospero at the end of the play did not, however, mean that the contradictions inherent in Shakespeare's conception of the role were ignored. They may not have been demonstrated in black-and-white terms, but they were clearly, even though sometimes subtly, suggested. Prospero's role as oppressor of Caliban was expressed in body posture, action, props, and tone of voice. He glided easily from the role of a tyrant into that of a gentle or angry father, and from the actor Carraro into the role of the artist/director. In his directorial role, he handed Ariel her costume for her role as "nymph o' th' sea" (1.2.301), in which disguise she then reeled Ferdinand in on a fishing rod from the depths of the orchestra pit. At various times during the performance Prospero stepped aside or joined the audience to observe the spectacle he created, from the chilling first moment to the climactic banquet scene, with blackened skies and a frightening horde of spirits. Out of this night, wrote Benedict Nightingale, swooped Ariel, transformed into a black harpy,

squawling and squawking out his accusations and threats. Once again, it was stunning; ... we were beginning to get a sense of character, atmosphere, and the issues ominously at stake.[23]

Strehler is one of the few directors with the imaginative generosity and craftsmanship to create such a spectacle, which balanced the illusionistic and anti-illusionistic elements in interpreting Shakespeare's text, and still managed to point the audience to the contradictions within Prospero's character.

A comparison of Strehler's productions of *King Lear* (1972) and *The Tempest* will demonstrate Strehler's flexibility and the thoroughness with which he reconceives the artistic requirements of each new production. Far from being a "captive of the past," this ability moves him very close to Brecht's precept of starting at point zero.

The two productions had many similarities: both made use of clown techniques, emphasized metatheatrical aspects of the texts, and the same actor, Tino Carraro, played Lear and Prospero. As mentioned before, Strehler also highlighted the male–female dichotomy of Shakespeare's texts by having a woman play both Ariel and the Fool. Despite their similarities, Strehler relied on radically different models. Prospero, for example, cast in the role of director who stands outside of the action and orchestrates it, often graphically moving his hands in time with the central action, contrasted with Lear, whom Strehler cast as a clown. Furthermore, the clown imagery used in the two stagings stemmed from two completely different theatrical traditions; *The Tempest* employed *commedia dell'arte* motifs, whereas *Lear* used clown characters from the circus tradition.

Even within the context of *The Tempest* Strehler used different clown traditions. Trinculo and Stephano were drawn directly from *commedia dell'arte*, whereas Ariel was presented in a French Pierrot costume traditionally associated with Jean-Gaspard "Baptiste"

Deburau, who performed during the early nineteenth century in
Paris (and who was popularized for modern audiences in 1945 by
Jean-Louis Barrault in Marcel Carné's film *Les Enfants du Paradis*).
There can be no denying that a relationship exists between the
various European clown traditions, but Strehler's choices were well
researched and precise and did not constitute a thoughtless takeover
or simple search for variety. Deburau marked an important development in the character of Pierrot. He liberated him from being a
low *commedia* servant, who was usually the recipient of physical
abuse from his master and the other *zanni*, and turned him into a
sophisticated trickster with supernatural qualities, who was more
likely to deliver a kick and disappear than to receive a kick and cry
about it. Deburau also brought a spiritual quality to the character
that has been associated with it ever since. His Pierrot had
thoughtful, sensitive eyes, and his movements, while often slapstick
and reminiscent of Arlecchino, were just as likely to be graceful and
poetic.[24] This version of Pierrot allowed Strehler to communicate
the superiority of Ariel as a character of dignity, if still a servant. By
contrasting his Ariel with the lumpen figures of Arlecchino/
Brighella and Pulcinella from the older Italian *commedia dell'arte*
tradition, which he chose for Trinculo and Stephano, Strehler
stayed true to the comic spirit of all three characters.

In contrast to the island of Strehler's *The Tempest*, which was filled
with light sporadically interrupted by shade, *King Lear* was presented in a circus tent with rope holds pulling down a canvas awning
and filled with darkness sporadically interrupted by points of light.
It can be seen from Strehler's successive productions of Goldoni's
The Servant of Two Masters that his concept of *commedia dell'arte* is
closely linked to visibility, thus the predominant darkness of *King
Lear* made the *commedia* style inappropriate. Strehler needed a clown
motif that suited the pervasive darkness of the play. He used,
therefore, the traditional figures of the *auguste* clown and whitefaced
clown which derive from the circus, and which fitted perfectly into
the relationship of Lear and his Fool. The *auguste* clown originally
interacted with the ringmaster, who had the utilitarian function of
keeping the show going and guiding the animal acts on and off with
his whip. The ringmaster was an authority figure and a part of
normal society. His whip was the symbol of authority over the
auguste clown and was frequently used in a comic, violent way
against him. When the animal acts at the circus were expanded, the

11   Carraro as Lear and Ottavia Piccolo as the Fool in Strehler's *King Lear*,
Piccolo Teatro, Milan, 1972. *Photo: Luigi Ciminaghi.*

utilitarian function of the ringmaster became more important, and
he had less time to devote to the clown. The clowns developed the
new character of the whitefaced clown to free themselves from their
dependence on the ringmaster. Yet the whitefaced clown inherited
many characteristics of the ringmaster; he was still an authority
figure who thought of himself as a "normal" person as opposed to
the *auguste* clown who was obviously antisocial. In this context, Lear
is, of course, the whitefaced authority figure who represents the
cultural norm, while the Fool is the *auguste* clown who represents
disrespect for cultural norms (see illustration 11). *King Lear*, already
structured as a voyage of discovery, allowed Strehler to use the
auguste–whitefaced clown relationship to communicate this voyage
in a similar way. Lear, who must be brought from the darkness of his
authoritarian normative view of the world to true enlightenment,
was educated by the Fool.

In Shakespeare's text of *The Tempest*, the characters of Trinculo and Stephano are already influenced by the Italian *commedia dell'arte* tradition. Strehler's twist was to portray them as *commedia* characters at an early stage in the tradition. They wore not the highly individualistic character masks of later *commedia*, but a more generic form of the half-mask. Nevertheless, Strehler's Trinculo had many similarities with the Pulcinella figure and Stephano with both Arlecchino and Brighella. Stephano wore a sailor-type hat, reminiscent of Arlecchino's, and Trinculo wore the distinctive tall hat unique to the Pulcinella character. Brighella, who originated like Arlecchino in Bergamo, is traditionally more crafty than Pulcinella, who comes from southern Naples; Strehler emphasized this point by having Trinculo/Pulcinella speak in a southern Italian dialect, while Stephano/Arlecchino/Brighella used a northern speech. Similarly, Brighella is normally presented as dishonest, unscrupulous, opportunistic, and vengeful, characteristics which Strehler found easy to emphasize in his Stephano. Pulcinella, on the other hand, is famous for his light quick movements, and the chief quality of his speech is "a kind of stupid wit or witty stupidity essentially gross and vulgar."[25] Trinculo's gestures made reference to bodily functions which stressed verbal puns in the Pulcinella mode. When he said, "Nor go neither; but you'll lie, like dogs, and yet say nothing neither" (3.2.18–19), Trinculo kicked back sand in a manner resembling a dog covering its urine.

Superficially, the fact that the director used the stylistic vocabulary of the circus in *Lear* and of the *commedia* in *The Tempest* might seem to corroborate Kott's contention that Strehler is the "prisoner of his past" – after all, both conventions involve a stylization of manner and costume associated with traditions of farce. But they were used to very different effect in the two productions. Strehler took Shakespeare's specification of Ariel as "an airy spirit" literally and had Ariel fly through the air, to the delight of the audience. Yet by exposing the "magic" which allowed her to soar through the heights on a simple rope, and by modeling Ariel after Deburau's Pierrot, Strehler used metatheatrical techniques to remind the audience that they were seeing a play in a theatre. The device created a distance between audience and stage necessary to reflect on the voyage of discovery presented in *The Tempest* in which magic, and thus escape, was ultimately rejected. The path towards an alternative solution had to be found by the spectators themselves. The Deburau Pierrot allowed Strehler at the same time to make a social statement about Prospero's assistant. The theatricality of *commedia* ensured that the audience was accompanied on its journey by the most delightful entertainment. The constructed circus-world of *King Lear*, in which Lear was cast as a clown, was the contrary meta-theatrical image to the magical island in which Prospero reigned as director. *King Lear* ultimately represented a voyage of escape, from darkness into light.

The use of magic and metamagic and farce and metafarce in these two productions may have made Strehler vulnerable to the criticism expressed by Kott and Planchon. The greatness of Strehler's directorial art, however, derives precisely from his understanding that there are no pure stylistic categories. The power comes rather from a dialectic between such categories. Brecht shared this view and his influence on Strehler is undeniable. Moreover, this dialectic has to be seen in conjunction with that which exists between psychologically based theories, such as those developed by Stanislavsky, and the theatricality of Copeau and Jouvet. With his production of *The Tempest*, the musician Strehler demonstrated how well he has mastered all these influences by presenting the multilayered text in a clear and highly entertaining way. Like Brecht, Strehler refuses to dismiss either "emotion" or "reason"; both directors keep emotions on a leash by a corrective use of *gestus*. Strehler's leash, however, happens to be longer.

NOTES

1 David L. Hirst, *The Tempest: Text and Performance* (London: Macmillan, 1984), 43. Quotations from *The Tempest* refer to the Arden Edition, ed. Frank Kermode (London: Methuen, 1964). All translations from the French and German are my own.

2 Unless otherwise noted, quotations from Strehler come from this interview.

3 On the occasion of his *Tempest* production, Strehler invited scholars and theatre practitioners to an international symposium on Shakespeare's work of his late period. Roger Planchon, one of the participants, summarized his thoughts about the subject which he had developed during the symposium, in a paper which he delivered to the French Shakespeare Society on 17 Nov. 1979, at the Ecole Normale Supérieure, Rue d'Ulm, in Paris. The text was translated into German by Marina Spinu, and published in *Theater Heute* under the title "Noch weiter – zurück zu Shakespeares Mythen, Göttern and Geistern" (Mar. 1981): 32–8.

4 Jan Kott, "Prospero or the Director: Giorgio Strehler's *The Tempest* (Piccolo Teatro di Milano)," trans. Barbara Krzywicka, *Theater* 10 (Spring 1979): 117–22 (quotation on 119). "This theater" refers to the Piccolo Teatro.

5 Planchon, *Theater Heute*, 37, 32, 34. The German translation uses both "das Übersinnliche" (supranatural) and "das Übernatürliche" (supernatural).

6 "Das Theater des Shakespeare" in Bertolt Brecht, *Werkausgabe* (Frankfurt am Main: Suhrkamp, 1967), 16: 585–94.

7 Lombardo's article, called simply "The Tempest," was included (without pagination) in the English program prepared by the Piccolo Teatro for the American tour of the production in 1984. Lombardo translated *The Tempest* for Strehler's production.

8 Giorgio Strehler, *Un théâtre pour la vie. Réflexions, entretiens, notes de travail*, trans. Emmanuelle Genevois (Paris: Librairie Arthème Fayard, 1980), 121.

9 "Prospero or the Director," 118.

10 See Hirst, *The Tempest*, 62; Kott, "Prospero or the Director," 117–18. The video of the production was made by Carlo Battistoni, who was also assistant director to Strehler for *The Tempest*. It is interesting that the usual process seemed to be reversed: film tends to belie the mechanisms of production, but this time the camera revealed more technical devices than the stage production did.

11 *Los Angeles Herald Examiner*, 9 July 1984.

12 *New York Times*, 27 July 1984.

13 Brecht, *Brecht on Theatre*, trans. John Willett (London: Methuen, 1964), 233.

14 Kott, "Prospero or the Director," 119. While Kott refers to Ariel as "he," and Shakespeare's text gives this support, Strehler's Ariel is – while not specifically feminine – clearly female. I find it natural, therefore, to refer to Ariel as "she" or "her."

15 *Ibid.*, 122.

16 John Willett offered the following definition of *gestus* in *The Theatre of Bertolt Brecht*, 3rd ed. (London: Methuen, 1967), 173: "It is at once gesture and gist, attitude and point: one aspect of the relationship between two people, studied singly, cut to essentials and physically or verbally expressed. It excludes the psychological, the subconscious, the metaphysical unless they can be conveyed in concrete terms."

17 *New York Times*, 27 July 1984.

18 *Los Angeles Herald Examiner*, 9 July 1984.

19 "Prospero or the Director," 120.

20 Telephone conversation between Pia Kleber and Michel Bataillon on 2 July 1991.

21 *New York Times*, 27 July 1984.

22 In an interview with Rosette C. Lamont, "Shakespeare with a Touch of Commedia dell'Arte," *New York Times*, 22 July 1984.
23 *New York Times*, 5 Aug. 1984.
24 See John H. Towsen, *Clowns* (New York: Hawthorn Books, 1976), 79–82.
25 Allardyce Nicoll, *The World of Harlequin* (New York: Cambridge University Press, 1963), 87.

CHAPTER 8

Between the curtain and the grave:
the Taganka in the Hamlet gulag

Spencer Golub

The cold prison of life surrounding Hamlet has made him its
prisoner, but the prisoner has become a rebel.

Nikolay Okhlopkov, "From the Producer's Exposition of
Hamlet" (1955)

The imagination and the spiritual strength of Shakespeare's
evildoers stopped short at a dozen corpses. Because they had no
ideology.

Aleksandr Solzhenitsyn, *The Gulag Archipelago* (1974)

As early as 1775, Hamlet's "To be or not to be" was translated into
Russian as "To live or not to live."[1] The social question of how one
lives in an oppressive culture engendered in Russians the existential
question of how one lives at all. Historically in Russia, personal and
social identity, already made fragile by the passage of time and the
inevitability of death, have been invalidated by the authority of the
state.

In his essay "Hamlet and Don Quixote" (1860), Ivan Turgenev
ascribed the term "Hamletism" to the condition of superfluity, of
unheroic self-absorption among members of the Russian intelli-
gentsia. Following the Russian Revolution of 1917, "Hamletism"
became synonymous with the retrograde self-advertisement and
morbidity of the politically disenfranchised and socially alienated of
all classes. The condition constituted one last ripple of individualism
in a sea of officially prescribed collective anonymity and pronounced one unfit and unworthy to participate in the new social
order. Still, as Hamlet's inner world "seized on the phantom" of his
father to achieve personal and social definition, so have Soviet artists
and audiences grasped at the Prince's lessons in conscience, in
reading their times, and in the tenuousness and untenableness of all
realities.[2]

While by now Russians generally consider Hamlet to have always

158

been one of their own, he was, in fact, slow to learn their language. *Hamlet* was first performed in Russia in 1748, in what has been called a "garbled translation" by the neoclassical man of letters A. P. Sumarokov. Sumarokov, who called Shakespeare "a boor," reduced *Hamlet's* varied language to a succession of uniformly stately rhymed couplets. He likewise "corrected" the plot, making Polonius rather than Claudius King Hamlet's murderer and ending the play happily by marrying Hamlet to Ophelia. Sumarokov admitted that his *Hamlet* "bears very little resemblance to Shakespeare's tragedy." Russia was first exposed to a playable *Hamlet* in the German translation by A. W. Schlegel and Ludwig Tieck (*c.* 1795). Mikhail Vronchenko published the first Russian translation (as opposed to adaptation) of *Hamlet* in 1828, but it was workman-like and unstageable. It was followed by Nikolay Polevoy's free and abridged translation, which was performed by "the Russian Kean," Pavel Mochalov, in an epochal production at Moscow's Maly Theatre in 1837, and continued to be used into the twentieth century. The nineteenth century also saw translations of *Hamlet* which combined Polevoy's and Andrey Kroneberg's (1849) poetic versions with Nikolay Ketcher's prose rendering. The first modern Russian translation was by the Grand Duke Konstantin Nikolaevich, the czar's cousin and a poet, who performed his *Hamlet* in 1902 at the Hermitage Theatre, St. Petersburg, with a company of military officers for an exclusive audience. In the twentieth century, there have been professional performances of *Hamlet* in Russian translations by Mikhail Lozinsky and by Anna Radlova, the wife of Soviet stage director Sergey Radlov.

It was not, however, until poet-novelist Boris Pasternak's highly idiomatic translation of *Hamlet* premiered in Vera Redlikh's 1939 production at the Red Torch Theatre of Novosibirsk that the Danish Prince was heard to speak fluent Russian. Russians familiar with the English text were startled at how well Pasternak had captured the essence and nuances of even the minor characters' speech. Mikhail Morozov, who completed a literal translation himself, remarked: "We have never been so intimately acquainted with the real persons of great tragedy. We had not even known that it was possible to be so closely acquainted with them." Pasternak's translation was published in 1940 and was introduced to the world via Grigory Kozintsev's 1964 film *Hamlet*. Although Pasternak also translated *Romeo and Juliet, Othello, Antony and Cleopatra, Henry IV,*

Parts 1 and 2, and *King Lear* for the Soviet stage, it was *Hamlet* which best captured his own celebrated social and moral dilemmas.

Pasternak viewed Hamlet not as a weak, vacillating figure but as someone who acts out of a sense of "duty and self-abnegation." "Hamlet," he stated, "is chosen as the judge of his own time and the servant of a more distant time." *Hamlet* is a drama of "entrusted destiny," the poet's heroic higher calling to a fate outside of his control, which makes him an avenger and yet which is served by his personal integrity. Pasternak likened both Hamlet and his original creation Yury Zhivago to the Christ at Gethsemane, who confronts his solitary fate with "resigned but dignified acceptance." This "passive sufferer" was offered by Pasternak as a positive alternative to the programed, unconflicted action of the new Soviet man.[3] The objective acceptance and self-denial of Pasternak's Hamlet proffered a different kind of heroic social ideal to the Russian public.

Pasternak's poem "Hamlet," ostensibly written by the eponymous hero of his novel *Doctor Zhivago*, was still banned at the time of Pasternak's death on 30 May 1960 and was recited illegally by the mourners at his funeral. The poem speaks of the poet's isolation and of the difficulty of life, two prevailing themes in Russian and Soviet culture, which became more pronounced during the gray years of Socialist Realism (1934–53), with its imposed anti-poetic resoluteness and concreteness:

> And yet, the order of the acts has been schemed and plotted,
> And nothing can avert the final curtain's fall.
> I stand alone. All else is swamped by Pharisaism.
> To live life to the end is not a childish task.[4]

The dilemma articulated and embodied by Pasternak impacted dramatically upon the consciousness of Yury Lyubimov, whose production of Pasternak's translation of *Hamlet* at Moscow's Taganka Theatre (29 November 1971 – 13 July 1980) was the most famous of his generation. When asked upon what principles the Taganka was based, Lyubimov quoted Pasternak's "Hamlet"'s opening lines:

> The stir is over. I step forth on the boards.
> Leaning against an upright at the entrance,
> I strain to make the far-off echo yield
> A cue to the events that may come in my day.[5]

Lyubimov, who had visited Pasternak in 1958 in internal exile at his home in Peredelkino, was saddened and angered by the humiliation that the poet had endured. He was confused by the two letters of self-criticism which Pasternak wrote, expressing culpability for having written the banned novel *Doctor Zhivago*. The book had won him the Nobel Prize for Literature in 1958, but he was forced by the Soviet government to turn it down.

Pasternak wrote that life is spent "in a struggle with one's self." Renato Poggioli remarked that Pasternak regarded "the self as an object rather than subject," a receptive vehicle for ego-less action in behalf of mankind, an entity to be valued for its sacrifice. Pasternak's heroic struggle in this direction led to courageous as well as compromised action. Pasternak's prototype in this regard was the actor, and he clearly regarded both Hamlet and himself as such. This reaffirmation of the actor's role, which countered its negative depiction in nineteenth- and twentieth-century Russian literature by Nikolay Gogol and Maksim Gorky, respectively, was furthered in the Taganka Theatre's production of the Pasternak *Hamlet*. The actor's brave act of self-nomination in "the spotlight's cold flame" (poetess Anna Akhmatova) exploded the purposeful misrepresentations which produced moral failure in Soviet life.[6] By 1971, the Moscow Theatre of Drama and Comedy on Taganka Square, which Lyubimov took over in 1964, had become a social and moral emblem for the Soviet avant-garde and for the Soviet theatre-going public, which fought to gain admission to its productions. It *was* Hamlet, a theatrical savior disguised as a social disorderer.

Following a two-year imbroglio over his proposed production of an adaptation which conflated several of Shakespeare's history plays into a single evening, Lyubimov turned to Pasternak's translation of *Hamlet*. In the beginning, many Taganka actors and its leading actress, Alla Demidova, had clamored to play Hamlet. Lyubimov selected Vladimir Vysotsky, he said, because he believed that as a poet, Vysotsky could best understand another poet (Hamlet via Shakespeare and Pasternak), and as a singer, he could discover the musical subtext in Hamlet's speech. In his career, Vysotsky wrote 900 songs and poems, which, in Lyubimov's words, offered "an irreplaceable chronicle of daily life in the Soviet Union of the past twenty years" (*c.* 1960–80). Demidova, who played Gertrude, recalled that the role of Hamlet came with difficulty to Vysotsky. It was too close to his own celebrated persona, which he did not want simply to replicate. Naturally, his interpretation of the role evolved over the course of ten years, but throughout, Vysotsky's was a

somewhat mature, thoughtful, even mournful Hamlet. He recog-
nized that in this life of struggle, the prisoner is punished for acting
independently and for speaking his thoughts aloud.

By design and historical circumstance, the Taganka, Lyubimov
and Vysotsky co-created a multi-voiced Hamlet, which perilously
advertised their iconic celebrity and contemporaneity. Lyubimov
had earlier investigated the "talent's crown of thorns" theme in his
stagings of plays featuring independent thinkers at war with authority, such as Brecht/Galileo (*Life of Galileo*, starring Vysotsky,
1966), Mayakovsky (*Listen!*, 1967) and Molière (*Tartuffe*, 1968).
Like Mayakovsky, the democratic voice of his generation and a
prince in the new Soviet society of the early 1920s, Vysotsky
manifested Hamletian disgust with the social mechanism and artistically critiqued it. Mayakovsky ended as a suicide. Like Molière, a
symbol of suppressed genius for Soviet artists, who collapsed while
playing Argan in *The Imaginary Invalid*, Vysotsky played Hamlet, his
favorite role, at the edge of his life. In his 217th and final performance of the role, on 13 July 1980 (he had rehearsed it for about two
years prior to performing it for ten), Vysotsky was ill. He period-
ically forgot his lines and had to rush off stage for medication.
During this performance, the heavy curtain which constituted the
production's major scenic device accidentally landed upon a coffin
on which Gertrude was sitting and revealed to her the ghost of
Hamlet's father, who had been hidden behind it. Twelve days later
Vysotsky was dead. With him died the production, since, by the
time of his death, Vysotsky *was* Hamlet for the Taganka company
and its audience.[7]

This Hamlet shared the courage of Vysotsky's convictions. His
antipathy to "stupidity, mediocrity, vileness" and "double-
dealing," as well as his reputation for "singing hooliganism," opting
for "honest death" over "tortured life," inverted Turgenev's model
of passivity, self-pity, and superfluity set forth in his seminal essay,
"Hamlet and Don Quixote" (1860). Vysotsky's poem, "My
Hamlet," written several years after the Taganka premiere, suggested his identification with and appropriation of the role.

When parts and props from this *Hamlet* were recycled in the
Taganka's commemorative production *The Poet Vladimir Vysotsky*
(1981), the conflation of actor and character into cultural icon was
complete. Both *Hamlet* and *Vladimir Vysotsky* marked the appearance
of a ghost and the disappearance of a man, the experiencing of an

absence. The "silence" which concluded *Hamlet* was extended into life and given a voice in *Vladimir Vysotsky*, as cast members took up their Hamlet's familiar stage position, seated on the floor, their backs against the theatre's back wall. Actors and audience together contemplated the passing of their Hamlet and perhaps of the Taganka's Hamletian moment of truth and actualization on the world's stage.

Vysotsky's Hamlet understood and accepted the existence and persistence of evil in the world. He did not seek to prove Claudius' villainy but rather to disprove it and so to break free from the tyranny of violence. This indirectly recalled the aftermath of the Russian Revolution, in which the party leadership debated and approved the moral and social efficacy of prolonged violence to counter lingering resistance. The danger of adopting the tyrant's means to overthrow him and by so doing becoming the tyrant had been the message of Evgeny Shvarts' fairy-tale plays of the Stalin era. Lyubimov believed that *Hamlet* called forth "a universe of unequalled violence" in Shakespeare's work but also offered the most direct and pervasive reference to the Divine Presence.

From the beginning, the Taganka Hamlet knew that he was a man alone, whose mission it was to teach people what troubled their souls, to help them to transcend mundane reality. Shakespeare has traditionally fed Russia's spiritual hunger. This interpretation clearly honored Pasternak's conception of Hamlet's role and suggested as well a sort of neo-symbolist God-seeking. Hamlet was infected with something of the spirit of the Thaw (i.e., post-Stalin) generation of the 1960s, which encouraged boundary-less art, with its boundless enthusiasm for life, its reckless openness, its belief in its power to help people to see and experience the world anew and to aspire to spiritual perfection via questioning and agitation. The ghost that haunted this Hamlet was not his father's but his brother's. His was a generational voice. "We see in his eyes," wrote Soviet critic Sergey Yutkevich, "the eyes of our contemporary."

Vysotsky's Hamlet was impatient with the "external obstacles" which mitigated his freedom to act. He moved through his "To be or not to be" soliloquy without pause, "resisting delusion," as he believed Russian culture had charged him to do. He whipped himself into the action, moving quickly, like the production's cinematic mise en scène, from moment to moment. As the years progressed, Hamlet's sense of urgency was intensified by Vysotsky's and his generation's sense that time was running out. Vysotsky, who began as a romantic rationalist, believing in the possibilities of this uncompromised life rather than in the possibly vain promises of the next (more the proto-Bolshevik Satin than the quasi-religious pilgrim Luka, in Gorky's *The Lower Depths*, 1902), eventually came to be imbued with the play's mystical irrationalism. Vysotsky became more aware of life as an unanswerable proposition. In ten years, the audience's social conscience had grown, in some measure as a result of Vysotsky's influence. They had been brought to the point where they understood the questions of man's value, of justice and violence, and could be asked once again, after a long, enforced respite, to confront and question the "imponderables." The social and philosophical implications of self-willed and externally enforced death, and of a spiritually deprived living death, which had fallen into programmed disuse as subjects for theatrical discourse, were revived. Once again, "to be or not to be" *was* the question, in a meaningful and not merely a conventional sense.

In response to a journalist's question of how he would stage Hamlet's most famous monologue, Meyerhold answered, "Radically. I would cut it [out entirely]."[8] Meyerhold understood that familiarity breeds contempt but also that in his day and especially in his voice, this question could not be asked. The prescribed, mythologized rationalism of a tyrannical world, Denmark or the Soviet Union, obviates the posing of rational questions, except, perhaps, in an irrational voice. Hamlet must be mad, which Russian culture suspected from the beginning, and the means by which his story is told must likewise be alogical and absurd. In his productions adapted from Bulgakov's *The Master and Margarita* (Taganka premiere, 6 April 1977) and from the works of Gogol (*The Inspector's Recounting*; Taganka premiere, May 1978), Lyubimov demonstrated his affinity for "madmen" and his understanding of the madness of modern Soviet history.

The Taganka production freed the play and the player from the imprisonment of *Hamlet*'s theatrical tradition, while locating the Prince in a metaphorical Soviet gulag (prison camp system). The Taganka reconciled the easy oppositions of power/powerlessness, will/will-lessness, activity/passivity, superman/common man projected upon *Hamlet* by Soviet criticism and engendered by the aura of "putrescent Hamletism" which, the late director Nikolay Akimov said, the play creates. Akimov's eccentric formalist *Hamlet* (Lozinsky translation, Vakhtangov Theatre, 1932) sought to remove the "tombstone of mysticism" fashioned for the play by Gordon Craig's 1912 Moscow Art Theatre and Michael Chekhov's 1924 Moscow Art Theatre 2 interpretations. Akimov's paunchy, "bourgeois-fied" Hamlet (played by the comedian Goriunov), victimized equally by his (feudally) "conditioned reflexes about the loss of his throne and the decaying action initiated by his humanist education," balanced unsteadily on the path that led to Socialist Realism in 1934. In his production, the "mad" Ophelia drowned while drunk, and the "mad" Hamlet pondered only whether to kill the king while getting drunk in a bar. Akimov's Hamlet was not so much a philosopher as "a political intriguer" (the Ghost was a political ploy perpetrated by Hamlet) whose actions became comprehensible to an unsophisticated audience. The production's composer Dmitry Shostakovich used Hamlet's recorder speech to ridicule proletarian musical hacks. Akimov's lavish sets reversed the severe constructivist experiments of the 1920s. Akimov, who was accused of demonstrating a "flagrantly nihilistic attitude toward the classics," cut most of the graveyard scene.

Sergey Radlov's 1938 production at his own theatre (Anna Radlova translation) signaled Socialist Realism's arrival in a mise en scène which meaningfully deployed individuals in relation to groups. The production's monumental character portraits, which threatened to crush Hamlet from above, prefigured Kozintsev's multiple iconic references to Claudius' (i.e., Stalin's) "revolution from above" and the resultant "cult of personality" in his film version (1964). It also underscored Russia's historical paranoia, in particular Stalinism's "introverted insularity," which was served by spying, conspiracy, and informing. These were time-honored national practices. Significantly, Soviet productions of *Hamlet* in the 1930s were not updated but were set in the Renaissance, thereby discouraging audiences from drawing parallels with contemporary figures and situations.[9]

Like the "spiritually dead people" who emerged from Stalin's prison camps, the mad, haunted Prince appears at Elsinore as "a corpse among the living, pretending to be alive and full of feeling." "But why pretend," asks camp survivor Evgenia Ginzburg, quoting poet Aleksandr Blok, "To be accepted by society, / One needs only to conceal the rattling of one's bones." Hamlet the prisoner, like these survivors, is "ennobled and purified" by his prison, and by "the climate of apparitions" (Pasternak) it engenders. His suffering, not his vengeance, reveals and frames his most human qualities.

The advent of apocalyptic time, signaled by the arrival of his father's ghost, "stopped the clock" of Hamlet's life, as the experience of arrest and imprisonment did that of the camp inmate. The prisoner's spiritual inner emigration laid bare the surreality of the material world outside. Hamlet's madness bears witness to his times rather than conspiring with them, revealing the horror of prison life, via the prisoner's "Aesopian" code, to a public still largely imprisoned. The madness resurfaced in Aleksandr Solzhenitsyn's accounts in the 1960s and 1970s of the Soviet gulag, exposing, as did Khrushchev's anti-Stalin "secret speech" of 1954, the real madness, the Soviet state's crimes against its own people. The prisoner's tale reinstates the individual's and society's human dignity. The story's theme, as Pasternak told Stalin in his telephone defense of imprisoned poet Osip Mandelstam (July 1937), is "life and death." While Stalin hung up on Pasternak, the dialogue between life and death registers in every scene of *Hamlet* and is summarized in the "To be or not to be" soliloquy. The Taganka *Hamlet* stressed the post-Stalin era's life theme, survival and salvation, rather than the Stalin era's death theme, revenge. Hamlet's action lost him his "seat near the columns" (Pasternak), his noble birthright, but gained him a noble rebirth, as the once solitary actor reabsorbed into the ensemble buried the Stalinist charge of cultish individualism in an open grave.[10]

Michael Chekhov's anthroposophic Hamlet had been inspired by the Ghost (a "pure shaft of light" symbolizing "the unalloyed voice of revolutionary conscience") to infiltrate and dissolve Elsinore's Gothic medieval darkness. Vysotsky's protest-singing Hamlet addressed the culpability of fathers (a role Stalin perfected in public and ignored in private), who had yet to confess their guilt. Hamlet's mousetrap play and the testimony of his overall action addressed the shadowy absence of a trial – that of Claudius for his brother's murder. His testimony of conscience sought to balance the "sincere confessions," which Stalinist forces coerced from prisoners and the rehearsed show trials, which displaced guilt from its rightful source and made a mockery of contrition. While the court at Elsinore dressed in bright colors, Hamlet wore black, mourning the absence of light, of honor, and of beauty. It was four years *after* the Taganka *Hamlet* premiered that Aitmatov and Mukhamedzhanov's *The Ascent of Mount Fuji* (1975) first openly discussed the (Stalinist) guilt of the previous generation. The Taganka Hamlet also was the sole mourner of the ghost of Russian humanism whose epitaph read: "And here art ends; here breathe the soil and fate" (Pasternak). It befell this Hamlet to resist the shadow life of neurasthenic non-resistance to evil, the retreat into "the bliss of penal servitude," that "kind sleep that makes the prisoner king."[11] It was incumbent upon this Hamlet to escape Claudius' mousetrap, the Soviet imprisonment, and to spring a trap of his own.

Vysotsky's uncompromising Hamlet was brilliantly served by Lyubimov's metaphorical "poor theatre" production. Lyubimov presented *Hamlet* "in a torn cloak," as a "rough-draft tragedy," a theatre of the poet and of the street, in accord with the troubadour tradition of his ensemble. Soviet dramatist Nikolay Erdman called Lyubimov, who staged "twenty-three adaptations from novels, poetry, and popular song" at his theatre, the Taganka's only resident playwright. His production of *Hamlet* embodied something of the "montage of attractions" approach pioneered by Meyerhold and his student Sergey Eisenstein in the 1920s and 1930s. Lyubimov attributed his rediscovery of their principles of construction to his work with Shakespeare and the latter's conception of time and space. Lyubimov's montage, breaking down the text into a series of brief episodes, constructed around a strong scenic metaphor, was designed to "shock" or "alienate" the audience and the text. It subverted reality via self-consciously advertised theatrical devices.

Beginning with his fourth production at the Taganka, an adaptation of John Reed's *Ten Days that Shook the World* (Taganka premiere, 2 April 1965), Lyubimov employed Meyerholdian machines for acting and Rembrandtian chiaroscuro effects. These devices exploded the theatrical framing of time and space into a prismatic extrapolation of historical, novelistic, and poetic essences. As the lapsed symbolists and proto-symbolists of the pre-revolutionary period had discovered (e.g., Aleksandr Blok in *The Puppet Show* and Nikolay Evreinov in *A Merry Death*), the torn-up stage, which defamiliarizes its own reality and conventions, allows for rapid and frequent tonal shifts, back and forth between tragedy and farce, reminiscent of Shakespearean technique.

David Borovsky's set for Lyubimov's *Hamlet* began upstage with the exposed, whitewashed wall of the theatre. Against this leaned roughly made metal swords and gauntlets, implements for revenge and torture. Hanging from this wall was a large, rough-hewn wooden cross, which, in a sense, mediated Hamlet's action. The set ended downstage in an open grave, in which the gravediggers dug real dirt. Likewise, a real skull was used for "poor Yorick." Lyubimov told Hedrick Smith:

We used skulls in several different scenes to make people think of the moment of death. Maybe if you think more about that, maybe you will be more decent in your life.[12]

The Stalinist prison camp inmate was intimately acquainted with the lessons and publicity of the grave. Failure to complete his work successfully was announced to the community by the appearance of a coffin bearing the prisoner's name. He was regularly crowded into "Black Marias" (prison transports), into prison cells "only as big as two good-sized graves," and held in descriptively named "kennels" and "standing cells," in which it was physically impossible to sit down. He was isolated and silenced, essentially buried alive. Stalin, "the gravedigger of the Revolution," buried millions of his "children" secretly. Meanwhile, Stalin publicly entombed Lenin, the spiritual brother who disowned him (King Hamlet to his Claudius), at the base of the Kremlin (fortress) wall. Hamlet witnesses the Ghost's extraordinary appearance; Soviet man witnesses the "technological miracle" which preserved Lenin's mortal remains.

The Taganka *Hamlet* began at the open dirt grave, at cockcrow, the point of both death and renewal. There, Vysotsky's Hamlet declaimed, to the accompaniment of his guitar, Pasternak's once forbidden poem "Hamlet" over the dead king and the dead poet. This action signified not so much a call to arms as a spiritual victory already won. Sometimes the actors, hidden in the wings, sang with him, improvising a musical dialogue on the theme of freedom. "The silence of the grave" and the "unanimity of belief" which blanketed Soviet culture for decades was broken. The prisoner's unspoken vow to "suffer in silence," a recognition of the fatality of "careless talk," and Pasternak's enforced creative silence during his lifetime, were evoked and laid to rest. The Taganka *Hamlet* immediately proclaimed its intention to tear down the wall of silence, which separated social classes, contemporaries, and artists from their audience.

However, the wall, in the form of a huge, mobile, coarsely woven hemp curtain, activated by an expensive aluminum track system, followed the Taganka Hamlet everywhere (illustration 12). It

12   Vladimir Vysotsky with Rosencrantz and Guildenstern before the dominating curtain in *Hamlet,* directed by Yury Lyubimov, Taganka Theatre, Moscow, 1971. *Photo: courtesy of Alma Law Archive.*

pushed him like Fate toward the womb-like grave, where the guilty and the just end and where it first encountered him. Ushered in by Yury Butsko's choral music, set to the accompaniment of piano, clarinet, violin, accordion, and contrabass, what appeared at first to represent the Soviet Hamlet's anonymous doom was revealed in the end to be his theatrical salvation.[13] Pasternak wrote that artists use metaphor as a spiritual shorthand measuring the distance "between man's short life and the immense and long-term tasks he sets himself." The curtain and the grave are custom-made metaphors, offering theatre and life a perfect fit. Lyubimov's and Borovsky's treatment of these two scenic metaphors subverted death's mystery and mastery over the Soviet imagination by reversing the theatre audience's anticipation of closure. As in Shakespeare's writing, which "makes vulgar mediocrity snort and rush in on the funereal solemnity of his finales," these metaphors, in their open-endedness, suggested that "no situation as seen by the artist or the thinker is final; every position is the last but one" (Pasternak).

Lyubimov's mise en scène questioned both "reality" and theatrical reality via an editing process which captured the discontinuity of the modern Soviet Hamlet's experience, while honoring Shakespeare's own subversive tactics. In performances of this production, Lyubimov began his notorious practice of signaling his actors with colored flashlight beams to indicate: (red) the performance is going badly; (green) all is well; (white) something in particular is off – the tempo-rhythm of the movement, the audibility of the voices, the naturalness of the acting. As aggravating to the actors but as purposeful was Lyubimov's habit of cutting scenes short at their emotional peaks, so as to effect what he considered to be a cinematic rhythm. Likewise, he rehearsed numerous scenic variants, in order to achieve a cinematic multi-facetedness of perspective. He rehearsed seventeen scenic variants of the scene between Hamlet and the Ghost.

In the climactic duel scene between Hamlet and Laertes, Lyubimov opted for "real" sound over choreographed fury. By striking their own rapiers and daggers together at opposite sides of the stage rather than engaging one another directly with their weapons, the duelists fully engaged the audience's imagination. The sudden outbursts of unrestrained flurries were unmitigated by the audience's and actors' normal fear for the participants' personal safety. This recalled an earlier Polish stage production of Dostoevsky's *Crime and Punishment*, in which Raskolnikov and the pawnbroker together stylized the horror of her axe murder in spatial separation accentuated by light. Perhaps, too, Lyubimov remembered a near-tragic dueling incident from his own acting career. Pasternak came to see Lyubimov, a famous romantic actor in his day, perform in his translation of *Romeo and Juliet* at the Vakhtangov Theatre. During a duel scene,

Lyubimov's rapier broke apart and hurtled into the audience, just missing the head of Pasternak, who was seated in the orchestra. Pasternak joked that Lyubimov had evidently failed to kill him.[14]

The Hamlet–Laertes duel represented a series of movements, rhythmically interrupted by alternating spurts of sound and silence, action and inaction, stitched together by an act of viewer montage. The viewers not only held the overall action of the play together in their minds, and by so doing co-created the performance, they grounded the isolated figure of Hamlet in the larger frame of the court at Elsinore, from which he was alienated. Lyubimov retrieved for the spectators the real danger of Hamlet's predicament from the staginess of his tradition. At the same time, he created a surreality, via the audience's direct participation in Hamlet's inner process and condition.

The Taganka's celebrated *Hamlet* curtain owed much to the pivoting and tracking iconostasis which Vadim Ryndin designed for Nikolay Okhlopkov's 1954 production at the Mayakovsky Theatre. Okhlopkov's *Hamlet*, like Lyubimov's, depicted humanism's victory over tyranny, the spiritual rebirth of Mother Russia embodied in an activist but non-ideological Prince. Both were Hamlets of the Soviet people's "own sufferings," of their "immature soul." In 1947, Okhlopkov had discussed a revolutionary Hamlet, cleansed of indecision in his commitment to complete his plan and, metaphorically, Stalin's Five-Year Plan. The healthy vacillation of Okhlopkov's 1954 Hamlet symbolized the director's abandonment of the pre-scribed certainty of Socialist Realism, his learning to balance, in the post-Stalin Thaw, his new-found freedom with the living memory of his historical imprisonment. Lyubimov's Hamlet, arriving at the end of the Thaw, during the Brezhnev "years of stagnation," stood in a sort of historical no man's land, in which his choices were clear but the state's response to and tolerance of these choices were not.

Lyubimov's and Borovsky's work on this production was likewise influenced by Peter Brook's minimalist *Hamlet*, which premiered in Moscow in 1955 on the first English company tour of the Soviet Union since the Revolution. The bare gray set which Georges Wakhevitch designed for Brook, allowing for rapid and "ingenious" scene changes, contrasted sharply with Okhlopkov's–Ryndin's maximalist plan, with its overbearing iron gates and catacombs, which transformed the world-as-prison metaphor into a literal and oppressive scenic metaphor. Ryndin's biographer, V. Berezhin, stated that his design "re-established the right of a stage setting to be metaphoric" in the post-Stalin Soviet theatre. Critic Aleksandr Anikst suggested that the monumental presence of the prison metaphor in Okhlopkov's mise en scène was intended to invoke its absence or obsolescence in the new free life of the Soviet artist. But whereas Okhlopkov's production utilized visual weight (which resulted in a ponderous tempo) to make its point, Lyubimov's stressed lightness (and speed). In Okhlopkov's production, as in Craig's before it, scenography overwhelmed acting, whereas in Lyubimov's the two collaborated with the audience to create meaning.

The old Taganka theatre, at which *Hamlet* was performed, did not normally make use of a stage curtain. Beginning with his 1969 production of *Mother*, adapted from Gorky's novel, Lyubimov made periodic use of a curtain of light, projected from instruments recessed in the stage floor and aimed at a 30-degree angle towards the audience. So, for the Taganka, the idea of a material curtain represented the invocation of an absent tradition. At the same time, the *Hamlet* curtain inverted the Elizabethan and the Taganka theatre's conception of an absent presence, a convention which the audience creates. The *Hamlet* curtain did more than reveal particular locales and scenes. It dramatized the appearing/disappearing action of theatre itself. In playing upon the expectations of the spectator, it rediscovered and reinvented him. Formalist critic Viktor Shklovsky wrote:

Art develops according to the technical possibilities of the time. The technique of the novel created the stock character. Hamlet was created by stage techniques.[15]

In its symbolic and (stage) managerial functions, the *Hamlet* curtain not only unfolded the play but, to an extent, created it. Theatre embodies the "Hamlet question." It transpires and quickly expires within the womb of time, occupying the stage between the matrices of a moving veil of mystery and illusion and a grave, as warm as a womb and as cold as death. Soviet history in particular has eavesdropped at the curtain and at the grave.

The *Hamlet* curtain was conceived to provide an Elizabethan-like continuous flow across an empty stage (Borovsky's idea) and to impersonate objects and locales which would otherwise have to be built and shifted – solid walls and tapestries, a shawl and swing.

Metaphorically, it suggested a giant snare or "mousetrap" and Hamlet's ensnared, intricately web-like mental and emotional condition. The latter function recalled the mobile, giant screens in Gordon Craig's monodramatic *Hamlet*. In Lyubimov's *Hamlet*, parallel actions were performed on either side of the curtain to create a cinematic split-screen effect. This suggested the "beehive effect" produced in Okhlopkov's *Hamlet* by exposing a cross-section of the inner workings of Elsinore castle to the spectator's gaze.

The *Hamlet* curtain was the tyrant's spider's web, the net in which he caught his subjects and the wall which crushed their spirits, stifled their cries and protected him from them. It was the wind against which the Prince bent his fragile figure and the cloak which protected him from it. It evoked the memory of the cloak with which the Prince shielded his father's ghost in Meyerhold's unrealized plan for staging the play. It invoked the spirit of the Ghost himself as a present absence – as death and the renewal of life, and the millennium and the Renaissance. It was Winston Churchill's "iron curtain" and the great storms of history and revolution that blew it away. It was God and Hamlet's and his world's fate, defined in and by time, space, and nature, and the veil of silence drawn before irrational truth and deathless mystery. It was Prospero's magic cloak, theatrical illusion as succor for and salvation from the tyranny of illusory reality and ineffable meaning. It was the funeral shroud in which Hamlet's corpse and that of his alter ego, Vladimir Vysotsky, were wrapped (the latter in his commemorative production) and the image of their unconquered spirits, which had flown. The curtain captured Hamlet's stitched-together life as dramatist and actor, son and lover, student and avenger, prince and rebel. It also suggested Gogol's capacious and ubiquitous overcoat, stitched together from Slavic traditions, superstitions, and conventions, out of which French critic Melchior de Vögué claimed modern Russian literature had tumbled. Gogol's overcoat doubled Prospero's cloak as the symbolic mantle of the poet and the language of poetry.

By becoming an agent in the action, the curtain ceded its conventional neutrality. It moved in every direction but the traditional one, that is, up and down. It "concealed" characters who remained in plain sight of the audience. It altered and questioned the vantage point of spectatorship, which must unify or select between competing character perspectives on stage. By cloaking himself in the curtain, Hamlet effectively wrapped himself in the spatial and temporal parameters of the present moment, from which he felt compelled to extricate himself but also to serve and to save.

While the movement of the curtain was meant to evoke "the breathing of unsolved mysteries," the breathing quickly became labored. The curtain represented another of Lyubimov's and his designer's habitual attempts to create actor-sensitive decor (following Meyerhold and Evgeny Vakhtangov), compliant with and expressive of the actors'/characters' wills. However, to the company members it seemed that the curtain had a will of its own, which it sought to impose upon them. The sound emitted by the tracking aluminum mechanism drowned out the actors' voices. The rhythm of the curtain's movement dictated the rhythm of the production, usurping an important part of the actors' roles. The curtain even received a curtain call.

Once, while the actors rehearsed Ophelia's burial scene, the aluminum mechanism collapsed, dropping the curtain over the entire stage in an eerie re-enactment of Craig's falling screen fiasco in the dress rehearsal for his *Hamlet*. While Lyubimov's actors escaped with minor injuries, the mechanism and the curtain did not, with the result that the production closed for six months. It was while nursing the tyrant back to health that the actors first came to forge a personal relationship with it as a fellow performer and to recognize it as being a boon to the production.[16] Inadvertently and ironically, the ensemble's rapprochement with the reconstitution of the tyrant realized one of Soviet history's most tragic themes.

In the Taganka *Hamlet*, the curtain lost its tradition of architectural permanence, and in its movement (and the ghostly memory of its permanence) underscored the impermanance of its realm, the stage. We theorize that the Elizabethan stage ended in a stationary scenic façade, anchored by a cosmic canopy. All of this was enfolded by a building whose shape was numerologically determined to reinforce the consistent code of permanence and order.[17] The disordered and disorderly Hamlet could be vicariously embraced by the Elizabethan audience as a hero of their collective imagining, even as the nightmare of irrationalism which he enacted was diminished by the orderly architectural semiotic which contained him.

In *Hamlet*, the Taganka performed the nightmare of Soviet imprisonment and historical erasure. The corpses of the dead, of the "superfluous," "former," and "non-people," which have littered

Soviet history, were swept from the stage by the giant curtain in the production's final image. But their ghosts had already taken flight in the theatre's enactment of tragic loss and heroic retrieval.

NOTES

I have made the transliteration consistent throughout the text and notes, except where publishers have employed different systems in rendering authors' names and the titles of their works.

1 Nikolay Okhlopkov, "Iz rezhisserskoy eksplikatsiy *Gamleta*," *Teatr* 1 (1955): 60, quoted in Michael Sidney McLain, "N. P. Okhlopkov: A Critical Life in the Soviet Theatre," Ph.D. diss., University of Washington, 1982: 246; Aleksandr I. Solzhenitsyn, *The Gulag Archipelago* (New York: Harper and Row, 1974), 173–4; James H. Billington, *The Icon and the Axe. An Interpretive History of Russian Culture* (New York: Random House, 1970), 354–5.

2 Richard Peace, *The Enigma of Nikolai Gogol* (Cambridge University Press, 1981), 175.

3 Pasternak reworked his *Hamlet* translation twelve times, first for director Vsevolod Meyerhold and then for the Moscow Art Theatre, prior to its performance in Novosibirsk. It was first published in 1940 in the journal *The Young Guard* and later that year by the State Literary Publishing House. A 50,000 copy printing was published by the Children's State Publishing House for secondary school students in 1942. Mikhail M. Morozov, *Shakespeare on the Soviet Stage*, trans. David Magarshack (London: Soviet News, 1947), 11, 13, 15–16, 20; Laurence Senelick, *Gordon Craig's Moscow "Hamlet". A Reconstruction* (Westport, CT: Greenwood Press, 1982), 78; Ernest J. Simmons, *English Literature and Culture in Russia* (New York, 1964), 206; Joseph Macleod, *The New Soviet Theatre* (London: Allen and Unwin, 1943), 210; Mikhail Morozov quoted in Joseph Macleod, *Actors Cross the Volga. A Study of the Nineteenth Century Russian Theatre and of Soviet Theatres in War* (London: Allen and Unwin, 1946), 265.

4 Yevgeny Borisovich Pasternak, Foreword, in *Boris Pasternak. Selected Poems*, trans. John Stallworthy and Peter France (New York: Norton, 1982), 41–2; Boris Pasternak, "Hamlet," "The Poems of Yury Zhivago," trans. Bernard Guilbert Guerney, in *Doctor Zhivago*, trans. Max Hayward and Manya Harari (New York: Pantheon, 1958), 433.

5 Mark Bly, "Lyubimov and the End of an Era: An Interview with Peter Sellars," *Yale/Theater* (1984): 9. The Taganka *Hamlet* premiered on 29 Nov. 1971 and closed on 13 July 1980.

6 Boris Pasternak, *Stikhovoreniya i poemy* (Moscow and Leningrad: Gos. Izdat. Khudozhestvennoy Literatury, 1965), 463; Renato Poggioli, *The Poets of Russia* (Cambridge University Press, 1960), 327; Billington, *The Icon and the Axe*, 562; Anna Akhmatova quoted in Nadezhda Mandelstam,

Hope Abandoned, trans. Max Hayward (New York: Atheneum, 1981), 319.

7 Alla Demidova, *Vladimir Vysotsky, kakim znayu i lyublyu* (Moscow: Soyuz teatralnykh deyatelei RSFSR, 1989), 75–6, 80; Youri Lioubimov, *Le feu sacré. Souvenirs d'une vie de théâtre* (Paris: Fayard, 1985), 121, 141–2; Alexander Gershkovich, *The Theater of Yuri Lyubimov. Art and Politics at the Taganka Theater in Moscow*, trans. Michael Yurieff (New York: Paragon House, 1989), 127–8 (originally published in Russian by Chalidze publications, 1986); Sergey Yutkevich, "Gamlet s Taganskoy ploshchadi," *Shekspirovskie chtenie 1978*, ed. A. Anikst (Moscow: Nauka, 1981), 85.

8 Gershkovich, *Theater of Yuri Lyubimov*, 5, 109–10, 115–16, 124, 126, 128; Demidova, *Vladimir Vysotsky*, 87–9, 91–8, 101; Lioubimov, *Le feu sacré*, 95, 193; Eleanor Rowe, *Hamlet: A Window on Russia* (New York University Press, 1976), 158.

9 Alma H. Law, "*Hamlet* at the Vakhtangov," *The Drama Review* 4 (Dec. 1977): 100–2; Nikolai A. Gorchakov, *The Theater in Soviet Russia*, trans. Edgar Lehrman (Freeport, NY: Books for Libraries Press, 1972), 340–1; Juri Jelagin, *Taming of the Arts*, trans. Nicholas Wreden (New York: E. P. Dutton, 1951), 35, 327; Macleod, *The New Soviet Theatre*, 152, 160–3; P. A. Markov, *The Soviet Theatre* (New York: G. P. Putnam's Sons, 1935), 92–3, 97; Andre van Gyseghem, *Theatre in Soviet Russia* (London: Faber and Faber, 1944), 102–5; M. S. Grigor'yov, *Sovetskiy teatr. K tridtsatiletyu sovetskogo gosudarstva* (Moscow: Vserossiyskoe teatral'noe obshchestvo, 1947), 323–5; Alex de Jonge, *Stalin and the Shaping of the Soviet Union* (New York: William Morrow, 1986), 223, 229–30, 242, 272–3; Rowe, *Hamlet: A Window on Russia*, 155; S. Nikulin, *Vysotsky na Taganke. Pervye roli* (Moscow: Soyuzteatr, 1988), 49–50.

10 Eugenia Semyonovna Ginzburg, *Journey into the Whirlwind*, trans. Paul Stevenson and Max Hayward (New York: Harcourt, Brace, and World, 1967), 70–1, 238–9, 341; Nadezhda Mandelstam, *Hope Against Hope*, trans. Max Hayward (New York: Atheneum, 1980), 146, 153–4; Boris Pasternak, "Translating Shakespeare," trans. Manya Harari, in *I Remember. Sketch for an Autobiography*, trans. David Magarshack (Cambridge, MA: Harvard University Press, 1983), 130.

11 Nikulin, *Vysotsky na Taganke*, 52; Billington, *The Icon and the Axe*, 515; Ginzburg, *Journey into the Whirlwind*, 89, 234; Mikhail Shvidkoi, "The Effect of Glasnost: Soviet Theater from 1985 to 1989," trans. Vladimir Klimenko, *Theater* (Fall 1989): 9.

12 Demidova, *Vladimir Vysotsky*, 82, 85; Gershkovich, *Theater of Yuri Lyubimov*, xii–xiii; Nikulin, *Vysotsky na Taganke*, 49–50; Hedrick Smith, quoted in Felicia Londré, "*Hamlet*," in *Shakespeare Around the Globe. A Guide to Notable Postwar Revivals*, ed. Samuel L. Leiter (Westport, CT: Greenwood Press, 1986), 145.

13 Ginzberg, *Journey into the Whirlwind*, 7–9, 100, 104, 165, 296, 316;

Mandelstam, *Hope Against Hope*, 162–3; Mandelstam, *Hope Abandoned*, 592; Tatiana Tchernavin, *We Soviet Women* (New York: E. P. Dutton, 1936), 243; Alex de Jonge, *Stalin*, 214; Yutkevich, "Gamlet s Taganskoy ploshchadi," 84; Nina Tumarkin, *Lenin Lives! The Lenin Cult in Soviet Russia* (Cambridge, MA: Harvard University Press, 1983), 81; Demidova, *Vladimir Vysotsky*, 80, 83–5; Lioubimov, *Le feu sacré*, 85; Nikulin, *Vysotsky na Taganke*, 49–50.

14 Pasternak, *I Remember*, 126, 149; Lioubimov, *Le feu sacré*, 39–40, 95–6; Demidova, *Vladimir Vysotsky*, 77–8, 83; Yutkevich, "Gamlet s Taganskoy ploshchadi," 88.

15 V. Berezkin, *Vadim Ryndin* (Moscow: Iskusstvo, 1974), 120–1, 131, 135, and Aleksandr Anikst, "Remarks at the Conference on Shakespearean Dramaturgy," 22 April 1962 (archives of the All-Russian Theatre Society) quoted in McLain, "N. P. Okhlopkov," 242–3, 245–8, 251–4. McLain offers an excellent, detailed description of Okhlopkov's 1954 production of *Hamlet*, "N. P. Okhlopkov"; Nick Worrall, *Modernism to Realism on the Soviet Stage. Tairov–Vakhtangov–Okhlopkov* (Cambridge University Press, 1989), 182; Nina Velekhova, "The Link of Time: Directing in the Soviet Union," *Theater* (Fall 1989): 30; Viktor Shklovsky, *A Sentimental Journey. Memoirs 1917–1922* (Ithaca: Cornell University Press, 1984), 233; Gershkovich, *Theater of Yuri Lyubimov*, 217.

16 McLain, "N. P. Okhlopkov," 246; Worrall, *Modernism*, 183; Yutkevich, "Gamlet s Takanskoy ploshchadi," 83; Lioubimov, *Le feu sacré*, 39, 95–6; Demidova, *Vladimir Vysotsky*, 77–8, 80, 83; Micky Levy, "David Borovsky Designs for Lyubimov: Recent Productions at Moscow's Taganka Theatre," in *Theatre Crafts* (Nov.–Dec. 1978): 35, 57–58.

17 George R. Kernodle, "The Open Stage: Elizabethan or Existentialist," *Shakespeare Survey* 12 (1959): 1–7.

CHAPTER 9

Woman scorned: Antony and Cleopatra at Moscow's Vakhtangov Theatre

Irena R. Makaryk

Writing in 1969, Irving Wardle, the *Times* literary critic touring Czechoslovakia, found that the theatre in eastern Europe was not a mere "adornment" to be forgotten in times of stress, but rather it was bound up with politics, and politics "are inseparable from the rest of life – and from the sense of history."[1] In the Soviet Union the apparent seamlessness of life and theatre has also been underscored by repeated assertions of the harmonious unity (rather than opposition) of performance and criticism. Sof'ia Nels, for example, claimed that all Shakespearean performances are closely tied to, and are an accurate reflection of, Soviet literary criticism. V. Kemenov went even further by insisting that there cannot be a conflict between Shakespearean scholarship and the staging of Shakespeare's plays.[2]

This chapter will focus on the consequences for the place of woman in such a totalizing view of theatre and criticism by examining the reviews of Evgenii Simonov's 1971 production of *Antony and Cleopatra*. In many ways synecdoches of "official" post-1934 Soviet readings of Shakespeare, these are necessarily and profoundly conservative, imposing, as they do, the grid of Socialist Realist "optimistic" tragedy on the play. In addition to confirming and supporting "high Soviet" clichés, formulaic readings logically lead to the espousal of patriarchal and centralist ideals.

Whether the reviewers tell the full story of the performance is difficult to say. Certainly unanimity is found not only among the critics describing this production, but also in the echoing confirmations of the later scholarly overviews of the period, as well as in the reminiscences of the lead actor, Mikhail Ul'ianov. However, traditionally Soviet reviewers have taken one of three possible stances: as "neutral" observers describing and evaluating performances; as "betrayers" criticizing an unorthodox production for its deviance; or as crypto-apologists "rewriting" productions in the terminology of the old formulas, thus shielding them from the attacks of officialdom. The task of deciphering which of the three aims the reviewer has taken up is made more difficult by the fact that the Soviet theatre has, since 1934 especially, been a resourceful one, often surviving by recourse to allegory, metaphor, and ambiguity.

Despite hints of departure from tradition, the Vakhtangov production was implicitly interpreted by three Moscow reviewers as observing the formula of traditional optimistic tragedy. What made these conservative readings possible was the continguity and complementarity of the vision of director, reviewer, and (later) scholar on one point: the decentering of Cleopatra. Thus the result is that performance and criticism coincided rather than parted company, supporting the anxious and insistent rhetoric of scholars like Nels and Kemenov. On all sides, Cleopatra was scorned as obstacle in the hero's path to glory; as foreigner; as woman who feels too much; as heroine much too closely allied to comedy for ideological comfort; and, finally, as nationalist who connives behind Antony's imperialistic back.

Perhaps not surprisingly, this approach to Cleopatra closely resembles the first (and male) rewriting of her history by Octavius Caesar whose narrative (as Lucy Hughes-Hallett has most recently and forcefully argued) was grounded upon four "universal" principles of Roman truth:

firstly, foreigners are inferior; secondly, women resemble foreigners in many respects, not least in their common inferiority to the Roman male; thirdly, a man who allows himself to be dominated by a woman is no longer a real man, and is most certainly not a real Roman; and fourthly, such a man cannot be considered accountable for his own actions – the guilt for his misdeeds is solely his female partner's.[3]

The influence of Caesar's implicitly anti-feminist narrative has had little difficulty crossing political or national boundaries. Sharing this common root, the Soviet view of the Egyptian queen does not significantly differ from a great many western interpretations of her.

A stage history of *Antony and Cleopatra* in the Soviet Union would be very brief, for productions are rare, not numbering much more than half a dozen.[4] This fact in itself bespeaks the influence of ideology on canon formation, both literary and theatrical. The "great four" –

Hamlet, Macbeth, King Lear and *Othello* – have proved more malleable than the late tragedies to the Soviet idea of "positive" tragedy. Soviet productions of *Hamlet* (especially pre-1960), for example, have insisted upon a "strong," "carefree" and "manly" Hamlet to whom "pessimism and will-lessness are foreign." Western interpretations of *Hamlet* have been vilified as "shallow psychological approaches" or, when they presented anything less than an heroic protagonist, as "bourgeois domestic drama."[5]

Unlike the "great four," *Antony and Cleopatra* has posed particular difficulties for an aesthetic which is hero-oriented. Iryna Vanina's comment about the major Shakespearean heroes who are "pure, strong, and decisive people" is a difficult view to sustain for Antony, who, for many western scholars, is deeply flawed and is "partly an object of scorn." In Laurence Olivier's assessment, Antony is "an absolute twerp ... A stupid man."[6] Yet, as we will see, the positive view of Antony is exactly the one which the Soviets attempted to endorse – although at least one Russian writer observed (à la Lytton Strachey) that there is also evidence here of "the soft, settling world" of Shakespeare's last years.[7]

Moreover, the flawed nature of Antony which Soviet productions needed to ignore, explain away, or reconstruct, is but one problem to address. By far the greater difficulty is presented by Cleopatra who shares the play with him. Quite unlike the more passive Desdemona, Cordelia, and Ophelia (but bearing some similarity to the equally problematic Lady Macbeth), Cleopatra has been perceived as a type of Kate – a scold, a harridan, a freak – who must be contained within the boundaries of a positive, Socialist Realist (or, more accurately, heroic realist) view of tragedy, where women are of little importance. (In this regard, it is not surprising that *The Taming of the Shrew* is one of the most frequently produced of Shakespeare's comedies.)[8]

Evgenii Simonov's *Antony and Cleopatra* opened the Vakhtangov's 1971 season with Mikhail Ul'ianov as Antony and IUliana Borisova as Cleopatra. The premiere of the play celebrated the fiftieth anniversary of the Vakhtangov theatre, once the Third Studio of the Moscow Art Theatre, where Evgenii Vakhtangov's exciting Expressionist productions – along with the work of Tairov and Meyerhold – created a golden first Soviet decade, one which Michael Glenny compares in its verve and innovation to the Elizabethan theatre.[9]

Deeply anti-naturalistic (he once referred to Stanislavsky's productions as "banal"), Vakhtangov's self-styled "imaginative realism" combined the fantastic and grotesque with the realistic. Not a supporter of an actor's theatre (like Tairov) nor a director's theatre (like Meyerhold), Vakhtangov came, toward the end of his short life, to be interested in the trinity of play–cast–audience – with the last element the most important. "Theatrical" and "modern" were two of his watchwords, suggesting that Vakhtangov's directorial style was closer to Brecht's than to his Soviet contemporaries.[10]

Simonov's directorial genealogy may be traced back directly to Vakhtangov through his father, Ruben, "the most talented of his [Vakhtangov's] students,"[11] who took over the theatre upon Vakhtangov's death. That Ruben continued the Vakhtangovian tradition even when it was clearly unpopular with officialdom is suggested by the comments of the theatre historian IU. Dmitriev, who condemned his stagings as "superficial" and "illusory"; Evgenii's productions, on the other hand, were praised for their realistic portrayals of life.[12] The apparently more palatable, conservative style of the younger Simonov may also be deduced by his posting from 1962 to 1967 to the Maly Theatre, recently referred to as a "second government" by Ul'ianov.[13] (One supposes that what Ul'ianov meant was that the theatre seemed to dictate what the audience was supposed to believe.) With the exception of this brief hiatus, from 1958 Evgenii Simonov has been with the Vakhtangov.

Simonov's productions, while varied, have been characterized as "optimistic," and tending toward a "lyrical, romantic tonality."[14] His directorial projects include both Soviet and world classics, but the play most often cited in connection with his successes is Aleksei Arbuzov's *An Irkutsk Story*, first staged in 1959 with Mikhail Ul'ianov and IUliana Borisova in the leading roles. Arbuzov's love story deals with the problems connected with a woman's developing social consciousness played out against the background of the construction of a large Siberian power plant. Valia, played by Borisova, meets and marries Sergei (Ul'ianov), a wise, honest, loyal, sensitive man who helps her overcome her own superficiality, uncovers her "hidden depths" and her true feelings for the masses. Sergei dies while saving drowning children. His meaningful death helps Valia in the final transformation from a kind of "operatic Carmen" to a sensitive being. Truly understanding Sergei at last, and with the help of Sergei's friend (who also loves her), Valia turns to the happiness of work: she joins the construction team as an excavator.[15]

By 1971, then, Evgenii Simonov and his lead actors, Ul'ianov and Borisova, had for nearly two decades been associated with conservative Romantic-Socialist-Realist productions. Borisova was usually cast as the weak or fallen woman of passion redeemed by the love of a good man, and Ul'ianov frequently played the heroic, romantic lead. In a recent interview, Ul'ianov referred to the theatre during these Khruschev–Brezhnev years as "an era of stagnation"[16] – by now a commonplace phrase applied to all aspects of Soviet life from the 1950s to the early 1980s. It would not be unusual, therefore, to read subsequent performances of Borisova and Ul'ianov in light of the official theory of "optimistic tragedy."

But the celebratory occasion of the premiere of *Antony and Cleopatra*, as well as the political times (just at the tail-end of the Thaw), suggests that Simonov may have been attempting to "feel out the dangerous spots of life" (to use Ul'ianov's phrase) by taking on a little-performed play; one which, at first glance, seemed so little amenable to the old readings. Z. Vladimirova may have alluded to this audaciousness when she observed that Simonov's production was a breakthrough both for the theatre in its artistic discoveries and for the actors in achieving a new maturity.[17] The choice of play, its translation, and the production's interpretive thrust indeed suggest a departure from Simonov's usual conservatism.

The translation was by Boris Pasternak, an important fact in itself, since Pasternak's name was a rallying-point for opposition to stultified authority. Pasternak regarded *Antony and Cleopatra* as the story of a "rake and a temptress," described "in the tones of mystery fitting to a genuine bacchanalia in the classical sense." For Pasternak, Shakespeare's much-touted "realism" and "objectivity" are found only in the histories. Here, Shakespeare was free to discuss the past because it was remote: "He could say whatever seemed good to him about politics, ethics, or any other thing he chose."[18]

The connection between past and present is one of the leitmotifs of the reviews of Simonov's production. Almost without exception, the reviewers insist upon the seamlessness of history, ideology, and performance: Shakespeare is their contemporary, as Antony and Cleopatra are Shakespeare's contemporaries; antique Rome and Egypt are but "masks" for the Renaissance. Moreover, in Vakhtangovian fashion, the performers did not forget themselves or their world: Ul'ianov is said to have played Antony "as a Soviet actor for whom the image of a democratic people's element was very close" (Vladimirova). How exactly he managed this, we are not told. What is important is that the reviewers felt that they must or could underscore the orthodoxy of all aspects of the production.

Perhaps the first thing to note about Simonov's production is the mise en scène, which suggested the masculine world to be encountered. The stage was built in the form of a golden half-circle divided into three parts by a series of wide sloped steps which led to the central acting space. Two gigantic warriors stood like statues on either side of the stage. A change of scene was indicated by the hanging of emblems on either side; Egypt was represented by an medallion bearing the profile of Cleopatra, Rome by the wolf. Conflict between Egypt and Rome was indicated by hanging both emblems at the same time. A leitmotif of stage business was the exchange of conversation by the "heroes–opponents" across the dead space of the center. The predominant sensibility, then, was Roman and masculine, and the Egyptian scenes, played out in the same space, were clearly aberrations or intrusions with no real locus (or reality) of their own. A further distinction between the world of man and woman was suggested by Vladimirova, who remarked that the Egyptian emblem along with a curtain drawn along stage rear represented a chamber in Cleopatra's palace (and thus suggested the woman's traditional domestic sphere of power), while the Roman emblem suggested the public places of Rome.

A favorite device of the Vakhtangov tradition, music (composed by L. Solin) was used throughout the production of *Antony and Cleopatra*. Mournful chords introduced the action, a dumb-show, in which the earth trembled, swayed, and broke up. This interpolated induction was meant to signify that "there is not and cannot be stability where there is no unity and trust between men" (Shirokii). The triumvirs – Caesar, Lepidus, and Antony – mimed an agreement with Pompey and embraced, delighting, we are told, in the fact that they had achieved peace without bloodletting (Shirokii). Such a masculine world, with its attendant concern with dissent and the breakup of a great empire, has obvious – although ambiguous – reverberations for the Soviets: was the audience meant to understand the crumbling to refer to the Soviet empire or to the west?

Unambiguous, however, was the place of woman in this

production. A tragedy of a great personality was the way that
Shirokii described *Antony and Cleopatra*. Vladimirova was even more
direct: she observed that the Vakhtangov "scorned" the "alliance of
the two characters, or names put forth by Shakespeare in the title of
the tragedy. In the performance, there was one hero – Antony."
Vladimirova went on to explain that Antony was "chosen" from the
"panorama" of the play as the main image, as "the sacrifice of
the tragic contradictions of the age." The phraseology sounds
Pasternakian; and one senses that Zhivago and Pasternak's Hamlet
shadow some of these descriptions. Yet while they clearly were bold
in alluding to some of the great Soviet contemporary concerns –
especially the relationship of the individual to the state – they did so
at a price: by marginalizing woman.

Marginalization was achieved in a number of complex ways, first
and perhaps most obviously by the rhetoric of difference. As
Frederik Barth has pointed out in his studies of ethnicity, boundary-
supporting verbal strategies tend to distance other human beings
from the speaker by insisting on difference. Such rhetorical strategies lead to stereotyping the other as "childlike, superstitious,
savage, dirty, or ignorant."[19] Similar conclusions have been drawn
by feminist critics who argue that the rhetoric of misogyny stresses
the otherness and hence lack of humanness of women, often by
employing onomastic means and, further, "by heirarchizing differences." As Luce Irigaray has pointed out, woman is not only Other,
but "quite specifically *man*'s Other: his negative or mirror image."[20]

This discourse of difference reverberated throughout the reviews,
where Antony was always portrayed as the measure of what Cleopatra was not. Thus he was a "titan" and great warrior of the age,
while Cleopatra and Caesar were "children of their time" (Vladimirova). In another mimed, interpolated ("characteristic") scene,
Cleopatra was described as having accepted a diadem from Antony
"with childish glee."[21] But Cleopatra was also "hard"; her
"womanly egotism ... [was] deaf to the needs of the world" (Vladimirova). As in the west, so in the Soviet Union: "what is praise-
worthy in Antony is damnable in Cleopatra."[22] Not entirely flaw-
less, Ul'ianov's Antony was nonetheless consistently exonerated on
all fronts. The reviewers perceived him as always acting reasonably,
honorably, and nobly. While Cleopatra intrigued, he wisely
manoeuvered; while she was faithless to him, he never betrayed her,
but acted out of political necessity.

"Lithe, evasive, cunning," to the reviewers Cleopatra was "a woman in all her weakness." Her "extravagant capriciousness" was contrasted to the nobility and sternness of Antony. She was illogical, but "more a woman than a queen, and where's the logic here?"[23] The aside implies intimacy with the (male) reader, a sense of shared values and point of view. Laughter both neutralizes but also ensures the reader's complicity in the derogatory statements.[24] Like Cleopatra, the female reader of the critics is decentered if not entirely absent. The review and the later scholarly appraisal become implicit pacts among them.

By contrast, the reviewers, and Ul'ianov himself in his later reminiscences, were fulsome in their praise of the Roman. Ul'ianov's Antony was "straightforward, adroit, strong ... a warrior";[25] a "great man," "great-souled," "understanding of the imperfect nature of mankind"; terrible in his rage, but also "gentle, sensitive in the movements of his soul"; he gave everything of himself without holding back (Shirokii); an "epicurean ... politician, warrior, beloved statesman; in a word, a complete man," one of "the titans of the Renaissance or of antiquity (which is a camouflage for the Renaissance)"; "a bold general and a wise politician" (Kulakovskaia). Without cruelty or treachery, Antony was frank and straightforward, like the contemporary hero, Yuri Gagarin.[26] Yet his great love for Cleopatra rankled. Boiadzhiev, like the historical Octavius Caesar, queried whether Antony had not, perhaps, lost his manly dignity.[27]

For Vladimirova, Antony was torn between "two abysses," Egypt and Rome, Cleopatra and Caesar. He thirsted after goodness and justice for all, but became "a sacrifice of the tragic contradictions of the age." Forced to act in a time when the ideas of the Renaissance had already been ruptured, he wanted to be a true son of his fatherland, to live both its sufferings and joys. The "egotism of Caesar and the divided soul of Cleopatra are the only borders of this world which overtake him" (Shirokii). Antony could "not see that the love of Cleopatra was deprived of spirituality and that the politics of Rome were framed by 'politicking'"; he loved his Cleopatra "not only sensitively, but in an elevated fashion, sincerely and greatly" (Vladimirova). For Antony, the "intrigues of the Queen of Egypt were foreign" (Kulakovskaia). Antony did not "break faith with Cleopatra – who led a cunning political game behind his back" (Shirokii). Antony married Octavia because of the demands of politics and out of "statesmanly necessity" (Kula-kovskaia).

The idealized portrayal of Antony is not unlike many western views of the Roman pointed out by Marilyn Williamson, L. Fitz, and, more recently, by Lucy Hughes-Hallett.[28] But the Soviet view arises from another source: not only from "mere" anti-feminism but also from officially sanctioned ideology. Ul'ianov's Antony closely matched the textbook description of the positive Soviet hero: a man of action "trailing clouds of glory," a determined, strong, even imperious leader, possessing a higher consciousness than those around him. The hero of Soviet formulaic fiction and drama usually finds himself in a new setting (a foreign land or any hostile surround-ings), where his task is to sway the backward, local masses, to make them accept his higher ideals. In the schema of optimistic tragedy, the hero is always unwavering, reliable, disciplined, and noble, while his opposition (the unformed masses, usually including a love interest) vacillate and complain until they finally recognize the greater way of the hero.[29] On the way to a "higher" consciousness, leisure and luxury of any sort must be rejected, as must spontaneity (*stikhinoe*) – the natural and elemental and hence the unexpected, inventive, undisciplined, passionate – in favor of the controlled, disciplined, stern.[30]

To succeed, the hero must abandon personal happiness and single-mindedly follow his goal. At the structural turning-point, the resistance to the hero's plans are overcome, a fact which results in "a flood of feeling and the establishment of a powerful emotional bond." This moment, argues Shkandrij, symbolizes "the triumph of the hero's point of view and the submission to his will of the masses, who fully repent their stubbornness."[31] Even if he loses his life, the hero's work is justified. Death (always a problem for Soviet literary theory) and self-sacrifice become palatable when their usefulness is underscored. *An Irkustk Story* clearly follows this pattern.

In such a scheme the "untamed" Cleopatra occupies a precarious place. Traditionally, in Socialist Realist models, the woman must succumb to the hero's point of view or be rejected by him; yet Antony inconveniently returns to Egypt (and therefore to luxury, passion, leisure) in the second part of the play. As a woman in an optimistic tragedy, Cleopatra must be kept in her secondary place; but as the great love interest of Antony, she must also be partially accommodated to the usual paradigms. This tension between ideology and the demands of Shakespeare's play is further evident in reviews, scholarly articles, and roundtable discussions, which opine that it is difficult to discern the essential conflict of the play.[32] What they allude to is the play's intractableness; its unwillingness to conform to the usual configurations.

That the ideological reading of *Antony and Cleopatra* is also necessarily patriarchal is continuously confirmed by the reviewers, who gave primacy to Antony, both in the order of presentation and the length. Borisova-Cleopatra was further decentered by Vasilii Lanovoi as Caesar who, in terms of space, occupied the second place of interest in reviews. A "sober politician,"[33] he was a "god of war, a fanatic, an ideologue" (Vladimirova) obsessed with power and the idea of greatness (Kulakovskaia).[34] Thus while Cleopatra existed on the boundary of Antony's world, Caesar (and the male world he represents) was seen as central to it. Commentaries on the play and on the production continuously emphasized the importance of male friendships, although the play gives ample evidence of the superficiality and convenience of male bonds. Most obviously, Pompey's dismissal of Menas' plan to murder his Roman guests (2.7) is not based on any idea of the indissoluble and holy bonds of friendship, but merely on the importance of the appearance of adhering to such ideas. The Soviet critics, however, ignored the Romans' hypocrisy, as they did their vulgarity, which they described as "manly" behavior.

Consistently implying that Cleopatra was that meddlesome element which came between true male friends, Vladimirova, for example, observed that Antony "tore" himself away from Cleopatra to "rush to help Caesar." For Shirokii, the real bond was not between Antony and Cleopatra, but between Antony and Caesar, the "true sons of the stormy Renaissance." Here the reviewers referred especially to Caesar's exclamation upon the death of Antony, "Now I cry: brother, counsellor, friend." What Shakespeare's play shows us, however, is that the values which Antony holds dear are precisely not those of Caesar. Antony's chivalric and quixotic attempt at settling the issue of the empire by a duel, and Caesar's subsequent scornful rejection of such folly, is only one instance in the play which reveals how far apart these men are. Antony's affiliations are to an old Rome of honor; Caesar's are to a new, shifting, changeable, *Realpolitik* version of empire.

The Soviet view of the play as a tragic tale of division among men (a slight reworking of the old western view of the play as a conflict between love and honor) is an idea underscored by Simonov's induction and by the uniformly applauded shipboard banquet scene, presented as the climax of the play. While Kulakovskaia, for example, without a trace of irony, applauded the "beautiful moment of unity" portrayed here, Boiadzhiev commended the "masculine, lively" quality of the banquet. Antony was the "soul of the warriors, beloved as leader, friend, brother ... And it becomes understandable why for them [the triumvirs] it was such a tribulation to give Antony away to the embraces of the 'gypsy.'"[35] In this latter telling comment, Cleopatra appears as the racial and generically foreign element which corrupts the hero and takes him away from his true (that is, masculine, Roman) setting.

The turning-point which corresponds to the formulaic shift in feeling and sense of unity between the hero and those around him is the death of Antony. It is only at this moment that Borisova's Cleopatra finally realized what Antony had been to her and how deeply she loved him. As Vladimirova pointedly observed, the death of Antony "allows them, the sinners" (i.e., Cleopatra and Caesar) to see the loss of the greatness of life. Vladimirova's phrase "the sinners" brings us back to an idealistic, ideological reading of the play. What is also significant here is the alliance of Cleopatra with Caesar – not with Antony. Implicitly, she is rejected. If "sinner" and "child," then Antony must be saint and "titan." The discourse of difference demands the extremity of hierarchization.

As tragic heroine, Cleopatra is also unnatural in her close affiliation with comedy. Rather than providing supporting scenes for the tragic hero, Cleopatra not only dominates the comic sequences and much of the rest of the action, but also fails to play the role of dignified heroine and source of pathos. Since Soviet literary theory has little room for comedy (although there is a long tradition of satire), the comedy of *Antony and Cleopatra* is generally perceived as destroying the tone of Shakespeare's play and placing the emotion of the main characters on slippery ground.[36] Humor, which leads to pluralistic thinking and multiple interpretations, collides with the strong desire for a single, controlled, didactic vision of the play based on simple binary oppositions easily resolved. Shakespeare's play, and especially Cleopatra, consistently defies such reduction. Tellingly, Boiadzhiev's later scholarly theatre history holds up *An Irkutsk Story* as a better example of the Vakhtangov's treatment of love, idealized and unsullied by comedy.

Associated with laughter, egotism, childishness, and unsettling passion, Cleopatra evokes the rhetoric of anxiety, as well as of difference. Described as being "coquettish, at times gentle, at times unbalanced" (Kulakovskaia), she is tentatively connected with mental disorder. Thus the reviewers complete the link between the alleged weakness of the female constitution (uncontrolled sexuality) and mental chaos. Such a disturbance was thought to arise particularly when women "attempted to compete with men instead of serving them," as Elaine Showalter puts it.[37] In *Antony and Cleopatra* this competition appears to reach its apex in the Omphale references, a pointer, for the reviewers, to the complete topsy-turvydom of this world.

A feminist deconstruction of the reviews may center on one final "dangerous spot" in the production: Cleopatra's political manoeuverings, another problematic strand in the complexity of her character, but also a potential emblem of subversion and instability. According to the reviewers, Cleopatra's duplicity and cunning, so foreign to Antony, were particularly shown when she "wishes to preserve her kingdom, and the crown of Ptolemy for her children" (Kulakovskaia). Thus Antony had political savvy, Cleopatra simply duplicity and slyness; moreover, there is an additional note of tribulation sounded: Cleopatra as nationalist.

To play Cleopatra thus is to embody the subversive Other in all its facets: as unbalanced woman and harridan, as foreign gypsy, as undignified comic fool, as passion personified, and as empire-destroyer and nationalist. If the point of optimistic tragedy is to celebrate a positive hero and his relationship to the masses, and, by extension, to celebrate the centralizing force and importance of the party, then the periphery (symbolized by Cleopatra) must be dismissed, submerged, or otherwise assimilated by the centralist impulse. The Socialist Realist paradigm upon which the reviewers conveniently draw is a myth of exclusion and exile, decentering the woman and assimilating her story into that of the positive hero.

Thus it is not surprising that in Simonov's production (or in the reviews) Cleopatra's love for Antony must have been at least partially open to doubt. When drawing attention to her undignified and comic behavior, reviewers uniformly questioned her love for Antony. Borisova's Cleopatra – the reviewers noted – only realized how deeply she loved Antony when he was dying. Then, she fell down and wept unrestrainedly at his feet. "Simple grief, as in thousands of women, made Cleopatra worthy of Antony" (Vladimirova). The emotionalism of the Siminov production took its cue from Plutarch, rather than from Shakespeare. However, Borisova's Cleopatra recovered quickly enough in order to try her charms once again upon Caesar, who could barely restrain himself from embracing her and submitting to her "play of eyes." According to Kulakovskaia, this was one of the best scenes of the play, with Cleopatra "kneeling before Caesar, womanly and mysterious." Failing to snare him, Cleopatra committed suicide. In Pasternak's translation, Caesar's last words are "Away from here – to Rome," a summary dismissal, tinged with disgust, of the spectacle of death and the uncontrolled, womanish passion of Egypt. (Shakespeare's text reads, "Our army shall / In solemn show attend this funeral, / And then to Rome. Come, Dolabella, see / High order, in this great solemnity" [5.2.361–4].) Denying Cleopatra grandeur even in death, the production succeeded in assimilating her story into the dominant male ideological discourse.

Yet all of the reviews concluded with the same encomium: a praise of the play's "humanism," which was equated with the triumph of great human emotions and the optimistic belief in mankind. The play was read as a poem dedicated to beauty and truth, and as "purification" – a process which submerges the ego (particularly to the demands and needs of society), and is symptomatic of Soviet optimistic tragedy rather than of Shakespeare's play. Simonov's is thus, finally, an old-fashioned romantic reading of the play, which in its belief in the transcendence of Antony's love shares a great deal more with Dryden's view (All for Love) than one would expect. It is not entirely a coincidence that the stress on the formulaic occurs in these reviews, not long after the short-lived Thaw had been declared an aberration. Among many other things, the Thaw (roughly 1956 to 1964, the period of some liberalization in the wake of Khrushchev's denunciation of Stalin) questioned the value of entrenched stereotypes, and the banality of contemporary literature and theatre. The renewed insistence on old models of literature in the 1970s may perhaps be seen as an attempt to validate the system, as a ritualized resolution of conflicts, or as an effort to smooth over the obvious fissures and dissent released in those years.

While *Antony and Cleopatra* has not been staged recently to the best of my knowledge, a new translation appeared in Soviet Ukraine in 1986 – the early phase of glasnost. It is instructive that both the translation and the commentary reveal a continuing difficulty with the figure of Cleopatra. Rather than deviating from Simonov's vision of the play, Olena Alekseenko's commentary focuses on Cleopatra's "weakness" and "femininity." Cleopatra's world is the world of "feeling." "Like the great Roman who wishes to have power over the world, so it is absolutely necessary that Cleopatra dominate Antony himself." Her whole character is "*a priori* unheroic ... womanly ... The retreat of Antony at Actium is the heroine's greatest triumph."[38] This interpretation of Cleopatra is borne out by Boris Ten's translation, which transforms Cleopatra's opening lines, "If it be love indeed, tell me how much" into "If this is love – is it great?" Her reply to Antony, "I'll set a bourn how far to be belov'd" is translated as, "But I want to delineate boundaries."[39] Cleopatra's amorous, witty play is metamorphosed into childish insistence.

The reviews of Simonov's production, and the later translations and critical comments, suggest the ease with which classics like Shakespeare may be assimilated into official ideologies when a totalizing view of the work is presented. Even as Simonov's production may have striven to speak to the present through Antony, ironically the very decision to center on the hero made it possible to endorse the old stereotypes and, by extension, to rewrite the play in reassuring, comfortable clichés. Perhaps a not unjust comparison might be made with another, more recent attempt to make Shakespeare speak to the present: Zeffirelli's film *Hamlet* which, in removing much of the mystery of the play and in casting Mel Gibson as Hamlet, curiously provides the viewer with a very old-fashioned, even Freudian production. Despite the prolific work of feminist theorists of the past two decades, the film presents yet another version of the weak and lustful queen.

Soon after the process of glasnost was initiated intellectuals were urged "to help in the cardinal processes of *perebudova* [perestroika],"[40] a plea which suggests that an idealistic and programmatic view of literature had not been unseated. However, by early 1990, theatre journals began to hark back to the rich period of the 1920s when Socialism promised much and allowed a rich variety of artistic freedom. It is on such fertile, contested ground, where canon, forms, and theories are questioned, that woman's place – as heroine, reader, reviewer – may once more be fruitfully reconsidered.

NOTES

1 Irving Wardle, "The Czech Dream," *The Times*, 29 Nov. 1969.

2 Sof'ia Nels, *Shekspir na sovestkoi stsene* (Moscow: Iskusstvo, 1960), 3; V. Kemenov, *Stat'i ob iskusstve* (Moscow: Iskusstvo, 1956), 66.

3 Lucy Hughes-Hallett, *Cleopatra: Histories, Dreams and Distortions* (New York: Harper and Row, 1990), 44.

4 Performances of *Antony and Cleopatra* are noted for 1923, 1934, 1960, 1961. See, for example, E. Time, *Dorogi iskusstva* (Moscow: Vserossiskoe teatral'noe obshchestvo, 1967); *Istoriia sovestkogo dramaticheskogo teatra*, 6 vols. (Moscow; Nauka, 1971). The play was not performed at all in Soviet Ukraine; see Iryna Vanina, *Ukrains'ka shekspiriana* (Kiev: Mystetstvo, 1964). Outside of the Slavic republics, *Antony and Cleopatra* seemed to gain some popularity during the period of the Thaw: in Uzbekistan (1964), Azerbaijan (1964), Yerevan, Armenia (1969), and in the Russian far east in Khabarovsk (1969). It was staged in Tallinn, Estonia, in 1955.

5 Nels, *Shekspir na sovetskoi stsene*, 254; Oleksandr Bilets'kyi, *Zibrannia prats'* (Kiev: Naukova dumka, 1966), II: 356; Nels, *ibid.*, 15.

6 Vanina, *Ukrains'ka shekspiriana*, 6; O. J. Campbell, *Shakespeare's Satire* (New York: Oxford University Press, 1943; rpt. New York: Gordian, 1971), 199; Laurence Olivier, *On Acting* (New York: Simon and Schuster, 1986), 162.

7 V. Shirokii, "Kraski tragedii. Antonii i Kleopatra," *Sovetskaia kul'tura*, 16 Sept. 1971: n.p.

8 The popularity of *The Taming of the Shrew* is evident in various accounts of Shakespeare in the Soviet Union and its satellites. See, for example, A. A. Smirnov, *Shekspir* (Leningrad and Moscow: Iskusstvo, 1963); Alexander Dutu, *Shakespeare in Rumania* (Bucharest: Meridiane, 1964), 234–9, who notes more than 411 performances of the play in Bucharest between 1956 and 1960 alone.

9 Michael Glenny, "The Soviet Theatre," in *An Introduction to Russian Language and Literature*, ed. Robert Auty and Dimitri Obolensky (Cambridge University Press, 1977), II: 273.

10 See Vakhtangov's own account in Evgenii Vakhtangov, *Stati i vospominaniia* (Moscow: Progress Publishers, 1982), comps. Lyubov Vendrovskaya and Galina Kaptereva, trans. Doris Bradbury, especially pp. 140–141, 155–158, and 262–265. Also see Nick Worrall, *Modernism to Realism on the Soviet Stage: Tairov–Vakhtangov–Okhlopkov* (Cambridge University Press, 1989).

11 Irina Makarevich, *Soviet Theatre; New Ideas* (Moscow: Novosti Press Agency, 1981), 48.

12 IU.A. Dmitriev, ed., *Istoriia russkogo sovetskogo dramaticheskogo teatra* (Moscow: Prosveshcheniie, 1987), II: 39.

13 Ray Conlogue, "Theatre in Russia Never Was just a Toy or Entertainment," *The Globe and Mail* (Toronto), 5 May 1990: c4 (an interview with Mikhail Ul'ianov).

14 Makarevich, *Soviet Theatre*, 50; Dmitriev, *Istoriia russkogo sovetskogo dramaticheskogo teatra*, II: 48.

15 The summary of the play's action is taken from G. A. Khaichenko, *Stranitsy istorii sovetskogo teatra* (Moscow: Iskusstvo, 1983), 176–9.

16 Conlogue, "Theatre in Russia," c4.

17 Z. Vladimirova, "Antonii, Kleopatra i drugie," *Moskovskaia pravda*, 10 Sept. 1971.

18 Boris Pasternak, "Translating Shakespeare," in *I Remember: Sketch for an Autobiography*, trans. David Magarshack (New York; Pantheon, 1959), 138–9.

19 Frederik Barth, *Ethnic Groups and Boundaries*, quoted in Werner Sollors, "Ethnicity," in *Critical Terms for Literary Study*, ed. Frank Lentricchia and Thomas McLaughlin (University of Chicago Press, 1990), 299.

20 Dympna Callaghan, *Women and Gender in Renaissance Tragedy* (Atlantic Highlands, NJ: Humanities Press, 1989), 124; Irigaray quoted in Toril Moi, *Sexual/Textual Politics: Feminist Literary Theory* (London: Methuen, 1985), 133.

21 G. N. Boiadzhiev, *Dusha teatra* (Moscow: Molodaia gvardiia, 1974), 318. For similar views, see the reminiscences of Mikhail Ul'ianov, *Moia professia* (Moscow: Molodaia gvardiia, 1975), especially 248–9.

22 L. T. Fitz, "Egyptian Queens and Male Reviewers: Sexist Attitudes in *Antony and Cleopatra* Criticism," *Shakespeare Quarterly* 28 (1977): 304.

23 Boiadzhiev, *Dusha teatra*, 319.

24 Callaghan, *Women and Gender*, 125.

25 Boiadzhiev, *Dusha teatra*, 318.

26 Dmitriev, *Istorii russkogo sovetskogo dramaticheskogo teatra*, II: 49.

27 Boiadzhiev, *Dusha teatra*, 316–21.

28 Marilyn L. Williamson, *"Infinite Variety": Antony and Cleopatra in Renaissance Drama and Earlier Tradition* (Mystic, CT.: Lawrence Verry, 1974).

29 For an excellent summary and analysis of the characteristics of Soviet formulaic prose fiction, see Myroslav Shkandrij, "Fiction by Formula: The Worker in Early Soviet Ukrainian Prose," *Journal of Ukrainian Studies* 7.2 (1982): 47–60.

30 See K. Clark, *The Soviet Novel: History as Ritual* (University of Chicago Press, 1981), 15–24, for a detailed discussion of the spontaneity–consciousness dialectic, especially as a parable of the Marxist–Leninist view of history.

31 Shkandrij, "Fiction by Formula," 50, 51. The death of Antony as the tragic culmination of "the theme of humanity and happiness" in the play is discussed by A. N. Doroshevich, "Tragicheskii geroi i ego antagonist v tragediiakh Shekspira (*Antonii i Kleopatra, Koriolan*)," *Nauchnye doklady vysshei shkoly filologicheskie nauki* 1 (1964): 103.

32 See, for example, IU. Vinogradov, "*Antonii i Kleopatra*," *Teatr* 6 (1970): 22. Also, L. Nimvitskaia, "Shekspir. Eshche Shekspir!," *Teatral'naia zhizn* 14 (1964): 14–15, for more about Shakespeare's "martial" humanism.

33 Dmitriev, *Istorii russkogo sovetskogo dramaticheskogo teatra*, II: 193.

34 See T. Kulakovskaia, "Vechno zhivoi Shekspir," *Sovetskaia Rossia*, 22 Sept. 1971.

35 Boiadzhiev, *Dusha teatra*, 318.

36 *Ibid.*

37 Showalter, *The Female Malady: Women, Madness, and English Culture, 1830–1980* (New York: Penguin, 1987), 74. On women and madness, also see Mary Jacobus, "The Difference of View," in *Women Writing and Writing About Women* (New York: Barnes and Noble, 1979), 10–21.

38 Olena Alekseenko, Afterword and Notes, *Antony and Cleopatra*, in Vil'iam Shekspir, *Tvory v shesty tomakh*, ed. P. A. Zahrebel'nyi *et al.* (Kiev: Dnipro, 1986), V: 676.

39 *Ibid.*, 418. Boris Ten's translation should be compared with the Pasternak translation used by the Vakhtangov troupe. Pasternak translates Cleopatra's opening lines as, "If it be love, then is it great or not?" And in response to Antony's reply, she remarks, "I want to know the extent of my charms."

40 *Literaturna Ukraina*, 16 Apr. 1987: 1.

CHAPTER 10

Hamlet *in postwar Czech theatre*

Jarka Burian

Czech productions of *Hamlet* since World War II have been notable for both their socio-political relevance and their artistically sophisticated mises en scène. In this they have essentially carried on traditions already established in the earlier years of the century. At times presenting a showcase of Czech cultural maturity, at other times venting the frustration and distress arising from harsh social and political conditions prevailing during their respective eras, and always revealing the distinctive artistry of their creators, Czech productions of *Hamlet* have served as a microcosm of the Czech theatre and its relation to the forces that have dominated the life of this nation in the heart of Europe. In a broader sense they also provide further testimony in the ongoing debate between those who see the challenge of staging Shakespeare in striving for maximal expressive fidelity to Shakespeare's presumed intentions as derived from his text and those who champion maximum freedom in handling the text in order to release the creative fantasy and vision of the director most fully.

Although the emphasis in this survey will be on several *Hamlet* productions since the 1950s, some consideration of general historical background and certain prewar productions provides a useful historical perspective. To begin with, one must recognize the great significance Shakespeare has held for Czech culture and Czech theatre. Lacking a sense of national identity since their defeat by the forces of the Habsburg Empire at the Battle of White Mountain in 1620, the Czechs began a slow revival of their culture and their political aspirations in the last decades of the eighteenth century. Czech theatre had no building of its own, no tradition in acting, and no stock of native drama. During the next 100 years, Shakespeare became a model and an inspiration for generations of theatre artists and audiences, especially in their efforts to free themselves from the hegemony of German culture and theatre. As Jan Mukařovský noted, "Czech theatre put on Shakespeare's plays not only in order to interpret to the full their philosophical and artistic message, but in order to place the Czech theatre itself on a high level of acting, direction, and staging" and "the growth of Czech theatre would be unthinkable without [Shakespeare]."[1]

The earliest production of *Hamlet* in Czech occurred in Prague in the early 1790s. Nineteenth-century productions were primarily notable for the increasing number of translations and the stage effectiveness of leading performers rather than for special interpretations or production concepts. More importantly, Shakespeare became progressively identified with the nationalist aspirations of the Czech people, who saw in his plays, especially in the tragedies and histories, many parallels to their own complex situation. On a more fundamental level, to translate and perform Shakespeare was a sign of cultural maturity. Nowhere was the connection between homage to Shakespeare and national pride more evident than in a Shakespeare cycle of four productions presented in 1864 to mark the tricentennial of Shakespeare's birth. The festivities included 230 costumed Shakespearean characters in a festive procession to the accompaniment of a march by Bedřich Smetana.

Early twentieth-century productions of *Hamlet* epitomized the increasing artistry and sophistication of interpretation evident in Czech theatre. At the same time, they placed less emphasis on the social relevance and the educative potential of the drama. The landmark production of *Hamlet* in 1905 in the National Theatre was hailed as the first great creative achievement of the Czech dramatic (i.e., non-musical) theatre. The production was dominated by the towering presence of Eduard Vojan (1853–1920), who combined the bravura technique of the romantic theatre with complex psychological analysis that led to a deep exploration of a character's intellectual and emotional life. The result was a Hamlet of great nobility, deep thought, and severe irony, isolated from others by the scale of his soul and the intensity of his suppressed grief. Concentrating on Hamlet's subjective, personal concerns, this turn-of-the-century *Hamlet* was essentially an apolitical production, evidence of which was the cutting of Fortinbras from the end of the play. Jaroslav Kvapil (1868–1950), the director, is acknowledged as the first great artist-director in Czech theatre, the one who brought the Czech dramatic stage to the attention of Europe. His blending of psychologically realistic acting with a sensitive orchestration of atmospheric lighting and selective, symbolist-influenced scenery created unified, carefully shaded productions in which considerable room existed for the creativity of individual actors.

Kvapil's and the Czech theatre's devotion to Shakespeare was most strikingly demonstrated in a 1916 cycle during which fifteen of Shakespeare's plays were presented in a six-week period in honor of the 300th anniversary of Shakespeare's death. Vojan's sovereignty among actors was reaffirmed by his playing of the roles of Macbeth, Hamlet, Lear, Othello, Shylock, Richard III, Benedict, and Petruchio during the festival. Although none of the productions was notable for its political slant, the cycle as a whole made a provocative political statement in itself, occurring as it did in the midst of World War I when Shakespeare's England was locked in bloody conflict with the Austro-Hungarian Empire, of which the Czechs were still unwilling members.

The next notable Hamlet was that of Eduard Kohout (1889–1976), in a production directed by the next great (some would say the greatest) Czech director, Karel Huro Hilar (1885–1935), in 1926 at the National Theatre in Prague. Hilar is chiefly identified with the Expressionist movement, but in 1926 he subordinated this tendency to what he called *civilism*, by which he meant a shift to concerns of everyday life after the devastation and hysteria of the war. Kohout represented a pale, sensitive youth, a "melancholy lyricist"[2] at a loss and impotent within the hostile, often grotesque world of the Danish court. In striking contrast to the manly, mature, philosophic Hamlet of Vojan, Kohout presented an inexperienced boy, alternately confused and vehement, tearful and explosive: a reflection of the young postwar generation and its resentment toward the alienating world it inherited. Not focused as exclusively on Hamlet as was the Kvapil–Vojan production, Hilar's *Hamlet* thereby also allowed the other characters to make a greater impact.

Hilar's direction involved what critics called a revue format, a series of rapidly changing scenes that deliberately accentuated contrasts in tone between the comic and the serious. The residue of Hilar's penchant for Expressionist staging was more evident in the scenography provided by Vlastislav Hofman (1884–1964), the first great Czech designer, whose own bent was toward heightened, bold expressiveness. Here, Hofman modified his often baroque effects and created a series of stark, austere settings based on a variety of silvery-gray screens, tall, thin prisms, wall units, and pieces of massive furniture mounted on easily movable platforms in the midst of black space, accentuated by harsh, sharply focused lighting that avoided almost all color. The settings were deliberately designed to facilitate the rapid, abrupt entrances of actors from behind the various units, but they also conveyed the sense of alienation Hilar was obviously seeking. Like the furniture, the costumes were a blend of period and modern in style. Hamlet's costumes included a short black jacket, vest, sweater, and basque cap; Gertrude wore a modern evening gown with train for the "mousetrap" scene. Although Hilar consistently eschewed a theatre of political, much less ideological, orientation, he was responsive to the social currents of his day. In this *Hamlet*, Hilar wanted a mostly young, postwar audience to identify with the world of the play on a personal level.

The last significant *Hamlet* before the German occupation was in fact not simply Shakespeare's *Hamlet* (however much edited) but a radical adaptation that combined elements of Shakespeare's text with one of Jules LaForgue's *Moralités légendaires*, a prose retelling of Hamlet's story with a modern psychological slant. The author of this hybrid, titled *Hamlet III*, was the celebrated avant-garde director E. F. Burian (1904–59). A committed Communist, Burian established his own theatre in Prague in 1933, modifying its name each year, D34, D35, and so on, the D representing the Czech word for theatre, "divadlo." A highly subjective, richly talented artist (he was a composer, poet, actor), Burian dedicated his theatre to a Marxist attack on the bourgeois society of his day, above all its fascistic manifestations. Frequently, however, Burian's Marxist commitment underwent crises arising from the clash of his artistic will toward free creation with the shifting demands of the Communist program. One such crisis occurred in the mid-thirties during the great Stalinist purges in the Soviet Union. Burian's idol was the renowned Soviet master director, Vsevolod Meyerhold, whose ongoing conflicts with Soviet bureaucracy culminated in Meyerhold's overt rejection of the official Soviet policy of Socialist Realism in the arts. As punishment and ultimate warning, the authorities took Meyerhold's theatre away from him. Strongly identifying with Meyerhold, Burian created *Hamlet III* in 1937 not only as a forceful attack against Fascism but also as a defiant statement in support of free artistic creation against any restrictions. Burian's Hamlet, dressed in white satin and with a dagger in one hand and a pen in the other, became not only a disillusioned, embittered intellectual, but virtually a terrorist, whose aim was to destroy a senseless world. The King and Queen were presented as crude murderers, members of a ruling class destined for extinction. A sole ray of hope in the world of this production lay in the Gravediggers, representatives of the people, whose children might one day overthrow the castle, instead of standing impotent before it. Attacked by Marxist critics, Burian eventually relented in his rejection of contemporary Communist policy for the arts, and ultimately spoke of the production as something of an aberration.

Nevertheless, the production was perhaps even more notable for the inventiveness and imagination of its highly stylized staging. The action took place on two turntables, sometimes silent, sometimes screeching in their movement. The acting frequently conveyed the impression of a waxworks of monstrous, dehumanized puppets, and Burian's own score for the production included sirens and other *musique concrète* sound effects. Operating on a very small proscenium stage, Burian pioneered in what we have come to know as multimedia theatre. His distinctive use of stage space, lighting, and especially projections in combination with the play of actors created highly metaphoric, theatrically synthesized performances that truly warrant the frequently abused term, "theatre poetry." One example in this *Hamlet* may stand for many others: on a relatively bare stage with black background and no curtain, the drowning of Ophelia was presented by an actress miming drowning behind bent wires and a scrimlike, lightly rippling white drape onto which was projected a specially made film of the enlarged details of an aquarium, in soft focus. Burian's theatrically creative imagination seemed to have an inescapable corollary: one rarely remembers any of Burian's actors. In his theatre, Burian was the dominating artist.

In wartime, occupied Prague, a 1941 production of *Hamlet* in the Vinohrady Theatre was chiefly notable for its scenography by František Tröster (1904–68), a significant designer and teacher whose career spanned the thirties to the sixties. Most of the acting occurred within an oval-shaped area on the stage floor, the closed end of the oval pointing upstage, the open end downstage. Mirroring this form was a configuration of draperies hung just beyond the upstage end of the stage oval. Varied colored lighting in conjunction with selective scenic elements placed beyond the draped oval created striking visual effects, such as the scene on the battlements,

Hamlet's encounter with Fortinbras on the plain, and the graveyard. Given the presence of the German occupation forces, the interpretation of Hamlet emphasized, with due caution, the helpless situation of an intellectual attempting to endure in a ruthless environment.

The first major *Hamlet* of the postwar Communist era was a response to the change from the hard Stalinist years of the fifties to a gradual softening of oppression and a corresponding loosening of tight controls of the arts, which had been most painfully apparent in the forced Socialist Realism that weighted like a heavy blanket on all creative activity. The late fifties saw the emergence of the studio theatre movement and its implicit rejection of traditional forms. It also saw the creation of striking evolution in scenography, which was perhaps nowhere more evident than in the work of Josef Svoboda (*b.* 1920), a trail-blazer of great subsequent influence in international stage design. Building on the visions and innovations of men like Adolph Appia and Gordon Craig, as well as on the Soviet avant-garde of the twenties, and the work of his own country-men, E. F. Burian and František Tröster, Svoboda developed an approach to staging which incorporated extensive use of contempo-rary technology. Scenography was to have a dynamic role in pro-duction, at times equivalent to the acting. Like the play of actors, scenography should also be capable of being modified and varied in response to the ongoing action – sometimes with sheer kinetic movement of scenic elements, and almost always with highly flexible lighting, including significant use of projections and other optical techniques. It is of course a new variation of "synthetic theatre," the premise of which is that theatre is an art of interacting, constantly variable components and relationships – an evolving gestalt in which the text may be the core or spine but by no means is the sole or even necessarily the main element. This concept or vision is cer-tainly not uniquely Svoboda's; it owes much to the strong structura-list tradition in modern Czech aesthetics and to the influence of outstanding Czech stage directors like Otomar Krejča and Alfred Radok, with whom Svoboda worked on many productions.

The National Theatre's production of *Hamlet*, in 1959 was directed by a contemporary of Svoboda, Jaromír Pleskot (*b.* 1922), designed by Svoboda, and had Radovan Lukavský (*b.* 1919) as a sober, older very disciplined Hamlet, who acted practically and decisively against a corrupt order only after careful analysis and reflection. Lukavský's journal of the production reveals the director's concept of Hamlet as a knight and Claudius as a politician. Hamlet the humanist discovered his dependence on and his responsibility to society. Hamlet became a "positive hero" in the best sense of the word: "Not mystic fate, but a clear mission."[3] The production had great appeal to its audiences, perhaps primarily because Lukavský's portrayal of Hamlet embodied many of the qualities most Czechs admire: a practicality based on thorough, sober reasoning; an independent intellect not subject to emotional indulgence; determined action at the right moment. Emerging from the dark Stalinist era, the production seemed to echo the need for sober, responsible action leading to a careful, rational liberalization of society. The production remained in the repertoire until 1965, by which time it had 171 performances, a record for Czech *Hamlet*s.

Svoboda's contribution reinforced the motif of an alienating though elegant and monumental environment. A total of twenty tall panels covered with a black plastic material and measuring approximately 3 by 9 meters each were situated in five planes parallel to and behind the prescenium opening. The twenty-four scene changes of the production were effected by laterally sliding the panels in differing configurations for each scene. Supplementing this architectonic, labyrinthine shaping of space was the reflective surface of the panels, which made them function as black mirrors, a striking vision in itself, but also highly conducive to certain lighting effects. For example, two spotlights reflected from the surface of a panel formed an abstract impression of two glaring eyes. This became the visual accompaniment to the Ghost's speeches, which were simply the recorded voice of Lukavský himself. Another example occurred during the "To be or not to be" sequence: Lukavský was essentially in silhouette, illuminated from behind by light *reflected* from one of the panels.

A provocative variation of the 1959–65 Prague *Hamlet*, as well as of Svoboda's ideal of scenography as an instrument to be placed at the disposition of the director, was the *Hamlet* created by the Czech team of Svoboda and Otomar Krejča (*b.* 1921) in Brussels in 1965. The impression of a hostile environment was strengthened and made more overt by the use of an oppressive wall constructed of rectangular, geometric masses that were individually movable along a downstage–upstage axis. Suspended at a 45 degree angle above this kinetic construction was a mirror that extended the full width and

depth of the wall; in effect, the mirror reflected the groundplan view
of the set to the audience. Thus, when the various pieces of the wall
moved forward or backward as much as two meters either way, the
spectator saw a double, now also vertical, movement of menacing,
monolithic objects vividly conveying the sense of a crushing, dehumanized world with which Hamlet must cope. The wall itself was
highly practicable; not only could action occur on top of the wall,
but individual pieces formed staircases, and the various positions of
the others could provide openings or hiding-places. Of particular
interest is that the mirror originated as a way of embodying Krejča's
directorial concept of the Ghost being an alter ego of Hamlet; in the
Ghost scenes, Hamlet was talking to himself, as the audience could
witness by means of the mirror.

The great breakthrough of the Prague Spring of 1968, toward
which the country had been painfully evolving for some ten years,
was aborted before any Shakespeare productions could celebrate or
respond to it. For most of the following twenty years, theatre was
once again forced to speak in cryptic, indirect terms; imagination,
much less any hint of criticism of the status quo, was regarded with
suspicion or simply censored. The leading directors were prevented
from working, as were many actors; it goes without saying that
playwrights who had in any way taken a critical view of the
twenty-year Socialist regime were banned from the stage. Václav
Havel was only the best known among many others. The goad for
most Czech productions of Shakespeare was likely to be the neo-
oppression of the Moscow-dominated Husák regime and the
depressing state of Czech culture and society.

In this context, the 1978 production of *Hamlet* by the Zábradlí
Theatre in Prague became a landmark. The theatre for which Havel
had been dramaturg and resident playwright was the site of a bitter,
grotesque caricature of traditional *Hamlet*s with their stress on the
eventual victory of humanistic ideals. Directed by Evald Schorm
(1931–89), a leading film director of the new Czech wave of the
1960s, who turned to studio theatre directing when he was barred
from film work after 1968, this *Hamlet* created a world dominated by
idiocy as much as evil. Going beyond the frustrated, impassioned
bitterness of E. F. Burian's prewar *Hamlet III*, it was a tragi-farcical
Hamlet, a cruel vision in the spirit of Jarry or Beckett. The characters, including Hamlet, seemed to be not individualized characters
with passion and conviction, but shards of humanity operating in a

fatalistic, absurdist universe in which the struggle against evil was at best quixotic. Most appropriately, Schorm chose the First Quarto *Hamlet* for his text. The unpoetic, unphilosophic near-melodrama of that version, as well as its condensed and swiftly moving action, lent itself well to Schorm's vision.

On the very small Zábradlí stage, the designer Jan Dušek (*b.* 1942) created a setting of white vertical panels made of buckram, an inexpensive, expendable material that was spattered with blood and was torn down during each performance. The panels made for a variety of easy entrances and enabled actors to hide and yet be seen. All furniture was constructed of varying configurations of boxes painted in military camouflage patterns; a sack of similar camouflage netting was suspended above the right side of the stage.

A basic parodistic tone was established at the start by presenting the Ghost loudly lamenting in full clanging armor. Costuming and makeup also signaled a deliberately eccentric approach: Hamlet had blackened eye sockets, black jeans, and a sweater; Claudius also had blackened eyes, a vest without a shirt, a blanket-like cape, and a very small crown; Horatio wore a safari outfit. Only the Players appeared in Elizabethan costumes. Hamlet himself was played as cool, reserved, matter of fact, and reasonable as he progressed without any particular hesitation or emotional stress toward what appeared to be a pre-programed death.

Symptomatic of the production as a whole was the graveyard scene. The Gravediggers were presented as circus clowns, in whiteface, with red balls for noses, making infantile non-verbal sounds, half-whistling, half-humming. They wore shorts, no shirts, and had gloves and long rubberized aprons curiously appropriate to their duties as exhumers. In jarring contrast to the stylized quality of the properties, costumes, and abstract white panels, Yorick's skull was ultra-naturalistic, muddy, and with stringy, matted hair. During Hamlet's subsequent scene with Osric, the Gravediggers rearranged the components of the setting for the duel. The duel itself was marked by a directorially imposed irony: both Laertes and Hamlet put on soft headcoverings that obviously blocked their vision: we witnessed a duel of two blinded opponents. At the culmination of the ensuing bloodbath the Gravediggers, who had been observing the duel, tossed Claudius back and forth before presenting him to Hamlet, who stabbed him. One of the Gravediggers then dragged on the bodies of Ophelia and Polonius and added them to the corpses of the dueling scene, while the other Gravedigger, still making infantile sounds, pulled down the camouflage net to cover all the bodies. Fortinbras entered in traditional armor, put on Claudius's crown, and presented the final speech in a cut-and-dried, mechanistic way, thereby suggesting that all the turmoil really hadn't made much difference and that a criminal had been replaced by a dehumanized puppet.

The Zábradlí *Hamlet* illustrates the special complication that was attendant on most Czech productions for the previous fifty years (that is, since the Munich dismemberment of the country): a need to communicate on more than one level, and in hidden, indirect, often cryptic terms because of severely oppressive conditions. A production, especially a revival of a classic, was expected to offer some comment or special perspective on the play in relation to the socio-political conditions prevailing at the time. By the same token, a Czech audience saw productions in at least two ways: it saw the inherent set of circumstances and characters in action as provided by the playwright, but it was also conditioned to perceive and appreciate the work of the director in setting up special parallels or resonances between the world of the playwright and the world in which they were living. The Zábradlí *Hamlet* seen by an American audience would probably have been taken as a jaundiced takeoff or burlesque of the play and/or the character, not as a despairing, grotesque comment on the current regime. To put it another way, the Zábradlí *Hamlet* to American eyes might have seemed a somewhat labored though ingenious parody with an enigmatic or questionable purpose; but to the Czechs it was an intensely bitter, grotesque reflection of their world and their predicament within it.

In striking contrast to the Zábradlí *Hamlet* was the 1982 National Theatre revival, which remained in the repertoire until December 1988. Not only was the text drawn from the more traditional Second Quarto and Folio sources, and the staging mounted in the much grander space of the Smetana Theatre building, but the entire aim of the production was more traditional in presenting Hamlet as a sympathetic, positive figure locked in a desperate, principled struggle to outwit evil forces, and succeeding. His and other lives are lost, but the clear point was that it was worthwhile. In his approach to *Hamlet*, director Miroslav Macháček (1922–91) seemed to challenge the premise that one must find a "new" way to interpret classic material in order to make it "relevant." He did not adopt any

striking view or concept or style, other than to emphasize the
humanity of the story and its characters as they were shaped by
Shakespeare and to relate the result as directly as possible to the
audience, on a traditional proscenium stage.

František Němec, an actor in his early forties, played Hamlet as a
masculine, often brooding figure, occasionally explosive, given to
darting and sprinting about the stage; he was frank, direct, intelligent and quick-witted, but neither a poet nor an intellectual. Warm
and responsive with friends and those he trusted, he was not neuro-
tic, indecisive, or isolated, but very much part of the court's life. The
implicit point was that Macháček viewed the play as a social
phenomenon rather than as a study of an unusual individual.
Reinforcing this approach was characterization that always stressed
the tangible humanity of the agents rather than some abstract
concept or special key to each figure. Outstanding examples were
Hamlet's two scenes with the Players. The bantering, exhorting, and
incidental by-play were those of old and tried friends. The scenes
glowed with an almost Dickensian life of their own; they were not
simply functional plot units with a few touches of humor. The First
Player's account of Hecuba was an impassioned, totally convincing
testimony that became reality to the First Player; his fellow actors
had to snap him out of his despair. The overall result of such
performances had the immediacy, color, and texturing of a genre
painting but without its excessive, naturalistic detail.

From one point of view, this *Hamlet* might be considered as
undistinguished insofar as it lacked a dominating metaphor, style, or
image, but the sheer involvement and intensity of the performers in
their moment-by-moment life on the stage prevented any such
negative judgments. One other theatrical technique contributed to
this effect and was crucial in this production: direct address to the
audience. Every soliloquy was overtly shared with the audience,
even Claudius' private confession of his rank offense. Hamlet did not
speak to himself or verbalize his inner thoughts in some sort of limbo;
he simply and impulsively took the audience into his confidence.
Macháček extended this technique to several other moments in the
play, presumably to increase the involvement of the audience. For
instance, at the end of act 3, scene 1, Ophelia, left alone on stage
after the exit of Polonius and Claudius, turned and stared in despair
at the audience. Horatio was included in act 4, scene 4, as Hamlet
was dispatched to England; left on stage as the others leave, he

turned to register dismay to the audience. And at the end of the play, alone and spotlighted on stage, Horatio appealed despairingly to the audience in mime. It is impossible to arrive at a neat interpretation of these various directorial touches, but it may be that Macháček, who was frequently in difficulties with authorities, deliberately avoided any sharp or overtly critical slant in the production, almost a complicity of allies against a common foe. Even though Fortinbras was presented as a noble, commanding figure rather than a Nordic fascist, the waste of humanity in the central action is what Macháček seemed to underline by his business with Horatio at the end, as if to say, "Must it come to this before a land is rid of its evil?"

To emphasize the human action of the play most forcibly, Josef Svoboda created an austere, virtually bare stage setting consisting solely of plain black drapes to enclose the action, and several shallow stairs running the full width of the stage. Minimal furniture and occasional touches of color (such as a rose-colored valance for the Players scene) were introduced into this space, which was illuminated with relatively high intensity lighting throughout. Moreover, the acting area was extended forward over the orchestra pit, so that much of the action took place between frontal side boxes of the auditorium at stage level. The consequent added exposure of the characters obviously reinforced the direct communion with the audience. Having abstained from many of his signature devices (projections, mirrors, kinetic scenery), Svoboda saved one striking effect for the very end. In his death throes, Claudius grabbed the black drape at the rear of the stage, pulling it down to reveal a massive staircase wreathed in smoke to heighten Hamlet's last moments, the entrance of the ruler-to-be, Fortinbras, and the mournful but grand movement of the soldiers bearing Hamlet's body up the topless stairs.

Considering the universal tradition of adaptations, even burlesques, of Shakespeare, and recalling E. F. Burian's *Hamlet III*, it is fitting to complete this survey with a glance at yet another approach to *Hamlet*, this one presented without costumes or scenery by three performers on a bare platform with a table and two chairs. It was the creation of Ivan Vyskočil (*b.* 1929), something of a maverick, gadfly, Renaissance man who has been operating on the fringes of Prague theatre since the late 1950s. A graduate of the theatre academy, and an initiator of the small-theatre movement of the

1960s, he prefers paratheatrical activities involving psychology and sociology to traditional dramatic and theatrical forms. A variant of what he calls his "text appeals," *Haprdáns* (an acronym of *Hamlet Princ Dánsky*) was a unique adaptation of *Hamlet* that was part lecture, part demonstration, and part editorial, which Vyskočil began performing in 1986. Assuming the central function of narrator-actor-critic, Vyskočil wittily reviewed some classic critical interpretations of the play before offering his own version of a *Hamlet* appropriate for our time: no longer a tragedy but, in line with today's standards, a normalized action in which much occurs but nothing of significance actually happens. First, he and his two co-performers (both women) presented a very funny, sardonic, 20-minute condensation of the main action that consisted of some dialogue and considerable narrative bridging, and during which each character was represented by a kitchen utensil: for example, a rather worn-out egg-beater for Hamlet, a wooden ladle for Claudius, a colander for Polonius, a whisk for Ophelia, and so on.

The *pièce de résistance* which followed was Vyskočil's revisionist *Hamlet*, a view behind the scenes during which we were shown moments of what really lay under Shakespeare's camouflaged version of events. Interspersed with running critical comment or quick asides implying contemporary parallels were Vyskočil's neo-*Hamlet* scenes between the main characters that revealed Hamlet with an Oedipus complex and an alter ego, and Claudius as a power-hungry, effective manager, who was manipulated by both Gertrude and Polonius, the powers behind the throne. In Vyskočil's version, Polonius was never killed; Hamlet received psychotherapy in England, returned normalized and completely adaptable (embodied as a brand new, shining egg-beater), and married Ophelia. A final scene revealed that Claudius, who remained as king, was really Hamlet's father, and that Polonius was looking forward to being a grandfather.

Haprdáns was far more than an ingenious charade; it represented but one more agile employment of *Hamlet* for purposes extending beyond the theatre. With wit and acumen, Vyskočil stressed often grotesque but also hilarious psychological and political tactics among the characters that made the play resonate, albeit indirectly, with the realities of Czech society before November 1989. His version has been running since 1986 and is but one of Vyskočil's presentations of a similarly idiosyncratic type.

Setting Vyskočil's eccentric adaptation aside, several concluding observations may be made with regard to this glance at Czech productions of *Hamlet*. First, the productions since World War II did not introduce approaches or tendencies that were not fundamentally present in one or more prewar productions; only the degree of sophistication in production techniques and the reference points or targets varied. On a more general level, because they were not really able to deal with the verbal beauties of image, metaphor, and sound patterns of Shakespeare in the original tongue, the Czech productions, perhaps like many foreign-language productions, tended to place greater emphasis on character interplay, theme, and overt stage action. Moreover, Czech theatre and its audiences, because of their historical and cultural background, were inclined to be especially sensitive to the social and political relevance of Shakespeare's works, particularly in a play like *Hamlet*, which is as rich in political implications as it is in psychological complexities. This tendency was particularly noticeable in periods of social and national stress, such as the era of 1948–89, which was dominated by an oppressive regime. As early as 1966, Zdeněk Stříbrný noted, "the tragedies of Shakespeare ... are ... courageous in their attack on the knotted complexity of life and history, and we ourselves are trying to grapple with this, too."[4]

Concurrently, however, there was a distinct tendency to place almost equal emphasis on the sheer production values of striking mises en scène, often with particular concern for the functional role of scenography. It is as if the Czech theatre artists were always conscious of a dual if not a triple responsibility: as interpreters of the dramatic values inherent in the text, as veiled commentators on forces influencing if not determining contemporary life in their land, and as artists who are ultimately as concerned with the aesthetic values of their efforts as they are with their socio-political relevance.

A final consideration suggests that unlike many other recent foreign productions of Shakespeare, which have often departed radically if not grotesquely from the original conventions and configurations of the plays, Czech productions have been notable for their relatively conservative, traditional (some might say outdatedly conventional) orientation. Even those productions that introduced striking shifts of tone and emphasis (e.g., the Zábradlí *Hamlet*) still maintained an essential fidelity to the basic structure and action of the play. They did not presume to use Shakespeare as a mere initial vehicle for their own radically subjective, often radically politicized, visions. Even Vyskočil's *Haprdáns*, which was not, strictly speaking, a production of *Hamlet*, implicitly retained the crucial elements and structural flow of Shakespeare's original in order to make its own points. This is essentially different from relegating Shakespeare's text to the role of a bare armature for surrealistic accretions, such as those evident in the productions of Peter Zadek, Andrzej Wajda, or Ingmar Bergman, which suggest a reluctance to acknowledge the special artistic challenge of revitalizing this difficult, often cryptic play on its own terms, but instead used the text as an occasion for the director's own (more important?) statement.

The Czech productions, on the other hand, seemed to rise to the challenge of staging *Hamlet* while still remaining close to its form and substance. They seemed to respect the text, in a double sense: not only what Shakespeare wrote but the way he wrote it. These productions drew on the Czech theatre's tradition of imaginative direction and expressive scenography to present in visual terms of line, mass, movement, color, and lighting – in concert with acting that was centered in psychological realism – a dynamic, often metaphoric embodiment of the respective concepts underlying the *Hamlet* productions noted here. In this sense, the Czech stagings of *Hamlet* may also be perceived as the aesthetic response of theatre artists to a universal masterwork of dramatic literature as much as they have been responses to external social and political pressures and their echoes within the play. The fact that they have shown relatively more fidelity to their source than have other postwar productions in Europe may owe something to the after-effects of an imposed policy of Socialist Realism, to a long affinity with a Stanislavskian acting tradition, and to a cultural tradition that values reason and moderation above impulse, passion, subjectivity. To these contributing causes must be added one other: with few exceptions (1968–9 and the very late 1980s), the Czech theatre since 1948 was not in communication with the iconoclastic post-modern movements that characterized so much of western theatre during the past thirty or so years. Now that the country is nearly wide open, it will be extremely interesting to see the extent to which this new freedom will be reflected in theatre, and in its new productions of *Hamlet*.

NOTES

1 Jan Mukařovský, "Shakespeare and Czech Theatrical Criticism," in *Charles University on Shakespeare*, ed. Zdeněk Stříbrný (Prague: Universita Karlova, 1966), 14, 21.

2 František Černý, *Měnivá Tvář Divadla* (The Changing Face of Theatre) (Prague: Mladá Fronta, 1978), 155.

3 Radovan Lukavský, *Hamlet: Pracovní Deník* (A Working Diary) (Prague: Divadelní Ústav, 1965), 105.

4 Zdeněk Stříbrný, "Shakespeare Today," in *Charles University*, 35.

PART III

Postmodern Shakespeare

A new set of theatrical responses is treated in this section: the deliberate, postmodern accenting of the strangeness of Shakespeare's texts and their interrelationship with other aspects of contemporary culture.

Marvin Carlson writes about three productions from the Paris director Daniel Mesguich, completely antagonistic to the habits of Anglo–American Shakespeare. Carlson sees Mesguich's work as a kind of end-point, an attempt to deal with an exhausted observance, particularly in its concern with the destruction of books: Mesguich's intertextual approach often uses actual books as cardinal stage devices. Wilhelm Hortmann also sees the visual as central to postmodern practice; his essay investigates the relationship of scenography to verbal text in some recent German productions, particularly an arresting *Twelfth Night* directed by Andrea Breth in Bochum.

Andrea Nouryeh introduces the subject of Shakespeare in Asia with a survey of Japanese performance; the history of Shakespeare's effect on Japanese culture, and Japanese theatre practice in turn influencing western understanding, is best demonstrated by Yukio Ninagawa's *Macbeth*. Patrice Pavis's intercultural treatment of three 1990 productions (by Peter Brook, Peter Zadek, and Robert Wilson) asks why directors and audiences, in a "postmodern no man's land," continue to return to Shakespeare. If his work is no longer performed in order to understand the text, and no longer performed in order to understand our contemporary world, what value can it hold in the theatre and in western culture?

Daniel Mesguich and intertextual Shakespeare

Marvin Carlson

Although almost all major modern French directors, from Antoine and Lugné-Poe to Mnouchkine and Chéreau, have included at least some Shakespearean works among their major undertakings, the French have never shared their enthusiasm that has made Shakespeare a central figure in German theatrical history. A director particularly associated with Shakespearean stagings is still a rather uncommon phenomenon in France, and probably no director of the current generation fits this description better than Daniel Mesguich. The association is a complex and ambiguous one, however, since Mesguich's Shakespeare is heavily influenced by contemporary French literary and psychoanalytic theory, resulting in radically untraditional productions that have inspired tremendous enthusiasm in some quarters and bitter protest in others.

Mesguich was born in Algiers in 1952 and moved with his parents to Marseilles ten years later. At 17 he entered the Sorbonne in philosophy and became a devoted student of Hegel. He then entered the Conservatory as a student of directing, working with Antoine Vitez. Upon his graduation he founded his own company, the Théâtre du Miroir, which attracted attention in the mid-1970s by its radical reworkings of Marivaux and Racine. These in turn led to an invitation in 1977 from Pierre Lavaudant, director of the state theatre at Grenoble, for Mesguich to come as a guest director for a production of *Hamlet*, his first Shakespeare.

The Grenoble *Hamlet*, actually entitled *Le Hamlet de Shakespeare*, brought Mesguich to general critical attention and fully displayed for the first time many of the features of his work. Like most of his productions, it stimulated very powerful reactions, positive and negative, both in March in Grenoble, and in November, when it was revived at the Théâtre des Amandiers in the Paris suburbs. Guy Dumur of the *Nouvel Observateur* spoke of this as a "disintegrated"

Hamlet, showing the influence of the French neo-Freudian Jacques Lacan. Mesguich, said Dumur, attempts "to penetrate the unconscious of Hamlet and Shakespeare by detonation, by throwing in a bomb to make everything fly apart."[1] Although the traditional text certainly undergoes a kind of disintegration in Mesguich's work, the intellectual process involved could as readily be thought of as agglutinative, of material being added and elaborated rather than broken apart or destroyed. In a special issue of *Silex*, the review of the Grenoble theatre, devoted to *Hamlet*, Mesguich spoke of two different texts of a classical work, the first being the written text. The second, his own concern, is "less immediately visible, deeper, often not written, sometimes not spoken, teased out by a variety of instruments (dialectics, linguistic science, psychoanalysis, historical materialism, and so on), made up of all the alluvial deposits which have accumulated and continue to accumulate around the first text and in its wake ever since it was first produced."[2] It was presumably to call attention to this "second text" that the Grenoble/Paris production of 1977 was called *Le Hamlet de Shakespeare* instead of *Hamlet*. The complexity of this accumulated text is particularly great in the case of Shakespeare, since the original works themselves were uniquely rich in the range of concerns explored and in the anticipation of future systems of thought. Mesguich has considered, for example, *A Midsummer Night's Dream*, but so far has not undertaken the project because it involves not only a complicated texture of dream analysis, but a complete mastery of "all the rules of Carnival, of the Tarot, of the Old Testament."[3] Mesguich has characterized Shakespeare as "the absolute writer, who always surprises and who has always anticipated everything, as if he had at hand a storehouse of everything to come – Freud, Joyce, Kafka."[4]

Each of the Mesguich Shakespeare productions has used a single but complex base setting, containing a number of areas and levels, continually restructured by a rich and complex play of lighting. The most striking feature of the *Hamlet* setting was a heap of stone ruins to the left, some traces of color still on the aging rocks. Columns, a sculptured lintel, a tattered curtain of one rich material marked this area as a stage, and so it was used in much of the production. The center and right of the stage suggested a dark exterior, with the sound of the sea roaring in the background. Perhaps the first shock of this production was the language, a kind of imitation Old French created by translator Michel Vittoz with Latin inversions of syntax, neologisms, echoes of archaic words, English terms, and recent Shakespearean translations. The reviewer for *Le Monde* speculated that Mesguich and his translator may have been in part attempting to recapture something of the poetic and intellectual richness this complex text may have presented to an average theatre-goer in 1603.[5] Rather more likely, especially in view of his reference to Joyce, Mesguich was interested in laying a thick web of verbal reference over the structure of a familiar action, calling up multiple references in the spectators' minds.

Other devices were clearly utilized to increase the texture of interreferentiality in the production. Elements of the "second text" of *Hamlet* – glosses and commentaries – were worked into the "first text." It was, the reviewer for *Le Monde* observed, as if the text of *Hamlet* were presented along with commentaries, criticism, and references "without putting these in notes at the foot of the page or the end of the book, but rather mixing them indistinguishably into the text itself, so that one could no longer tell what was text and what Freudian, Lacanian, and other glosses."[6] In addition a new character, an "Archidame," was added specifically for the purpose of introducing material from contemporary authors that did not relate directly to *Hamlet* but was connected thematically with certain scenes or with their interpretation by Mesguich. Often on a small balcony overlooking the stone stage, the Archidame presented selections from Marguerite Duras, from Cixous's *Portrait de Dora*, from Godard's "La Chinoise."

Characters and actions were, like the language, presented in unconventional, and often in complex, refracted, and ambiguous forms. Two characters played Hamlet (dressed in rose rather than the traditional black), and a clown (Yorick?) often parodied them, making an ironic third. There was no Ghost – instead Hamlet confronted his double, appearing not on the ramparts but on the internal stage. There were also two Ophelias, a blond and a brunette, appearing nude in the mad scene. Gertrude, seemingly near to Hamlet in age, also appeared nude in the bedchamber scene, its Freudian theme of incest markedly apparent. Many sequences were presented, or parodied on the smaller internal stage, perhaps most strikingly the "To be or not to be" speech which was given here not by Hamlet, but by one of the Players, for the entertainment of the court. Although most of the play's memorable moments and sequences were retained, Mesguich, as in his subsequent

Shakespearean offerings, radically altered the rhythm of the text by interpolations, cutting, rearrangement, and even repetition of sequences. A number of scenes were given twice, for emphasis or to stress different elements. Perhaps most striking, when Hamlet found the King in prayer he "killed" him several times, each time with Claudius springing back to life as if in a rewound film.

In the summer of 1981, after a similarly deconstructed interpretation of Claudel's *Tête d'or* had augmented his reputation, Mesguich was invited to stage *King Lear* at the Avignon Festival, the leading showcase in France for experimental new productions. Major critics were less kind to *Lear* than they had been to *Hamlet*: Guy Dumur in the *Nouvel Observateur* called it "a massacre of a great work." Pierre Marcabru in *Le Figaro* conceded a brilliant use of space, visual imagination, and texture of light and sound, but likened the audience's experience to that of a child in front of a Christmas shopwindow, dazzled by the display but left with little of substance. All at last was reduced, in Marcabru's opinion, to "hollow formalism" in which the director "sought to define his existence by the destruction of his enemy, the author."[7]

Certainly Mesguich's *Lear*, like his *Hamlet*, provided much to offend those who expected a traditionalist treatment of the text, but his visual and textual innovations clearly proved more attractive to the Festival audiences than they did to these reviewers. *Lear* proved the leading attraction of the summer, without a seat or even a stair-tread unoccupied for any of its performances. As with *Hamlet*, Mesguich embedded the Shakespearean work within a web of associative materials, critical, cultural, and artistic, now including his own previous Shakespearean staging. Once again certain scenes were severely cut and other sequences repeated several times. Costumes were elaborately theatrical but suggestive of no particular period. Among the major features of the setting by Thierry Delory was a little cemetery with miniaturized oblique walls that served in this production a function similar to the small theatre in *Hamlet*. The production began with the emergence from this cemetery of a sepulchral figure carrying a skull. This was Yorick, who, like the Archidame in *Hamlet*, provided during the course of the play a series of related observations from modern authors – Aragon, Barthes, Camus. A traditional clown costume was worn not by Yorick but by Lear, whose entrances, exits, and gestures, like those of most of the characters, were as a rule highly stylized and grotesque.

And once again Michel Vittoz provided the translation, another complex verbal structure based upon the original but with continual elaboration and distortion of syntax and semiotics. In this production the verbal text was still further distanced by the use of chest microphones employed so as to produce a kind of spoken chant with few modulations except for violent eruptions of sound or abrupt silences. The tension between silence and speech, and the inadequacy of speech to bring the reality of what is thought and felt out of the domain of silence, has been a central concern of much modern theory and, Mesguich has suggested, of much great theatre, especially in plays like *Lear* and *Hamlet* where silence, the unspoken, and the inadequacy of speech are pivotal matters. Silences were of considerable importance in the Mesguich *Lear*, but in fact there was rarely a moment devoid of sound. An extremely elaborate tape created by Daniel Deshays accompanied the action, a montage superimposing a distant piano, snatches of symphonic music, a bit of rock, the passing of a distant train, and piercing bird cries.

Mesguich has spoken of encouraging his actors to determine their work on a principle of resistance, as if the words betrayed by indirection what they really wanted to say but repressed. *Lear* and *Hamlet* clearly sought to provide glimpses of this suppressed world by verbal play, disjunctures, unexpected associations and disassociations, theatrical strategies similar to the literary strategies of post-structuralism. Clearly, such an approach has little concern with psychological interpretation, indeed with interpretation in any conventional sense, even with the telling of a story. Shakespeare's plots remain, as overarching frameworks, but attention is focused upon the plays of elements, linguistic, visual, emotional, and semiotic, within these organizing structures.

In the spring of 1985 Mesguich mounted his third Shakespeare, *Romeo and Juliet*, at the Théâtre de l'Athénée in Paris. Once again intertextuality was a major organizing principle of the interpretation, but this time manifested in a much more directly theatrical way. The adaptation, by Gervais Robin, moved away from the linguistic thickness of the earlier Vittoz texts, but still took considerable liberties with the original. In a program note the adapter spoke of the universality of this story, known, at least in its broad outlines, to almost everyone. Romeo and Juliet have become paradigmatic lovers who, Robin suggested, "haunt our theatres, our films, our books."

The Mesguich production made literal this "haunting," and, in accordance with its director's interest in the "second text," emphasized also that our present reception of this familiar story is now itself haunted by other related stories of frustrated love, by Cyrano and Quasimodo, by lovers in other Shakespearean tragedies, and in the works of Chekhov, Marivaux, Racine. In earlier Mesguich works such related texts might have been suggested by verbal echoes, embedded in the Vittoz adaptations of Shakespearean lines or set apart in specific speeches by interpolated characters like the Archidame or Yorick. Here the ghostly figures of characters from these related texts physically appeared, moving in and out of the shifting world of Romeo and Juliet and our perception of it.

The setting, more elaborate and more openly metaphorical than those of the earlier productions, was perfectly suited to these manifestations. It was a huge labyrinth, an enormous library with corridors filled with hundreds of books, leading off in all directions in a manner somewhat suggestive of Brugel's *Tower of Babel* (illustration 13). From time to time shrouded ghosts from these innumerable tomes wandered about the balconies, walkways, and major acting areas of the stage like figures in a Strindberg chamber play. In this intertextual labyrinth, the focus upon the story of Romeo and Juliet appeared as the result of the choice of some mysterious higher power. In the opening scene a book fell to the stage from the flies and was opened by the servant/clowns Abraham and Gregory, who moved in and out of this production in a manner somewhat reminiscent of Stoppard's Rosencrantz and Guildenstern. They began to read, developing a complex verbal routine out of Shakespeare's joking puns which built gradually into a quarrel and then into the public confrontation between the rival houses which opened the major action of the play.

The ball scene became the locus in this production of the intertextual process. The sequence actually began with Mercutio's Queen Mab speech. Upstage center a section of the library approached by a rather erratic group of stairs could be closed off with curtains to form the familiar Mesguich inner stage. Behind this were more rows of books, but they could be covered by an inner backcloth to emphasize the stage image. For the Queen Mab speech, Mercutio conjured up in this space against a theatrical night sky a parade of the personifications of his fancy, a parade that spilled down the stairway and became the costumed guests at the ball. As the ball

13   *Romeo and Juliet*, directed by Daniel Mesguich, Théâtre de l'Athénée, Paris, 1985. The Capulet ball. *Photo: Brigitte Enguerand.*

progressed, its guests began to perform scenes suggested by their costumes but also related in some manner to the frustrated love motif of the overarching play. Thus Juliet appeared as Nina in *The Seagull*, while other actors played the Lady Anne scene from *Richard III*, the rejection of Nero from Racine's *Britannicus*, a lovers' quarrel from Marivaux, and finally, from *Hamlet*, the scene in the Queen's bedchamber, which Mesguich again saw in deeply Freudian terms.

Some of these scenes were performed for the entertainment of the other guests, like charades at a party, but at other times several scenes were played simultaneously in different parts of the stage, their lines interlocking and seemingly commenting on each other. Romeo, the outsider, participated in none of this, playing his only real party scene (the pilgrim speeches) with Juliet. He was last seen by Juliet amid the thwarted lovers of Chekhov, Marivaux, and Racine, gathered on the up-center stage, each acting out his or her agony to an absent lover, while downstage "Hamlet" tried in vain to make Gertrude see this intertextual version of his "ghost."

No other section of the production was elaborated in such baroque complexity as this, but every scene contained images of striking beauty and originality. The costumes were almost entirely of black or of grays and greens so dark as to appear black, with red accents, especially in handkerchiefs and in the dropping of red petals, vividly suggesting splashes of blood. The stage floor was covered in white sand against which these elements stood out sharply and in which swords, books, and so on were from time to time buried or discovered. As in the earlier productions there was an almost continuous musical score, exactly calibrated with the actors' movements, also adding powerfully to the overall effect. For example, a recurring motif was a repeated tentative touch, as when the Nurse found the presumably dead Juliet, a motif chillingly reinforced on each occasion by an exactly corresponding musical chord. At the end of the production, the dead lovers were led off into the depths of the literary labyrinth in a kind of dance of death by some of the other ghostly literary figures who haunted the production, apparently to join them in their Pirandellian half-existence as permanent fictional "characters" in this Borgesque library.

From 1986 until 1988 Mesguich served as director of a national dramatic center, the Théâtre Gerard-Philipe at Saint-Denis, in the suburbs of Paris. One of his first creations here was a restaging of *Hamlet*, utilizing the Vittoz adaptation. This time Mesguich himself, whose reputation as an actor is also considerable, played the title role as well as directing. This production was considered by some critics to be more modest, less flamboyantly imagistic than Mesguich's first *Hamlet*, less oriented towards the play's mythic dimensions than towards its personal, social, and theatrical concerns. Nevertheless, the new interpretation was unmistakably Mesguich's. The subject of *Hamlet*, he observed at this time, is "the monstrous alchemy of appearance and reality." As had been the case in previous Mesguich productions of Shakespeare, appearance and reality often shifted abruptly, interpenetrating in highly theatrical terms. When Hamlet stabbed Polonius, the tear in the arras ripped through the castle wall as well, creating a seeming crack in the universe itself. Francisco and Bernardo in the opening scene themselves turned out to be apparitions, fading upon the crowing of the cock. Ghostly doubles haunted central characters, Rosencrantz and Guildenstern were clearly a single figure doubled, and Hamlet, instead of being two characters as in 1977, was a fragmented small crowd, including a complete skeleton (of the dead Hamlet?) that Hamlet carried about with him. In an interview Mesguich suggested that the greatest difficulty in *Hamlet* was losing oneself in it, since the play was infinite in its speculations, and the character Hamlet stood at the center of this infinity, reflecting all other characters. Remember, said Mesguich, that the play begins with the question "Who's there?" "That is the central question. Who is Hamlet? The eye of the cyclone, everyman, the touchstone of all those who surround him. One cannot say he is mad, violent, feigning. Nothing is certain, nothing crystalized, nothing set. One does not interpret Hamlet, one makes of it what one is."[8] The play began with a doubling of the theatre itself and a foregrounding of this central question. The curtain rose to disclose another curtain, soon tossed by wind and swirling fog, with the sound of the sea in the background. The second curtain rose on an abandoned and decaying stage, filled with fog which slowly dispersed as the cry "Who's there?" was repeated again and again from scattered offstage voices.

Inevitably Mesguich's reinterpretations of classical works have aroused questions about his responsibilities to the original text, and his strong directional vision has aroused questions about his relationship to his actors. His attitude toward both matters was clearly expressed in comments on *Lorenzaccio*, which he staged in the same season as the 1986 *Hamlet*:

We must remember that we are presenting a nineteenth-century play about the sixteenth century after having known Einstein, Freud, and Marx – I respect the tradition, but I do not want to be its ventriloquist. A text is by definition open and plural. When it is put on stage, it is as though a newborn child takes its first breath. A performance is always signed by someone. When the director is not visible, the dominant ideology provides the backing. The same is true for the actors. Those who are not directed also obey someone invisible. It is true that during rehearsal I explain a good deal. I speak knowing that between saying and doing there is a gulf. That gulf is the actor's freedom.[9]

The "opening" of the text, both by exposing hidden meanings and by insertion of material from other texts, has encouraged some of Mesguich's commentators to apply to his work the fashionable term of deconstructionist. "It is an accurate label to a point," Mesguich has remarked, "but I don't do in theatre what Jacques Derrida does

in his writing." Certain concepts, Mesguich suggests, have come
into his work from Derrida, as well as from Roland Barthes, Gilles
Deleuze, and other contemporary theorists. Their influence is indirect, a tool, but this intellectual basis Mesguich sees as essential
to his vision. "I try for a theatricality pushed to the edge, almost
a violence, where you can feel the pure pleasure of acting. But it has
to be intelligently thought out, otherwise it's only an animal
pleasure."[10]

In the fall of 1989 Mesguich returned to the Athénée in central
Paris for his most recent and most critically acclaimed Shakespeare,
Titus Andronicus. Leading Parisian reviewers, such as Michel
Cournot, Pierre Marcabru, and Marion Thébaud, several of whom
had expressed misgivings about Mesguich's radical reworkings of
Hamlet and *Lear*, united in calling this production one of the most
brilliant and challenging on the contemporary French stage, the
greatest achievement to date of "a great poet of the theatre," and
"by far the outstanding production" of this difficult play "among
those stagings in a number of countries over the past twenty
years."[11] This achievement was all the more remarkable since the
rarely performed *Titus* has traditionally been considered the most
difficult and problematic work in the Shakespearean canon. Those
with a longtime interest in the work of Mesguich recalled that he
first gained a certain notoriety in Paris through a shocking scene in
his Conservatory production of *La jalousie de Barbouillé* utilizing
realistic blood and viscera, and some speculated that the ghastly
events of *Titus* might have encouraged Mesguich to return to such
horrors. Others, anticipating an eventual Mesguich Shakespeare
cycle, looked upon *Titus* as a difficult but unavoidable item in this
series. Both views underestimated the seriousness and depth of
intellectual commitment of Mesguich to all of his projects.

Mesguich, unlike many interpreters, did not consider *Titus* a
crude or ill-formed early work, but a significant philosophical
drama, already the work of a genius of the theatre. Despite his
productions of *Hamlet* and *Lear*, Mesguich has shown a strong
directional interest in the early works of major dramatists, like
Chekhov's *Platonov* or Claudel's *Tête d'Or*, in which the seeds of the
later and better-known works can be discerned. In *Titus* he sensed
"the kernel, the matrix of the entire Shakespearean continent," the
source from which flow *Richard III*, *Macbeth*, and *Lear*. He saw it not
at all as a simple Grand Guignol tragedy of blood, but as a highly

calculated study of barbarism, with a "calculated, gradual, and inexorable escalation of crime, almost mathematical in its rigor."[12]

The concept of barbarism was central to Mesguich's interpretation of *Titus*. He found the recent RSC production of the play (directed by Deborah Warner) disappointing, in that it stressed the barbarism in costume and gesture, but in a deracinated way, without reference to the civilization from which this barbarism had departed. Mesguich considered it critical that the play was set in Rome, a cradle of civilization, the master city, a metaphor for Shakespeare of high culture and civil organization. *Titus*, however, shows a late Rome, in which this culture and civilization have created their own barbarism, a new surge of cruel and elemental forces springing up amid, and in part defined by, the no-longer-understood relics and ruins of the past. This is not a pre-civilized barbarism, but a post-civilized one. When rituals are retained, their "civilized" meanings are forgotten, and they become elemental acts – the symbol becomes flesh, the cooked becomes the raw. In Mesguich's production, this phrase was enacted literally at the beginning of the play when the only dimly understood ritualized "sacrifice" of the symbolic ram was interrupted so that the victim could become the flesh-and-blood captive, Tamora's son. The horror of the play, Mesguich has commented, comes not from the spilling of blood itself, but from the "marriage of the ritual and the real, the marriage of theatre and of civilization with the raw, with flesh and blood." Thus the interplay of barbarism and civilization blended in this production with the common Mesguich fascination with the interplay of theatre and reality, seeming and being, the living and the dead.

The tension between barbarism and civilization was symbolically centered in this production in a common Mesguich symbol – the book. The posters for *Titus* showed rows of ancient, leather-bound books on the shelves of a library and two huge nail-like spikes propped against them. These books and spikes served as a kind of visual polarity in the production, the books recalling the almost-forgotten past civilization in the ruins of which this barbaric action unfolds, and the spikes the all-too-physical reality of the present, as the weapons of choice for the play's multiple murders and assassinations. The entire action took place in a strange, haunting setting conceived by Louis Bercut, and strongly recalling the setting for Mesguich's *Romeo and Juliet*: another library, an immense baroque

14 Christian Blanc as Titus in the library in Mesguich's *Titus Andronicus*,
Théâtre de l'Athénée, Paris, 1989. *Photo: Marc and Brigitte Enguerand.*

room not seen head-on, but fallen on its side, so that at the back of
the stage the sky was seen through an arching dome with a center
open ellipse (illustration 14). Despite the visual echoes in the rows of
leather-bound books, the library served as a quite different metaphor in these two productions. *Romeo and Juliet* was presented as part
of an intricate network of literature, a functioning system which
became manifested on the stage as characters and scenes from other
books, other plays, other stories, interacted with those of Shakespeare's tragedy. No such communication was possible in *Titus*,
where the books represented an almost forgotten past, now scarcely
accessible. Just as the characters were unable to relate physically to

the spatial orientation of the library, they were unable to relate to its contents, even to the point of remembering precisely what function books served. When in Mesguich's barbarian world "symbol became flesh," books became simple physical objects, to be utilized as hiding-places, weapons, or objects to be mutilated or destroyed, not as repositories of hidden information about alternate worlds. The lapse from civilization to barbarism was for Mesguich most clearly captured in the replacement of what the library represented by the physical violence of this new world. "Blood on a book," he has said, "is more frightening than the worst of slaughterhouses."

Like *Romeo and Juliet*, Mesguich's *Titus* began with a book falling from the flies, but the image was a very different one. Descending electronic chords with ominous string tremolos beneath, a recurring musical motif, sounded in the darkness, and the curtain rose to reveal a crumpled shape lying center stage on the bookcases. The figure arose, revealing itself as a thin, bowler-hatted turn-of-the-century gentlemen, holding a dove in his hand, an image strongly suggesting a painting by the Surrealist Magritte. The mysterious gentleman gave a single line, "All is departed." In the bookcase above his head, which formed the ceiling of the set, a book caught fire and dropped flaming to the floor beside him, again suggesting an image from a Surrealist painting. The curtain fell, ending the first scene.

All of these images appeared again and again during the production. Falling, flaming books marked several of the murders, and the play ended in a flaming apocalypse. The mysterious gentleman, played by Mesguich's dramaturg, Philippe Noël, was identified in the program simply as "Le Monsieur." He served in part, like Mesguich's earlier Yorick or Archidame, as a kind of choric figure for the introduction of intertextual allusions, but he also moved gradually from scenes of his own into the action of the play, taking on certain functions of the clown, bringing Titus the heads of his sons and delivering Titus' message to the Emperor. Among the external sources most quoted by Le Monsieur was Kafka, an author of particular interest to Mesguich, especially in this production. Mesguich's first major undertaking as a director was an adaptation of Kafka's *The Castle* in 1972, and he has acknowledged Kafka as one of the continuing influences on his work, especially in *Titus Andronicus*, which he has characterized as "Kafka through Shakespeare." A quotation from Kafka appeared in the program and was also quoted by the chorus-clown Le Monsieur during the production itself: "Life is an eternal detour which does not allow us to understand even the direction from which it departs."

Two interlocking themes informed Mesguich's concept of barbarism in *Titus*, and both contributed importantly to the visual symbolism of the production. One was the loss of contact with the older civilization represented by the library and specifically its books; the library literally self-destructed during the production, not only through the spectacular self-combusting books, but in the more mundane, but equally chilling sifting down of dust and crumpled plaster from cracks above the stage at the ends of certain scenes. The second theme was the loss of understanding of ritualized abstraction and its replacement by cruelty and bloodshed as word became flesh. Perhaps the most poignant illustration of the loss of relationship to the books that surrounded these characters was the scene of Bassianus' death. As he expired, the horrified Lavinia kept thrusting a book at him, as though she felt somehow it had the power to cure him if she only knew how to use it. When this failed, she cast the useless book aside, and over his dead body opened her mouth in a silent scream reminiscent of Helene Weigel's famous moment in *Mother Courage*.

The dead rarely disappear from Mesguich's dramatic world, and they were particularly evident in *Titus*. Among the elements in the strange distorted library were two huge darkened glass cases, one on each side of the stage, framed by baroque marble pillars and seeming to contain some kind of preserved or mummified exhibits. After Bassianus' death, he appeared among the "specimens," which we then realized included bones and skulls, in the large glass case to our right. The previously killed son of Tamora also appeared, in the opposite case, his makeup suggesting that decomposition had begun, and in many of the subsequent scenes both corpses watched with interest from these enclosures. They were soon joined by others, such as the two sons of Titus, one falling into each glass case when they were trapped in the pit. From time to time, the dead left these habitations, however, to rejoin the living, as in the striking scene (3.1) where Titus appealed in vain to passing Roman citizens. In this version, Titus sat center stage facing down left, and as he tried vainly to gain their attention, the entire cast, living and dead, filed past him, moving diagonally from down left to the up right exit. Later it was the corpses, at Titus' instruction, who shot the arrows with threatening messages into the city, after which they joined in a round of ghastly laughter, like the crackling of dry leaves.

As in the earlier Mesguich Shakespeare productions, the general progression of scenes and much of the original dialogue was retained (for this production Mesguich prepared his own text), though the actual articulation of scenes was much altered. Mesguich divided the play into approximately twenty-five brief scenes, some exactly corresponding to scenes in the original, but most shorter, and a few totally of the director's invention. After each of these the curtain fell rapidly, and the audience sat a moment in darkness registering the invariably striking visual images of the scene just completed. A number of the scenes were very short, little more than striking vignettes, like the first, or the one immediately following, composed only of balanced diagonal crosses by the rival princes, identically dressed in dark robes and blood-red sashes, and repeating their claims in identical words. Sometimes a curtain interrupted a scene, which continued after a short pause with the positions of major characters shifted, or sometimes, as in the earlier Mesguich interpretations, a gesture or a sequence was repeated for emphasis or to underline certain elements in the plot. When, for example, Saturninus turned from Lavinia to Tamora as his Empress, he first made a sweeping exit up-stage left with Lavinia. The curtain fell, then rose on the same configuration, and the exit was identically repeated, but this time with Tamora.

For most of the scenes, the stage remained essentially empty, defined, according to Mesguich's usual practice, by the actors' bodies and striking lighting effects, but there were some notable exceptions. The forest was represented by broad bands of white fabric criss-crossing the stage, and the rape of Lavinia was represented by her being caught in the center of the stage by the sons, and all three wrapping themselves in the fabric, torn loose from its fastenings at the edges of the stage. Both Aaron and the sons of Tamora, captured and dispatched by Titus, were shown in captivity in much the same way, like flies in the center of the stage, wrapped in a spider-web of chains that stretched away in all directions. The notorious banquet at the end converted the baroque library into something resembling a Renaissance hell scene. The ghastly pie served by Titus was decorated with the same ram's skull which marked the sacrifice that opened this cycle of horror. As Titus began to speak of Virginius, smoke began to rise from an up-stage pit

behind him. Soon flames appeared here also. As Lavinia, then
Tamora, then Titus, then Saturninus were stabbed, each fell across
the table forming a heap over the ram's head, and as each fell,
portions of the library burst into flame, and books and plaster
continued to fall. Fires higher than the table erupted from the
up-stage pit, and other fires surrounded the fallen figures, as the last
remnants of the library and its civilization disappeared. Grotesque
waltz music was heard under the riot of destruction, and over it the
voice of Marcus with a final question and a challenge:

> Now judge what cause had Titus to revenge
> These wrongs, unspeakable past patience,
> Or more than living man could bear.

No further Shakespearean works are in Mesguich's immediate
plans, though he is considering undertaking *The Tempest* at some
time in the future. He has expressed a keen interest in two recent
Italian productions of this work, by Giorgio Strehler in Milan and
Leo De Berardinis in Bologna. When asked recently what other
contemporary directors he found of most interest, he perhaps not
surprisingly mentioned two who share with him a strong personal
vision and powerful sense of visual poetry in the theatre – Robert
Wilson and Tadeusz Kantor. A quotation from Kantor appeared in
the program for *Titus Andronicus* and, indeed, seems even more
appropriate as an epigram for the work of Mesguich than for that of
its speaker: "I attach a far greater importance to the text than those
who boast of faithfulness to the text, who think of it as a point of
departure ... and who go no further than that." In a 1988 interview, Mesguich characterized as "grotesque" the idea that a work,
especially a rich work like the plays of Shakespeare, was possessed of
some self-sufficient and hermetic meaning with which each new
production must be in harmony. Later in the interview he was asked
for his view of Peter Brook's decision never to present *The Merchant of
Venice* because of its antisemitic elements. Mesguich likened this
prejudice to that against Wagner, whom he has successfully produced, responding, in a kind of artistic credo "One must never close
books; one must open them."[13]

This emphasis upon opening interpretation and expanding a text
outward rather than seeking an inner, "essential" meaning associates Mesguich, of course, with a great number of figures in the
modern and postmodern artistic and interpretive worlds, but the

position he holds is in a number of ways unique. While he shares with Wilson and Kantor, and for that matter with Brook, a brilliant and individualistic visual sense and the capacity to bring to life a series of astonishing and memorable stage images, he differs from each of these other masters of the contemporary stage in the type of visual structure created. The difference may be clearly seen in the most recent Shakespearean productions of each of these major directors: Mesguich's *Titus*, Wilson's *King Lear* in Frankfurt (May 1990) and Brook's *The Tempest* in Paris (October 1990). Although Wilson's production ran for almost four hours, he cut the original text radically, converting the remainder into a series of highly stylized tableaux, many of great, if rather cold and abstract, beauty. Brook presented a much more faithful text (translated into French, of course), and drew his visual vocabulary from the same minimal, earthen, flowing, vaguely Indic world that formed the basis of his *Mahabharata*, to which *The Tempest* suggested a kind of visual sequel.

In his willingness to take liberties with Shakespeare's text, Mesguich is much closer to Wilson than to Brook, but the *type* of variations and elaborations that he creates is different from either. In addition to the striking visual sense that Mesguich shares with Wilson and Brook, which results not only in original visual images of great power and beauty as well as in evocative visual echoes of previous theatre and works of art, Mesguich has a keenly developed *literary* and *theoretical* imagination. In the network developed in his plays there are thus not only the visual allusions, but literary and critical ones, most notably in the insertion of non-Shakespearean dramatic material and critical texts. It is this consciously intertextual dimension of Mesguich's work that ties him most closely into the theoretical background of his time and explains why names like Barthes and Derrida tend to appear as French reviewers attempt to discuss his productions and their approach. It is extremely appropriate that the setting for two of the most recent, and most highly acclaimed, Mesguich Shakespearean productions have been labyrinthine libraries. For the Anglo-Saxon member of the audience this sort of approach may seem particularly French – suggesting Barthes's *plaisir du texte*, a sensual enjoyment not only of such traditional elements as sound and visual image, but of the intellectual play of literary structures and literary allusions. The artists quoted in the program for *Titus* provide an excellent insight into the range of Mesguich's artistic interests and into the overlapping concerns with a highly visual art, and yet one that is closely tied to modern literary experimentation as well – Borges, Pasolini, Jabès, Kantor, Brecht, Mayakovsky, Fellini, Kafka. The modern English production of Shakespeare, after a rather brief flirtation with concept production, has clearly returned to the traditional emphasis upon character and the star actor. Recent French Shakespeare – Vitez, Lavelli, Mnouchkine, Savary – though on the whole considerably more imaginative and more striking visually than English production, has really not engaged the textual tradition and textual echoes of these seminal works. Mesguich's approach, despite its close intellectual and artistic ties with postmodern currents in other fields, remains unique.

In the summer of 1990 at the Avignon Festival Mesguich was interviewed by a *Figaro* journalist who tested whether the passing years, a growing reputation, and a position teaching in the Conservatory had softened Mesguich's youthful radicalism in respect to Shakespeare by asking Mesguich his current view of certain iconoclastic statements from 1977, in connection with his *Hamlet* project. The first was that Shakespeare owed more respect to Mesguich than Mesguich to Shakespeare, the second that the goal of "understanding" a play was a feature of bourgeois drama that had little to do with great works.

Mesguich continued to defend these views. Concerning the first he quoted Pascal, who defined himself as "In the camp of the moderns, that is to say, the ancients." By this, Mesguich explained, Pascal meant that he felt himself older than Aristotle or Shakespeare since he had the advantage of the historical and cultural tradition of which they were only a part. As for understanding a play, Mesguich explained that to understand suggested an intellectual possession, while the best art always expanded beyond any individual grasp. The simplest, the clearest phrase ever written, "to be or not to be," eludes our certainty of understanding. The theatre should recognize this and seek not to explain written texts but to "render them incandescent.'[14] Clearly the visionary young director of the 1970s has not disappeared in the established Conservatory professor of the 1990s, and the French stage can doubtless anticipate further incandescent Shakespeare from Daniel Mesguich.

NOTES

1 Guy Dumur, "Alas, poor Hamlet," *Nouvel Observateur*, 28 Nov. 1977: 112, and "Les Urgences de Daniel Mesguich," *ibid.*, 3 Jan. 1986: 55.

2 Quoted in Dumur, "Les Classiques dans tous leurs états," *Nouvel Observateur*, 22 Aug. 1977, 61.

3 "La Fête à Shakespeare," interview with Mesguich and Shakespearean scholar Daniel Sibory, *L'Evénement du Jeudi* 193 (14 July 1988): 89.

4 Quoted in Marie Francoise Lecière, "Daniel Mesguich: éclairs et éclats," *Le Point*, 13 July 1981: 61.

5 Michel Cournot, "*Le Hamlet de Shakespeare* mise en scène par Daniel Mesguich," *Le Monde*, 18 Nov. 1977: 34.

6 *Ibid.*, 34.

7 Dumur, "Le Clown et la salopette," *Nouvel Observateur*, 25 July 1981, 58. Pierre Marcabru, "Shakespeare fait le trottoir," *Figaro*, 13 July 1981: 13.

8 "Hamlet c'est moi," *20 Ans*, Dec. 1986.

9 Dumur, "Urgences," 55.

10 Quoted in John Strand, "Re-presenting France's Favorite Playwright," *Passion* (London), Nov. 1986: 36.

11 Cournot, "La Magie de *Titus Andronicus*," *Le Monde*, 21 Oct. 1989: 16; Pierre Marcabru, "Un tragique hébraïque," *Figaro*, 19 Oct. 1989: 35. Marion Thébaud, "Daniel Mesguich et la barbarie," *Figaro*, 17 Oct. 1989: 37.

12 Mesguich, director's notes from a flyer circulated by the Théâtre de l'Athénée.

13 Mesguich, "La Fête," 88.

14 Frédéric Ferney, interview, "Daniel Mesguich: le feu sacré," *Figaro*, 23 July 1990: 36.

CHAPTER 12

Word into image: notes on the scenography of recent German productions

Wilhelm Hortmann

DESIGNING FOR SHAKESPEARE: THE BREAK WITH TRADITION

"One board, two casks and a passion." Audiences have never been satisfied for long with the kind of theatre implied in Lope de Vega's definition. The Elizabethan public was no exception. The change in audience expectations, as Bernard Beckerman has shown, took place during Shakespeare's own lifetime and is reflected in the way the author addressed his public.[1] Very roughly, the audience of the young Shakespeare consisted of listeners, that of the old of viewers. It is true that the transformation of the "gentle hearers" of the earlier plays into the "gentle spectators" of *The Winter's Tale* or even into "Those that come to see / Only a show or two" (*Henry VIII*, Prologue) was not altogether consistent. Nevertheless the increasing importance of the visual aspect of theatre as compared to the auditory is undoubted. When the open platform was relinquished for the indoor stage with proscenium arch, wings, and backdrops, the actor, formerly supreme, had to compete for attention with the scene painter and, soon afterwards, at the height of the baroque period, with the engineer and his stunning special effects, ranging from thunder and lightning, erupting volcanoes and other spectacular fireworks, to airborne motion and waterfalls.

Spectacle and illusion, however, though growing temptations, were not unopposed. As early as 1812 Friedrich Schinkel, the great architect of classical Berlin, claimed that "to achieve true drama" the theatre would have to get rid of its present craze for "decoration," and he praised the ancients for whom "a symbolic indication of the place of action ... was quite sufficient to stimulate the productive imagination of the spectators."[2] "True drama" versus "decoration" – the opposition is still unresolved. Goethe felt it when he boasted of his ability – given the right play – to captivate an audience with no more than actors on a naked platform, while at the same time requesting for his own *Faust* all the suggestive magic of which the stage machinery of his time was capable.[3]

Contemporary directors feel it: Peter Zadek rendered *Measure for Measure* (Bremen 1967) on a bare stage, while his productions of *The Winter's Tale* (Hamburg 1978) and *The Taming of the Shrew* (Berlin 1981) were a feast for the eyes. Two souls would seem to be at strife in the director's breast, that of the intellectual and that of the sensualist, the one thinking in words, the other in images. Their unappeasable conflict has been responsible for a wealth of theatrical achievement as well as a succession of far-reaching reforms all aimed at engaging that elusive quantity, "the productive imagination of the spectators."

We take up the story in the Germany of the early 1960s when young rebels in various provincial theatres broke with a tradition for the production of the classics that had become established during the 1950s. At that time the German theatre struggled hard to recover the lost humanist ethos, and in this process of vicarious expiation of the guilt the nation had contracted under the Nazis, the reverence extended to the classics played an important part. Many Germans felt that classic works enshrined a timeless heritage of cultural and moral values, and many directors thought that heritage could best be transmitted by respectful renderings on non-specific sets from which concrete historical associations had been carefully deleted.

To the young revolutionaries in the 1960s and 1970s (Palitzsch, Zadek, Minks, Heyme, Stein, *et al.*), this orientation of German postwar theatre toward restoration was ideologically suspect. They regarded it as an attempt to re-establish prewar values on the basis of a diffuse cultural idealism, which would have to be stopped. The classics, they argued, had been spiritualized and put on a pedestal, and this had domesticated and emasculated them. To recoup their original explosive power and make them reveal their inner material contradictions they would have to be inserted into a radically contemporary cultural context. In many cases this meant subjecting them to the shock-treatment of politicizing, (psycho-)analyzing, and even brutalizing, if necessary. Under such stress, the order and harmony traditionally regained in the fifth acts would show up for what they were, fraudulent shams. Only by thus reawakening the troublesome potency of the classical works, it was thought, could the spectator be existentially involved again and activated or – if he remained incorrigibly bent on culinary entertainment or lofty ritual – be driven from the theatre.[4]

Spectators were not only confronted with drastically altered and deliberately rough texts, they were also scandalized by having their visual expectations brutally thwarted. In this period of bitter strife, heated controversy, and aesthetic turmoil, the very basis of theatrical communication was changed. Eventually, after a decade of critical, subversive, debunking productions a new theatre aesthetics had come into existence, purposefully disjunctive, off-center, disruptive even, but also open to novel combinations and telling surprises and enjoying an almost unlimited freedom of expression.

In this process the traditional relationship between text and visual presentation was profoundly altered. Traditionally, set design plays a supportive role only. Its importance increased when the textual message began to be distrusted. In debunking productions the crude means of manipulating the verbal language soon turned stale, whereas the scenic language afforded unlimited possibilities for transmitting the new visions and for bodying forth the forms of interpretations hitherto undreamt of. The images began to lead a life of their own, scenography became the central concern of directors, the visual appearance of a production often overwhelmed the mental appeal of the text and the art of the actor. However, the new scenic language comprising the whole realm of optical signs (decor, projections, props, stage architecture, costumes, movement, lighting, etc.) proved difficult to understand. Since its inventors employed a new grammar and used an unfamiliar vocabulary to transmit radically changed meanings, they often left audiences guessing, and antagonized many. In retrospect, the period dominated by this struggle to redefine the theatre's social function and culminating in many taboo-breaking productions can be seen as the most thrilling aesthetic adventure on the German stage since the explosion of theatrical creativity during the Weimar Republic in the 1920s. It resulted in an extension of the aesthetic canon (traditionalists complained of its near-suspension), creating an attitude of experimentation and innovation which spread beyond the avant-garde and left its imprint also on more "conventional" forms of theatre.

In the following I want to examine this new alignment of "word" and "image." The examples are drawn from both avant-garde and mainstream theatre, a distinction that became more difficult to make as soon as scenography was freed from its subservient role and began to grapple with the director's art in an exhilarating and, as we shall see, hazardous joint venture. The selection of examples is necessarily personal, and the makeshift categories under which they are subsumed should not be mistaken for general principles. Denis Bablet, the great authority on twentieth-century stage design, doubts whether the scenographic impressions we derive from the present can be marshaled into a systematic order at all, since they represent the work of literally hundreds of highly individual artists each at a particular stage of development and cooperating in changing alliances and conjunctions with personalities of equally distinct artistic mold and temperament, the directors.[5] Thus it is little more than impressions that will be offered on the following pages.

OPTICAL ALIENATIONS, SCENOGRAPHIC TRANSFORMATIONS

The change of heart about the classics was almost always underscored by powerful visual signs. Thus Peter Palitzsch, for his version of *Henry VI* (*Krieg der Rosen*, Stuttgart 1967, set design: Wilfried Minks) had a frieze composed of skeletons, severed limbs and broken implements of war mounted across the stage and kept in view all the time (illustration 15). The message that aristocratic power games result in nothing but carnage and waste needed no further laboring. In Roberto Ciulli's *As You Like It* (Cologne 1974, set design: Bert Kistner) the forest of Arden was represented by a huge felled tree on whose leafless and ice-glazed branches the banished Duke and his listless companions in heavy greatcoats perched like owls in winter. On this clinically white stage the transforming power of love could not operate, and was not meant to. It could only be vivisected, with the foreseeable result of discovering at its core aggressive sex, neurosis, and freezing self-isolation.

Occasionally, when such optical alienation effects limited to single components were thought insufficient, the message was brought home in a more radical fashion. The Romanian director Petrica Ionescu's *As You Like It* (Bochum 1976) was performed on a set (designed by Hans Peter Schubert) suggesting a vandalized slaughterhouse or a war-damaged factory, with burst pipes, torn-off tiles, and heaps of rubble. Like Clifford Williams' version in London in 1967, it was played by an all-male cast. But Ionescu's Celia and

15 *Henry VI* (*The War of the Roses*), directed by Peter Palitzsch, Stuttgart, 1967, designed by Wilfried Minks. *Photo: Werner Schloske, courtesy Schauspiel Stuttgart.*

Rosalind were muscular fellows who could have taken on the wrestler Charles themselves; they acted like tough infantrymen, as did
most of the other characters. Apparently the underlying idea was of
a group of hard-boiled soldiers, survivors of an atomic war, killing
time by performing a comedy they could not understand any more
since women and love had been dead for a long time. Whereas
Williams' production was interested in examining acting conventions, Ionescu's rendering proclaimed the human and cultural losses
and the destruction of value in the wake of ultimate war. Under the
conditions generated by this catastrophe the delicate gradations of
love from earthy to courtly in the original turned into an absurd,
cynical, or despairing repetition of once meaningful interactions.
The forest of Arden was reduced to a few sickly plants under plastic
covers, watered hopefully but without success by the shepherds.
Genetic change had turned them back into satyrs, frightened earth
creatures emerging briefly from their holes in the ground for hurried
copulation and conversation. The unambiguous set precluded all
versions of pastoral and proclaimed the doom of a degenerate
civilization.

Central images or novel visual settings chosen to express a particular directorial interpretation need not be of such portentous cast
to work, but they must be of a quality to tempt the spectator's
imagination to develop them further, otherwise even the most
ingenious idea for a central image or revisualization can turn into a
straitjacket. A case in point was Peter Siefert's *Troilus and Cressida* at
the Mannheim National Theater in 1983 on the set designed by
Günter Kupfer. At first glance it seemed a bright idea to move Troy
to Atlantic City and to present the decay of authority among Greeks
and Trojans as crumbling command structures in rival crime syndicates. The Trojan headquarters were in a bar where Pandarus
mixed the drinks, Priam in a wheelchair tried to keep peace among
his sons, and a peroxide Helena rose from a shell like a Hollywood
vamp turned Venus. The Greeks camped in a trailer on the beach,
held their council of war in deckchairs around a wobbly folding
table, arranged the duel between Hector and Ajax as a boxing
match with running bets, sent Diomedes, a leather-clad macho with
Elvis Presley hairstyle, to pick up Cressida in a Buick convertible
flying the syndicate's pennant, and Achilles finally put Hector out of
business with a sawnoff shotgun.

This clever transposition of the play into such an apparently suitable modern setting did not, however, throw a new light on the precarious subject-matter and the dubious moral status of the characters. On the contrary, it tended to reduce the necessary ambivalence to clear-cut single meanings. The spectators were fully occupied trying to place the many iconographic allusions of the production, to paintings (e.g., Edward Hopper's *Nighthawks* with Troilus at the bar), to scenes from Humphrey Bogart and Elvis Presley films, to television spots. But the crackle of minor shocks of recognition seemed to make true cognition impossible and superfluous. The range of associations opened up by the central scenographic metaphor – Greeks and Trojans as rival syndicates – proved too flat and insignificant. If "degree" only means the control of power within the syndicate instead of the universal principle of order in nature and the commonwealth, or if the theme of love is too quickly released from its iridescent ambiguity into sexual plainness, then this proves that the dominant image which produced such reductions was wrong. By keeping spectators under a barrage of visual surprises and forcing them to register and decode dozens of one-to-one correspondences, the production allowed no freedom for imaginative discovery.

It would appear, then, as if a design conceived as an elaborated and specific system of visual correspondences is a mixed blessing: it makes its point, clearly and unequivocally, yet the pleasure of spotting the pictorial references is offset by a loss of imaginative freedom, understood in the literal sense of being given the chance to supplement the images on stage with individual additions and proliferations. Apparently, the spectator's creative imagination must have room to play around the central image. There must be empty spaces on the scenographic canvas, suggestive indeterminacies, as it were; the full canvas produces claustrophobia by forcing views and denying visions.[6]

Such counterproductive effects can also occur when productions – without being fully translated into a new setting – are dominated by a single powerful pictorial or spatial symbol. For Otomar Krejča's *Hamlet* (Düsseldorf 1977), Thomas Richter-Forgach had designed an architecturally intriguing set of movable segments which easily formed interiors, platforms, and niches, while two constantly used flights of stairs afforded a diagonal articulation of the scenic space. The stage ceiling was a huge mirror slanted towards the auditorium. Krejča had already experimented with such a mirror construction twelve years before in Brussels, on a set designed by Josef Svoboda. Now, the dimensions were larger and the mirror extended across the whole width of the stage, so that the audience saw what happened on the stage and behind the stage at the same time. By means of the mirror the actors kept watch on each other so that, at times, they acted in two directions at once, horizontally to the present members of the cast and vertically towards the mirror trying to keep track of absent characters. Similarly, the spectator had two pictures on the retina all the time, the action in front, and the view from above via the mirror. Obviously this was meant to be a *Hamlet* in which everyone kept everyone else under close and suspicious surveillance, a state of affairs for which the mirror was both visual aid and symbol. It fulfilled both functions to perfection and thus – scenographically – ruined the production despite the efforts of the cast. The double vision focused attention on elements of plot and intrigue, on externals, without opening up vistas towards "that within which passes show," without allowing the imagination to reach those areas of the play that lie beyond the visible.

A high, gray, brick wall with a narrow opening in the middle was the dominant feature in Rolf Glittenberg's set for Jürgen Flimm's *Hamlet* at the Thalia-Theater in Hamburg (1986). Lighted only from the side, it had a sinister aspect, and being pushed far forward it pinned the action down to the narrow strip of proscenium and forestage. This set provided no galleries, no interiors, no hiding-places, only a bare acting space, public and without secrets, under the threat of the terrifying wall. Was there a Denmark behind it? A pointless question when all action referred to the wall only: the actors pressed close to it when they did not want to be seen, cowered down by it in moments of emotional stress, and finally were propped up against it as corpses by Fortinbras. The wall was insurmountable and inexplicable. It seemed as if it might move forward at any moment and obliterate everything. The visual impact of this symbol dominated and doomed the human relationships from the start. The wall in its inescapable presence obstructed the outlook on other dimensions and lay like a blight on the spectator's soul. Its rigid denial of space crippled the imagination and reduced the play to an exercise in deliberate pessimism, a *Hamlet* between wall and pit. The wall was certainly of profound symbolic significance, but as a central image it was utterly wrong if it made us forget that it is inner rather than outer walls which Hamlet has to overcome.

ON PRODUCTIVE INDETERMINACY

How to turn the stage from mere acting area into a "living space" and thus to achieve the central purpose of all scenography seems a target easier to miss than to hit. Both total and partial transpositions into novel settings can create unwanted side-effects, as can the choice of the wrong symbol. Success seems to depend less on the *degree* of scenic physicalization than on the way the spectator's imagination is engaged. Is it stunned, bludgeoned, or merely kept occupied, or has it been enlisted to cooperate creatively? Why some designs release such productive audience participation and others don't is difficult to say. Some of the most lasting impressions of Shakespeare performances in Germany in recent years have derived from productions whose scenographic realizations could not be put under a general formula. They all, however, contained discrepant elements, unintegrated material, and the irritation thus set up in the minds of the spectators seemed to stimulate audiences to project imaginatively beyond the visible and beneath the surface. Artistically, the two successful examples described below represented totally different scenographic solutions; yet they had in common a sensation of productive restiveness virulent enough to make the spectator an active partner in the theatrical event.

In Dieter Dorn's production of *Troilus and Cressida* (Munich 1986) mild visual alienations were employed to keep this sensation alive and to refocus attention on the text and the action. Devising an appropriate design for this play has always been a problem. Historical costumes are liable to make an audience – like Max Reinhardt – rebel against the staginess of the "cursed theatre Greeks," modern uniforms may evoke the wrong associations, while the choice of a completely different frame of scenographic reference – as in the Mannheim production – can rob the play of important dimensions. Jürgen Rose's design avoided the trap of a too-definite visual setting; it was marked instead by a contradictory, yet suggestive, indeterminacy. The sides of the stage were formed by cloths smeared with many colors, at the rear there was a paper-covered sliding door of similar aspect for the rapid exits and entrances, on the floor flat raised segments in an irregular pattern. The abstract quality of the set was faintly reminiscent of action painting and *informel*, and denied any representational orientation. The costumes, too, had been carefully kept from definitely indicating place or

16 A battle scene from Dieter Dorn's *Troilus and Cressida*, Munich, 1986, designed by Jürgen Rose. *Photo: Oda Sternberg.*

period. The men wore what looked like battledress trousers, their bare trunks were encased in tight leather belts and straps or covered by tunics of indistinct patterns somewhere between heraldic designs and camouflage spots, the more warlike sporting Indian braves' headbands. Pandarus and Cressida were clad in flowing robes of rough weave and patterns derived from African and Mexican tribal handicraft textiles, their foreheads were decorated in oriental fashion with strings of pearl – altogether a powerful blend of incompatibilities. The impression of vital eclecticism was reinforced by entrances of the Kabuki type (rapid movement, rigid bodies) of several of the figures, which recalled Ariane Mnouchkine's *Richard II* seen in Munich two years before on her widely acclaimed tour.

The unresolvable ambiguity of the mutually exclusive stylistic elements made it impossible for the spectator to find correspondences. The prevalent optical impression was of something archaic and passionate, of eruptive ferocity barely restrained, of a primitive culture in its harsh exoticism (illustration 16). The contradictory associations evoked by costume and set refused to be combined into a definite (and thus restricting) image; they formed instead a complex referential potential which – since visually unappeased and unresolvable – focused attention on the text. Apparently the directorial decision to allow the play to speak for itself (by no means a self-evident one in the present theatrical climate in Germany) directly influenced the design. Dieter Dorn obviously thought Shakespeare's treatment of the themes of war, obedience, love and fidelity ambivalent enough and not in need of improvement from the vantage point of ideologically superior minds. He therefore avoided direct pictorial references to warring nations past or present. Instead, he created an emotionally charged but somehow abstract visual setting which – precisely by its indeterminacy – produced a heightened imaginative responsiveness to the inner meaning of the play and to its projection through the actor's art in word, gesture, and movement.

TWELFTH NIGHT AT BOCHUM: POSTMODERN SHAKESPEARE AND THE PICTORIAL IMAGINATION

As we have seen, the desire to remain true to Shakespeare is often better served by a visual environment that sets up certain irritations or countercurrents than by traditionally supportive illustrations. The debunking director will naturally try to broadcast the ideologically suppressed subtext by indicative and disruptive scenographic metaphors. But what if there are nothing but subtexts? Deconstructing directors who see the dramatic text as a system of interactional strategies accompanying an endless succession of theatrical self-projections can no longer claim to speak for a deprived minority or to do battle for a suppressed viewpoint. Their postmodern consciousness will reject such stances as no longer viable in a pluralistic world. They will not mourn a vanished centrality or a unified ideological perspective but affirm plurality instead as a positive chance to enter into multiple and polymorph language games, types of action, and ways of living.[7] Such convictions do not simplify the directorial task. To create a gripping theatrical event the director now has to aim at two contradictory achievements at once: to extract from the play its wealth of readings, in other words, to dissolve it into the many private worlds of the characters and their self-deluding subterfuges, and at the same time to make the vital themes of the play felt as existential concerns.

This cannot be achieved on a bare stage or in a minimalist setting. It needs the full support of a rich pictorial imagination. The postmodern theatre is above all a theatre of images. This is a consequence of the radically altered conception of character in postmodern aesthetics. In the classical tradition a character has to penetrate appearances and to surrender all potential selves in order to arrive at his true identity. In postmodern thinking the character possesses only temporary identities, multiple selves, and their role strategies.

Whereas the classical character tries to discover his ultimate center of gravity in "self"-searching soliloquies, the postmodern character has to establish himself to us in a different manner: he has to reveal himself to us as the combination of numerous fantasies, projections, stylizations, adopted stances, as a network of temporary and largely imagined selves from which there is no escape. There is no ultimate reality to arrive at. That is why the opposition of appearance and reality can no longer be employed as an analytical instrument. According to postmodern thinking we are all caught up in, in fact, constituted by, our fictional selves, and when we try to discover truth or to experience a genuine emotion the chances are we pursue illusions and deceive ourselves. To the philosopher this may be a sad conclusion, to the dramatist and director it is a godsend. Not only is all the world a stage, not only are all the men and women merely playing the seven parts enumerated by Jaques, each character, in addition, is intent on performing self-chosen roles in fictions of which he or she is largely unconscious. A situation rich in deep comedy, and a glorious vindication of theatre as a philosophical metaphor, applicable even to postmodern man.

But how is this conception of character as a succession of self-projections to be realized on the stage and to be made productive? The most effective means are theatricalization and "quotation." Some observations on Andrea Breth's production of *Twelfth Night* (Bochum 1989, set design: Gisbert Jäkel) may illustrate how these methods were employed.

Feste, carrying a pig's-bladder lantern, drew the curtain. The meaning was obvious: the wise fool inviting other fools, the audience, to watch a performance. On the forestage, in an armchair,

17   Sebastian rowing in the sea. A visual prologue to *Twelfth Night*, directed by
Andrea Breth, set by Gisbert Jäkel, Bochum, 1989. *Photo: Klaus Lefebvre.*

Orsino: in features, wig, and posture recalling Dürer's famous
Christ-like self-portrait. Orsino, like Christ, a sufferer for love?
Behind him was a huge imitation of a stage portal through which, on
the center stage, there was a jumble of upturned armchairs on which
indistinct figures acted out a strange dance like puppets on strings:
figments of Orsino's imagination moving to the tune of the music
that is the food of love? Behind them, against a backdrop which
changed color several times during the performance, a female figure
with bow and arrow, Cupid perhaps, imperceptibly moved across
the field of vision. The whole was a case of theatre within theatre
multiplied: the Fool presenting the Duke, the Duke presenting the
theatre of his mind with references to painting, religion, and
mythology. Before the scene between the castaways Viola and the
captain, the audience was treated to a poetic storm at sea preceding
the shipwreck. This was represented by ten rows of cardboard waves

(in the manner of the famous Hokusai print) being pulled up and down on visible strings with a dolphin on a stick jumping the crests (illustration 17). When it ended, the imitated stage portal had disappeared and the upturned armchairs now looked like a rocky coastal landscape. At the same time a huge circular hole in the ceiling became visible, suggesting a sky in Magritte colors, with an immobile figure hanging over the rim and looking down on the stage. An actor? A puppet? A celestial observer? Once again, the principles of theatricalization and quotation had been put to work without, however, all the references being decodable, let alone combinable to a single unified meaning.

For act 2, scene 3, the scene of midnight caterwauling in Olivia's house, the set showed a lonely street at night with Toby and Andrew Aguecheek like Beckettian tramps warming themselves at a burning brazier, while Malvolio descended to upbraid them from a staircase

18 Malvolio (Jochen Tovote) reads the letter in front of a movie audience in Breth's *Twelfth Night*. Photo: *Klaus Lefebvre*.

at the back which suggested Piranesi's *Carceri*. The *coup de théâtre* was the subsequent letter scene. For this scene the stage was rebuilt into a cinema of the 1950s, its armchair seats slanting towards the audience (illustration 18). There was an usherette selling cigarettes and ice-cream in the central passage, Fabian (a mafioso from B-films of the period) tinkling away on the piano at the back, Aguecheek munching popcorn and enjoying the performance, that is, he watched Maria and Toby using Malvolio for a movie of their own while the latter, totally caught up in his own scenario, was impervious even to the most obvious deceptions.

Quite clearly the principle of theatricalization here attained a new quality. Usually it works through the anti-illusionist display of the way stage effects are achieved, or it relies on the never-failing means of the play within the play to make its point that appearance and reality are difficult, if not impossible, to tell apart. Presenting the duping of Malvolio as an action taking place in a 1950s cinema is at first glance no more than a variation on this well-worn theme. That a new dimension is involved becomes obvious when we realize that we, the audience, are the screen onto which these "games" or "performances" are projected, and that our collective memory is the receptacle from which their iconography is taken. This is an enormous radicalization of the theatre metaphor, going far beyond Pirandellian puzzles. No longer are characters in search of an author, they are shown to be their own "authors" in that they freely adopt scenarios and choose "self"-projections, neither of which are, however, altogether of their own devising: a complicated state of affairs. On one level it means that characters exist and act in different scenarios at once, their own and other people's. At another level it is a question of "images," their sources, and their power of evocation and suggestion.

The first aspect can be said to have been prefigured by Shakespeare himself. The most telling example occurs in *A Midsummer Night's Dream*. The whole piece is composed of plays within plays. The mechanicals perform "the most lamentable comedy" of "Pyramus and Thisbe," possibly Shakespeare's self-parody of *Romeo and Juliet*. The many interruptions from their audience turn the mechanicals into figures in a play or game "performed" by the court, just as Pyramus and Thisbe remain figures in a play performed by the Athenian craftsmen. The young couples who mock their primitive idea of dramatic fiction were themselves victims of a fiction only the night before, in a play staged by Oberon and his assistant Puck, who, as he says, puts on slapstick comedies for his private entertainment by playing tricks on simple country folk. Oberon and Titania perform *théâtre intime*, the well-known marital jealousy game with the Indian boy and Bottom as stakes. Theseus and Hippolyta, emerging from mythology, play Duke and Duchess. The realities of one group exist as fictions in the games performed by the others. And whoever feels this as too fantastic is requested by Puck in the epilogue to imagine to have dreamt it all. A reassuring conclusion? On the contrary, it is the most daring extension of the theatre metaphor: if the spectators can dream such convoluted epistemological and ontological complexities, perhaps it is we, the audience, who are the authors. If so, the circuit of metamorphoses between fictions and realities is finally closed.

The second aspect, the question of images and their origin in postmodernist productions like the Bochum *Twelfth Night*, is even more complicated. If we act in our own and everyone else's fictions it follows that we are also our own directors. Since in a play the characters for obvious reasons are bound to the overall scenario or prefixed dramaturgy, the fact that they also partially determine their own mise en scène can only be realized through self-projection or self-stylization. To make this apparent on the stage, images have to be found. In traditional productions the images are selected to give concentric support to the accepted meaning of the play, to represent its structure in a typologically ideal form. Under postmodernism the images have become emancipated, they live and shine in a Garden of Eden coexistence of high and low, ancient and modern, learned and simple, crude and refined. The pluralism that exists in the minds of the spectators is reflected in the heterogeneous iconography on the stage. The pictorial allusions in the Bochum production to Dürer, Caspar David Friedrich, Hokusai, Magritte, Piranesi, and Edward Hopper had no common denominator. Neither had the numerous references to films. What nevertheless stopped these diverse visualizations from degenerating into an aesthetic chaos was the haunting quality of the individual self-stylizations, the suggestive power of their iconography, and their ultimately enigmatic character.

Two examples of many may illustrate this. For the scene between the Duke and Cesario (2.4) what appeared like a group of monks or hooded figures with Venetian masks carried the Duke in a sedan-chair onto the forestage, to Gregorian chant and organ music. There the sedan-chair was turned into a fourposter bed with a nightblue, starspangled back and canopy, on which the Duke in a flowing mantle, his white shirt open at the breast, reclined in the last paroxysm of suffering for love with Feste kneeling to him as to a saint to deliver his mournful hymn to death, "Come away, come away, death, / And in sad cypress let me be laid." The whole made a most beautiful tableau: the soulful Dürer-Christ-Orsino on his Calvary of love, his dependants on their knees and only St. John-Cesario, his favorite disciple, beckoned to sit on the edge of the bed to deliver his message, increase the agony, and for one trembling moment to become the vicarious object of his master's deep desire. It was a scene of utter artificiality, and at the same time utterly convincing. Convincing, however, not as unmediated, genuine expression, as the spontaneous overflow of a powerful feeling, as it were, but convincing as a reflection of this emotion through art, as a perfect stylization which transmitted not the emotion itself but its multivalent and suggestive image. It was as such that the scene received enthusiastic applause.

The self-stylization of the other sufferers for love in the play, above all Malvolio and the sea captain Antonio, was brought out by similarly elaborate foils. Malvolio in haughty self-righteousness dwelt in distant and removed regions symbolized by the Piranesi associations of the black, dimly visible staircase at the back. Before he condescended to speak, he literally had to descend. He communicated with others as with himself in an affected nasal singsong, a trick of voice and a part of his put-on style that he dropped at last under the impact of pain and shame. That a lover of such elevation and refinement should have his most private wishes published to all the world as in a common movie show was an extra twist of the knife. Yet his confession of love for his mistress Olivia, the peak of irreality and delusion, was also his moment of highest truth. Was there a heart after all beneath the insufferable poses? No, it was only that the stylized projection of himself as a man with a heart was artistically convincing.

Antonio's motiveless love of Sebastian has worried critics and directors and sent them motive-hunting. Gay Antonios have abounded. Andrea Breth's explanation of the character was much more subtle and an ironic revelation of flattering masculine self-images: she had Antonio cast himself for the role of danger-braving

19 Antonio (Manfred Böll) and Sebastian (Stephan Ullrich) in 3.3, among cardboard figures in an Edward Hopper coffee shop. *Photo: Klaus Lefebvre.*

bloodbrother ready to follow his friend into the jaws of the lion. Their meeting (3.3), with the exchange of money and the appointment to meet at the Elephant, was blown up into a conspiratorial assignation taking place in an Edward Hopper bar with ingenious *trompe l'œil* effects (illustration 19). Antonio's rejection of the apparently ungrateful Sebastian was as wildly excessive as his previous protestations of love and friendship. What literally knocked him over was not seeing Sebastian in Olivia's arms, but having his romantic image of himself as truest of friends shamefully betrayed, punctured by the commonplace solution of the mistake.

Two questions remain, that of the authenticity of emotion and of the origin of the images in postmodern productions. In the eyes of postmodern directors, genuine emotions, authentic feelings, the thrills of unique singularity and identity, are outmoded and futile demands made on the theatre. Their favorite tools, theatricalization and self-projection, turn the assumed emotion of a character into a stylized artefact. When supported by all the possibilities of cultural reference at the disposal of a well-funded theatre and when well acted, a new kind of authenticity can result: expression and emotion become inseparable, style becomes matter. We live in a world where everyone knows, actors as well as spectators, that we all act out self-images and pursue our own self-projections. Authenticity under such conditions can no longer be a question of the actor making himself feel the genuine emotion by Stanislavsky's method of psychological immersion and fusion. Nor can it be a question of the actor merely presenting the result of his analysis of the emotion, in the manner of Meyerhold or Brecht. Adapting a famous phrase of T. S. Eliot's, the actor has not a personality to express but a medium, and this goes for the director also. What is demanded is the authentic expression of the medium. When successfully done it will convince the spectator. This conviction – in a postmodern production – extends to the artefact, not the emotion. The well-devised artefact vindicates whatever emotion was to be projected, not the other way round. The Bochum *Twelfth Night*, however, managed at times to break through its own aesthetic program when, for very brief moments, it allowed its most impassioned self-deluders, the Duke, Malvolio, Antonio, to catch glimpses of possibilities of spontaneous feeling. These occurred when they were in contact either with Viola and Sebastian who were wisely exempted from the heavy self-stylization of the others, or with Feste who was wise enough to exempt himself.

The profusion of pictorial allusions in Andrea Breth's *Twelfth Night* calls for comment. They were derived from many fields, mainly from painting (with artists from the Renaissance to the present day, as already enumerated), from films (*Casablanca*, Hollywood gangster movies, Tarkovsky), from mythology (Cupid/Eros: with bow and arrows, with broken wings; the huge owl hovering over several sets, perhaps even the dead horse among the rocks on the coast of Illyria), from religion (the monks, Gregorian chant, Christ-Orsino, St. John-Cesario), from literature and theatre (the Beckettian tramps), from everyday surroundings (a slanting revolving door in the middle of the stage leading nowhere for some of the scenes, as well as figures reading *The Financial Times*; the 1950s cinema). Why were so many cultural traditions quoted? Were all these allusions really necessary to tell the story of *Twelfth Night*? Or was it just an exercise in postmodern mannerism, the designer's nightmare journey into the regions of surrealist phantasmagoria? Of course the story *Twelfth Night* can and will be told more simply and with sparer means. But if the basic presupposition is that we shield ourselves from contact with essential experience or reality by interposing the most elaborate stylizations and self-projections, then these have to be physicalized somehow. The most effective means to do so are visual ones. The image-making faculty that Coleridge hailed as a divine gift, under a different aspect proves to be a curse: we are enmeshed in images, we cannot – or only rarely – penetrate them and reach through to "reality." Virginia Woolf claimed that the "ordinary mind on an ordinary day" received "a myriad impressions" falling into it like "an incessant shower of innumerable atoms" and that it was enclosed by them as in a "luminous halo."[8] What the mind receives, according to Virginia Woolf, are sense impressions. What the mind produces, according to Suzanne Langer, are images. Waking or dreaming, the mind is ceaselessly at work generating images.[9]

This anthropological theorem of man as an image-making animal has far-reaching consequences. In the course of history the human race has developed highly expressive and articulate symbolisms, discursive and non-discursive ones. In the latter (poetry, music, the visual arts) it has accumulated a storehouse of images which is constantly restocked and forms the collective source of cultural reference. Formerly each period, social group, or artistic school was intent on making its own distinct contribution to this storehouse as hallmark of its particular identity. In the period of *post-histoire*, when history is being replaced by international crisis management and social engineering, identity becomes negotiable and the corresponding images can be selected from the well-stocked shelves of the past. The electronic media permit us to rifle the storehouse; they permit us, without the slightest effort, to parade the greatest artistic monuments of human self-definition for our inspection, to upset their order, to reshuffle and even distort them. At a time when channel-switching spectators are quite conversant with the idea of multiple and temporary identities for themselves, it is not surprising that the theatre will draw its scenographic metaphors from many sources. In real life when people meet, the images they have styled themselves on often diverge atrociously. A Dürer-Christ-sufferer for love may very well fetch up against someone whose self-projections were spawned in shallower waters. So why not in the theatre? What used to be a comedy of confused identities can now be seen and produced as a comedy of diverging image worlds or assumed styles. In an age and at a point in cultural development when the core of a character is no longer authentic identity but self-stylization on borrowed images, the story of the self-deceptions of Orsino, Malvolio, Olivia, and Antonio may well have to be told in this new radicalized form. As long as the ideal of personality was that manner and essence should converge, Buffon's famous definition "le style, c'est l'homme-même" was applicable. Now it is a matter of "des styles, c'est l'homme postmoderne," and this plurality of styles cannot but inform the staging of Shakespeare. The scenographic images employed in this process do not solve the problem, however; they are part of the enigma itself.

NOTES

1 "Shakespearean Playgoing Then and Now," in S. Homan (ed.), *Shakespeare's More than Words Can Witness: Essays on the Visual and Nonverbal Enactment in the Plays* (Lewisburg: Bucknell University Press, 1979), 142–59. My essay contains some material from articles published in German, notably from "Spielorte und Bühnenräume: zur Szenographie von Shakespeare-Inszenierungen der jüngsten Vergangenheit," *Shakespeare Jahrbuch/West* (1989) and "Die Macht der Bilder – Szenographische Notate zu einigen jüngeren Shakespeare-Inszenierungen," *Kunstgriffe. Festschrift für Herbert Mainusch*, ed. Ulrich Horstmann and Wolfgang Zach (Frankfurt am Main: Peter Lang, 1989). I have tried to avoid overlap with my reviews of West German Shakespeare productions between 1980 and 1986 in *Shakespeare Quarterly* and with the examples described in my "Changing Modes in *Hamlet*-production: Rediscovering Shakespeare after the Iconoclasts," in *Images of Shakespeare*, ed. Werner Habicht, D. J. Palmer, Roger Pringle (Newark, NJ: University of Delaware Press, 1988), which may be consulted for a more complete picture.
2 Quoted after Ernst Schumacher, "Szenographie *der* Veränderung, Szenographie *in* Veränderung," *Maske und Kothurn* 27 (1981): 361.
3 See Goethe's letter to Heinrich von Kleist of 1 February 1808 and "Vorspiel auf dem Theater," the induction to *Faust*.
4 For the radical break with tradition on the German stage during the 1960s and 1970s, see Günther Rühle's two-volume *Theater in unserer Zeit* (Frankfurt am Main: Suhrkamp, 1982), and *Deutsche Dramaturgie der Sechziger Jahre*, ed. Helmut Kreuzer (Tübingen: Niemeyer, 1974).

5 Denis Bablet, *The Revolutions of Stage Design in the Twentieth Century* (Paris: L. Amiel, 1976), 257.

6 Simon Williams in *Shakespeare on the German Stage, 1586–1914* (Cambridge University Press, 1990), 212, makes a similar point with reference to Max Reinhardt's earlier tendency to overproduce when he speaks of "that particular attribute of the theatre by which a complete representation of any play may defeat its own purposes by being too complete. In the theatre, sustaining the illusion depends partially on the willing effort of the audience and this effort can only be released when some part of the world on stage is absent."

7 For a comprehensive and readable survey of postmodernism, see Wolfgang Welsch, *Unsere postmoderne Moderne* (Weinheim: VCH, 1987).

8 "Modern Fiction," in Woolf's *The Common Reader*, 1st series, (London: Hogarth Press, 1925).

9 Suzanne Langer sees "symbolic transformation" as a basic activity of the human mind. On the complex connection between symbol, image, and myth in the "presentational" symbolisms of art, see chaps. 6 and 7 in her *Philosophy in a New Key. A Study in the Symbolism of Reason, Rite, and Art* (Cambridge, MA: Harvard University Press, 1942).

CHAPTER 13

Shakespeare and the Japanese stage

Andrea J. Nouryeh

"Translating Shakespeare into Japanese is a wild shooting at a target in which there is neither bull's eye nor central circle."[1] This typifies the general opinion of practitioners in the art of converting Shakespeare's poetry into contemporary Japanese. Unlike European translations which can draw from common Christian symbols, climate, and topography, and have linguistic correlatives, Japanese translations must be adaptations in which much of the verse, imagery, humor and cultural context of the original plays is lost. It might appear that an attempt at translation is therefore futile, yet Shakespeare's plays have been repeatedly rendered successfully, almost poetically, in Japan since Commodore Perry landed in 1853.

The staging of Shakespeare's plays in Japanese has almost as long a history. Early productions were of free adaptations taken from Charles Lamb's *Tales from Shakespeare* rather than complete translations. The first, appearing in 1868, was a Kabuki-style *Julius Caesar* which served as a protest play against the bureaucratic "law and order" government in power at the time.[2] Seventeen years later, an adaptation of *The Merchant of Venice, Sakuradoki Zeni no Yononaka* or "The Season of Cherry-Blossoms, the World of Money,"[3] gained popularity as a simple revenge comedy like those written for the Kabuki theatre.

There is an affinity between the plays of Shakespeare and those of Kabuki which has ensured Shakespeare's current status as the most popular playwright in Japan. One obvious aspect of this affinity is thematic: the familial bonds, civil war, violence, bloodshed, betrayal, and vengeance which come out of the struggles of feudal societies. Another aspect is that the plays' narratives focus on the heroic deeds and tragic mistakes of historical or legendary figures. Both the Elizabethan and Japanese dramatic traditions show the supernatural's effects upon the natural world, balance tragic with comic scenes, and present refined and barbaric sides of human behavior in the same play.

Theatre scholars have not only pointed out these similarities in content but also in the Elizabethan and Japanese stage traditions. Such experts as Yasuo Suga and Leonard Pronko[4] have acknowledged that in both traditions plays were staged against the setting rather than in it; both depended upon the display of costumes as part of the spectacle; and both relied upon an open stage, a placeless scaffold, without scenery and without a front curtain. According to their analyses, players in these theatres were dancers and acrobats who used exaggerated facial expressions and large gestures along with color, makeup, and costumes to indicate character and emotion. They cite the use of non-performing stagehands – the stage keepers of the Elizabethan public theatres and the *kurogo* or "black clothes men" of Kabuki – who appeared on stage in full view of the audience, yet did not detract from the stage action.

It is curious then that since the beginning of the twentieth century until the mid-1970s, the stagings of Japanese productions of Shakespeare have avoided any elements of Kabuki and Noh. This phenomenon can best be explained by the pervasive influence of Shōyō Tsubouchi, Japan's foremost Shakespeare scholar, and a playwright, critic, and novelist as well. With his vast knowledge of Elizabethan theatre, he sought to use Shakespeare as a "textbook" or model for the creation of a new literary Japanese drama. To this end, he founded a literary department at Tokyo Professional School (later Waseda University) in 1883 in which Shakespeare became a major part of the curriculum. Rejecting the free adaptations of Shakespeare which were currently prevalent, he translated the plays himself to make them accessible to the Japanese public. To further his aspirations, Shōyō established the Bungei Kyōkai, a literature and art society, to study Elizabethan drama in depth. In 1911 the society produced his translation of *Hamlet*, the first westernized presentation of a Shakespeare play in Japan. This production marked the beginning of *shingeki*, the new dramatic form in Japan emphasizing translations of European plays staged in western style.

Shōyō's approach to Shakespeare continued to prevail as *shingeki* troupes began to produce the literary, yet stageworthy translations of Shakespeare's plays which began surfacing after World War II. These new texts were in colloquial Japanese, ensuring that the plays would be easily understood by the audience. However, the productions which utilized them imitated western style and eschewed any references to Japanese theatrical traditions. Settings and staging techniques of London productions which had been observed and painstakingly documented were carefully reproduced on the Japanese commercial stage, despite the fact that *Throne of Blood*, Kurosawa's 1957 landmark adaptation of *Macbeth*, showed innumerable possibilities of juxtaposing Kabuki with Shakespeare. Instead of utilizing these texts as a way of commenting on contemporary life, productions by *shingeki* troupes underscored the idea held since the late nineteenth century that Japanese culture still had much to learn from the "superior" western drama.

The first departure from this fidelity to British Shakespeare occurred when Terence Knapp began his search for a "Japanese" style for the *shingeki* Shakespearean productions he directed for the Tokyo theatre company Gekidan Kumo, and its offshoot, Gekidan En. Knapp, a former member of the National Theatre in Great Britain and Head of Acting Studies at the University of Hawaii, had come to Japan in 1966 as a professional actor and a student of traditional Japanese theatre. While fulfilling his acting engagement, he also taught movement and voice production to members of Gekidan Kumo. Eight years later he was commissioned as the company's director for their production of *Twelfth Night*. Rather than stage the expected reconstruction of a British production, Knapp tried to present Shakespeare in "the context of the modern Japanese situation ... to incarnate Shakespeare in the body of Japanese actors so that Shakespeare could be a really living, immediate dramatic experience to the Japanese audience."[5]

For the 1977 Gekidan En production of Tetsuo Anzai's translation of *Measure for Measure*, Knapp was still looking for an indigenous Japanese performance style, although he set the production in the Vienna of the 1920s. To elicit a more instinctive and intuitive connection for the actors with their roles, he put the actors through a series of improvisations during rehearsals. For example, one exercise was to play the scenes in the style of a samurai film; another was to change the setting to the Edo period and adapt the scenes and characterizations to feudal Japanese. The meanings of the lines and scenes were made more explicit when the actors had full use of their own gestures and behavior patterns.[6] In production, this understanding of character and lines gave the actors an intensity that had not yet been witnessed on the commercial Japanese stage.[7]

Knapp and Anzai collaborated once again for Gekidan En on *Much Ado About Nothing* in 1979, the first "Japanized" production of Shakespeare to be produced on the commercial stage since the turn of the century. It was a direct outgrowth of the improvisations done for *Measure for Measure*. Knapp's production concept centered on the idea that the play would be a storybook tale – conflicts and problems would appear suddenly like thunderstorms on a sunny summer day and disappear quickly, restoring the celebratory spirit which opens the play. A secondary aspect of his concept was that this production should come up out of "the wellspring of Japan's own cognizance."[8]

To accommodate the director, Anzai chose to set the play in Yokohama during the Meiji period, about 1895. He found plausible analogues for Shakespeare's characters in Japanese folk heroes or character types from this period. There were only two changes: Balthazar became Don Pedro's geisha and Antonio became Leonato's sister. The choice of the Meiji period (1867–1912) was ingenious because it signaled a cultural transition. During this time in Japanese history, feudal traditions were being challenged by the influx of western ideas and fashions which followed Commodore Perry's landing in this city in 1853. Thus, the social hierarchy requisite for the characters' relationships in *Much Ado About Nothing* and Beatrice's outspoken independence would not be anachronistic in the production.

There were also other advantages to the choice of period. The Sino-Japanese War had just ended in a victory for the Japanese, and provided a perfect pretext for festivity and celebration.[9] In addition, the Meiji period was rife with the pretentious posturing of the noblemen and merchants of Yokohama who were trying to attach western culture to themselves as if with glue. Since Meiji art, fashion, and music exhibited a preposterous quality of unassimilated European and American elements in the midst of 300-year-old traditions, these elements provided a wealth of possibilities for comedy. Victorian gowns with their bustles, crinolines, poke bonnets, and military uniforms with their hussar jackets with epaulettes, boots, and plumed hats were haphazardly worn on top of or under kimonos. To this was added the incongruity of hearing "Sigh No More Ladies" played on the samisen, and hearing German brass-band polkas, waltzes, and late nineteenth-century tunes like "Annie Laurie" in a Japanese context.

Further, the period also provided the inspiration for the set.

Leonato's house was framed by a border design created by a false proscenium of summer flowers. Behind the veranda of the palatial house was a garden of wisteria with a revolving rose arbor in and out of which Beatrice and Benedick chased each other during their teasing scenes. For the production's finale, the *o-bon* festival ritual song and dance, the set was lit by lanterns which shone throughout the garden. The entire effect of the stage picture was reminiscent of Meiji period wood-block prints.

While Anzai created a successful adaptation with little alteration to Shakespeare's text, Knapp created a production that revealed the warmth and lightness of the comedy at the heart of the play.[10] He gave the actors the opportunity to develop their roles from their own experiences rather than impose English characterizations upon them, as had been done by *shingeki* directors before him. Using improvisations in which actors played their roles as Italians, as feudal samurai, and as characters in Meiji Japan, Knapp helped them find appropriate gestures and voices. Improvisation was also used to overcome Knapp's unfamiliarity with the stage movement required by performers wearing traditional costumes. For example, in one scene he had wanted the actors to kneel or sit in the garden, a posture difficult to execute in wooden shoes and kimonos. While improvising, the actors brought out a blanket, placed it on the floor, took off their shoes, and then knelt down and drank sake together.[11] In this way the actors' solution to the problem was integrated into the production.

Knapp also experimented with different physical and vocal styles. For the first appearance of Don John, for example, he used Kabuki. The production assistant demonstrated traditional stances and use of the voice, which were copied by the actors for this scene. For the Watch, Knapp experimented with the English technique of using dialects to draw out low comedy. He asked the first watchman to use the colorful Osaka dialect. Then each actor found a dialect for his own character. Eventually the scene emerged with a variety of speech patterns that greatly augmented the comic effect.

Yet, despite his incorporation of Japanese acting styles and dialects, despite the great pains he and his collaborators had taken to recreate rituals, customs, and dress appropriate for the time and place in which the play was set, Knapp had not created a truly Japanese production of Shakespeare. These inclusions, no doubt, added a dimension of familiarity and facilitated a deeper understanding of the play. However, Knapp's *Much Ado About Nothing* was still essentially an imitation of western Shakespeares;[12] it was no more than a lively, well-acted, de-Anglicized version of the play with interesting, albeit culturally accurate, window-dressing.

Knapp wanted to test Shakespeare's universality, to see if Shakespeare speaks to all cultures in the same way. He thought that the text – the original plot, situation, character interrelationships, emotional context, humor and theatricality – could surmount cultural difference and emerge unimpeded by translation and adaptation.[13] He fell short of the mark because his notion of universality was restricted by his English perspective of the play. This is first evident in his fairy-tale visualization: he rejected the designer's cold gray set design and the historically accurate yet somber costumes because they did not conform to his idea that the production reflect a sunny and nonsensical tone. Secondly he imposed a western perspective on the "silliness" of the Japanese people of the Meiji period, who took western and eastern modes of fashion "and lumped them all together hugger-mugger," as he put it.[14] True, traditional costumes and those of the period helped symbolize the essential conflict between Japanese values and western culture in this production, and even some attention was paid to affirming *bushidō*, the samurai code of honor, yet little emphasis was placed on the meaning that the Meiji period had for the contemporary audience.

For example, Knapp made no attempt to show the effects of the Meiji governmental mandate to modernize Japan, begun in 1868, as a way of maintaining independence from western economic and political domination. He also failed to point out the careful and deliberate imitation of European and American models of education, law, economics, art, literature, and politics that was taking place. During the Meiji period, Japan was transformed from its position as an isolated feudal society to its place as a modern, industrial power in less than fifty years, what Will Durant referred to as a "hectic and artificial metamorphosis."[15] However, Knapp ignored the fact that the rapidity with which this change was accomplished left little room for the Japanese people to reconcile their past traditions with this arbitrary imposition of western urban industrialization. Thus he neglected to note that the Meiji period sowed the seeds of self-doubt and a sense of humiliation that continued to plague the Japanese people after 100 years. That Knapp was setting *Much Ado About Nothing* in the period which established

Shakespeare's dominance as the exemplary literary playwright had tremendous political and social implications for his audience, yet his conception of the production did not allow for any of these issues to be addressed seriously.

While the *shingeki* troupes like Gekidan En were disregarding the growing antagonism toward the continued westernization of Japanese culture in the 1960s and 1970s, an alternative theatre was developing out of campus uprisings across Japan. Reacting to American involvement in the civil disorder in Vietnam, Japanese students expressed vehement anti-American sentiment and a growing national pride. Their marches, demonstrations, and guerrilla theatre performances criticized the pro-western elitism of powerful Japanese merchants and manufacturers. Witnessing the effectiveness of the theatrical medium as a political tool, young student directors like Tadashi Suzuki and Yukio Ninagawa at Waseda University determined to forge a new kind of Japanese theatre. While addressing the political and social issues concerning the youth of Japan, they would incorporate and thus revitalize the suppressed traditions of Kabuki and Noh in their productions.

At the forefront of the little theatre movement, Suzuki and Ninagawa abandoned careers on the commercial stage and formed their own avant-garde companies. For Suzuki, this meant moving to the mountains of Toga where he explored the connections between Noh and classical Greek drama and developed a rigorous program of physical training for actors for this new style. For Ninagawa, it meant creating a directing style for his company's productions which became a blend of oriental and occidental music, acting, staging techniques, and spectacle.

Within a decade, the little theatre movement began to affect how Shakespeare was being staged in Japan. The director most significantly altered by the new trends was Norio Deguchi, once associated with two prominent *shingeki* companies. In order to create productions of Shakespeare which were contemporary rather than imitative of what could be seen in London, he started his own Troupe Shakespeare Theatre. His purpose was to stage Yushi Odajima's translations of Shakespeare's plays in a style which would best suit their colloquial language. Over a six-year period, from 1975 until 1982, the company performed all of Shakespeare's plays in their 110-seat basement theatre. Their productions, characterized by their simple jeans and tee-shirt costuming and use of rock-and-roll music, came close to "the Japanese sensibility of the young."[16]

With Yukio Ninagawa's transition from his avant-garde company to the commercial stage in 1974, the impact of the little theatre movement was strengthened. Invited by Tadao Nakane, producer of the Toho company, to direct *Romeo and Juliet* in Tokyo, Ninagawa embarked on a mission to create "a theatre free of the limitations imposed by language and nationality."[17] This led to the creation of productions of western plays that abandoned the "falseness" and ossified western realism typical of *shingeki* stagings. Instead, Ninagawa developed a directorial approach that neither emulated realism nor reproduced traditional theatrical styles. Thus, *Romeo and Juliet* was presented as a contemporary Japanese love story between two ordinary young people and was marked by the use of Elton John's music. Continuing in collaboration with Nakane, Ninagawa directed a star-studded *King Lear* in 1975 and *Hamlet* in 1978. The latter was characterized by a blending of Japanese and western elements: Claudius' heavy red and blue Kabuki makeup and the traveling players' singsong vocal style, characteristic of Bunraku and Noh, were added to atmospheric lighting effects, complex set designs, realistic crowd scenes, and western music.[18]

In 1980 Ninagawa directed *Macbeth*, as translated by Yushi Odajima, his most important interpretation of Shakespeare to date. Placed in Japan during the latter half of the sixteenth century, the Azuchi-Momoyama period, the production drew on the parallels between the civil wars in medieval Scotland and a period of corruption in Japan when rival warlords continuously fought for power and when subordinates overpowered those to whom they owed allegiance. Ninagawa's reading of the play rested on the premise that Macbeth's murder of Duncan was one of these historic acts of overthrowing the established hierarchy. However, Macbeth's corruption went beyond denial of his samurai code of rank and honorable conduct, which obliged him to seek redress for any attacks on the honor of himself, his family, and his superior and, if necessary, to die while doing so. For Ninagawa, Macbeth's greater treachery came with his assassination of his friend and equal, Banquo, and his gratuitous killing of Lady Macduff and her children. By underscoring this difference, he hoped to emphasize the human qualities which universally motivate people to commit such heinous crimes – lust for power, greed, suspicion, and envy.[19]

Further, the director felt his role was to bring something of the world of the Japanese past back to his contemporary audience. To this end, he set the production in an oversized *butsudan*, the Buddhist altar found in many homes through which each family maintains contact with the souls of its ancestors.[20] This became a dominant image in the production. As a gong sounded and chanting was heard, two women, doubled over with age and dressed in ordinary kimonos, hobbled through the auditorium and onto the stage. They pushed open the great ornate doors to reveal latticed opaque windows, like huge *shōji* screens, which filled the proscenium opening. Functioning as a scrim behind which stage action was often illuminated, these screens symbolized the separation between the past and the present, between illusion and reality. Thus, as the two women opened the altar doors, they began an epic ritual which appeared to be coming out of the collective memory of the Japanese people.

Seated at either side of the screens, the two old women drank tea, ate rice with chopsticks, sewed or knitted, and made origami figures, while they observed the action. Once or twice they crept to the screens and peered through them to get a better look. When Macduff's family was killed, they became a silent chorus visibly weeping or gasping with horror in reaction to Macbeth's many acts of violence and his death at the hands of Macduff. In the final moments of the play, as Malcolm took the crown and began to address the crowd, the two old women closed the gates, ending the story while he was still speaking. It was as if these struggles for power that plagued Japanese's history did not end with Macbeth's downfall. Though the tale seemed to come out of Japan's past, this final gesture made it appear that the struggles which the audience and these women, representatives of the masses, had witnessed remained unresolved even today.

A second dominant image in the production was the cherry blossom. To the Japanese these beautiful flowers signify mortality. They embody both nature's benevolence and malevolence; their appearance is deceptive and, therefore, evokes something sinister. In fact, when they are in profusion, it is believed that the sight of the blossom can turn men mad.[21] Ninagawa capitalized on all of these meanings. When the witches first appeared on the heath, seen through the screens, there was thunder and a shower of cherry blossoms. Later, as first Duncan and then Macbeth took the throne, a backdrop with a painting of huge cherry blossom branches against a gilded background dominated the stage. Banquo's fight with the three assassins took place under a cherry tree and he was murdered in a shower of white petals. Near the play's end, Birnam Wood came to Dunsinane as a profusion of cherry branches in blossom. Throughout the action, the scattered petals remained as a reminder of the violent deaths and madness spawned by Macbeth's ambition.

A further visual image was a vibrant red color, used to symbolize death, madness, and disorder. Ninagawa began with the blood-soaked bandages of the messenger bringing news of Macbeth's bravery to Duncan. This was picked up in the vivid red of Macbeth's and Lady Macbeth's kimonos and the red lining of their cloaks. Lady Macbeth's silver-gray cloak lined in blood-red was particularly significant. First worn on the night she helped Macbeth kill Duncan, the robe became associated with the bloody murder and the sexual passion between husband and wife. Later, at the end of a very poignant sleepwalking scene, Lady Macbeth exited dragging the cloak behind her. Its exposed lining became the trail of blood which had destroyed her sanity. After her suicide, Macbeth took up her empty cloak, caressed it and placed it upon his back as a mantle of grief. In death as in life, they remained bound together by their love and their guilt. The final and most significant use of red was in the lighting of a huge, red, cratered moon hanging as a backdrop. First seen when Macbeth met the three witches and heard their prophecy, it reappeared as Macbeth faced Macduff, his mortal enemy. At the moment Macduff dealt him the fatal blow, the moon drained of color as if instantly purged. The nightmare of murderous ambition had finally ended.

In addition to the spectacle related to Japan's past and the vivid symbolic imagery, Ninagawa borrowed much from Kabuki. He used its comic servant to serve as the drunken porter and its mad-women (played by male actors) to serve as the three witches. Kabuki also supplied him with the pantomime horses ridden by Macbeth and Banquo on the heath. Further, it gave the production some of its significant gestural language, most notably the unique stylized poses of the *mie* and the high, sharp kicks, acrobatic flips, and gleaming samurai blades of the *aragoto* to evoke a real sense of danger in the stage fights and battle scenes. Relying on the traditions of vertical space in Japanese theatre, Ninagawa staged much of the action close to the floor with the actors either crouching, kneeling, or standing with their legs wide apart and knees bent.

Against this Kabuki style, Ninagawa set many representational and blatantly emotional elements. The first of these was the use of realistic sound effects – the crows announcing Duncan's approach, the owl's scream upon Duncan's death, the dawn birdsong the following morning, and the sound of approaching horses. Second, there was the use of western classical music – selections from the Fauré *Requiem*; Purcell's *Chaconne*; a Brahms sextet; and chamber music by Schubert, Corelli, and Bach. These served almost like a movie score, underlining the emotional states of the characters while presenting an intercultural commentary on the action. Third, Ninagawa used a realistic acting style to accentuate and illustrate the intense love and physical passion between Macbeth and Lady Macbeth. Their encounters were filled with fondling and explicit caresses, what usually on the Japanese stage would merely be suggested by symbolic gesture. Working against the cultural expectations of his audience, Ninagawa had his actors play Lady Macbeth's drunkenness, hysteria, and madness, and Macbeth's fear, guilt, and bravery in the face of defeat in a style which would openly portray the characters' motivations and emotions. Witnessing these outward displays of passion and inner feeling, the audience would be disquieted at the same time they were feeling empathy.

With this inconsistent and eclectic style for *Macbeth*, Ninagawa wanted his Japanese audience to be uncomfortable, to be shaken out of complacency, to question their wholesale acceptance of western values at the expense of those which had been upheld for centuries. By asking his traditionally trained actors to work toward psychological realism in their performances and, conversely, those trained in psychological realism to work for stylization in their performances, he created a hybrid way of playing that seemed to overthrow the preeminence of either style, to upset his audience's preference for uniformity, and to highlight his message about the need for Japanese people to recover their lost traditions.

Besides the incorporation of Kabuki in his earlier Shakespeare productions, and of Noh in Ninagawa's most recent staging of *The Tempest* in 1988, productions of Shakespeare's plays in Japan since the mid-1970s have reflected the reawakened interest in indigenous theatre forms. Notable is the revitalization of the art of traditional puppetry in productions of Shakespeare plays performed by Japanese puppet theatres. For example, the Doll House troupe's *A Mid-summer's Night's Dream* in 1977 updated Bunraku in order to take advantage of the trick elements built into the life-sized mannequins in a way to enhance the fantasy of the play.[22] A further example is the Yokiza Marionette Theatre Troupe's *Hamlet*, directed by Toshiyuka Fukuda in 1986. This production not only incorporated puppet drama but reaffirmed the trend begun by Ninagawa that Japanese stagings of Shakespeare could speak directly to contemporary issues. Staged as a "play within a play," this *Hamlet* used a puppet version of Shakespeare's play to comment on changes which had occurred in the lives of a Japanese marionette troupe from World War II until the present. The interaction of puppet characters and human actors was played as if it were taking place over time from the 1940s until the 1980s. Costume changes and projected images of historical events like Mishima's suicide and the riots of the 1960s maintained the appropriate time frame. Thus, Fukuda's *Hamlet* was adapted so that the play could serve as a metaphor for life in postwar Japan.[23]

Unique in this trend of creating productions of Shakespeare plays which reflect Japanese traditions and social concerns was Tadashi Suzuki's "postmodern" adaptation of *King Lear* staged in 1984. This was Suzuki's second attempt at staging a Shakespeare play since his 1973 production of *Macbeth* and was unlike any production of Shakespeare in Japan which had preceded it. In contrast to directors who had relied upon the many contemporary translations of Shakespeare plays available, Suzuki created his own text for what he entitled *The Tale of Lear*. He flagrantly cut and rearranged Shakespeare's play, forgoing the linear narrative. What resulted was a distillation of the play to its spiritual and emotional essence.[24]

Suzuki altered the play using the prevalent attitudes of his Japanese audience: their intolerance for father–daughter conflicts, their expectations that aging rulers would abdicate power as a matter of course, and their acceptance of illegitimate offspring as rightful heirs in ruling families and warrior classes. With this in mind, the director reduced the confrontations between Lear and his daughters and gave the Gloucester subplot more weight.[25] Concerned with the play's theme about the dissolution of society, a theme Suzuki felt was important for the contemporary world, his script focused on the evil in human relationships which precipitates society's downfall. To heighten his bleak vision, he eliminated the character of Kent, the only real voice of sanity and loyalty in the original. In this way there was no character to provide relief from the destructive machinations of the other characters.

In his casting choices, Suzuki worked against representing Shakespeare's characters realistically. Lear was an old man, not a king, who was a patient in a mental hospital. Yet the young actor who played him came out without stage makeup, the only indication of his age being his antique kimono. Attending Lear was his nurse, the Fool, who was played by a male actor. Yet this character was dressed in a female nurse's uniform. The audience's perception of the play's gender issues was further distorted with Suzuki's casting of Goneril, Regan, and Cordelia as "super-masculine men" in kimono and beards.[26] By fictioning the characters as signs of old age, madness, and human evil,[27] Suzuki challenged the audience to respond less to human representations than to the signs themselves.

Taking further license, Suzuki modified Shakespeare's plot. The conceit of his version was the conflation between the patient Lear's memories and the events in the Lear story that the nurse was reading in "her" book, "The Tale of Lear." As the old man began to remember his past, he also imagined himself to be the betrayed and impotent king he was hearing about. Acting out his distorted reminiscences and hallucinations, he died believing himself to be the hero of the story.[28] The production unfolded as a pageant of tableaux using the stylized stomping movements and intense vocalizations which have characterized Suzuki's distinctive method of training performers. *The Tale of Lear* became a modern ritualized enactment of madness and death which both mirrored and revitalized the essential qualities of Noh drama.

What made Suzuki's approach to staging Shakespeare unique was that he took the original play and chose not to direct it as written or translated but as a jumping-off point to explore its universal themes. He was attracted to the play not only because it deals with the dissolution of social order but also because it deals with an important modern enigma: to live in isolation is often unbearably difficult, yet to live in groups means being subjected to the inevitable struggles for power that group interaction implies.[29] Thus Suzuki used the play to investigate the madness of the political power games that human beings play around the globe. He wanted to address these issues with his Japanese audiences, but he also saw how Shakespeare's *King Lear* could be used to shed light on the disintegration of the family and social fabric of American culture.[30] For this reason, he chose *The Tale of Lear*, adapted into English and played by an American cast when it toured the United States in 1987, to serve as his English-language directing debut.

Rather than remain hampered by translators' questions about rendering Shakespeare as close to the original as possible, the director took Shakespeare's text, reshaped it, and made it his own. Like the director Lee Breuer, who staged *King Lear* as a story about a southern matriarch, Suzuki was not intimidated by Shakespeare's stature as a great western playwright. Instead, he read the play in light of his own culture and his perception of the contemporary world.

The history of Shakespeare in Japan reveals the dilemma inherent in Japanese culture for the past 125 years. As Japan shook off its isolation to become a modern industrial power by embracing the best of European and American culture, it placed its own heritage at risk. This is no better illustrated than by Shōyō's championing of Shakespeare as the school for Japanese letters. At first the exposure to Shakespeare had been popular and natural; audiences were allowed to experience the parallels between the feudal societies of Elizabethan England and Japan and between the Elizabethan and Japanese stage traditions without apparent mediation. However, this facile acceptance of Shakespeare was shortlived. As Shōyō's didactic purpose for translating and staging Shakespeare's plays as models of western civilization and dramaturgy took over, the Japanese theatrical traditions receded, then withered. This is most apparent in the period between 1911 and 1974 when *shingeki* troupes dominated the Japanese stage and when productions of Shakespeare were relied upon to mediate western ideals and standards for Japanese society. This mediation had two major consequences. First, it imposed western taste while it belittled Japanese sensibility. Second, it generated a paradox: despite the ease with which the Japanese used western modes as their standards for theatre, they were unable to reconcile them with Japanese culture. This approach took hold despite the warnings voiced in 1905 by two of the greatest modern Japanese writers, Natsume Sōseki and Mori Ōgai, that the wholesale adoption of any such western writer as Shakespeare would displace the integrity of the Japanese mind.[31]

As a result, after one hundred years, Shakespeare has come to occupy a vital part of the Japanese literary tradition and to achieve popular status among theatre-goers. Even the anti-western and nationalistic sentiments of the protests of the 1960s and 1970s could not detract from that status. In fact, contemporary directors who rejected the *shingeki* tradition of restaging European productions of the plays as unresponsive to Japanese concerns could not abandon the works of Shakespeare. By identifying themes which had significance to Japanese mores and customs, and by developing production styles which balanced Japanese stage traditions with western realism, these directors bridged the chasm created by differences in language and in culture. Through this hybrid style and emphasis on Elizabethan themes which have parallels in Japanese literature and theatre, they were able to address the crisis at the heart of their culture, namely the ongoing emulation of western values to the detriment of a distinctly national identity. Hence their productions of Shakespeare's plays served not as didactic tools to understand the west but as instruments to enlighten the Japanese audience about itself.

NOTES

1 Toshikazu Oyama, "On Translating Shakespeare into Japanese," *Shakespeare Translation* 2 (1975): 30.

2 Yasumari Takahashi, quoted in "Is Shakespeare Still Too English?," in John Elsom (ed.), *Is Shakespeare Still Our Contemporary?* (New York: Routledge, 1989), 84.

3 Yoshiko Kawachi, "Shakespeare and the Modern Writers in Japan: Translation and Interpretation by Shōyō, Ōgai and Sōseki," *Shakespeare Translation* 7 (1980): 30–1.

4 Yasuo Suga, "Theatre Ways, the Elizabethan and the Japanese," *Shakespeare Studies* 2 (1963); Leonard Pronko, *Theater East and West* (Berkeley, CA: University of California Press, 1967).

5 Tetsuo Anzai, "Adapting *Much Ado* to Japan: Personal Reflections," *Shakespeare Translation* 7 (1980): 10.

6 *Ibid.*, 11.

7 Donald Richie, "Unbuttoned *Measure for Measure* Now Playing at Kinokuniya Hall," *Japan Times*, 12 Apr. 1977.

8 Terence Knapp, "The Karasawagi Journal," *On-stage Studies* 6 (Summer 1982): 95.

9 Anzai, "Adapting *Much Ado*," 13; Samuel L. Leiter, *Shakespeare Around the Globe* (Westport, CT: Greenwood Press, 1986), 513. This is not unlike A. J. Antoon's choice of the victory of the Spanish-American War for his setting of the New York Shakespeare Festival 1972 production of *Much Ado*.

10 S. Agnes Fleck, "A Japanese *Much Ado*," *Shakespeare Quarterly* 32 (1981): 367.
11 *Ibid.*, 366.
12 Takahashi, "Is Shakespeare Still Too English?," 88.
13 Knapp, "Karasawagi Journal," 107.
14 *Ibid.*, 91.
15 Will Durant, *The Story of Civilization: Our Oriental Heritage* (New York: Simon and Shuster, 1954), 916.
16 Takahashi, "Is Shakespeare Still Too English?," 85–6.
17 Taken from program of *Ninagawa Macbeth* seen at the Brooklyn Academy of Music, Oct. 1990.
18 For a thorough description see B. S. Field, Jr., "A Tokyo *Hamlet*," *Shakespeare Quarterly* 30 (1979): 277–9.
19 Interview with Yukio Ninagawa, Brooklyn, NY, 26 Oct. 1990.
20 Descriptions are gleaned from the production at the Brooklyn Academy of Music and from reprinted reviews from London and Edinburgh newspapers gathered in *London Theatre Record* ("Edinburgh Theatre Festival," 11–31 Aug. 1985, and "Macbeth," 9–23 Sept. 1987); *The Times*, 26 Aug. 1985, 13 Sept. 1985; *The Times Literary Supplement*, 13–19 Nov. 1987; *Plays and Players* 385 (Oct. 1985): 22, 408 (Sept. 1987): 6–7, 410 (Nov. 1987): 18–19; *Shakespeare Quarterly* 37 (Summer 1986): 227; and *Drama* 159 (1986): 38.
21 The explanation of the blossoms' significance was printed in the programs prepared for Edinburgh and London performances.
22 Kazuki Hasebe, "Recent Shakespeare Translations and Stage Productions in Japan," *Shakespeare Translation* 5 (1978): 65.
23 For more complete descriptions see Susan Chira, "In Japan, A *Hamlet* set in '45," *New York Times*, 22 Mar. 1986; and James Shapiro, "*Hamlet* in Tokyo," *Shakespeare Quarterly* 37 (1986): 489–91.
24 Marie Myerscough, "East Meets West in the Art of Tadashi Suzuki," *American Theatre* 2 (Jan. 1986): 9.
25 Hank Dobin, "Shogun Lear," unpublished paper presented at the Shakespeare Association of American conference, Mar. 1990.
26 Arthur Holmberg, "The Liberation of Lear," *American Theatre* 5 (July/Aug. 1988): 16.
27 *America's Arena* 6 (June 1988): 12. In this newsletter published for the Arena Stage, Suzuki is quoted as arguing that in the all-male tradition of Japanese theatre, the actor must "approach the role as a pure fiction."
28 Dobin, "Shogun Lear," 3.
29 Holmberg, "Liberation of Lear," 14.
30 *Ibid.*, 14.
31 Kawachi, "Shakespeare and the Modern Writers," 42–3.

CHAPTER 14

Wilson, Brook, Zadek: an intercultural encounter?

Patrice Pavis

An intercultural Shakespeare? Should we really be surprised after the endless experiments that have been tried out on the world's most frequently performed dramatist? In fact, some of the most stimulating productions have come to us from cultures or theatrical styles that call on forms and traditions foreign to the English tradition. Yet intercultural theatre is not an acknowledged genre in criticism; at the most it represents an important, if little known, trend in contemporary theatre practice. It is from this standpoint that I will examine three contemporary productions, neighbors in the new European territory: Robert Wilson's *King Lear* in Frankfurt (June 1990), Peter Brook's *The Tempest* in Paris (November 1990), and Peter Zadek's *Measure for Measure* in Paris (March 1991).

Wilson, Brook, Zadek: three personalities who defy comparison, three stars whose only common traits are to have been the *enfants terribles* of the very institution which now recognizes them as major participants, and to have each encountered Shakespeare in the course of their artistic careers. Theirs is a Shakespeare reduced to the lowest common denominator, no longer the object of a re-reading of the text, but rather the object of cultural confrontation and of intercultural theatrical practice, albeit in different or even contradictory ways. If these productions can be compared at all, it is not because of the directors' dramaturgical analysis or because of their historical reading of the plays, but by virtue of their intercultural practice – whether that is explicit, as in the case of Brook, or implicit, as in Zadek and Wilson.

Wilson does not choose one cultural tradition over another; he has no interest in reprocessing elements specific to identifiable cultures.[1] Brook, on the other hand, welcomes numerous traditions and alone merits the title of intercultural director. Zadek, trapped among the English, German, and French acting traditions, vacillates between a conditioned Brechtian reflex – which consists of breaking up the fable and its political inscription, the better to reconstruct it ideologically – and a unifying and soothing aesthetic of bad taste and kitsch, opening up the text to all sorts of playful excesses.

The absence of conscious dramaturgical analysis, or at least its reduction to a secondary role, does not help with the comparison of the three different plays and their differing productions. This is even more the case because the productions no longer ask to be accepted as authentic (re)readings of Shakespeare's text, a text which has become very difficult to read even for specialists, and was already difficult in the lifetime of the author.

Nor is it any easier to pick out the cultural allusions and exchanges in the productions. No semiotics of culture exists that is sufficiently precise and methodical to permit an analysis of specific theatrical modes and their relationships with surrounding cultures. Lacking a complete (and easily repeatable) method of evaluating cultural exchange,[2] in this essay I will examine the following benchmarks:

1 The global discourse of the production.
2 The use of actors.
3 The relationship of the performance to the text and its translation.
4 The theatrical representation of culture: the manner in which the production shows culture (or cultures) on stage.
5 The type of interculturalism and its relationship to Shakespearean tradition.

WILSON: *LEAR ET DELIRE*

1. Except for a workshop with students at the University of California in 1985 on the same play, Wilson had never staged Shakespeare. He has worked on classical texts for no more than ten years, though he has staged writers and composers as diverse as Euripides, Gluck, Charpentier, Ibsen, Chekhov, Debussy, Strauss, and Wagner. He works more and more for the institutionalized German municipal theatres (*Stadttheater*) which have permanent companies.

With a commission from the Frankfurt Schauspielhaus, a director might stray far from Copeau's ideal – the ideal of classical *Bildung* – which prods and questions the text until it is forced "to give up its secret, by dint of intelligence and respect."[3] The purpose of Wilson's directing is not to elucidate the text, nor to discover a hidden aspect within it, but rather to set the characters' words in a spatial and gestural arrangement that is strictly controlled. The same abstraction and stylization govern his use of architectonic and luminant space as govern his arrangement of bodies and voices. Distributed according to a rigorous and abstract plan on the stage, the actors often create frozen tableaux and perform strange gestural routines, which are disconnected from any feeling and remote from ordinary content. The actions, the lines, the scenes are not linked by the thread of an easily readable fable. The geometry of gestures, of attitudes and movements, the circuit of sounds throughout the stage and the house, the intentionally mechanical delivery – these all create the impression of a straitjacket for expression, an armature that picks up all the variations of intensity *en bloc*, without individualized discrimination.

2. Human psychology is replaced by imperceptible variations of color on the cyclorama which encloses the space. The stage is a machine which absorbs the living, material forms of the actors and of the spoken text, in order to reposition those forms within the overall visual and auditory dynamics of the production.

The actors in *King Lear*, however, could not manage to restrict their emotions and speech within the severe limits imposed by this arrangement. They quickly fell back into pathos and externalized signs of emotion, hinting at a half-psychological, half-philological interpretation of their roles. Their classical training ill-prepared them for Wilson's requirement that they act not in accord with what they felt but only in accord with what they could show. As soon as they got into their roles they lost the aesthetic precision and impassivity Wilson desired, and damaged the remainder of the performance with unwarranted and invasive emotions.

Take, for instance, the case of Marianne Hoppe, the *grande dame* of German theatre. Cast in the role of Lear, she managed as well as could be expected to maintain a balance between psychological acting and a delivery that repeated the same intonations and vocal effects *ad infinitum*, adopting a limited number of vocal and postural attitudes (plaintive or angry poses, for example). According to Heiner Müller,[4] Wilson had not had the good fortune to see the UFA films in which Hoppe always acted with the grandiloquence appropriate to heroic popular drama, and therefore has not been encumbered by the cultural connotations of that thirty- or forty-year era. It all sounds very different to the German ear.

The anti-psychological method of the production required the actors to exercise greater control – not necessarily a mechanical frigidity, but at least a distance from their roles. Wilson, either through compromise or surrender, was not consistent in his own strategy: he did not achieve the dissociation of word and gesture, of speaker and presenter, of signified and signifier, of text and enactment. He allowed the actors to reconstitute themselves as anthropomorphic entities, and to use cheap effects of character and individuality. Questions about motivation and meaning continually resurface.

3. They had never really disappeared, however, despite (dare I say it?) all of Wilson's efforts. Listening to the text in Baudissin's German translation, spectators tended to apply motivation and meaning to the action on stage whether they wanted to or not.

The choice of this nineteenth-century translation, much more literary than the one by Schlegel in common use, was surprising, especially when we know that Wilson had commissioned an adaptation from Heiner Müller, who was not able to complete his task in time. Baudissin's translation retains cultural connotations which simply do not mesh with Wilson's theatrical rhetoric. Just as the production was relatively abstract and depersonalized, so the text is complex, diffuse, and long-winded, clearly situated within the tradition of neo-romantic acting. The translation, which explains motivations with philological care, seemed an intruder in Wilson's stripped-down and glacial scene, damaging the performance instead of nurturing it. The visual and sound effects were so consequential that the production could have dispensed with verbal accompaniment entirely: a foreign language, or a text sung like an oratorio, might have been more appropriate. And yet an abridged version of the literal translation had been prepared by the dramaturg Helen Hammer, who further adapted Shakespeare's text, reducing it to nothing but the pillars of the argument and the rhetoric of the sentence. Because the text was boiled down to essentials, eliminating expressions which might slow down primary information, it maintained the underlying shape of the dialogue, the design of the syntax, and the basic rhetorical structure.

Thus the simplified syntax did not fit inside Wilson's theatrical figuration nor utilize the same rhythmic and semantic moorings. The theatrical image was much more fragmentary, discontinuous, and abstract than the verbal text. Verbal rhythm and visual rhythm were not modeled upon one another; and their asynchronicity was problematic because it appeared more accidental than critical or productive.

4. Taken all in all, culture was represented in an antithetical manner. The cultural baggage of the Shakespearean tradition and the world of Lear and of kingship were hardly shown; any rare glimpses escaped as if by accident. Conversely, the world of lines, of forms, of gestures and sounds referred to our own contemporary, anonymous, and dehumanized society, to "design" effects, to a streamlined universe from which all warmth and humanity have disappeared. Wilson neutralized all cultural effect in the text, all connotation, all local color, by converting Shakespeare's specific political fable into a story about the universal relationships of the family.

What was readable came from the visual order, not the textual. If no recognizable reading was suggested, there was at least great coherence in the lighting, in the centering/decentering of the action, in the scenic distribution of volume and form. The electro-acoustic music by Hans-Peter Kuhn, circulating through the space without illustrating action or mood, focused the entire production and made it dynamic.

The adapters of reception (i.e., some elements in the production which are supposed to facilitate reception for a disoriented public) were not tied to one particular cultural practice but were formal and aesthetic. They aimed solely at reinforcing the harmony of propor-tion and the correspondence between the various elements (space, lighting, stage objects, gestural choices). Other adapters – involun-tary and parasitical, these: the psychologizing of the acting and the humanizing of character relationships – reintroduced a reading of the tragedy that was banal and familiar. A poem by William Carlos Williams, "The Last Words of My English Grandmother," spoken by Hoppe, positioned Wilson's reading of the play by describing the final moments of an old woman who has lost her taste for life ("rolled her head away"), and who denounces the lack of under-standing of young people ("Oh you think you're smart / you young people, / she said, but I'll tell you / you don't know anything"). With the same vacant air, Lear confronted no one, not even his own shadow. A culture of interaction or of confrontation gave way to high-tech indifference. The violence was less that of the cruelties inflicted upon Lear than that of the coldness of human kinship and

the neutralizing of emotion. It was this culture of human relationships which was most visibly absent in Lear's universe.

5. The production was the complete opposite of intercultural communication. Wilson was not interested in adapting one foreign
culture (English, or literary/literate) to another (German-American,
or post-industrial/postmodern). His culture did not aim at setting
up communication between groups or different contexts, as in Brook
and, to a lesser extent, in Zadek. It was a culture manufactured out
of a collage, out of a syncretism of divergent traces built on a
thoroughly mastered and coherent aesthetic, an aesthetic which
itself is situated "beyond good and evil" of existing cultures, in a
postmodern no man's land. Here lies the radical difference between
Wilson and Brook: interculturalism would not know how to be
postmodern, to the extent that it refuses to reduce and collect
cultures without taking account of their origins and purposes.

Wilson attempted to put into parenthesis all culture and all
meaning conveyed by the dramatic text: the production was not a
decoration and illustration of the text, but a device allowing it to be
heard, as if the quiet and the space which surrounded it opened for
the spectator a direct access to the text. The scenographic images
were never of great visual impact, nor did they paraphrase the text;
the moving screens which continuously centered and recentered the
stage were present only in order to modify this device for listening to
the text.

Despite all this, the text of *King Lear* was regarded as sacred,
precisely because all the paraphernalia declared it to be abstract,
irreducible to a single interpretation, and enigmatic by nature. Such
a relativism discourages any particular reading entirely and transforms the text into a simple affair, summarizable in a few commonplaces scattered about like scraps of shed skin. Despite the abstract
wrapping-paper of a production conceived as installation art, all the
commonplaces of traditional Shakespearean interpretation were
here once again: violence, madness, aging, the tragic – so many
notions which the production wanted to get rid of, and which our
general, popular culture regularly dishes up with a variety of sauces.
The return of suppressed psychological and philological aspects of
the Shakespearean text produces all this poetic and human cargo as
soon as the spectator hears it.

So we have in fact a very classical reading of the text, the kind of
reading expressed in Dullin's idea that "*King Lear* is one of the most

Elizabethan of Shakespeare's plays: it is, on the one hand, his
naïveté on the level of the strictly dramatic action, and, on the other,
his extraordinary sophistication on the level of the intellect, which
astonish and repel us."[5] In Wilson, intellectual sophistication is
translated into an aesthetic sophistication of tableaux. Performance
is no longer in vassalage to text. Wilson's *Lear* is the sign of a change
towards a different culture of meaning and interpretation, towards a
postmodern relativism – as if a larger entity with indefinable contours, culture-as-a-whole, were replacing an entity grounded on the
sign, the text, the word, the relationship between signifier and
signified.

BROOK HARVESTS *THE TEMPEST*

No one knows this culture with indefinable contours, or how to draw
its complete dimensions, better than Peter Brook, the magician of
Les Bouffes du Nord. It was with *The Tempest* that Brook began his
work with actors culled from different corners of the world, at the
Mobilier National in Paris in 1968. Going well beyond his two
tentative attempts at the play at Stratford in 1957 and in 1963, he
tried to "create" actors capable of finding within themselves unexpected resources. In 1968 he wished "to see whether *The Tempest*
could help the actors find the power and violence that is within the
play," he said; "whether they could find new ways of performing all
the other elements which were normally presented in a very artificial way ... and whether the actors could extend their range of
work by using a play that demanded this extension."[6] Brook thus
forced the actors to go beyond themselves in order to note how many
cultures could go to rack and ruin, to note how a primitive society of
islanders might pass from an Edenic state of nature and sensuality to
an explosion of the instincts.

After the long series of developments with the International
Centre for Theatre Research, and a detour in form for *The Mahabharata*, *The Tempest* of 1990 presented instead a universal reconciliation
among peoples as well as reconciliation inside each person. Prospero's island, a rectangle of sand where a rock was discreetly placed
upstage as if to suggest shattered illusions, was a utopian place where
history's wounds were healed, where the natives, like the travelers,
lived in a sensuality of the concrete and in an eternal present of
reconciliation.

1. The entire production was steeped in concrete thought. Nothing was said or thought which was not also signified by a visual or tactile materiality of signs: sand, light, the musical and vocal decor. The abstraction of this parable, its hermetic symbolism, was redeemed by a concrete use of the stage and a warm simplicity in the acting. The natural world and the invisible world converged in the world of illusion. Brook has as much nostalgia for "the England of Shakespeare [where] ties with nature, with the natural world, had not been broken," as for the utopian world where "for an actor raised in a climate of ceremony, of ritual, the road that leads to the invisible world is often direct and natural." Though cut off from society and from history, the natural world of the island was not a universe closed in upon itself; unlike Strehler's famous production (1978), it was not a place where the spells of theatre, illusion, and art took hold. For Brook "the essential theme is not the illusion of the theatre, not the stage, but life."[7] Prospero's (and perhaps Shakespeare's) renunciation of the world of magic and illusion became Brook's renunciation of theatrical virtuosity – with a concomitant deepening and revitalizing of interhuman and intercultural communication.

2. For Brook everything stems from the actor, who must be capable of furnishing the space, the silence, and the fable with lucidity and lightness. The text, Brook said, "must be played lightly, and without embarrassment about its unreality, which is why our stage is not a world of real perspectives and distances, but a sand carpet, a playing field."[8] This lightness was sustained by the open space, the subtle moods and variations of the lighting, the rhythmic and musical commentary.

The actors are very different from one another, not only in their ethnic origins, but even more in their physical and vocal qualities: it's not enough just to compare the morphology of the different African actors when thinking about their individual selves. Despite such diversity, all the actors have been marked by their common work with Brook: a very quick acting style, constant contact with the audience, an exteriority of effects, and, for the African actors (according to Brook), "a different quality from white actors – a kind of effortless transparency, an organic presence beyond self, mind or body, such as great musicians attain when they pass beyond virtuosity."[9] This presence gave to the powers of Prospero (Sotigui Kouyaté) an effect of the marvelous without spectacular exoticism.

His quotidian magic was the opposite of theatrical illusion, and retained an authenticity that allowed the actor to perform African songs, to put pebbles on the sand, or to invoke the reality about him without giving the impression of representing a fiction – as if he were acting under his own name inside a theatrical ceremony.

The casting also upset the traditional perspective that sees Caliban as a black slave colonized by the noble and white Prospero. Indeed Kouyaté, a lanky actor from Burkina Faso who is a "griot by birth,"[10] played the role of Prospero – big switch here – with a highly European vocal and gestural rhetoric, such as one might see at the entrance exam for a conservatory, as if the African griot, by some perverse neo-colonial effect, felt himself obliged to "act European." His highly spiritual fragility contrasted with the Herculean strength of Mamadou Dioume in the role of Antonio, and with the twirling loquaciousness, the vital and earthy force of the aerial trickster Ariel (Bakary Sangaré). In the same paradoxical spirit, Caliban (David Bennent) was played by a German actor who looked like a little boy from back home. The change in perspective was not systematic, however, and thus did not assume a dramaturgical meaning, since the role of the usurper Duke was enacted by one of the Africans (Dioume is from Senegal), which literally challenged any vision of "black and white" in the play. Far from strengthening a political, ideological, or racial conflict, the actors instead told a marvelous tale. But the actors told it from their own separate perspectives, and with a very sensuous way of speaking the text, taking pleasure in pronouncing each syllable, without distancing themselves from the phonetic systems of their mother-tongues.

3. Here the translation by Jean-Claude Carrière is clearly a delight for the African or Asian mouth. The materiality of the text is not flattened by an overly fluid or facile adaptation. Certainly, Carrière has suppressed, restructured, or simplified some "obscure dialogue," reduced the number of the "other lords," and suggested an acting version quite separate from the traditions of literal translation. Nevertheless, these rearrangements remain minor, while the essential is preserved: what Carrière himself has called "des mots rayonnants"[11] – points of radiance, or radiating words – preserve the semantic and rhythmic supports of the original. We can judge this a little in the final words of the play:

And my *ending* is *despair*

Unless I be relieved by *prayer*,
Which *pierces* so, that it assaults
Mercy itself, and frees all *faults*.

Ma *fin* est *désespoir*, à moins qu'à
    mon secours,
ne vienne la *prière*
si *perçante* qu'elle s'élance
à l'assaut de la *pitié* même
et de tout *méfait* nous délivre.

Carrière has even more deftly resisted the temptation to adapt the play by practicing transculturation upon it, since the story is set in no man's land, on a utopian island, and since it could not be inscribed with a determined cultural context without losing its parable-like character. Despite the references to Naples and Milan, the play welcomes a variety of cultural identities: it is located in a place that is as much another part of the world as another part of oneself. Thus the cosmopolitanism of the actors and the cultural syncretism of the staging were both legitimized by the translation.

The cultural transfer took place on the levels of vocal enunciation, of mise en scène, and of the acting, not on the level of the literal contents of the fable. The actors represented neither their original cultures nor a context which had to be identified in order to situate the fable. The large number of cultural allusions warned against any unilateral reading. At the same time the allusions revealed an underlying common ground, universalizing the conflicts and the human relationships.

4. The theatrical representation of all these cultures, therefore, never served as a mimetic figuration, nor one idealized by exotic effects, nor (as in Strehler) a created metaphor of the world viewed as a stage. It placed itself instead under the sign of an immediately comprehensible acting convention, elementary in its use of universal referents which were also reminiscences of previous productions; the sand to demarcate the island, brought back from *Carmen*; the bamboo poles, borrowed from *The Mahabharata*, to construct and dismantle the ship, bit by bit; the fruit on a tray, suggesting the utopian mirage of a civilization with abundant fruit ripe for picking (cf. the end of *The Mahabharata*); musicians sitting on Persian carpets as in *The Conference of the Birds*. All these elements have become Brookian signs of cultural otherness, modeling and semanticizing cultural indexes already present in Brook's idiom.

Each new production nonetheless uses a basic culture which receives and modifies the others: Persian for *The Conference of the Birds*, Indian for *The Mahabharata*, African for *The Tempest*. The

African animism and the marvelous lent themselves admirably to this use of the convention, and initiated a new type of communication: Prospero questioned his daughter while holding an amulet over her head; Miranda relived her childhood by closing her eyes (1.2). Just before freeing Ariel, Prospero held him tightly in his arms, both staring straight ahead.

The African tonality did not rule out other borrowings, much more localized: Korean masks, a Zen garden, the rather Indian cut of the African bubus, etc. Images from western culture appeared in traditional representations: St. George overcoming the dragon (1.2); Ariel as the angel of the Annunciation in a white gown; Miranda the bride in white; Caliban and Ariel, perched on top of a pillar, looking like devil and angel; Stephano and Trinculo improvising in gibberish and with Neapolitan gestures (2.2).

Despite all the allusions to these varied practices, the theatrical readability was as comfortable as that of an extravaganza intended for an audience of children. The modification of the text in translation, the coherence of the "squalls of signs" carried by perfectly adjusted and targeted vectors, and the uninterrupted flow of transcultural allusions – all assured the greatest readability. The return to the supernatural and to the naïve resulted in an interpretation of great freshness. It dispensed with the serious dramaturgical analysis which, as was sometimes the case in the 1960s, saw Prospero as colonizing exploiter, Caliban as an exploited colonial, and Ariel as an intellectual engaged in the struggle for national liberation ...

5. Brook is no longer alone in this rejection of the theatre of interpretation; he has received the support for some time now of some of the directors who were earlier most involved in dramaturgical research and political activism, such as Peter Stein.[12] Brook, who has never believed in preparation based on a scrupulous philological reading of the text, has also never been party to the facile convention of the postwar English theatre which claims to let the text speak for itself (a slogan that Wilson frequently uses today!).

Brook's relationship to the Shakespearean tradition is highly ambiguous: according to his conception of transcultural communication, Brook relativizes all Eurocentric claim to release the enigma of the text. At the same time, Shakespeare is for him so mysterious and complex that one cannot interpret him with words and ideas; at best, his potential force can be unleashed thanks to the presence and vivacity of actors: "even though Shakespeare's words are inevitably coloured by their period, the true richness of this writing lies at a deeper level, beneath the words, where there is no form, nothing but the vibration of a great potential force."[13] As if he mistrusted all artistic forms and all readings of the text that might weaken this force, in *The Tempest* Brook made these traditions and cultures meet beyond specific forms, at the "pre-expressive" level, as Eugenio Barba would say. The proof of this intercultural pudding is – as we might expect – in its enabling the ludic encounter of actors drawn from the most varied of backgrounds, and in its making their exchanges both obvious and "natural." The clarity and spontaneity of the acting, together with the readability of the networks of signs, in this case re-established the kind of dramatic coherence that one no longer expected to see, and which conveyed itself with all the more force as a result. In this sense, the intercultural aesthetic of Brook should be seen as an appropriate response to the contemporary crisis of meaning, but a response which does not opt for the "have-you-seen-me" relativism of the postmodern.

A MADE-TO-MEASURE ZADEK

The traitor in our three-person drama, the villain of the piece, is obviously Peter Zadek, who has the bad taste to make child's play of all cultures: Jewish, English, German, French, and, above all, kitsch. It's not at all clear that his production of *Measure for Measure* should be called intercultural theatre, even in the sense of a meeting of cultures and of acting techniques "drawn from elsewhere," as in Brook. Here the intercultural was present more in linguistic transfer than in actual transculturation. Zadek's experience at the Théâtre de l'Europe in Paris revealed the difficulty of interculturalism in the "narrow" sense – that, for example, of an Anglo-German director who customarily works in Germany and who was invited to direct an English author using French actors for a French audience. The numerous problems of this recent project, which was coldly received by audiences and by the critics, were not all intercultural in nature, but the inherent difficulties of the multinational enterprise weighed still more heavily on the result.

1. In a play which deals with good and evil, and which clearly differentiates the good characters from the bad, it was surprising to find a production with no guiding force, no coherent discourse, nor – when all is said and done – any pertinent view of the work. Despite

the series of gags and mini-shocks (of no great consequence these, especially in light of what Zadek pulled off with his *Othello* and *Lulu*), one could not see where the interpretation of the text was leading; the actors were left to themselves, boredom soon set in, and the evening dragged on. The global rhythm of the production was rather turgid and above all it was badly managed, since, instead of cooperating, supporting, or confronting one another, the subordinate rhythms (those resulting from the different systems of signs, and those of the actors taken individually) canceled each other to create a generalized arhythm. The "discord between the rhythm of the play and its production,"[14] which Zadek knows to be fatal to any Shakespearean production, was as damaging to the reading of the text as to the mise en scène he offered.

The absence of any central thesis is most likely connected to the "artistic lightness" which Zadek claims when he tries to say extremely difficult things. This lightness or "opening up of the staging"[15] is supposed to replace the Brechtian period when theatrical interpretation closed the text and allowed an authoritarian solution to its conflicts and contradictions. It is also a heritage of Zadek's training in England, a country where theatre has remained entertainment, a craft rather than an art, and where performance does not carry any philosophical or political message:

I believe that a very important aspect of my work in the theatre – that which can be called the "opening up of the staging" – stems largely from my encounter with those English traditions that I have absorbed in part – one might even say that it has to do with those typically English rules of the game which are designed for living together in society, with my hereditary tendency (which I got from my German parents) to think in moralizing terms.[16]

It remains to be seen how this Zadekian conflict between "opening up" and moralizing is resolved on a case-by-case basis. In the Paris *Measure for Measure*, the conflict was complicated by the presence of totally dissimilar actors and of an audience with unusual expectations. But both actors and audience were situated entirely within the western method of producing classical texts: no extra-European form of culture was presented to *defamiliarize* the perceptions of the spectator and put the fable in a different context. The audience was thus at the mercy of the production's discourse, yet the choices were not backed up or clarified. In this *Measure for Measure* those choices were barely readable and rather contradictory, limited to allusions and isolated effects. The Duke, for example, was seen as a disquieting manipulator: but his cunning, his vanity, and his duplicity were suggested without always being carried through or applied inside a global and systematic discourse. No historicizing of the play attempted to explain the political stakes, no moral thesis was advanced, no explanation at all was offered for the relationship between political power and desire – the very subject-matter of the play. On the contrary, the action was illustrated with the naïveté and the limitless imagination that Zadek has always claimed for his Shakespeare. He remarked on his production of the same play in Bremen in 1967: "In Shakespeare great naïveté and sophisticated subtlety are conjoined. There are no theories, no moral lessons, no aesthetic principles, and no modish staging which can replace a lack of imagination with the usual superficial effects."[17] But where has the German Zadek gone? Where is Germany going? Is it playing tricks with us again?

2. The answer appears to be simple: he could not, or did not know how to, use actors from a tradition totally different from that of their English or German counterparts. The former he values when they are capable of lightness, the latter when they add to this quality a physical presence and an "opaque" corporeality (such as Ulrich Wildgruber, Eva Mattes, or Hans Mahnke do). In his initial experience with a production of *Measure for Measure*, under the direction of Neville Coghill at Oxford in 1944, Zadek found an axiom that has stuck with him, and which defines his approach to Shakespearean actors fairly well: "I love it when Shakespeare is played by gifted amateurs, because he has no need of the slick assurance of professionals ... "[18]

Zadek could not recapture this direct, unpretentious acting or this corporeal robustness using French actors who were completely lacking in the "lightness of amateurs" and who possessed very strong vocal identity: the timbre, intonation, and the rhythm of elocution of actors such as François Marthouret, André Marcon, Phillipe Clévenot, or Roland Amstutz are instantly recognizable, whatever their roles. The formal, neoclassical perfection of their diction tended to interfere with the direct, shocking, and provocative side of the production. Their vocal signatures were not utilized in an ensemble fashion, which might appear to be the result of dramaturgical analysis, or in a system of cultural allusions. Other actors made such pallid appearances that their characters lost all consistency and remained almost voiceless. Such was the case with Isabelle Huppert, the celebrated film actress, in the role of Isabella (despite an interesting interpretation which suggested that her moral intransigence depends upon obscure motivations), and with Jean-Pierre Jorris, long associated with Vilar, in the role of Escalus, both of whom went totally unnoticed. Indeed all the actors were left to themselves and to their well-known vocal signatures; but such freedom seemed more an abdication of staging than a deliberate choice to open it up. Opening up the staging should at least be perceived as an intentional process which facilitates the re-reading of the text. This was not the case, despite a translation that would lend itself well to a global appropriation of the play.

3. Jean-Michel Déprats has retranslated much of Shakespeare for the most important French directors of the past twenty years, and with great felicity. He is even behind the translation of *Measure for Measure* by Jean-Claude Carrière, used in Brook's production of 1978.

Déprats's interest is in translating for the benefit of the source language and not for that of the target language and culture. He refuses to reduce or assimilate the cultural characteristics of the original work, which often creates problems for the target audience. He is particularly fond of translating in a homogeneous way the radiant and recurrent words which underlie the Shakespearean text, so as to preserve its construction and its signifying rhythm. He thus abandons the play on words in French which Carrière, who is much more "target-oriented," particularly likes. Déprats protects both the structure and the rough patches of the original, maintaining the proportions and logic, especially the rhythmic logic, of the English text.

The work of Déprats, as much dramaturgical reading as philological concern, marks a renewal in the approach to French Shakespeare (already started by the translations of Bonnefoy and Vittoz) in that it breaks with the aesthetic of Good Taste, and breaks with the assimilation of Shakespeare into French "genius." It finds a use for literalness, and rediscovers the theatrical form of the text, its source of energy, its color, the movement of the words and the "physique of the language."[19]

Sadly, Zadek paid little attention to the characteristics of this translation in his work with the actors. He drowned the materiality of the text in the jumble of his effects and the lack of attention which resulted from them. Instead of anchoring the acting in the body and reclaiming its internal logic, he ran after the instantaneous meaning and the isolated, discontinuous effect. It would seem that he didn't understand the cultural resonances of some of the wordplay in the translation. Two examples:

(a) "Pompey the Bum" quite naturally became in Déprats "Pompey Le Cul" (2.1), and every experienced French ear at once heard the slang expression "pomper le cul," in the sense of "exhausting or wearing someone out."

(b) When Angelo suggests a way of saving her brother to Isabella, he does not beat around the bush: "Fit thy consent to my sharp appetite" (2.4). Déprats made this wonderful discovery: "Plie ton consentement à mon désir aigu." The French words here have productive double meanings, polite and sensual, so that they reconstitute some of Shakespeare's bawdy ambiguity. Déprats's line could be rendered in English as "Give your consent to my strong wish," or as "Fit your accord around my pointed desire."

In both these cases, the French audience got the wordplay immediately, but neither the actor nor the production exploited it with the slightest allusion, by expression or by gesture. It's hard to believe that the purpose here was to avoid being redundant or too explicit, in order to make it "light."

In short, there was a complete disparity between the translation and the staging. This lack of coordination was as damaging to the text as to the ingenuity of the production. Unlike Wilson's aesthetic, here the discrepancy between text and staging was not the result of a deliberate choice (the desire to avoid the redundant, for example), but rather the mark of an inability to enrich one by the other.

4. Building upon bizarre profusion and bad taste, Zadek made unreadable on stage a dramaturgical design that appears in the play to be a blueprint for symmetry and exchange: the opposition between power and license, truth and lies, good and evil. Any oversimplified dialectic was challenged, since for Zadek, despite the allegory of this medieval morality play, things are not always so cut and dried. Thus it was with irony and antiphrasis that he set the altar of the blessed Virgin and the public urinal on opposite sides of the apron, to signify that they represent two sides of the same coin. Such a frontispiece aped the opposition between high and low, between spirit and body; it asserted that everything is equally

perverted, that glory conceals misery, the sublime the sordid. Every-thing on stage was fake: the set made of meticulously ugly card-board, the garish costumes that shocked the eye, the hypocritical and obscene emotions.

5. And so the thesis of the show was that it is all the same, everything is rotten, everything is relative. Whereas Brook sought a general reconciliation among human beings, races, classes, conspira-tors and victims, Zadek saw only discord, incompatibility, and indifference. Whereas the intercultural sought a place of harmony and experimentation, here there was nothing but a banal and expensive international co-production which debased all local or national tradition and devitalized all cultural exchange.

How can we explain this pathetic result, this magnificent mess, when we consider that the artists involved are normally excellent? Was it the result, perhaps, of confining the exchange to the Euro-pean setting, and further disallowing any national tradition the opportunity to assert itself? Or because the production was not enlivened by sufficiently strong visual thinking like Wilson's, or by a transcultural and mystical universalism like Brook's? Or simply because the Théâtre de l'Europe is a technocratic creation which prefers to rely on big names (Shakespeare, Zadek, Huppert) without taking chances, instead of looking for what they might bring to an exchange? In the case of Zadek, interculturalism demonstrated the most debilitating characteristics: those of an international pro-duction imposed from above and assembled purely for reasons of prestige, an enterprise which, as it proceeded with its work, took no care over the result of such exchanges or over the value of the techniques and practices of its constituent cultures. It seems that only a permanent troupe with the orientation of Brook's at the CICT can measure up to such a complicated process.

In these three intercultural experiences, so powerfully different from each other, and in the innumerable other productions throughout the world in which the name of Shakespeare is mentioned, is there anything that still might concern that little dramatist from Strat-ford? Who knows, maybe!

It's clear that the work of the classic of all classics is no longer a model to follow, nor a score to be performed; it is instead an entire culture of otherness, similar and different, unrepresentable and unattainable, ready to lead us on to an infinity of other cultural enterprises. The variable now is not the political teaching that the dramaturgy carries, nor the cultural and philological character-istics that all these foreign expressions discover in it, but rather the theatrical and aesthetic practices that can be manufactured out of it. In this sense, Shakespeare is now a machine to make theatre, to reveal other cultures, to observe their constant changes. As if the truth no longer came from Stratford-upon-Avon, but from cultures affected despite themselves by Stratford, cultures which have the strength to resist it and at the same time the longing to consult it.

We notice this when comparing the way in which "we" and "the others" employ references to Shakespeare. For "the others" – in Africa, in India, or in China,[20] and in many Third World countries – Shakespeare is used as a militant discourse in adaptations of the Brechtian type. For "us," as we have just seen, the intercultural experience, as yet barely acknowledged, is often politically naïve on a grand scale. Its supreme naïveté lies in thinking that "the cul-tural" replaces politics, and that "cultures," particularly minority cultures, make all political analysis invalid.

"Elsewhere," just as "here," Shakespeare remains the classic *par excellence*, the obligatory reference point for all scholars. Shake-speare is the ideal testing-ground for an act of cultural banality (Zadek); or for trying out other cultures, notably African cultures because they are especially syncretic and oral (Brook); but also for maximizing the purely aesthetic in the tradition of the avant-garde (Wilson).

Is it still really necessary to be interested in Shakespeare, if his work is no longer examined for itself or for its relationship to our own condition? Perhaps the question is immediately disqualified, because it is insufficiently postmodern: now we should ask not *what* the text means or *what meaning* it can convey, but *where* it can lead us. This highly pragmatic question brings us back to stage practice, in order to see what use production can make of the text, without knowing in advance whether it will try to read and interpret it.

Of these three directors, perhaps only Brook trusts Shakespeare's text – but sadly it is a blind trust, for he has decided once and for all that everything is in Shakespeare and, conversely, Shakespeare is in everything. The intercultural packaging of *The Tempest* only con-firmed what was already known about the text; for all that, it was not a practice thought out in advance but had to be invented and tested on the spot. It fit wonderfully into the cultural patchwork of this variegated production and in the quotidian magic which the actors displayed.

At the opposite extreme, Zadek refused to countersign the moral theorem that the fable of *Measure for Measure* would like to impose on him: the absence of direction for the actor and of a coherent reading left the audience perplexed: was it because of the bankruptcy of all ideologies resulting from the collapse of the Soviet empire, or just a botched-up job of directing?

Wilson almost managed to make us forget Shakespeare, but – sadly – not quite. The cultural reminiscences carried by the text, and by the embryonic fable and reading in his production of *King Lear*, could not stop spectators from sobering up quickly and remembering their duties as model readers.

Whatever the amazing ambiguity, the universal complexity, or the strange familiarity of Shakespeare, it is still necessary to encounter him. But the encounter can no longer be between the devouring west and the troublesome east or south. It now must be between the politically radical thought of the Third World and the universalizing and humanist thought of the west, the consumer of all cultures.

Shakespeare, again, as the mediator between these two types of thought? It is the price of becoming unique, universal, and intercultural.

Translated by Ann Tyrrell Kennedy and Dennis Kennedy

NOTES

1 In this earlier productions like *The Civil Wars* or *The Knee Plays* the borrowings are much more obvious. On this subject see Christel Weiler, "Japanese Traces in Wilson's Production," in *A Reader Intercultural Performance*, ed. P. Pavis (London: Routledge, due 1994).
2 I have elsewhere proposed the following "hourglass" model:
   (1) cultural modeling, sociological, anthropological codifications
   (2) artistic modeling
   (3) perspective of the adapters
   (4) work of adaptation
   (5) preparatory work by the actors
   (6) choice of theatrical form
   (7) theatrical representation/performance of culture
   (8) reception-adapters
   (9) readability

(10) reception in the target culture

(11) given and anticipated consequences.

See P. Pavis, *Theatre at the Crossroad of Culture* (London: Routledge, 1992), 185.

3 Copeau, "La mise en scène," *Encyclopédie Française* (Paris, 1935), 17:1764–5.

4 "Shakespeare stört eigentlich die Aufführung," Gespräch mit Heiner Müller über Wilsons Frankfurter Lear (von Moritz Rinke), *Deutsche Bühnenkunst*, July 1990: 83.

5 Charles, Dullin, *Ce sont les dieux qu'il nous faut* (Paris: Gallimard, 1969), 204.

6 Brook, quoted in Margaret Croyden, "Peter Brook's *Tempest*," *The Drama Review* 13.3 (1969): 125.

7 Brook, "Une énigme," in Shakespeare, *La Tempête*, trans. Jean-Claude Carrière (Paris: CICT, 1990), 3–4.

8 Quoted in Michael Kustow, "Sovereign of the Enchanted Isle," *The Observer*, 14 Oct. 1990.

9 Quoted in *ibid.*

10 Sotigui Kouyaté, "Je suis griot d'origine," *Libération*, 12 Oct. 1990.

11 See Brook, *The Shifting Point* (New York: Harper & Row, 1987), 94.

12 On the meeting between Peter Stein and Peter Brook, see Gerhardt Stadelmaier, "Das Ballett der Königsdiener," *Frankfurter Allgemeine Zeitung*, 15 Nov. 1990: "The two heroes, Brook and Stein, show one of their ancient masks: on the one side is the naïve old man, on the other the man who thinks he knows everything. After that they join forces to take a stand against the German theatre of interpretation and signification."

13 Quoted in Kustow, "Sovereign of the Enchanted Isle."

14 Peter Zadek, *Das wilde Ufer: ein Theaterbuch* (Cologne: Kiepenheuer und Witsch, 1990), 186.

15 *Ibid.*, 205.

16 *Ibid.*, 210.

17 *Ibid.*, 81.

18 *Ibid.*, 136.

19 See Jean-Michel Déprats, in a program note for the production: "A text by Shakespeare above all is a text written for mouths, for cheeks, for sighs. To translate it for the stage is to be asked to write in an oral and gestural language, muscular and lively, capable of offering to the performer an instrument for acting that is vigorous and precise. To use a theatrical text, written by an actor for actors, is to try to preserve or recreate the theatricality inscribed in the original text."

20 Cf. Parasuram Ramamoorthi, "Macbeth: A Transcultural Experiment," paper at the Eighth Symposium of Theatre Critics and Scholars, Novi Sad, June 1991; and Yu Weijie, "Topicality and Typicality: The Acceptance of Shakespeare in China," *The Dramatic Touch of Difference*, ed. Erika Fischer-Lichte, Josephine Riley, and Michael Gissenwehrer (Tübingen: Narr, 1990).

Afterword: Shakespearean orientalism

Dennis Kennedy

Any approach to Shakespeare that inquires about his prevalence in world culture is obliged to notice that he is not valued everywhere. Claims of Shakespeare's universality cannot be substantiated, at least on a literal level, since there are numerous areas in which he is not read, performed, or studied with enthusiasm: by the enormous populations of the Islamic countries, for instance (where no dramatist is highly valued, though poets certainly are), in much of Southeast Asia, in most of Africa. But neither the British nor North Americans have to travel far to see signs of Shakespeare's limits. Because of the native force of neoclassicism, France proved particularly resistant until the second half of the twentieth century. Most pointedly, Shakespeare is infrequently performed in the Iberian languages – and it's worth mentioning that more people in the world speak Spanish as their first language than any other European tongue. Samuel Leiter's *Shakespeare Around the Globe*, a guide to "notable" productions since the war, selects twenty-one performances from the German-speaking countries and fifteen from France, but only four from Spain and none at all from Portugal or from the entirely of Latin America, from El Paso to Tierra del Fuego. Shakespeare's relative absence in Central and South America may result from competing colonial allegiances, as Gary Taylor asserts,[1] though it is just as likely connected to the existence of a competing canon of Spanish Renaissance drama.

As no one reason accounts for the naturalization of Shakespeare in diverse foreign cultures, so no single reason explains his alienation in others. This is most apparent in Asia, where the responses to Shakespeare have been almost as varied as the histories of the peoples who make up the continent. Obviously Shakespeare in India has been a vastly different enterprise than Shakespeare in Japan or Shakespeare in China. But regardless of the target country, the extreme process of alienation required of the text in transference to such remote settings has often made English-speakers uneasy. Shakespeare productions in Japan at the turn of the century, for example, were treated with jocular arrogance in the London press, accompanied by photos of actors in national dress and imperious captions. Kurosawa's Shakespeare films still meet resistance in some western quarters on the grounds that they are so thoroughly bound to the samurai ethos and to Japanese traditions of performance that they cannot be appreciated outside that environment.

Part of this response is culturally instinctive, the common inclination of the west towards things eastern. As Edward Said shows, the history of orientalism has been the history of the intellectual ownership of the east by the west. Western culture since the eighteenth century has imported its Orient, Said says, "domesticated for local European use."[2] With Shakespeare there may also be a lingering resentment that Asian nations could turn the tables on Britain by appropriating one of its own cultural monuments. Some Shakespearean commentators have been heartened by Asian attention, seeing it as proof once more of their subject's universal appeal; a more thoughtful response might be to wonder what "Shakespeare," exactly, has been transferred and appropriated by eastern cultures, and for what reasons.

Shakespeare in Asia cannot be detached from larger questions relating to interculturalism and cultural imperialism. This is immediately apparent historically. As I note in the Introduction, Shakespeare's arrival in Europe was brought about by factors that had nothing to do with his Elizabethan condition or his position in England in the eighteenth century; the nationalist needs of central and eastern Europe made Shakespeare useful, and ultimately the heart of a new literary and theatrical movement. But generally speaking, in Asia this was not the case, for Shakespeare arrived in most Asian (and African) environments in the baggage of empire. Whereas in Europe the Shakespeare project embraced the translation and outright appropriation of the texts, in Asia the imperial mode tended to bring them in the original language as a demonstration of the linguistic and cultural superiority of the conqueror. This was most notable in India, of course, where the insertion of the Shakespearean master text into native life paralleled the insertion of the power of the master race. Obviously this is a complex subject, one that draws not only upon the history of Shakespeare in the

Orient but also upon large administrative, educational, and cultural systems relating to the importation of dominance. But as the Indian feminist critic Ania Loomba has revealed, the continued presence of Shakespeare in English in India is part of a domestic reproduction of patriarchal British hegemony.[3]

The performance and study of Shakespeare everywhere, however, are part of a large and highly diverse pattern of material and intellectual enterprises, and the Shakespeare industry – which of course includes this book – has more at stake than the cultivation of the words written by a dead English dramatic poet. These thoughts, which are now common among critics of established or canonical literature, cannot be ignored when thinking about Shakespeare's position in Asia. If any performance of Shakespeare outside of English requires cultural transfer with its attendant cultural loss and replacement, surely his performance in Asia requires a lot: the entire range of Christian-European reference, including the dramatic, mythic, folkloric, and fabulistic postulates of Shakespeare's plays, suddenly becomes extrinsic or even spurious.

To what extent are western Shakespeareans prepared to acknowledge and understand that extreme kind of transculturalism, especially when it violates accepted standards of interpretation? Though westerners have a new, refreshing openness to eastern cultures, we have not abandoned the imperial mentality entirely. The east, which in the past was literally there for the taking, now seems metaphorically there for the taking. When large numbers of British, European, and American scholars flew off to Tokyo to discuss the universality of Shakespeare at the congress of the International Shakespeare Association in 1991, some saw an excellent symbol of the internationalism and the trans-political appeal of their discipline. Others saw the disturbing perseverance of western imperialism, or at the least a kind of cultural opportunism quite familiar in the history of the west's relations to the east. (In fact it was none of these: such gatherings are enabled by institutionalized power structures. An international meeting of scholars discussing Shakespeare proves nothing in itself about Shakespeare's universality, or about cultural imperialism; it only proves that there are sufficient numbers of scholars with funding and vested interests to make such a meeting economically feasible.)

It has become necessary, I think, for Shakespeareans everywhere to be more overt about the motives behind the study and reproduction of Shakespeare, even when the motives are worthy. It's not enough any longer to assert that Shakespeare is deserving of study and performance because the plays are great, or reflect the best of western culture. We must become more honest about ourselves than that, more historically grounded about our own positions as institutionalized commentators or theatre practitioners, more willing to engage in dialogue with those who do not love Shakespeare or do not believe his work to be self-evidently valuable. Is it possible that Shakespeare dominates our stages too much, to the exclusion of other deserving material, and dominates our classrooms to the detriment of alternative artistic structures? Is it possible Shakespeare gets performed so much because Shakespeare can attract funds? Is it possible that there is too much Shakespeare? Is it even possible, as Gary Jay Williams has recently asked, to "imagine a world without Shakespeare?"[4]

Shakespearean scholars rarely ask such questions, but others are beginning to ask them, and will ask them with growing force. The old humanist project, that until recently controlled British and American universities and the international study of Shakespeare, insisted that because its messages were not overtly political they had no political content. But all messages have political content, if only by virtue of what they omit or by virtue of political ideas that they instinctively reproduce. And the enforced study of Shakespeare in Britain and America has long been used, normally in an unconscious manner, to support traditionalist notions of class distinctions, the merit of high art, the social worth of advanced education, and the value of the arcane.[5] Looking at the history of Shakespeare abroad, especially in tense intellectual arenas like those in eastern Europe since the Second World War, makes us realize that Shakespeare can be made to represent other political meanings as well, both overtly and covertly. Those meanings are often drastically foreign to the Anglo-American tradition, and sometimes much more dangerous than what we are accustomed to, as many of the essays in this volume have shown. Foreign experiences with Shakespeare are more capable, it seems, of restoring some of the original peril of the plays.

These issues are most clear when they are applied to China, a country whose dominant values and postwar history have been extraordinarily dissimilar to those of the west. But before I address Chinese Shakespeare, I'm going to speak briefly about something

that is deeply related: what I call Shakespearean orientalism. By
that I mean the importation of eastern modalities into Shakespeare
performance in the west. While there are a number of examples that
could be cited, by far the most important and influential are the
three productions directed by Ariane Mnouchkine between 1981
and 1984 for the Théâtre du Soleil, located just outside of Paris,
which self-consciously drew upon intercultural aesthetic strategies.
Her productions traveled in Europe, and were given prominence in
Los Angeles in 1984 as part of the grand cultural display called the
Olympic Arts Festival.

The western tendency to seek artistic renovation in eastern styles
has a long history, but contemporary usage is connected with new,
postmodern circumstances. It's often mentioned in commentary on
postmodernism that much of our current mode of perception is
conditioned by the rapidity of electronic communication and the
frequency of global travel, circumstances that have altered, perhaps
for ever, long-standing notions about human separateness and geo-
graphic isolation. Not all of these changes have been voluntary or
virtuous, and some have been going on for a while now: ours has
been the century of global disruption, the century of the refugee. But
the recent influx of Asian and Latin American peoples into the US,
of Indian subcontinental peoples into Great Britain, and of African,
southern Mediterranean, and Middle Eastern peoples into western
Europe, has created a climate where distinct, separate cultures
begin to blend into one another, through borrowing, appropriation,
and imposition. (This is most apparent in the altered dining habits
in the west, which have in many cases incorporated the culinary
diversity provided by immigrant ethnic groups: perhaps the super-
market shelves of Britain and North America are the best index of
the growth of interculturalism.) The population influx has put
enormous pressures on the ideal of unifying diverse tribes into a
single national entity, the political equivalent of modernism. The
transfer of one cultural tradition to another is a fact of life for
resettled peoples, and for their host countries; indeed the west has
been using the east to spice its food, its clothing, its speech, and its
art for some time already.

Significantly, Mnouchkine came to Shakespeare only when she
got stuck trying to write an original play for her theatre on the
tragedy of Southeast Asia in our time. Most curiously, considering
Mnouchkine's own political commitment and the history of Shake-

spearean production since the war, she turned to Shakespeare because of what she called his ideological neutrality, turning her back on the Brechtian and the Kottian methods. "Shakespeare is not our contemporary and must not be treated as such," she said in an interview; "he is distant from us, as distant as our own profoundest depths." Her program, which originally was to have included six plays, was offered "hoping to learn how to represent the world in a theatre," as she wrote in the note for the opening production.[6] Thus her notion of Shakespeare's utility was grounded in his timelessness, which she thought required an abstract style, one that evoked images rather than messages. Already thinking about the east, and steeped in Asian theatre from her studies in the 1960s, Mnouchkine manufactured an eclectic orientalism to uncover the mythic dimensions she sensed in the text.

Kicking high and chanting in elevated speech, accompanied by cymbals and gongs, her actors burst through the accepted conventions of Shakespearean playing like Kabuki players through a paper screen. *Richard II* (1981) was a self-consciously mixed metaphor in which French actors borrowed elements from Asian performance to create a vision of the English medieval court. Sophie Moscoso, who collaborated with Mnouchkine on a number of aspects of the productions, put it this way:

In order to work on these war-like heroes, we needed to find a grand epic form. Ariane suggests inspiration from Japanese theatre forms, Noh and Kabuki, the origins of theatre and a theatre of origins; above all, it's a theatre of mask and of the masque.[7]

Character was established by mask or mask-like makeup, and by non-psychological patterns of gesture and movement; emotion was signified through formalized song and dance; the tragic dimension was conveyed through ritual conjurations like those in Noh and Kabuki, with some additions from the Indian Kathakali dance-drama and from Chinese Opera. To appropriate Shakespeare, Mnouchkine first appropriated the cultural details of the east, transforming both in the process.

The Shakespeare cycle continued with *Henry IV, Part 1* (1982), and a hauntingly beautiful Indian *Twelfth Night* (1984), then was abandoned. The sensory power of these productions was overwhelming – perhaps especially when performed on tour in other countries, where the French language was not well understood –

and the boldness of the scenographic and performance methods without rival in contemporary Shakespeare. Some spectators, of course, noted with melancholy the losses in verbal and intellectual dimensions. What is undeniable, however, is that Mnouchkine's intercultural tactics, alongside those of Peter Brook, have vastly expanded the visual and cultural references available for Shakespeare in our time.

I've gone on about this because I think Mnouchkine's Shakespearean orientalism has affected and slightly corrupted our ability to understand Shakespeare in Asia. What Mnouchkine did was to take a style, or rather a series of separate styles, and detach them from their origins and cultures. Kathakali dance, after all, has no relation to Chinese Opera other than a tendency to bright colors and conventionalized, athletic movements: external relations, nothing essential. This is the same type of appropriation the west has always perpetrated on the east, the same inclination that Edward Said discusses. It is the equivalent of serving an "oriental dinner" planned and prepared by European cooks at which Moo Goo Gai Pan, Mutar Panir, and Shrimp Tempura appear on the same plate, to be eaten with knife and fork. There is nothing morally wrong with it; in my own case, I found Mnouchkine's productions highly appealing – as I found *Les Atrides*, her four-part version of the *Oresteia* and *Iphigenia in Aulis*, which used the same methods. But however tasty the oriental Shakespeare at le Théâtre du Soleil might be, it achieved its success through enormous cultural dislocation.

Certainly Mnouchkine managed to estrange Shakespeare for her audiences, to point out the wondrous otherness of the fables. There was no danger that a comfortable Anglo-centricity would overtake the responses to these productions. Nonetheless, her insistent imposition of superbly foreign modes on the history plays tended to detach them from *any* political and historical meanings, Elizabethan or contemporary. *Richard II* was a dangerously political play in Shakespeare's time because it acts out the deposition of a king, an action not many monarchs like to see represented on the public stage. The well-known performance in 1601, timed to coincide with the attack on the queen's authority called the Essex Rebellion, got Elizabeth's ire up and Shakespeare and his company in deep trouble. As we have seen in this volume, Stalin banned *Hamlet* during the war for much the same reason, because it might provoke rebellious discontent. But Mnouchkine was concerned with style, and substituted a powerful aesthetic experience for a social one. Jan Kott's dismissal of her productions – "fake Japanese and fake Shakespeare" – is hardly surprising.[8]

When we turn to Shakespeare in China, instead of in a western dream of the Orient, we find the story is vastly different. While indigenous theatrical styles have been used for Shakespeare performances, in China these styles naturally carry their meanings with them and thus can never be merely aesthetic devices. In some ways Mnouchkine looked to the Orient because she felt western traditions for classic theatre were exhausted; in this light what is most interesting is that China is without a Shakespearean traditon. As Qi-Xin He has noted, the first translations date only from 1903 and Shakespeare remained marginal, especially in the theatre, until very recently.

The importation of Shakespeare into China, then, followed neither the nationalist model established in central Europe in the eighteenth century, nor the imperialist model of the nineteenth and early twentieth centuries. Instead it followed almost directly the political condition and changing circumstances of the country. When foreigners and foreign culture were excoriated in China, Shakespeare was essentially ignored. After the revolution of 1949, however, Shakespeare became immediately important – chiefly because Chinese literary scholarship followed that of the "elder brother," the Soviet Union, and Shakespeare was an important writer for Soviet critics and Soviet theatre. In keeping with the orthodox Marxist approach, one of the chief issues for Chinese Shakespearean criticism after the revolution was the question of whom the dramatist wrote for. Bian Zhilin, the leading Chinese Shakespearean of the period, concluded in 1956 that Shakespeare "had written for the people, not for the ruling class, and that Shakespeare opposed the feudal system in the early part of his career and exposed the evils of capitalism in the later part."[9] Needless to say, this was not an opinion shared by the dominant Anglo-American scholars of mid-century. A few student productions of the plays were mounted, and some popular films were made that were based on Shakespeare's stories.

All of this came to a sudden end in 1966, when the Cultural Revolution stopped the study and reproduction of almost all artistic material for a violent decade. For twelve years there was effectively no Shakespeare scholarship, and, as Qi-Xin He writes, "even

Shakespeare's name vanished from the lips of a population of nine hundred million people."[10] A world without Shakespeare was not an imaginary game for the Chinese. Foreign literature, banned as "feudal, bourgeois or revisionist" by the Cultural Revolution, started to appear slowly after 1976. A crucial moment occurred in November 1979 when the Old Vic Company presented *Hamlet* with Derek Jacobi, with simultneous Chinese translation through earphones, in Shanghai and Beijing. Thereafter local productions increased, both professional and amateur, some Shakespeare films were again shown, and revised versions of the plays in translation were newly published.

This movement climaxed in 1986 in the first Chinese Shakespeare Festival, again seen in both Shanghai and Beijing. A total of twenty-eight productions of eighteen different plays were mounted between 10 and 23 April, some of them in a quasi-western style, some in traditional Chinese Opera style.[11] An interesting insight about practical theatre conditions in China can be gained from the production of *Titus Andronicus* at the Shanghai Drama Institute. It was directed by Qi-Peng Xu, and designed by Mao-Sheng Hu in collaboration with my own former student at the University of Pittsburgh, Ming Chen. The design was a huge set of permanent steps with many mobile columns, much influenced by the Czech scenographer Josef Svoboda, who had visited Shanghai some years earlier. Thus the look of the play was modernist and European, indebted to Appia and Craig, but the columns, which were moved to numerous locations throughout the production, mystified western visitors who attended. How could such monumental pillars be so gracefully shifted, they wondered, what kind of mechanism had the Chinese theatre developed unknown to the west? Mao-Sheng Hu, who is professor of design at the Institute, told me the secret: the columns were moved by large numbers of stagehands, who stood patiently and invisibly behind each of them throughout the performance. In China, he noted, technology may be backward but labor is plentiful and cheap.

In a flurry of new Shakespearean activity after the Cultural Revolution, one of the most intriguing performances was a *Measure for Measure* by the People's Art Theatre Company in Beijing in 1981, translated and directed by Ying Ruocheng. Two British artists participated: Toby Robertson was "Visiting Director" and Alan Barrett designed the set. This play, with its disturbing morality, incomprehensible Elizabethan references, and bitter-sweet conclusion, is often difficult for western audiences. Imagine the difficulties it imposes for Chinese spectators untutored in its dramaturgy, its themes, and its Christian backdrop. Yet in China drama has always been assumed to concern the present, and recent events seemed to prepare the audience for *Measure for Measure*. In England and America the play appears to be about personal corruption; in more difficult regions it appears to be about politics. External conditions control how an audience views art; as Athol Fugard said in another context, "there are no non-political stories in South Africa." The exploration of "governance" and its "properties" was particularly sensitive in China in 1981, a country that had just gone through one of the most profound political and cultural upheavals in human history. Robertson has noted that the trial of the Gang of Four, which was "looming over all of China" at the time, seemed to condition everyone's response to the play. Thinking of Angelo's abuse of power and the Duke's trust, one intelligent spectator said, "it's a wonder Shakespeare could guess what the Chinese villains would do and say several hundred years later."[12]

To encourage his audience to see the play in a contemporary light, Ying Ruocheng abandoned Shakespeare's biblical title and called the play *Please Step into the Furnace*. The phrase alludes to a well-known story about a corrupt administrator in the Tang dynasty. When a wise judge asked him what he would do with a recalcitrant criminal, he suggested that the felon be placed in a large heated urn until he confesses his misdeeds. The judge then ordered that such an urn be prepared, and invited the wicked official to climb in. Thus Ying's title immediately conveyed to the Chinese audience the common parable of a cruel master caught in his own trap, the engineer hoist with his own petard.

The translation further emphasized contemporaneity by using Beijing street dialect for the bawds, contrasting this to the formal elegance of the courtly characters. As Carolyn Wakeman noted, the production deliberately strove to make the actors look natural, to emphasize that they were Chinese under their western characters, not "a race apart." "The costumes, timeless and traditional, subtly encouraged recognition of the play as a mirror of the spectators' world," even suggesting in some instances "details of clothing common on the streets of Peking today." In a noisy second scene, when Claudio and his mistress Juliet were "paraded in tall white dunces' caps before a crowd of curious spectators, the action would, however unconsciously, have evoked scenes of public criticism and humiliation familiar from the recent Chinese past."[13]

The performance apparently had a great effect on all levels of society, suggesting that Chinese audiences might be more ready to accept Shakespeare's strange fable than western audiences are. One sign can be found in the treatment of the Duke. In western interpretations he is a problematic figure, for his toying with Isabella's emotions and her brother's life seems cruel, and his authoritarian patriarchy seems at odds with his merciful and rather spongy nature. He is often treated as a charcter who knows himself only slightly more than Angelo does himself, and maybe even less – at least Angelo is driven by a passion he seems to understand. But in Ying Ruocheng's production there was no overt or implied critique of the Duke's authority; his methods and power were accepted as just and proper, not questionable or perverse. The performance script had been molded to insure thus: in cutting some 500 lines from the text, the production eliminated most references to God, to prostitution, and statements "which might have contradicted current political concepts in China."[14]

The acceptance of authority, strongly encouraged by Confucius, is still expected in Chinese society, at least by the government. When authority is not accepted, as in the democracy demonstrations of 1989, dissent is likely to provoke severe and long-lasting retribution. I write this on the third anniversary of the events known in China as "June 4," and a newspaper report confirms the continuation of the tendency. "Many Chinese believe that talking about the Tiananmen crackdown will accomplish nothing," Nicholas Kristof writes, "and will simply risk punishment."[15] The Tiananmen Square Massacre had an immediate impact on Chinese Shakespeare: the second Shakespeare Festival, which was planned for 1990 and was to be larger and more international than the first, was immediately canceled and has not yet been rescheduled.

Earlier I asked if Anglophone Shakespeareans are really prepared to accommodate the challenges to Shakespeare reception that are presented by performances in Asia. Generally speaking, I think we are not. As Patrice Pavis notes in this volume, we have not even begun to develop a theory of cultural exchange that might help us understand what happens when Shakespeare travels abroad, and so far there has been little interest among Shakespeareans in such an enterprise.[16] A theory that can explain how "Shakespeare" operates in Mnouchkine's orientalism, in Ninagawa's occidentalism, and in what Pavis calls "the politically radical thought of the Third World" may be too much to ask for – yet it is the most important task Shakespeareans face. It is much more important than linguistic analysis, textual examination, psychological assessments, historical research, or any of the Anglo-centered occupations scholars have traditionally valued and perpetuated.

If we are to make the study and performance of Shakespeare fully contemporary and fully international we must worry less about his textual meaning and more about his prodigious appropriation (or misappropriation) in a global context. Shakespeare is not everywhere, but he is certainly more places than any other dramatist and perhaps more than any other artist. He can be seen in the strangest company: at an inaccurate reconstruction of the Globe Theatre in Tokyo and selling tinned tuna on American television; in schoolrooms in Lagos and in Madras; in the books of Allan Bloom and of Alan Sinfield. After dominating our stages, he has reappeared as a near-obsession for contemporary British and American filmmakers, some of whom carry Shakespeare like the anxious burden carried by the romantic poets: in Woody Allen's *A Midsummer Night's Sex Comedy*, in William Reilly's *Men of Respect*, in Peter Greenaway's *Prospero's Books*, and, most surprising of all, in Gus van Sant's *My Own Private Idaho*. His work has become the closest thing we have to a common cultural inheritance, but it is an inheritance that is thoroughly redefined by each culture that receives it.

Shakespeare's genius did not lie in anticipating all future history, as the Chinese spectator at *Measure for Measure* thought. I have been arguing that the universality we so often admire derives not from Shakespeare's transcendence but from his malleability, from our own willingness to read in the pastness of the texts and find ourselves there. What selves we find depends on who we are: thus the Shakespeare seen in China should *not* be the Shakespeare seen in London, or Paris, or Los Angeles. Shakespeare performance in English, especially in the well-established theatres, has again become tame and expected. Generally speaking, it has ceased to be a political challenge, and rarely is an intellectual one. Perhaps intercultural performances, which force the issue of Shakespeare's foreignness and urge audiences to reassess comfortable attitudes about the integrity of culture, can teach us how to regain some of what we have lost, as

those foreigners Brecht and Kott did after the war. The most
extreme examples of foreign Shakespeare can show us what we miss
most of all in the Anglo-American theatre: the power of danger, the
cruelty of power, the real prospect that a dead English playwright
might still shake audiences to the bone, get the censor riled, make
the Queen angry, get the actors arrested, and make us want to do
something besides sit back and politely applaud.

NOTES

1 Gary Taylor, *Reinventing Shakespeare* (New York: Oxford University
   Press, (1989), 379. Samuel Leiter proposes that the "dearth of success-
   ful Spanish-language productions" is due to "the lack of worthwhile
   Spanish translations of the plays" – *Shakespeare Around the Globe: A Guide
   to Notable Postwar Revivals*, ed. Leiter (New York: Greenwood Press,
   1986), x. Actually Shakespeare is performed with some regularity in
   Latin America, but not nearly to the degree he is in North America or
   Europe. According to *The World Almanac and Book of Facts 1993* (New
   York: World Almanac, 1992), 606, there are currently 320 million
   native speakers of Spanish; next in line among European languages is
   English with 316 million. Portuguese claims a further 165 million native
   speakers.
2 Edward Said, *Orientalism* (New York: Random Hosue, 1978), 4.
3 Ania Loomba, *Gender, Race, Renaissance Drama* (Manchester University
   Press, 1989), 10–37.
4 Gary Jay Williams, "Queen Lear: Reason Not the Need," *Theater* 22.1
   (Fall/Winter 1990–1): 78.
5 See Taylor, *Reinventing Shakespeare*; Graham Holderness (ed.), *The
   Shakespeare Myth* (Manchester University Press, 1988); and Michael D.
   Bristol, *Shakespeare's America, America's Shakespeare* (London: Routledge,
   1990). Hugh Grady's *The Modernist Shakespeare* (Oxford: Clarendon
   Press, 1991) deals with some of these issues in the context of modernism.
6 Quoted in David Bradby and David Williams, *Directors' Theatre* (New
   York: St. Martin's Press, 1988), 100, 98. I discuss Mnouchkine's work
   further in *Looking at Shakespeare* (Cambridge University Press, 1993).
7 Sophie Moscoso, "Notes de Répétitions," *Double Page* 32 (1984): n.p.
8 Jan Kott, in John Elsom (ed.), *Is Shakespeare Still Our Contemporary?*
   (London: Routledge, 1989), 16.
9 Quoted in Qi-Xin He, "China's Shakespeare," *The Shakespeare Quarterly*
   37 (1986): 154.
10 *Ibid.*, 155.
11 The festival is treated in "Shakespeare in China," a special section of
   Shakespeare Quarterly 39 (1988): 195–216; reports are provided by
   J. Philip Brockbank, by Zha Peide and Tian Jia, and by Edward Berry.

Two further short reports (by Huang Zuolin and by Yang Hengsheng) are contained in "On China's First Shakespeare Festival," *China Reconstructs* 35 (July 1986): 40–3.

12 Paul Allen, "Interview with Athol Fugard," *New Statesman and Society*, 7 Sept. 1990: 38. Toby Robertson, in Elsom, *Is Shakespeare Still Our Contemporary?*, 83. The Chinese spectator is quoted in Carolyn Wakeman, "*Measure for Measure* on the Chinese Stage," *Shakespeare Quarterly* 33 (1982): 501.

13 Wakeman, "Measure for Measure on the Chinese Stage," 502. Robertson says the title of the play was *Three Men in a Vat* (Elsom, *Is Shakespeare Still Our Contemporary?*, 83), but he seems to have misremembered.

14 Qi-Xin He, "China's Shakespeare," 155. A parallel treatment of the topic is provided by Yu Weijie, "Topicality and Typicality: The Acceptance of Shakespeare in China," in *The Dramatic Touch of Difference: Theatre, Own and Foreign*, ed. Erika Fischer-Lichte, *et al.* (Tübingen: Narr, 1990).

15 Nicholas D. Kristof, *The New York Times*, National Edn., 5 June 1992: A4.

16 Recent books that deal with issues of interculturalism in the theatre include Pavis's *Theatre at the Crossroads of Culture* (London: Routledge, 1992) and *A Reader in Intercultural Performance*, ed. Pavis (London: Routledge, due 1994); *The Play Out of Context: Transferring Plays from Culture to Culture*, ed. Hanna Scolnicov and Peter Holland (Cambridge University Press, 1989); *Interculturalism and Performance*, ed. Bonnie Marranca and Gautam Dasgupta (New York: PAJ Publications, 1991); and the volume edited by Fischer-Lichte, cited above. Shakespeare receives little attention in these works. Phillip B. Zarrilli's recent essay is useful: "For Whom Is the King a King? Issues of Intercultural Production, Perception, and Reception in a *Kathakali King Lear*," *Critical Theory and Performance* , ed. Janelle G. Reinelt and Joseph R. Roach (Ann Arbor: University of Michigan Press, 1992).

Index

Shakespeare's plays are listed by title; the major productions discussed are further identified by directors and dates. Page numbers in **bold** refer to illustrations.